PSYCHOLOGY AND SOCIAL RESPONSIBILITY

PSYCHOLOGY AND SOCIAL RESPONSIBILITY

Facing Global Challenges

Edited by
SYLVIA STAUB and
PAULA GREEN

NEW YORK UNIVERSITY PRESS
New York and London

NEW YORK UNIVERSITY PRESS
New York and London

Library of Congress Cataloging-in-Publication Data
Psychology and social responsibiliy : facing global challenges /
edited by Sylvia Staub and Paula Green.
p.   cm.
Includes bibliographical references and index.
ISBN 0-8147-7931-X—ISBN 0-8147-7941-7 (pbk.)
1. Social psychology—Moral and ethical aspects.
2. Psychotherapy—Moral and ethical aspects.   3. Responsibility.
4. Social conflict 5. Nonviolence.   I. Staub, Sylvia, 1936–   .
II. Green, Paula.
HM251.P8343   1992   91-39723
302—dc20   CIP

New York University Press books are printed on acid-free paper,
and their binding materials are chosen for strength and durability.

Manufactured in the United States of America

c 10 9 8 7 6 5 4 3 2 1
p 10 9 8 7 6 5 4 3 2 1

Contents

PART SIX
PREPARING THE NEXT GENERATION

PART SEVEN
CONCLUSION

Foreword

Herbert C. Kelman

This volume addresses a broad range of current issues bearing on the human condition. In many ways, it complements and supplements the book of readings, *Psychology and the Prevention of Nuclear War,* edited by Ralph White and published in 1986. In the five years that have elapsed since publication of that earlier volume, our world has experienced changes, which the present volume explores.

In my preface to the White volume, I argued that "for intellectual, pragmatic, and moral reasons, the prevention of nuclear war must be seen in the broader context of war prevention in general." I insisted that there must be better ways of solving problems that war and that "psychological analysis, in particular, can contribute to the discovery of such alternatives." I concluded with the hope that, "having been mobilized by the threat of nuclear war, . . . we will extend our inquiry to the abolition of war in general as a social institution and as an instrument of policy." The centrality of such an agenda has been brought home by the events of the past year.

It is hard to remember that it was only a short while ago that the world looked bright and hopeful. The Cold War had come to an end. A process of democratization was sweeping through Eastern and Central Europe, as well as the Soviet Union itself. Several bitter regional conflicts of long standing were moving toward peaceful resolution, often with the help of a newly vitalized United Nations. Peace had suddenly become a respectable and even a fashionable concept. In the United States, we talked about the uses of the peace dividend for the betterment of our society, and throughout the world there was increasing hope that we would enter a new era of international cooperation in the solution of global problems of security, health, welfare, protection of the environment, and equitable distribution of resources.

Barely a year later we found ourselves in the midst of a vicious war, initiated by the outrageous acts of aggression against its neighbors by the president of Iraq, heavily armed with the help of all of the world's major powers, including Germany, the United States, and other Western countries; and made inevitable by the decision of our own administration to pursue a military solution before giving nonviolent and diplomatic efforts a chance to resolve the crisis peacefully. Fortunately, at the time this preface is being written, the war is over; it was mercifully quick and succeeded in liberating Kuwait and apparently neutralizing Saddam Hussein's military capabilities. The notion, however, that it was a "clean" war with minimal costs is an illusion that can be sustained only from the narrow, short-term perspective of the military victors.

The war exacted enormous costs in the number of human beings killed and wounded, the suffering and displacement of vast populations, the destruction of society, and the degradation of the environment. Its impact on the political stability of the Middle East and the possibilities for resolving the outstanding problems of the region is still unknown; much will depend on the postwar policies pursued by the administration. On the other hand, there is little doubt about the opportunity costs of the war: massive resources have been used in the prosecution of this war and will almost certainly be used for the preparation of future wars rather than for the betterment of the human condition through efforts to advance social justice, human welfare, and the quality of life. From a longer-range perspective, we have wasted an opportunity to develop and apply mechanisms of creative conflict resolution and genuinely collective security. Instead, we have reinforced a model of the "new world order" for the post-Cold War era based on the primacy of military force, on the dominance of the United States, and on a disregard of regional concerns and sensitivities.

It is easy to react to the developments of the past year with cynicism and despair. The specter of nuclear weapons and other nonconventional weapons of mass destruction is still very much with us despite the end of the Cold War. Conventional warfare, particularly in its high-technology format, is hardly an acceptable alternative for the decent and wise conduct of international relationships. The promising changes in the Soviet Union and in Eastern and Central Europe have been thrown into doubt by the reemergence of vested interests and profound ethnic conflicts. The global and domestic problems of economic justice and human rights are still low on the agenda of political decision makers. Nevertheless, we cannot afford to conclude that changing the world is an impossible task.

The events of recent years have demonstrated that change is possible and, indeed, significant changes have taken place. The difficulties and the reverses that we have encountered along the way are merely reminders that changes in human consciousness and in entrenched social institutions come slowly and only as a result of great effort. Thus, an alternative to responding with cynicism and despair is a renewed commitment to continuing the process of working for change. In the coming phase of these efforts, we need to go deeper and confront the collective habits, the institutional structures, and the parochial thinking that have kept us from grasping the implications of the new world we live in. We have to challenge the continued acceptance of war as an instrument of policy and the continued failure to act on the realities of global interdependence. We have to develop multinational mechanisms for peaceful resolution of international conflicts and for dealing constructively with problems arising from poverty, hunger, and homelessness, violation of human rights, ethnic and religious discrimination, the growing number of refugees, and hazards to health and the environment. We have to take responsibility for the world we hope to leave to coming generations through participation in collective efforts that challenge the established ways of doing business, and through fostering institutional and educational changes conducive to empowerment of our own and the world's population.

These are issues to which psychologists, as well as other social scientists and mental health professionals, can make important contributions and to which the present volume addresses itself. The book could not be appearing, therefore, at a more timely moment in human history. Moreover, the contributors are all high-level professionals who have combined scholarship with activism throughout their careers. I feel confident that this collection of their essays will inform the activist community and the general readership of some of the psychological underpinnings of war and peace and other global issues confronting us today; that is, that it will inspire fellow-professionals to pursue the sociopolitical implications and applications of their work, and that it will introduce students to new approaches to global issues and to the possibilities for merging professional careers with social responsibility.

HERBERT C. KELMAN
Richard Clarke Cabot Professor of
Social Ethics, Harvard University
President, Psychologists for Social
Responsibility

Acknowledgments

This book was inspired by a conference entitled "Psychology, Peace and Social Responsibility," which we, the editors, were involved in organizing and which took place at Hampshire College in Amherst, Massachusetts, in December 1988. The success of and enthusiastic response to that conference persuaded us to edit a book on the theme of the relationship between psychology and social responsibility. We wish to thank Virginia Senders, who coordinated the conference with us and whose energy and creativity contributed so much to the success of that conference. We also wish to thank the members of the Conference Committee, whose hard work and dedication also made that conference possible: Kathryn Arbour, Ruth Backes, Peter Corbett, Anita King, Harold Rausch, Patricia Romney, Amy Rosebury, Suzanne Slater, and Susan Theberge.

We are grateful to Michael Klare and Adi Bemak, of the Five College Peace and World Securities Studies Program in Amherst, for their generous support and cooperation in cosponsoring the conference.

In addition, we thank Jason Renker, our editor at NYU Press, for his belief in the value of this project and for his help throughout the process of putting the book together. We thank Edward Emery for his helpful comments on sections of the manuscript, and Anne Anderson, coordinator of the National Office of Psychologists for Social Responsibility, for her suggestions and support. Lastly we thank John Mack for his support, advice and commitment to this project from its beginnings.

Each of us has some personal thanks to offer:

I, Paula, have felt especially supported in my writing and activism ventures by the wisdom, compassion and dedication of the two people I live with: my husband, Jim Perkins, and our housemate and friend, Eric Kolvig.

I, Sylvia, wish to thank my husband Ervin Staub for his support, encouragement, and invaluable advice, and for sharing his knowledge and experience with me at every step of the way. I am also grateful to my sons, Adrian and Daniel, for their continuous interest and enthusiasm in this project, and to my good friend Sarah Conn, for her love, support, and inspiration in this and all of my work.

Contributors

George W. Albee, Ph.D., is Professor of Psychology at the University of Vermont and president of the Vermont Conference on the Primary Prevention of Psychopathology. He is the general editor of a series of books on the prevention of psychopathology as well as numerous articles on political action and social policy as efforts at achieving a just society. He is past president of the American Psychological Association and currently serves as president of the American Association for the Advancement of Applied Preventative Psychology.

Susan M. Books is a clinical psychologist in private practice in Cambridge, Massachusetts. She has been a social activist since 1967, when she tutored migrant children. She has researched long-term commitment to social activism with women who were involved in the antinuclear movement. She is also a member of the Boston Women's Peace Research Group.

Sarah A. Conn, Ph.D., is a clinical psychologist and psychotherapist in private practice in Newton, Massachusetts. For the past three years, she has taught a course on global awareness, social responsibility, and psychotherapy at the Center for Psychological Studies in the Nuclear Age at Cambridge Hospital, Harvard Medical School, and a course on global issues and social change at Tufts University. She has conducted workshops and has published several articles on these subjects. She is also a member of the Boston Women's Peace Research Group.

James A. Dyal, Ph.D., is formerly Chairman and Professor of Psychology at the University of Waterloo in Ontario and is cochair of the Research Task Force of Psychologists for Social Responsibility.

Priscilla Ellis, Ph.D., is a clinical psychologist in private practice with Newton Psychotherapy Associates, codirector of the Social Research Institute of New England, and codirector and coresearcher for the Atomic Veterans Family Project. She is a member of the Boston Women's Peace Research Group.

Susan T. Fiske, Ph.D., is Professor of Psychology, University of Massachusetts at Amherst. Her published work addresses many aspects of ordinary people's political and social thinking. Her major research focuses on interdependence and stereotyping. She has also conducted research on citizens' perceptions of nuclear threat.

E. Scott Geller, Ph.D., is Professor of Psychology at Virginia Polytechnic Institute and State University, and has pioneered the application of behavioral science toward solving safety, health, and environmental problems in corporate and community settings. He is a Fellow of the American Psychological Association, editor of the *Journal of Applied Behavior Analysis,* and associate editor of *Environment and Behavior.*

Lane A. Gerber, Ph.D., is the Pigott-McCone Professor of Humanities and Professor of Psychology at Seattle University and is a Clinical Faculty member of the University of Washington Department of Psychiatry and Behavioral Science. He is the author of *Married to Their Careers* and of articles on the practice and teaching of psychotherapy and on psychological aspects of medicine. He serves on the boards of the Seattle chapter of Educators for Social Responsibility, and of Seattle Peace Theatre. He established the volunteer mental health service center of the Refugee Clinic at Harborview Hospital.

Paula Green, Ed.D., is Associate Adjunct Faculty in psychology at Antioch New England Graduate School. She maintains a small clinical practice and devotes much of her time to writing, teaching, and traveling internationally as an activist in the movements for nonviolent social change. She is currently on the National Council of the Fellowship of

Reconciliation and is director of Karuna Center, which offers workshops in communication, reconciliation, and peacemaking.

Herbert C. Kelman is Richard Clarke Cabot Professor of Social Ethics at Harvard University and President of Psychologists for Social Responsibility.

Phyllis La Farge is the author of *The Strangelove Legacy: Children, Parents, and Teachers in the Nuclear Age* and has published articles about nuclear age education in the *Bulletin of Atomic Scientists*, the *Annual Review of Peace Activism*, and the *Family Resource Coalition Report*. She is a contributing editor to *Parents* magazine.

Robert Jay Lifton, M.D., is Distinguished Professor of Psychiatry and Psychology at the Graduate Center of the City University of New York and director of the Center on Violence and Human Survival at John Jay College of Criminal Justice, CUNY. He held the Foundations' Fund Research Professorship of Psychiatry at Yale University for more than two decades. He has been particularly interested in the relationships between individual psychology and historical change in problems surrounding the extreme historical situations of our era, and has taken an active part in the formation of the new field of psychohistory. His most recent books are *The Nazi Doctors: Medical Killing and the Psychology of Genocide*, and *The Genocidal Mentality: Nazi Holocaust and Nuclear Threat* (with Eric Markusen).

John E. Mack, M.D., is Professor of Psychiatry at Cambridge Hospital, Harvard Medical School, and founding director of the Center for Psychological Studies in the Nuclear Age. He is the author of *Prince of Our Disorder: The Life of T. E. Lawrence, Nightmares and Human Conflict*, and *The Alchemy of Survival: One Woman's Journey*.

Sally A. Mack is a social worker and peace activist. She is affiliated with the Child Development Unit at Boston's Children's Hospital, conducts a seminar on social and psychological issues in medical practice for third-year medical students, and has a private practice in psychotherapy. She is an active member of Social Workers for Peace and Nuclear Disarmament.

Joanna R. Macy, Ph.D., is Adjunct Professor at the California Institute of Integral Studies in San Francisco, and at the Starr King School for the Ministry in Berkeley. She is the author of *Despair and Personal Power in the Nuclear Age, Dharma and Development, World as Lover, World as Self*, and *Mutual Causality: The Dharma of Natural Systems*. She is the founder of the Nuclear Guardianship Project.

Douglas McKenzie-Mohr, Ph.D., is Assistant Professor of Psychology at Wilfrid Laurier University in Ontario, Canada. His primary research interest is in the contribution that psychology can make in resolving international conflict peacefully. Presently he is the co-chair of the Research Task Force of Psychologists for Social Responsibility and a research scholar at the Center for Psychological Studies in the Nuclear Age at Harvard. He is actively involved in Canadian peace groups.

Bianca Cody Murphy, Ed.D., is Assistant Professor of Psychology at Wheaton College, where she teaches a course on psychology in the nuclear age. She is a counseling psychologist in private practice and codirector of the Atomic Veterans Family Project, a research project on the psychological effects of exposure to nuclear radiation. Her publications include book chapters and articles on teaching about nuclear issues, working with families exposed to environmental contaminants, and the application of family-systems thinking to nuclear issues. She is past co-chair of the Nuclear Issues Study Group of the American Orthopsychiatric Association, a founding member of Division 48, the Division of Peace Psychology of the American Psychological Association, and an active member of Psychologists for Social Responsibility.

Jonathan W. Reusser, A.C.S.W., B.C.D., is a family therapist and is on the faculty of the Graduate Program in Counseling Psychology at the University of Massachusetts, Boston, where he teaches courses in family therapy. He is codirector of the Atomic Veterans Children's Project. His interest in the impact of broader social issues on parenting skills has led him to do research on family responses to the threat of war and to organize seminars and teaching materials for parents. He is a member of the Nuclear Issues Study Group of the American Orthopsychiatric Association and the Nuclear Issues Task Force of the American Family Therapy Association.

Jeffrey Z. Rubin, Ph.D., is Professor of Psychology at the Fletcher School of Law and Diplomacy, Tufts University, and executive director of the Program on Negotiation at Harvard Law School. Past president of the Society for the Psychological Study of Social Issues and vice-president of the International Society of Political Psychology, Rubin has written extensively on interpersonal and international conflict and negotiation. Among his recent books are *Leadership and Negotiation in the Middle East* (with Barbara Kellerman), *Social Conflict: Escalation, Stalemate, and Settlement* (with Dean G. Pruitt), and *When Families Fight* (with Carol Rubin).

Richard C. Sherman is a clinical social worker and a former teacher and director of the Greater Boston Physicians for Social Responsibility. He now heads the Social Workers for Peace and Justice of the Massachusetts chapter of the National Association of Social Workers. He also maintains a private practice in Newton, Massachusetts.

Brett Silverstein, Ph.D., is an Associate Professor of Psychology at the City College of New York. He is a member of the steering committee of Psychologists for Social Responsibility (PsySR) and of the Task Force on Peace of the Society for the Psychological Study of Social Issues (SPSSI). He organized and directs the Enemy Image Project co-sponsored by PsySR and SPSSI.

Sylvia Staub, Ed.D., is a clinical psychologist in private practice in Amherst, Massachusetts. She is a co-founder of the Western Massachusetts chapter of Psychologists for Social Responsibility and is committed to exploring the connections between psychological theory and practice and the larger contexts of the social world.

Ervin Staub, Ph.D., is Professor of Psychology at the University of Massachusetts, Amherst. He taught at Harvard and has been Visiting Professor at Stanford, the University of Hawaii, and the London School of Economics and Political Science. Since the late 1960s, he has been conducting research on and developing a theory (personal goal theory) about personal and social determinants and development of helping and altruism, and about passivity in the face of others' needs. His books include the two-volume *Positive Social Behavior and Morality* and *Roots of Evil:*

The Origins of Genocide and Other Group Violence, which explores the origins of genocide, mass killing, torture, and war and the evolution of caring and nonaggressive persons and societies.

Janet Surrey, Ph.D., is director of Psychological Services, Adult Outpatient Department, McLean Hospital, research consultant at the Stone Center, Wellesley College; and Instructor in Psychology, Department of Psychiatry, Harvard Medical School. She has spoken and written extensively on topics related to the Stone Center relational theory of women's psychological development. She is coauthor of *Woman's Growth in Connection* and is on the advisory board of Women's Action for Nuclear Disarmament. She is also a member of the Boston Women's Peace Research Group.

Roger Walsh, M.D., Ph.D., is a professor in the Departments of Psychiatry and Philosophy at the University of California at Irvine. His personal and research interests include the nature of psychological well-being, meditation, Asian psychologies and philosophies, integrating different schools of psychology and psychotherapy, and the psychological causes and possible cures of our contemporary global crises. His books include *Beyond Ego: Transpersonal Dimensions in Psychology; Beyond Health and Normality: Explorations of Exceptional Psychological Well-being; Mediation: Classic and Contemporary Perspectives; A Gift of Peace; Staying Alive: The Psychology of Human Survival;* and *The Spirit of Shamanism: A Psychological View.*

Steven J. Zeitlin, Ph.D., is a family therapist and research associate at the Center for Psychological Studies in the Nuclear Age, and an affiliate of Harvard Medical School at Cambridge Hospital. His research has focused on family response to significant stress including the death of a parent and to global threats such as nuclear war. He has written several articles and is the coauthor of *No Reason to Talk About It: Families Confront the Nuclear Taboo.*

PSYCHOLOGY AND SOCIAL RESPONSIBILITY

INTRODUCTION: TOWARD A SOCIALLY RESPONSIBLE PSYCHOLOGY

Sylvia Staub and Paula Green

This book is intended as a call to action for the creation of a "socially responsible" psychology. The psychological disciplines have clearly left their mark on twentieth-century society in nearly every facet of social life. In child-rearing, family life, personal relationships, education, industry, business, management, marketing, and in countless other aspects of everyday life, the skills and knowledge of psychologists and mental health professionals are sought and applied. The basic premise of this book is that psychology, in all its forms, is relevant not only to these everyday issues and problems but also to the major global crises and challenges that face the world today. All the disciplines within psychology and the mental health professions have an important role to play both in our understanding of the causes and effects of social and global problems and in helping to develop effective ways of responding to these problems. Our primary purpose in creating this book is to demonstrate some of the contributions that psychology has made in this direction, to propose new ways that psychology can contribute, and to point to some of the ways that individuals who work in these fields, or are preparing to work there, can participate in the work for global transformation and survival.

Most of the twenty chapters that follow are original contributions written specifically for this book. Their authors include psychiatrists, clinical psychologists, social psychologists, social workers, family therapists, a scholar of comparative religion and general systems theory, an environmental psychologist, and a writer on issues of peace and global education. This book brings together for the first time many of the leading writers and thinkers from the psychological and mental health fields who have a reputation for combining professional commitment and achievement in the social and behavioral sciences with concern and involvement in social issues.

THE CHALLENGES WE FACE

Widespread public awareness is finally developing about the gravity and magnitude of the social, economic, and environmental problems that beset us today as a species. The dangers of armed conflict in an age of nuclear, chemical, and biological weapons; a broad range of serious ecological crises; depletion of natural resources; uncontrolled population growth and increasing economic disparity among the peoples of the world —these are but a few of the problems. In this book we want to draw attention to the important psychological *implications* and *effects* of global issues. Our country has recently experienced an intense and frightening period of armed conflict in the Middle East, and we are still dealing with its myriad consequences. For many of us, this experience has heightened an awareness of our common vulnerability and feelings of fear, anxiety, and dread as we contemplate the threats, both military and environmental, that were raised by the conflict. It also brought home to many of us the interdependence of the issues as well as the nations in today's world —that we indeed can be said to be living in a "global village." We hope, in this book, to provide the reader with some insights into the profound psychological impact of living in this "global age."

In putting together this volume, we also intended to call attention to some of the major psychological forces and processes that we now know contribute to the *creation* of our major social and global problems. Since all the major threats to human survival today are caused by human behavior, the challenge lies in identifying these psychological root causes and discovering ways of controlling or ameliorating them.

CREATING A "SOCIALLY RESPONSIBLE" PSYCHOLOGY

The proposal of a "socially responsible" psychology raises for many a basic question: What *is* the relationship between our "professional" roles and duties—as researchers, teachers, or psychotherapists—and our roles and duties as responsible citizens? Is it possible to heal the split between these two identities that so many of us feel? Is there a professional model of social responsibility that would enable us to be engaged as professionals in socially relevant issues, without compromising our commitment to "objectively verifiable" knowledge?

Psychology's expressed commitment to bettering human life goes back to the earliest days of the profession. According to Morawski and Goldstein, "the mandates for socially responsible practices . . . became and remain visible in the constitutional declaration of the APA (American Psychological Association) and . . . are still construed as a significant function of contemporary psychology" (1985, 276–77). This function, though, has historically been seen by psychology as limited to providing "facts" rather than "values." But as Prilleltensky writes, "The persistent refusal of psychologists to elaborate on the role of values in their disciplines has been one of the most influential factors interfering with an understanding of psychology in a social context" (1989). He argues that socioeconomic, cultural, and political factors have shaped the methods and content of psychology to a very large extent, and that the belief that psychology is immune to ideological or value influences is a serious error in its perception of itself.

Perhaps in this perceived split between facts and values lies the framework for the long-held distinction between acting as a "professional" within the psychological disciplines and as a "socially responsible" citizen in the outside world. Thus until recently there have been few serious or consistent attempts in psychology to integrate concern for social issues with the practice of one's profession. One exception is the Society for the Psychological Study of Social Issues (SPSSI), which was founded in 1936. It is an organization of psychologists and allied scientists whose members have in common an interest in conducting research, education, and training on psychological aspects of important social issues. SPSSI also works to affect public policy within social and governmental agencies, based on the findings of psychological research. But as Argyris (1975), Sampson (1977), and Sarason (1984), note, most psychologists have concentrated on the task of "objectively" acquiring and disseminating knowledge without concern about its social relevance.

A belief in the necessity of "value-neutrality" has characterized psychological research and practice. But Prilleltensky argues that psychology is instrumental in maintaining the societal status quo by "endorsing and reflecting dominant social values (and) disseminating those values in the persuasive forms of so-called value-free scientific statements." He further argues that by exposing the mechanism of the prevalent ideology, "psychology can make a meaningful contribution to the course of social change" (1989, 799). We will take a brief look at some of psychology's recent efforts at studying critical social issues and problems for the purpose of effecting broad social change.

PSYCHOLOGY AND NUCLEAR ISSUES

In the decade and a half following World War II, psychologists became involved in research concerning nuclear war, but this research largely supported government policy in an attempt to "socialize Americans to the benefits of atomic weaponry and energy" (Morawski and Goldstein 1985). This was followed by a brief period, in the early 1960s, of research on the psychological dimensions of international relations in the nuclear age, for the purpose of developing diplomatic strategies for preventing nuclear war. Here, for the first time, "psychologists began to promote prevention of, rather than preparation for, war" (Morawski and Goldstein 1985). This work was critical of American foreign relations and of the policy of deterrence (Deutsch 1961; Osgood 1962; Milburn 1961).

After this early period of activity, research by psychologists on nuclear issues and concerns did not reemerge until the early 1980s, when a reawakening to nuclear issues occurred both among the general public and in the psychological fields. These years saw the founding of national professional organizations devoted to research and debate on the nuclear threat and other major social issues. One of these organizations, Psychologists for Social Responsibility (PsySR), was founded for the express purpose of using psychological principles and tools to promote conversion from a war system to a world dedicated to peace and social justice:

Our primary goal is to draw on the knowledge, perspectives and practices of psychology in preventing war and building authentic security. Our programs for pursuing these goals blend research, public education and civic dialogue with activity. (*Newsletter of Psychologists for Social Responsibility*, Fall 1990)

A further focus of research on nuclear issues during this period of the early 1980s was the study of the psychological effects of living in the nuclear age. A leader in this movement is the psychiatrist and psycho historian Robert J. Lifton, whose research and writing (1979, 1982; Lifton and Falk 1982) centered on the psychological mechanisms that have allowed us to live with the possibility of nuclear war and on the broad and pervasive psychological consequences of living with this threat. In the opening chapter of this volume, Lifton argues for the need for a major shift in our thinking, away from a "genocidal mentality," with its dependence on nuclear weapons for a feeling of strength and safety, to a "species mentality," in which we recognize our shared fate on earth.

Another body of research related to the issue of nuclear weapons during the 1980s focused on the reactions of children and adolescents to the threat of nuclear war (Schwebel 1982; Beardslee and Mack 1982; Escalona 1982) and some of the developmental consequences of the impact of living in a nuclear age on children and adolescents. In chapter 19 of this volume, Steven Zeitlin summarizes much of the psychological thought and research regarding ways in which living in the nuclear context affects young people, and ways that the older generation can help the younger generation to deal with these issues.

Related to these developments in the early 1980s was the emergence of the "despair and empowerment" movement, which has consisted largely of group workshops that focus on the "psychological and spiritual work of dealing with our knowledge and feelings about the present planetary crisis in ways that release energy and vision for creative response" (Macy 1983). These workshops were mainly conducted by members of a national network of peace and social activists called "Interhelp." The ideas behind despair and empowerment work were developed by Joanna Macy, a teacher of comparative religion and general systems theory, and the founder of Interhelp. In chapter 2 in this volume, Macy highlights the philosophical, psychological, and spiritual bases of this work and presents her analysis of our responses to global perils and of our personal resources for social action.

PSYCHOLOGY, INTERNATIONAL CONFLICT, AND CONFLICT RESOLUTION

Beginning in the 1960s, psychologists began to criticize the behavior of national leaders (Frank 1960) and the creation of "good guy/bad guy" dichotomies, such as that between the United States and the Soviet

Union (White 1965). During this period, Bronfenbrenner (1961) introduced the concept of "mirror imaging," referring to the phenomenon
that the United States and the Soviet Union holds the same negative
misperceptions of each other. The need for psychological expertise in the
conduct of foreign policy was argued for by several psychologists during
this time, and several models for resolving international tensions were
developed (Deutsch 1961, 1963; Frank 1960, 1961; Osgood 1962). In
1965 Herbert Kelman edited an important collection of writings on international conflict from a psychological perspective (Kelman 1965), and in
1967 Jerome Frank's book, *Sanity and Survival: Psychological Aspects of
War and Peace,* appeared. The 1980s ushered in another flowering of
research on the psychological study of international conflict. By the mid-
1980s a body of research and writing had accumulated on the subject of
international conflict and war, and in 1986 a collection of these writings
was gathered by Ralph White in an edited book, *Psychology and the
Prevention of Nuclear War.* Included in this area is the study of conflict
resolution and negotiation. In chapter 5, Jeffrey Rubin presents an overview of this research and gives his view of a psychological perspective on
conflict and negotiation as it applies to international relations.

AGGRESSION, ENEMY-MAKING, AND PEACE

Two important areas of study within psychology that have broad social
import are the study of human aggression and of the psychological mechanisms involved in the creation of enmity between groups and nations.
In chapter 4, Ervin Staub explores some core issues in this area of
research and defines conditions that lead individuals and groups to turn
against each other. He also offers a vision, based on the study of helping
behavior and cooperation, of how groups can develop positive relations
with one another.

Psychologists have also done a great deal of research on the causes and
effects of "enemy imaging," the process wherein people come to identify
a group as an "enemy." Brett Silverstein, in chapter 6, reviews this
research and suggests ways that psychologists, through research, teaching, and community intervention, can help society resist the insidious
processes of enemy-making.

The proliferation of research conducted by psychologists on issues of
peace and related subjects prompted the American Psychological Associ-

ation to establish, in 1990 the Division of Peace Psychology, whose purpose is to encourage psychological research, education, and training on peace and nonviolent conflict resolution and related issues. In the *Research Directory* published by PsySR in 1990, indexed by topic, over two hundred psychologists are listed as conducting research on topics related to critical global issues, including, for example, images and perceptions of the nuclear threat, the development of enemy images, nuclear policy decision-making, patriotism, peace studies, and peace education.

PSYCHOTHERAPY, MENTAL HEALTH, AND SOCIAL ISSUES

In the 1980s, after a long period of almost exclusive absorption with the "internal," intrapsychic dynamics of the individual, some psychotherapists began to pay attention to the social, economic, and political contexts of their patients' or clients' lives, and evaluate the impact of these "external" factors on their emotional and psychological well-being. This growing movement harkens back to the "social context" perspective on mental health issues championed by Alfred Adler, who had been one of the original members of Freud's psychoanalytic circle around the turn of the century. Adler has been described as a "social activist in theory and practice." To him, mental health implied "socially affirmative action," and social responsibility was seen as "fundamental to the practice of psychology" (Rudmin and Ansbacher 1989).

The honest psychologist cannot shut his eyes to social conditions which prevent the child from becoming a part of the community and from feeling at home in the world, and which allow him to grow up as though he lived in enemy country. Thus the psychologist must work against nationalism when it is so poorly understood that it harms mankind as a whole; against wars of conquest, revenge and prestige; against unemployment which plunges people into hopelessness; and against all other obstacles which interfere with the spreading of social interest in the family, the school, and society at large. [Adler 1935, quoted in Rudmin and Ansbacher 1989]

Adler was ousted from the Psychoanalytic Society in 1911. Consequently his perspective on the importance of social issues in mental health was overshadowed by the more dominant views in psychoanalysis and the other psychotherapies that emerged in the early part of the century. These views, held by Freud and his followers, emphasized that the intrapsychic dynamics of the individual and the effects of early childhood experiences with one's primary caretaker, usually the mother, were the sources of emotional difficulties, psychopathology, and poor adjustment.

It was not until the development of family-systems theories and the family therapy movement, which began in the 1960s, that this individual, or at best dyadic, frame of reference began to be broadened to include the impact of the family as a whole on the psychological development and functioning of individuals. As mentioned above, this lens has been further broadened as clinicians have begun to consider the impact of a broad range of social, political, and experiential factors on their patients' lives. The impact of sexism, racism, physical and sexual abuse, alcoholism, poverty, various man-made and natural disasters, and the nuclear threat have all recently become the focus of study in clinical practice and research. The challenge of addressing the effects of these and other social factors in mental health practice and theory has been taken up by practitioners and researchers with a broad range of approaches: psychoanalytically oriented therapists (Levine, Jacobs, and Rubin 1988), family therapists (Mirkin 1990), feminist therapists (Laidlow, Malmo et al. 1990), and psychotherapists with other theoretical perspectives (Porter et al. 1986). Part Three, entitled "Mental Health and Psychotherapy in a Global Context," contains four chapters, each of which presents a new and innovative approach to the integration of political and social concerns with the practice and issues of psychotherapy, including individual psychotherapy, family therapy, and community mental health approaches.

PSYCHOLOGY AND THE ENVIRONMENT

An issue that has recently begun to attract the attention of behavioral scientists is that of the psychological and cultural factors related to environmental degradation and global environmental change. Many natural scientists in governmental agencies and foundations concerned with the environment claim that they would welcome psychological research on "everything from how to change people's behavior to understanding what the psychological impact will be of the changing environment on our children" (Rudmin and Ansbacher 1989). The National Science Foundation, for example, is offering research grants for studies that will help explain how "individuals and institutions affect and respond to environmental processes at a multinational or global scale" (Rudmin and Ansbacher 1989). Among other questions psychologists are asked to tackle are: What are the psychological causes of behaviors that contribute to global warming? How does the perception of risk affect the public's response to climate change or other environmental issues? Part Four, which we call "Psychology and the Environment," presents two different perspectives on psychological aspects of environmental problems. In chapter 11, John Mack calls for a new vision of our relationship to the earth as a whole, for a psychology of environmental responsibility, while in chapter 12 Scott Geller offers a behavior-change perspective on solving these problems.

ACTIVISM, COMMITMENT, AND EMPOWERMENT

Given the magnitude and importance of the challenges we face today, one may well ask: What motivates and sustains individuals in their involvement and commitment to social action? What circumstances and experiences move people from inactivity to activity, from a feeling of powerlessness to a feeling of empowerment? What are the emotional, social, and cultural supports that are necessary for developing and sustaining commitment and involvement in these critical and complex issues, whether as private citizens or as professionals? These are questions about the psychology of activism. In Part Five, "Empowerment and Activism," four chapters address these questions, each in a very different way—ranging from personal accounts of the development of commitment to activism, to reviews of psychological research on factors related to social activism.

EDUCATION FOR SOCIAL RESPONSIBILITY

Educators have shown a rapidly growing interest in global issues as well, which has given rise to a movement to incorporate into elementary, secondary, and college and university curricula instruction and discussion of these issues, including the responsibilities of citizenship. One of the earliest and most successful organizations to do this on the elementary and secondary level is Educators for Social Responsibility (ESR), a professional association of educators. ESR was originally founded in 1982 to introduce the topics of nuclear weapons, nuclear war, and conflict resolution into the public schools. It gradually expanded its mission to create new ways of teaching to promote active and socially responsible participation in global issues, including topics such as cooperative learning, nonviolent conflict resolution, and environmental education. In chapter 17, Phyllis La Farge provides a broad overview of the important work being done in the teaching of social responsibility and global issues in the schools.

Another important development took place in the 1980s at colleges and universities around the United States and Canada as courses began to be offered in departments of psychology, political science, international relations, and interdisciplinary studies that included material on the psychological aspects of war and peace, conflict resolution, peace psychology, nuclear weapons issues, and the psychological effects of living in a nuclear age. The number of courses offered that focus on or at least include these topics has been steadily increasing since the early 1980s. In chapter 18, James Dyal and Douglas McKenzie-Mohr describe the role such education plays in shaping the worldviews of high school, college, and university students.

In this introduction, we have tried to give a brief overview of the themes that will be discussed in the following chapters. We hope that this book will inspire students, teachers, researchers, and practitioners, in psychology and related fields, to participate in creating a new "psychology for our time," as called for by John Mack in the concluding chapter. In his essay, he describes an emerging view of the human psyche, self, or individual as a "far-reaching field, interdependent, interconnected, and interpenetrated by other minds or psyches." This shift in the notion of self implies that social responsibility "is not simply about caring for the other outside of oneself; it means to be concerned for one's self in the other." The new ways of dealing with social and global problems that this book presents call for nothing less than a transformation of the psychological professions, so that social responsibility enters the very core of our professional identity.

REFERENCES

Argyris, C. (1975). Dangers in applying results from experimental psychology. *American Psychologist, 30,* 469–485.

Beardslee, W. R., and J. E. Mack. (1982). The impact on children and adolescents of nuclear developments. In R. Rogers, ed., *Psychosocial Aspects of Nuclear Developments.* Task Force Report #20. Washington, D.C.: American Psychiatric Association.

Bronfenbrenner, U. (1961). The mirror image in Soviet-American relations: A social psychologist's report. *Journal of Social Issues,* 17(3), 45–56.

Deutsch, M. (1961). Some considerations relevant to national policy. *Journal of Social Issues,* 17(3), 57–68.

———. 1963. On changing an adversary. *American Journal of Orthopsychiatry,* 33, 244–246.

Escalona, D. (1982). Growing up with the threat of nuclear war: Some indirect effects on personality development. *American Journal of Orthopsychiatry,* 52(4), 600–617.

Frank, J. D. (1960). Breaking the thought barrier: Psychological challenges in the nuclear age. *Psychiatry,* 23, 245–266.

———. (1961). Emotional and motivational aspects of the disarmament problem. *Journal of Social Issues,* 17(3), 20–27.

———. (1967). *Sanity and Survival: Psychological Aspects of War and Peace.* New York: Random House.

Kelman, H., ed. (1965). *International Behavior: A Social-Psychological Analysis.* New York: Holt, Rinehart and Winston.

Laidlow, Malmo, et al. (1990). *Healing Voices: Feminist Approaches to Therapy.* San Francisco: Jossey Bass.

Levine, H., D. Jacobs, and L. Rubin (1988). *Psychoanalysis and the Nuclear Threat.* Hillsdale, N.J.: The Analytic Press.

Lifton, R. J. (1979). *The Broken Connection: On Death and the Continuity of Life.* New York: Simon and Schuster.

———. (1982). Beyond psychic numbing: A call to awareness. *American Journal of Orthopsychiatry,* 52(4), 619–629.

Lifton, R. J., and R. Falk (1982). *Indefensible Weapons.* New York: Basic Books.

Macy, J. R. (1983). *Despair and Personal Power in the Nuclear Age.* Philadelphia: New Society Publishers.

Milburn, T. W. (1961). The concept of deterrence: Some logical and psychological considerations. *Journal of Social Issues,* 17 (3), 3–11.

Mirkin, M., ed. (1990). *The Social and Political Contexts of Family Therapy.* Boston: Allyn and Bacon.

Morawski, J. D., and S. E. Goldstein. (1985). Psychology and Nuclear War. *American Psychologist,* 40(3), 276–284.

Osgood, C. (1962). *An Alternative to War or Surrender.* Urbana: University of Illinois Press.

Porter, K., D. Rinzler, and P. Olsen. (1986). *Heal or Die.* New York: Psychohistory Press.

Prilleltensky, I. (1989). Psychology and the status quo. *American Psychologist,* 44(5), 795–802.

Rudmin, F. W., and H. L. Ansbacher. (1989). Anti-war psychologists: Alfred Adler. *Psychologists for Social Responsibility Newsletter.*

Sampson, E. E. (1977). Psychology and the American ideal. *Journal of Personality and Social Psychology,* 35, 767–782.

Sarason, S. B. (1984). If it can be studied or developed, should it be? *American Psychologist,* 39, 477–485.

Schwebel, M. (1982). Effects of the nuclear war threat on children and teenagers: Implications for professionals. *American Journal of Orthopsychiatry,* 52(4), 608–618.

White, R. (1965). Images in context of international conflict: Perceptions of the U.S. and U.S.S.R. In Kelman 1965, 236–276.

———. (1986). *Psychology and the Prevention of Nuclear War.* New York: New York University Press.

PART ONE

PSYCHOLOGICAL PERSPECTIVES ON A GLOBAL AGE

Each of us is called on to do something that no member of any generation before ours has had to do: to assume responsibility for the continuation of our kind—to choose human survival. . . . For the risk of extinction is not just one more item on the agenda of issues that face us. Embracing, as it does, the life and death of every human being on earth and every future human being, it embraces and transcends all other issues. —*Jonathan Schell*

This part consists of three chapters that take a bold look at current threats to human survival and offer some visions for constructive response.

In the first chapter, Robert Jay Lifton examines our current "genocidal mentality" and proposes the need for a "species mentality" that will lead us out of the abyss of global holocaust and into acknowledgement of our shared fate. He urges professionals in all disciplines to engage in the "universalistic activities" of species self and planetary transformation. In chapter 2, Joanna R. Macy describes the paralyzing consequences of repressing and denying our fears and anxieties about global crises. She presents the "despair and empowerment" work she developed, in which feelings are acknowledged and shared with others, leading to the discovery of inner resources for constructive action on issues of global concern. In chapter 3, Roger Walsh presents his view of the causes of contemporary threats to human survival from a wide range of psychological perspectives, including cognitive, behavioral, social learning, and psychodynamic, and suggests the necessary steps for the development of a psychology of human survival.

1

From a Genocidal Mentality to a Species Mentality

Robert Jay Lifton

In a posthumous essay, Robert Lowell wrote that since 1936 the earth's surface seems to have sagged and cracked. He was referring to the years of Hitler, Stalin's purges, Buchenwald, the atomic bomb, and the threat of nuclear war—things that still preoccupy us. We therefore must address our concerned scholarship and our activism—and we need lots of both, never one without the other—to precisely this menace, these threats.

Let me begin with an image. In Haifa, Israel, a few years ago I was interviewing a Jewish dentist who had survived three years, rather miraculously, as a prisoner in Auschwitz. This was part of my study of Nazi doctors (Lifton 1986). The interview was very painful for him as he told me in great detail about what he had to witness and do in order to survive there, and it was very valuable for me. At the end of that interview he looked around his very comfortable house, high on that hill overlooking the beautiful Haifa harbor, sighed deeply, and said, "This world is not this world. This world is not this world."

What he meant by that was that however comfortable and safe one's surroundings may seem, once one has known Auschwitz one knows that there is menace underneath. And I thought about that because it was the same kind of feeling I got when I talked to people in Hiroshima much earlier, in 1962 (Lifton, 1968 [1982]). They too could be comfortable in pleasant surroundings (by that time), but underneath was their sense of menace derived from what they had gone through and what they knew threatened the world.

There is an American Zen Buddhist monk who has taken up an antinuclear position, who has made a vow to himself that he will never engage in any conversation with anybody without mentioning the danger of nuclear weapons. That means, of course, that he makes a perfect pest of himself. He cannot get into a taxicab without raising the question of nuclear weapons. There are probably a lot of people he encounters who wish he would go away.

After having lived and worked in Hiroshima, I did not find that so strange. I found myself—without having articulated that vow—doing something similar: never in any way addressing the whole issue of nuclear weapons without some mention of Hiroshima. Now I extend my vow. Whenever I deal with these questions, and it has to be often, I also bring in the *species self*—a sense of one's self (that is, one's way of symbolizing one's own organism) as related to the sense of self of everybody else on the planet. This is the direction of possibility beyond, and instead of, holocaust. Species consciousness and the species self are possibilities already taking shape.

The species self plays an important role in my recent book, with Eric Markusen, *The Genocidal Mentality: Nazi Holocaust and Nuclear Threat*, on the European Holocaust and its lessons for our nuclear predicament (Lifton and Markusen 1990). But in all my work, I talk about the need for a larger sense of human connectedness, or what I call the sense of immortality, the symbolization of immortality that we all need; the sense we require of living on in our children and their children, or in our people, in our group (Lifton 1979 [1984], 1987). This sense of immortality through the species self is then extended outward, so that it includes living on in our children and their children, in our group and country, but also living on in humankind. Thus we sense that something of us continues if humankind continues.

But one must look *into* the abyss in order to be able to see beyond it. From the Nazi Holocaust, one can find certain principles and parallels that we need to grasp, that are relevant to what is happening in regard to our nuclear stance.

People can relate to the world in a dangerous way, with what I call the *genocidal mentality:* a mind-set that includes individual and collective willingness to destroy, according to certain standards of necessity, entire human populations. When one begins to consider the genocidal mentality, it has to do with a genocidal readiness. The Holocaust in Europe did not just happen; there was a genocidal readiness established through an ideology, through various institutions that were built up, and through certain bureaucratic circumstances. The genocidal mentality is a collective process; it has to do with structures and groups' collectivities and, above all, with ideology.

There is one very important difference between the Nazi situation and the nuclear one. In the Nazi situation, there was a clear distinction between victims and victimizers: the Nazis were the victimizers and those they preyed upon—Jews, gypsies, Russians, Poles, homosexuals, Seventh Day Adventists, and others—were victims. But once nuclear weapons are brought into use, there is no longer any distinction between victimizers and victims. There is a strange reluctance to give up that distinction, as one can see in the care taken to build deep, concrete shelters for our military and political leaders so they can continue to run the nuclear war after it has begun and everybody else is dead. That is their illusion, but also a reflection of the inability to face that very simple and formidable development in the distinction between victimizers and victims. And of course, the breakdown in distinction is epitomized by global ecological consequences of large-scale nuclear weapons use: detonate a certain amount of megatonnage and the whole world may be destroyed or at least no longer able to sustain life.

Genocide is arranged at the highest intellectual levels. Franklin Littel wrote about the Nazi Holocaust that "the death camps were planned, built, and operated by the men and women of the modern university." This made him, appropriately enough, raise some questions about the modern university. We should recognize in this genocidal mentality a fundamental wrongness and absurdity that informs everything we do. We do have to proceed with day-by-day actions, starting from where we are, but we must also recognize that the whole structure is absolutely absurd and unacceptable, and has to be changed. Absurdity is a beginning source of wisdom.

To look at the history of how we got to this absurd situation, we can study the strategic bombing in the middle and end of World War II (Lifton and Markusen 1990, 17–21). This is a crucial and neglected dimension that people are rediscovering. It is usually said that the Nazis engaged in immoral bombing, and we imitated them. that's too simple. Yes, the Nazis did engage in immoral bombing and lots of other immoral actions. But the policies for strategic bombing were formed between the wars. They are an outgrowth of the military's romance with air power; indeed, area bombing of civilians began almost with the invention of the airplane at the turn of the century. These policies were developed more by England and then the United States than by any other countries. Democratic countries, unfortunately, are capable of genocidal actions: after all, it was the strategic bombing policy that led to, and prefigured, the Hiroshima and Nagasaki bombings.

An aspect of our own relationship to this problem is what I call "false nuclear normality." This is a very simple but still neglected idea. All through the nuclear age, various signals have been given out in our society about what is acceptable, appropriate, and normal behavior from us, the citizens of the United States. In the early days of nuclear strategy, during the late 1950s and early '60s, Herman Kahn and others had the country almost convinced that the reasonable or normal man or woman was to join in a "rational assessment of how best to prepare for and win a nuclear war." To refute this intellectually, and to cry out with passion against it was in some way, by their judgment, "emotional" or "irrational." It was not "normal," it was "deviant."

Those who grew up during that time remember very well the "duck and cover" drills, because the preparation for nuclear normality began early in the schools. An associate of mine, Michael Carey has done a wonderful study of people of that generation, his generation (Carey 1982, 20–24). By interviewing people who underwent those school drills, he came to the sense that yes, they were terrified. They did not really believe that putting a piece of paper over their heads and closing their eyes would protect them from all the nuclear dangers; but they did not know *what* to believe because their authorities, the teachers, were telling them just that. They were confused. They had nightmares, but the message was: to be a normal child, you're not supposed to be afraid. However, the nightmares continued, often into adolescence, and when questioned about it all kinds of fears and imagery flowed out.

Recent work by William Vandercook, a historian in Chicago, has demonstrated that there was a systematic effort to impose that nuclear normality on the country. A committee was even officially established by the National Security Council consisting of psychiatrists, ordinary doctors, social scientists, and retired generals whose charge was to evaluate how people respond under the threat of mutual annihilation, and how to help them be strong in relationship to this threat and to behave well should a nuclear war occur (Vandercook 1986). They issued reports and hemmed and hawed and invoked American patriotism and many other things, but the gist of it was they could not really think of a way because Americans did not believe in the key to the whole project: effective civil defense. Americans have never believed in civil defense, and the absurdity of civil defense has always epitomized the absurdity of the nuclear arms race, and has always served as a point from which we can undermine and sabotage the false claims to civil defense, to nuclear safety, to nuclear normality.

Just as that first wave of nuclear normality was being combatted, a second wave appeared—in a way a more serious one. The second wave of nuclear normality can be epitomized by the phrase, "living with nuclear weapons." That was the title of a very unfortunate book that came out of the Kennedy School of Government at Harvard University, and in its last paragraph concludes that living with nuclear weapons is our only hope—that there is no greater test of the human spirit (Carnesale et al. 1983). I reject that living with nuclear weapons is our only hope, and think that the test of the human spirit is to get rid of the weapons.

One can tell the wrong-headedness of anyone concerning nuclear weapons (or anything else) by their attitude toward humor. And that particular Harvard study assaulted two of the most important expressions about nuclear weapons we have had so far, the lyrics of Tom Lehrer and the film, *Dr. Strangelove: Or How I Learned to Stop Worrying and Love the Bomb*. The Harvard study called these messages nuclear escapism. What the authors did not realize was that when Tom Lehrer wrote his wonderful lyrics, "we will all go together when we go," and "Hey mom, I'm off to drop the bomb"; or when *Strangelove* depicts that wild Air Force officer going down with the Texas yodel as the bomb explodes into a vast nothingness, these are bitter condemnations through humor, mockery, and satire of the absurdity of the entire nuclear weapons structure.

Joseph Nye, who is one of the leading Harvard spokesmen, has written a book called *Nuclear Ethics* (1986), which, I think is something of an oxymoron. He raised a question in response to Jonathan Schell, who had made a perfectly reasonable statement in saying that if any policy has a possibility of leading to the destruction of the world, then we should treat that policy as though it *would* lead to the destruction of the world. In other words, stay away from it. But Nye asks, "Would it follow we have no right to gamble because if we lose the game would be over? It does not follow from the fact that extinction is an unlimited consequence," he continues, "that even a tiny probability of extinction is intolerable, and that our generation has no right to take risks" (Nye 1986, 63–64). And then he says, "In this risk-taking we should not be too beholden to future generations. How do we know what future generations will feel?" Otherwise we are in danger of "establish[ing] a dictatorship of future generations over the present one." It may be true that we don't know exactly what future generations will feel, but I think I can speak for future generations when I say I know they would like to be here.

The third wave of nuclear normality is the one about the "Star Wars" system. First it's canceled, then it's on again, and continues to change its line repeatedly. Is it protecting people? No, it turns out to be protecting weapons. Is it a defensive system? Actually, it turns out to have a few offensive gimmicks as well. But the central point about Star Wars is that it expresses a comprehensive illusion about the central fact of the nuclear age: absolute, universal vulnerability. That is what Star Wars denies in its vast, elaborate pseudotheological system. Thus, it can be made a criterion for nuclear normality: Isn't it abnormal to oppose a shield against nuclear weapons?

These descriptions of nuclear normality (and they are psychological as well as political as they set forth their criteria) develop from our dependence on the weapons themselves, on the perverse ideology of *nuclearism*. Nuclearism really means exaggerated psychological, political, and military dependence on nuclear weapons, even the passionate embrace or near worship of the weapons as a solution to a wide variety of human dilemmas, most ironically that of "security" (see Lifton 1984, chap. 23). Nuclearism always insists that the development of weapons becomes the normative principle.

There are certain patterns that inform the genocidal mentality. There is first the issue of historical trauma and response. One cannot begin to understand the Nazi Holocaust without understanding the traumatic

experience of the German people, World War I, and their demoraliza-
tion.

In the case of nuclear weapons, the trauma is more subtle and less
appreciated. Ironically, the historical trauma has been our own use of
weapons. Paul Boyer's excellent book, *By the Bomb's Early Light: American Thought and Culture at the Dawn of the Atomic Age* (1985), gives
one a very vivid sense of the extent of the American trauma after Hiroshima. For instance, within a day or two there were expressions of great
fear in the newspapers. As the New York *Herald Tribune* put it, "It was
weird, incredible, somehow disturbing. One forgets the effect on Japan
or on the course of the war. One senses the foundations of one's own
universe trembling" (quoted in Lifton 1979 [1984], 371). And there were
many responses like that, expressing the fear: Why *wouldn't* we be next
as victims of the bomb once this weapon has been created? But that fear
was of course submerged in the waves of nuclear normality that I have
tried to describe.

And instead of taking appropriate directions toward peace, we embraced the very source of the fear, the weapons themselves, so the
ideology of nuclearism rose out of the first wave of nuclear fear. And then
we call upon the weapons, the object of that fear, to save us, to protect
the peace, to keep the world going, as something close to salvation.

In both Nazism and nuclearism there is some sort of identification
with ultimate power and with the claims of science, and the glue is
ideological. Both need professionals. There are professional killers one
can draw upon—soldiers, people from the ranks, ordinary people—and
train them to be killers. (That has always been done in wars but people
can be trained for genocide as well.) But you also need killing professionals, people who will apply their professions to genocidal purposes. The
Nazi doctors did that within a biological idiom. The parallels here are the
weapons designers among nuclear physicists and nuclear engineers, and
the weapons strategists themselves among physicists, social scientists,
economists, and others.

Nuclear weapons designers and strategists are not Nazis, and in fact
the difference is very important. Nazi ideology was vicious from the start.
The viciousness of nuclearism is less obvious. These are decent people
who can be likable and articulate, and who can wish for peace, who make
these weapons and who write draconian scenarios of their use. Thus, it is

a case of lending their professions to a genocidal project. And it is the tragedy of American physics, just as it was the tragedy of J. Robert Oppenheimer personally, that American physics, and especially nuclear physics, came of age at the time of (and with the construction of) that first atomic bomb.

Nazi doctors in Auschwitz adapted to their extreme environment by evolving what I call the "Auschwitz self." These Nazi doctors, most of the time living in Auschwitz and Poland, conducted selections, sent arriving Jews to the gas chambers, and really supervised the whole killing project by declaring people dead in the gas chambers. The sequence of their lives became routine. They engaged themselves actively in the killing as their job in Auschwitz, and then three or five days a month went on leave back to Germany, where they would be ordinary fathers and husbands, visiting their children and wives. That was their prior, relatively more humane self. Their second or "double" self was their Auschwitz self. These selves can function relatively autonomously. Nazi doctors did have a conscience, but instead of standing between them and their victims as a conscience should, it functioned in connection with their loyalty to their organization, to their institution, to the world of Auschwitz.

When one looks at nuclear physicists who have been involved in weapons work in some of the work of Steven Kull and some of my own interviews with them, one sees considerable *doubling* (the formation of a functional "second self," related to but more or less autonomous from the prior self) in them, as well as in the weapons designers and weapons strategists (Lifton and Markusen 1990, 13, 148–155; Kull 1988). For instance, one leading physicist went to work on the hydrogen bomb, even though he was opposed to the bomb. He did so because he felt that the Russians would make it in any case, and some other physicists had convinced him that they needed him and that the bomb could be made. He was working on it, hoping all the time it couldn't be made. But then a military committee came down to Los Alamos where he was working, and they began to express awe and enormous pride and loving feelings toward this new weapon, which they were eager to have, and he felt increasingly anxious as he heard them speak because he knew the weapon was horrible. He kept his silence. In keeping his silence, he was in a sense maintaining an adaptation to that environment. Through this doubling, he maintained a sense of self in his work but did not take it home, enjoyed his family in a human way, and went for long walks in the spectacular Los Alamos hills, as did many of those physicists. But in maintaining that doubling, he maintains his entire adaptation to the Los Alamos environment and the entire nuclear weapons situation. There are many other examples of a parallel nature that one could describe.

In addition to the activity of professionals—that is, *professional killers* and *killing professionals;* it is the second group that we have to be most concerned with, being closest to ourselves—is the development of what may be called societal momentum toward genocide when genocide was not necessarily intended.

For instance, even the Nazis had not clearly come upon their decision to kill all the Jews—the Final Solution—until sometime in early 1941. That has been fairly well established by historians. Of course they had a murderous ideology and everything was in place for that possibility. But it was the ebb and flow of bureaucratic problems and ideological radical-ization that led to that decision, which wasn't clearly intended, at least not consciously, in those earlier years. A similar kind of process of societal momentum toward nuclear genocide could readily take place. The INF (Intermediate Range Nuclear Forces) Treaty, signed in 1987 by Presidents Reagan and Gorbachev, even with all of its deficiencies—the worst of which is that it lessened the urgency of the anti-nuclear move-ment, and it should not have—is nonetheless a useful step, because it at least interrupts some of that societal momentum toward crossing a certain genocidal threshold.

However, it does not address deterrence. Deterrence is a policy based upon the necessity of dissociative psychological processes in people, especially in those who maintain the policy. *Dissociation* (of which dou-bling is a form) means some part of the self is separated from other portions of the self. To maintain and support deterrence, one has to block out a crucial dimension of it: you have to be ready to use the weapons, and willing to use them. The readiness and willingness to use them, the genocidal mentality, is what the American people dissociate from. The process of *psychic numbing* or diminished capacity to feel—usually in-volving separation of thought from feeling—is, as I speak of it, an aspect of dissociation in Americans' maintaining support, as far as it goes, for deterrence.

We should not make the mistake of thinking that deterrence is a peaceful structure. As structured now—and despite the remarkable recent changes in East-West relations—it is a genocidal structure; it is part of the genocidal mentality, and we must go beyond it.

Now, finally, the good news. We have come to recognize, through research studies, that there is lots of anxiety about nuclear weapons. But that anxiety is useful, at least the tension and fear, because it's a break from the sustained numbing that prevails and from nuclear normality.

Once one takes in the truth of nuclear threat, namely the imagery of extinction, the capacity of the weapons to destroy the world and all or most of the human and animal populations on the earth, then one develops an idea that I call "shared fate." We recognize that our fate is in common with that of the Soviet Union or any other nation, and therefore, I say to my Soviet counterpart, or he or she to me, "If I die you die. If you survive I survive." And once one moves toward shared fate, one has taken a step toward the species self and species consciousness, because one recognizes that my sense of self is in relationship to the survival of every other sense of self, every other self on the planet. That form of self-image takes shape in me with that recognition. This is not an idealistic but a pragmatic statement. In that sense, ironically, the truth about the destructiveness of the weapons leads us to an insight about shared fate on this planet. (And many planetary problems press themselves on us, toward which only species consciousness can offer us anything like a resolution. Consider very obvious situations such as Chernobyl. It is a species problem, not a Soviet problem or a European or an American problem; it's everybody's problem. There are many other examples, like the pollution of waterways, the "greenhouse effect," destruction of the ozone layer, or even the AIDS epidemic, that are species problems and have the same effect.)

For that insight to develop and grow—and it is within us in various haphazard ways—we must continue to take in the nuclear and other global threats. The awareness of shared fate takes shape individually and collectively and is being recognized and thought about. We have seen it expressed, for example, in the selection of Nobel Peace Prize recipients, and the Nobel Peace Committee is not exactly a radical group. It has given an award to International Physicians for the Prevention of Nuclear War, to Elie Wiesel, and to other peacemakers in the world for whom shared fate is a theme.

Shared fate means moving toward a broader human identity. It is important to make clear that as one moves to a more inclusive sense of self, or a more inclusive human identity that does indeed take in all of humankind, one is not giving up or surrendering one's more immediate identities. One remains a Russian or an American or a Dane or a Chinese or a Nigerian or whatever one is. One remains a professional if that's what one is. Or if I speak personally, I remain an American, a Jew, a psychiatrist, a professor, a father, a husband, a writer, a Moriano Ouncon fan, a tennis fanatic, and a sometime cartoonist, among other things. But all of these are joined in with a species consciousness, so that I am for myself very importantly a member of the human species.

When one moves toward a species self, one can reject the perverse ideology of nuclearism and the equally perverse criteria of nuclear normality and the genocidal mentality, and move toward what is a species consciousness. Obviously we never do things perfectly, to put it mildly, as human beings, we will move back and forth and grope, as we are doing now, toward species consciousness and species self. But even a partial groping, with significant elements of species consciousness, can go a long way in terms of political and ethical decisions and policies that we adopt.

One can call upon the professions for their potential movement toward species consciousness, or call it species professionalism. All the professions at their most ideal have that species consciousness. A physician is supposed to be a healer on a universal basis—not a killer, and not a healer only of some. I remember one riveting scene from a film that was taken of a visit by the physicians' antinuclear movement to the Soviet Union a few years ago. It showed Evgueni Chazov, leader of the Soviet delegation, and Sid Alexander, leader of the American delegation, each leaning over a very, very sick man in a Moscow hospital. Each of them put a stethoscope on the man's chest and back, and you could see each one completely immersed in that medical problem. And for that moment, Russian and American distinctions, even nuclear weapons, were forgotten. All they cared about was how they might treat this man so that he might continue his life.

That kind of species commitment is at the heart of all professions. We surrender it too easily in the name of power, money, or some sort of professional compliance with the powers-that-be. One could say the same of science. Instead of addressing itself to weapons making, or a deadly and murderous biology, as in the case of the Nazis, science could recall that it is from its beginnings a universal language and a universalistic activity. There are scientists who are addressing themselves to that universalism in Europe and in the United States. The environmental and nuclear weapons problems are two central issues that science can begin with because they are by definition universalistic in their effects, and they cannot be approached in any other way.

Not only professionals but all people should strive toward species consciousness and the species self. There is first of all its compelling, pragmatic logic. There are the historical forces that can contribute to a species self. There are also many tendencies, sometimes called "postmodern," to look at things holistically. We saw many of these in the late '60s and early '70s and they are still very much with us. They include interest in community and in overcoming some of the fragmentation, scientism, and technicism of the modern era. They are timely as well, and this is a timely moment for species consciousness.

Indeed, one could call it a species moment, a moment of species possibility. One can look at it in evolutionary terms. As an evolutionary step we require species consciousness if the human species, and the other species—for whom we have considerable responsibility on this planet—are to survive. There is a question of evolutionary adaptation here. When Nazi doctors did what they did, and when nuclear physicists involved in weapons making and others involved in weapons strategy do what they do, they are adapting to an immediate environment and an immediate national ethos. But that adaptation is maladaptive to the larger future; immediate adaptation to genocidal potential threatens the overall human adaptation.

We can say, finally, that the species self is a biological truth and a psychological possibility. It's a biological truth because it avoids what Erik Erikson has called "pseudo-speciation": different communities or nations or groups treating other communities, nations, or groups as though they were a different species. But they are not, of course; we're all part of the same human species. And psychologically, in the imperfect way that I just described, we are capable of species consciousness. We all have some of that and we can develop more as we move toward a species self.

At the end of my study of Nazi doctors, I referred to a talk I had with a Jewish doctor who survived an Auschwitz incarceration. He told me his story and became my friend. He described how at a certain point he and a few other prisoner doctors were overwhelmed with moribund patients (prisoner doctors were actually allowed to do some medical work in Auschwitz) clamoring for relief. He and his friends did what they could. They dispensed the few aspirins they had and ran out of them, but then made a point to offer a few words of reassurance and hope. Almost to his surprise, he found that his words had an effect; as he put it, in that situation they really helped. By maintaining one's determination to try to heal, even under the most extreme conditions he was able to conclude, "I was impressed with how much one could do." The lesson applies to all of us. He was living out the words of Samuel Beckett: "In the end it's the end that is the worst. . . . you must go on a little more; you must go on a long time more."

REFERENCES

Boyer, Paul. (1985). *By the Bomb's Early Light: American Thought and Culture at the Dawn of the Atomic Age.* New York: Pantheon.

Carey, Michael J. (1982). Psychological Fallout. *Bulletin of the Atomic Scientists,* 38, 1.

Carnesale, Albert, et al. (1983). *Living with Nuclear Weapons.* Cambridge: Harvard University Press.

Kull, Steven. (1988). *Minds at War: Nuclear Reality and the Inner Conflicts of Defense Policymakers.* New York: Basic Books.

Lifton, Robert Jay. (1982). *Death in Life: Survivors of Hiroshima.* New York: Basic Books.

———. (1984). *Broken Connection.* New York: Basic Books.

———. (1986). *The Nazi Doctors: Medical Killing and the Psychology of Genocide.* New York: Basic Books.

———. (1987). *The Future of Immortality.* New York: Basic Books.

Lifton, Robert Jay and Eric Markusen. (1990). *The Genocidal Mentality: Nazi Holocaust and Nuclear Threat.* New York: Basic Books.

Nye, Joseph S. (1986). *Nuclear Ethics.* New York: Free Press.

Vandercook, William F. (1986). "Making the Very Best of the Worst: The 'Human Effects of Nuclear Weapons' Report of 1956." *International Security,* 11.

2

Planetary Perils and Psychological Responses: Despair and Empowerment Work

Joanna R. Macy

CONCERNS FOR THE WORLD

We live in an extraordinary time—here at this moment on planet Earth. From news reports and from our environment, we are bombarded by signals of distress—of toxic wastes and famines and expiring species, of arms and wars and preparations for war. These boggle the mind and stir within us feelings of dread, anger, and sorrow, even though we may never express them. By virtue of our humanity, we share these deep responses. Though our styles of response may differ, we are all citizens of the same planet, all trying in our different ways to cope with a deep, inchoate, and collective sense of danger. For to be conscious in our world today involves awareness of unprecedented peril.

This peril, as I see it, comes from three different directions. Each constitutes a development of catastrophic proportion, each increases daily in intensity, and each has become a standard feature in our psychic landscape. Let me review them.

1. *The threat of nuclear war.* The U.S. government bases its power

This chapter is adapted from chapters 1 and 2 of *Despair and Personal Power in the Nuclear Age,* by J. Macy (1983), Philadelphia: New Society Publishers, with permission of the publisher.

and policy on the credibility of this threat. With expenditures in the trillions of dollars, weapons of mass destruction proliferate. Nothing in history suggests that they will not be used, or unleashed by accident. Our awareness of this is so potent and pervasive that, according to polls, the majority of the public expects a nuclear war to occur within their lifetimes, that they will not survive it, and that civilization as we know it will end.

2. *The progressive destruction of our life-support system.* Toxic wastes . . . acid rain . . . rising rates of radioactivity . . . loss of topsoil and forestland . . . spreading deserts . . . dying seas . . . expiring species of plant and animal life. These facts assail us through news reports and our own sensory experience in the air we breathe, the water we drink, and what we see happening to our environment. These developments, arising from our ways of consumption and production, prefigure yet larger-scale disasters.

3. *The growing misery of half the planet's people.* Prevailing economic patterns impoverish the Third World, causing hunger, homelessness, and disease. In no period of history has so large a proportion of humanity lacked the means for a decent and healthy life. With growing disparity between "haves" and "have-nots," with the spread of totalitarian regimes and the use of detention and torture on an unprecedented scale, deep rage erupts, turning our planet into a tinderbox.

PAIN FOR THE WORLD

These developments are facts of life in our present world. They shape the wider context of our lives. Whatever policies we may advocate in response to them, they are part of the story we are living now together. To be aware of them at any level is to feel pain for our world and our collective future. The pain is all the more poignant, since these developments render questionable for the first time in recorded history the survival of our species and of our planet as a viable home for conscious life.

Until now, every generation throughout history lived with the tacit certainty that other generations would follow. Each assumed, without questioning, that its children and children's children and those yet unborn would carry on—to walk the same earth, under the same sky. Hardships, failures, and personal death were ever encompassed in that vaster assurance of continuity. That certainty is now lost to us whether we work in the Pentagon or in the peace movement. That loss, unmeasured and immeasurable, is the pivotal psychological reality of our time.

"Well, this isn't the first time people expected the end of the world," some of us say. And that is true; at the first millennium and during the Black Plague in Europe there were groups who announced and prepared for that event. But they saw it as the act of a divine being—of a just and wrathful God who was ready to punish the beings he had created and loved. In other words, it was seen within contexts of meaning that lent dignity and continuity to human life. Today, however, the pervasive inklings of apocalypse are bereft of meaning; they are not only bolstered by the projections of scientists but imbued with the absurdity of collective suicide.

The responses that arise, as we behold what we are doing to our world, are compounded by many feelings. There is fear—dread of what is overtaking our common life, and terror at the thought of the suffering in store for our loved ones and others. There is anger—yes, and bitter rage that we live our lives under the threat of so avoidable and meaningless an end to the human enterprise. There is guilt; for as members of society we feel implicated in this catastrophe and haunted by the thought that we should be able to avert it. And above all, there is sorrow. Confronting so vast and final a loss as this brings sadness beyond the telling.

Even these terms, however—anger, fear, sorrow—are inadequate to convey the feelings we experience in this context, for they connote emotions long familiar to our species as it has faced the inevitability of personal death. The feelings that assail us now cannot be equated with dread of our own individual demise. Their source lies less in concerns for the personal self than in apprehensions of collective suffering—of what happens to others, to human life and fellow species, to the heritage we share, to the unborn generations to come, and to our green planet itself, wheeling there in space.

What we are really dealing with here is akin to the original meaning of compassion: "suffering with." It is the distress we feel in connection with the larger whole of which we are a part. It is our pain for the world.

No one is exempt from that pain, any more than one could exist alone and self-existent in empty space. It is as natural to us as the food and air we draw from our environment to fashion who we are. It is inseparable from the currents of matter, energy, and information that flow through us and sustain us as interconnected open systems. We are not closed off from the world, but integral components of it, like cells in a larger body. When part of that body is traumatized, we sense that trauma too—in the sufferings of fellow-beings, in the pillage of our planet, and even in the violation of future generations. When the condition of the larger system falters, sickens, as is happening in our present age of exploitation and nuclear technology, the disturbance we feel at a semiconscious level is acute. Like the impulses of pain in any ailing organism, they serve a positive purpose; these impulses of pain are warning signals.

Yet we tend to repress that pain. We block it out because it hurts, because it is frightening, and most of all because we do not understand it and consider it to be a dysfunction, an aberration, a sign of personal weakness.

REACTIONS TO PERIL

So, as a society we are caught between a sense of impending apocalypse and the fear of acknowledging it. In this "caught" place, our responses are blocked and confused. Look at the following comments that are frequently made when the possibility of mass annihilation is mentioned:

"It's too horrible to think about. I just block it out."
"Everything I do seems pointless. It could all go at any time."
"Maybe it won't land here. Maybe we'll survive."
"It won't ever be dropped. No one's that crazy."

Do these responses have a familiar ring? Perhaps you have heard similar comments when issues of human survival surface in the course of a conversation.

Looking both at our reactions and our lack of reaction to the peril of our time, we find three widespread behaviors: disbelief, denial, and double life.

1. *Disbelief.* Even though much of my life is taken up by this issue, I still find it hard to believe that nuclear weapons actually exist. Their existence is maddeningly abstract; I've never seen a bomb, let alone an explosion, except on film. I especially find it hard to believe that after millions of years of the evolution of life on earth, after millennia of civilization, of spiritual and artistic geniuses, Shakespeares, Mozarts,

Einsteins, we should come to this—that we should be developing and deploying instruments to blow up our world. That these instruments are real, that by human intention they are poised off-shore and targeted at me now, that we are similarly aiming them at conglomerations of other human beings, is—very frankly—a fact that for most of my waking hours I am unable, at some level, to take seriously.

2. *Denial.* Such quasi belief can of course lead to denial. Not so long ago, it was the possibility of annihilation itself that we tended to disclaim. Then, with the acceleration of the arms race and the talk of "limited nuclear war," we did not deny the danger so much as what is at stake. We heard sober assessments that a hundred million dead are an "acceptable" and "survivable" loss. Stunned by the prospect of so immense an atrocity, the human mind is tempted to acquiesce to the triviality of its own existence. It is tempting to say, as Lifton reports hearing in the halls of his university, "What's so special about human beings?"

3. *Double life.* And so we tend to live our lives as if nothing has changed, while knowing that everything has changed. This is what Lifton (1979) calls a "double life," and we all lead it to some extent. On one level we maintain a more or less up-beat capacity to carry on as usual— getting up in the morning and remembering which shoe goes on which foot, getting the kids off to school, meeting our appointments, cheering up our friends . . . and all the while, there is this inchoate knowledge that our world could go at any moment. Awesome and unprecedented in the history of humanity, it lurks there, with an anguish beyond the naming. Until we find ways of acknowledging and integrating that level of anguished awareness, we repress it; and with that repression we are drained of the energy we need for action and clear thinking.

Each of us has had the experience of responding to emergency. We may have rushed to douse a fire, or pulled a friend away from a moving truck, or raced to a child who fell into deep water. Each of us has the capacity to drop everything and act. That power to act is ours in the present situation of peril, all the more so since we are not alone. No outside authority is silencing us; no external force is keeping us from responding with all our might and courage to the present danger to life on Earth. It is something inside us that stifles our responses. What is it that leads us to repress our awareness of danger, miring so many of us in disbelief, denial, and a double life?

CAUSES OF REPRESSION

The reasons for repressing our awareness are not hard to find. Some typical examples were expressed during a Despair and Empowerment workshop, a process I will describe later in this chapter. After a morning of sharing deep personal feelings about the planetary crisis, from nightmares of nuclear holocaust to anguish for oppressed peoples, the question was raised: "Why in our daily lives do we avoid expressing these deep concerns?"

Within minutes dozens of responses came forth:

"I don't want to spoil the time we have left."

"People would see me as a doomsday cartoon figure."

"I don't want to depress myself."

"I want my kids to be happy, I'm afraid of showing them how afraid I am."

"If I spoke my fears, they might come true."

"The future is too overwhelming to talk about."

"I don't want to appear weak or emotional."

There are specific reasons why we avoid naming our innermost concerns, and there are many kinds of fear that inhibit us from acknowledging and expressing these concerns.

Fear of Pain

Our culture conditions us to view pain as dysfunctional. There are pills for headaches, backaches, neuralgia, and premenstrual tension—but no pills, capsules, or tablets for this pain for our world. Not even a stiff drink helps much. As Kevin McVeigh says in his despair and empowerment workshops: "Instead of survival being the issue, it is the feelings aroused by possible destruction that loom as most fearful. And as they are judged to be too unpleasant to endure, they are turned off completely. This is the state of psychic numbing."

To permit ourselves to entertain dread for the world is not only painful but frightening; it appears to threaten our capacity to cope. We are afraid that if we were to let ourselves fully experience our dread, we might fall apart, lose control, or be mired in it permanently.

Fear of Appearing Morbid

"Be sociable," "Keep smiling," our society tells us with its cult of optimism. "If you can't say something nice, don't say anything at all," as I was admonished as a child.

A sanguine confidence in the future has been a hallmark of the American character and a source of national pride. The successful person, as we conclude from commercials and campaigns, brims with optimism. In such a setting feelings of anguish and despair for our world can appear to be a failure of maintaining stamina and even competence.

Fear of Appearing Ignorant

Our culture also conditions us to expect instant solutions. "Don't bring me a problem unless you have the answer," Lyndon Johnson used to say during the Vietnam War. Similarly today, many feel that we should not complain about a situation unless we have already evolved a "solution" to it. It is hard to express our dread of nuclear holocaust, for example, without finding ourselves enmeshed in an argument over the requirements of national defense and challenged to produce an immediate alternative strategy to secure American power. If we have not evolved a panacea, along with an impressive command of facts and figures about military hardware and the history of the arms race, we can feel stupid, frustrated—as if our concerns were without grounds.

Fear of Guilt

To acknowledge distress for our world opens us also to a sense of guilt. Few of us are exempt from the suspicion that as a nation—through expedience, life-style, and dreams of power—we are accomplices to catastrophe.

"I wasn't out of high school when I went to see 'Hiroshima Mon Amour,'" writes Christina Robb in the *Boston Globe* (1982). "I was an American. America had invented, designed, manufactured, used and stockpiled incendiary devices that made the ovens of Auschwitz look like campfires. How could I unknow this knowledge? I didn't want us to be bad. I didn't want to feel so guilty so young. I locked my guilt in with my fear of nuclear war."

Similarly, we cannot attend to the spreading hunger in the Third World and our own country—or the trade of toxic chemicals—without feeling somewhat implicated. And that makes their horror yet harder to face. As Peter Marin (1981) wrote in an essay on moral pain, "Many of us suffer a vague, inchoate sense of betrayal, of having somehow taken a wrong turning, of having somehow said yes or no at the wrong time and to the wrong things, of having somehow taken upon ourselves a general kind of guilt, having two coats while others have none, or just having too much while others have too little—yet proceeding, nonetheless, with our lives as they are."

Fear of Causing Distress

Pain for the world is repressed not only out of embarrassment and guilt, but out of compassion as well. Reluctant to burden loved ones with our inklings of apocalypse, we would protect them—both from the distress we feel and even from the knowledge that we bear it. We don't want them to worry on their own account or on ours. And so, partly out of concern for them, we keep up the pretenses of life-as-usual.

For parents the psychological burdens of our time are especially heavy and poignant. Not only do the threats to our future hit us with visceral impact as we picture (or try not to picture) our children in scenes of deprivation and horror; we also try to stifle that dread for the sake of our children's present happiness and sanity. This burden is all the weightier for those who believe that it is the role of the parent to be all-wise, all-protective, and in control.

Fear of Provoking Disaster

There is also the superstition that negative thoughts are self-fulfilling. "To speak of doom will make it more likely to happen" is the kind of rejoinder many of us often encounter, when we express dread for our collective future.

But in fact it is just the opposite. Psychoanalytic theory and personal life experience show us that it is precisely what we repress that eludes our conscious control and tends to erupt into behavior. "When an inner situation is not made conscious, it happens outside as fate," Carl Jung has said. Unfortunately, many of us, ignorant of this fact, make the one who expresses alarm over the prospects of nuclear war feel guilty of somehow contributing to the very fate we fear.

Fear of Appearing Unpatriotic

Deep in many of us, deeper than our criticisms and disappointments about national policies, lies a love of country. It is woven of pride in our history and heroes, of gratitude for what they won for us. Particularly in America, built as it was on utopian expectations, this love of country seems to require of us a profound and almost religious sense of hope—a belief in our manifest destiny as a fulfillment of human dreams.

To entertain feelings of despair over our country's present condition and future prospects seems almost un-American. If I allow these feelings to surface, am I lacking in allegiance? If I express them, am I a peddler of doom, sapping our confidence as a nation, weakening our will? Am I giving comfort to the enemy? Many would say so, now in this time of crisis. Many would have us silence our fears and doubts lest they erode our sense of national virtue and our determination to prevail.

In paying heed to these voices, we overlook an essential element in the American character: our capacity to speak out, to "tell it like it is." Since the time of the pilgrims we have been a people who refused to be silent, who rang alarms with Paul Revere, who called for defiance with Patrick Henry, who with Abraham Lincoln, Emma Goldman, Martin Luther King Jr., and countless others gave voice to the future by speaking out. But in this juncture of history, many of us muffle our concerns, shift our gaze, because we are fearful of appearing unpatriotic.

Fear of Religious Doubt

Many of us think (or try to think) that "God won't let this happen" when images of mass annihilation break through our defenses. Even just entertaining these images can seem to challenge our belief in a loving and omnipotent deity, and in the goodness of creation itself. Are feelings of despair over the growing possibilities of disaster a sign of inadequate faith?

Throughout history, of course, the fact of human suffering has always tested our belief in a divine order. The issue is known as theodicy: how to square the existence of evil with an existence of a benign and powerful God. The struggle with this issue has deepened the heart, broadened the mind. It has brought us back again and again to a core truth in each major religious heritage—and that is the deep, indeed sacred, power within each of us to open to the needs and suffering of humanity. That power—a wellspring of love, compassion, and service—is proclaimed in the psalms and prophets of Judaism, in the cross of Christ, in the path of the Buddhist bodhisattva, in the brotherhood at the heart of Islam. Yet we tend to forget those summons to take within ourselves the travail of our world. Assuming, perhaps, that our God is too fragile or too limited to encompass that pain, unsure whether God will meet us in the midst of such darkness, we hesitate to let ourselves experience it, lest our faith be shattered or revealed as inadequate.

Fear of Appearing Too Emotional

Many of us refrain from expressing our deep concerns for the world in order to avoid creating the impression that we are prey to our feelings.

For centuries the dominant Western white male culture has erected a dichotomy between reason and emotion. Assuming that reality can be apprehended in an "objective" fashion, it has accorded higher value and trust to the analytical operations of intellect than to the "subjective" realm of feelings, sensations, and intuitions. Such dichotomies are no longer found to be valid; for advances in subatomic physics, depth psychology, and general systems theory reveal the fallacy of "objectivity." But old mental habits die slowly. Many of us, schooled in the separation of reason from feeling, discount and discredit our deepest responses to the condition of our world. Dread of nuclear holocaust? Grief for expiring species? Horror for the millions in hunger? These are "only" feelings, frequently dismissed in ourselves and in others as self-indulgent, "idealistic," and "irresponsible."

Given the different ways the sexes are socialized in our culture, men suffer more than women from the fear of appearing "emotional"; displays of feeling can cause men to be considered unstable, especially in work situations. Yet women experience this fear too. They often withhold their expressions of concern and anguish for the world lest these be treated condescendingly, as "just like a woman."

Sense of Separate Existence

We have been conditioned to assume—thanks to the individualistic bias of our culture—that we are essentially separate selves, driven by aggressive impulses, competing for a place in the sun. Our affective responses to the plight of our world are interpreted reductionistically in the light of these assumptions, and given short shrift.

We have trouble crediting the notion that concerns for the general welfare might be genuine, and acute enough to cause distress. Assuming that all our drives are ego-centered, we tend to wonder if feelings of despair for our planet are not manifestations of some private neurosis. Do we find ourselves weeping for the Afghans or the peasants in El Salvador or for decimated dolphins? Perhaps we suffer from a hangover of Puritan guilt. Maybe we are sexually unfulfilled or were toilet-trained too early. Thus we are tempted to discredit those feelings that arise from solidarity with our fellow-beings, dismissing them as some kind of personal morbidity. "Even in my therapy group," writes a teacher, "I stopped mentioning my fears of nuclear war. The others kept saying, 'What are you running from in your life by creating these worries for yourself?'" In chapters 7 and 10 of this book, Lane Gerber and Richard Sherman discuss this tendency to exclude global and social concerns from the relevant domain of psychotherapy.

Many of us, conditioned to take seriously only those feelings that pertain to our individual needs and wants, find it hard to believe that we can suffer on behalf of society itself—and on behalf of our planet—and that such suffering is real and valid and healthy.

Fear of Feeling Powerless

Probably the most frequent responses to the subject of the nuclear threat (or acid rain, or world hunger, etc.) is to the effect that "I don't think about that, because there is nothing I can do about it."

Logically, this is a nonsequitur: it confuses what can be thought with what can be done. And it is a tragic one, for when forces are seen as so vast that they cannot be consciously contemplated or seriously discussed, we are doubly victimized—impeded in thought as well as action.

Resistance to painful information on the grounds that we cannot "do anything about it" springs less from powerlessness—as a measure of our capacity to effect change—than from the fear of experiencing powerlessness. The model of the self that predominates in Western culture is: "I am the master of my fate and the captain of my soul." It makes us reluctant to engage in issues that remind us that we do not exert ultimate control over our lives. We feel somehow we ought to be in charge of our existence and emotions, to have all the answers. And so we tend to shrink the sphere of our attention to those areas in which we feel we can be in charge.

EFFECTS OF REPRESSION

Let us now consider the costs we incur when we repress in these ways our responses of pain for the world and alarm for the future. What does it do for us to block out not only deep, recurrent responses of fear, anger, and grief, but even the very instinct for self-preservation in the face of possible annihilation?

The repression takes a mammoth toll on our energies. A marked loss of feeling results, as if a nerve had been cut. As Barry Childers has said, "We immunize ourselves against the demands of the situation by narrowing our awareness." This anesthetization affects other aspects of our life as well—loves and losses are less intense, the sky is less vivid—for if we are not going to let ourselves feel pain, we will not feel much else either. "The mind pays for its deadening to the state of our world," observes Robert Murphy, "by giving up its capacity for joy and flexibility."

This state of absence, or at best this dulled human response to our world, is called "psychic numbing." Robert Lifton, who coined the term in his study of Hiroshima survivors, now applies it to all of us—recognizing that everyone in this planet-time, by the simple fact of being threatened with horrors too vast to contemplate, is a victim of the bomb. "The very existence of nuclear weapons," says Norman McLeod, "is an assault on the human heart." Under such an assault we tend to shut down and finally shut off.

In the following sections we will be exploring the various forms of psychic numbing in order to put our ear to the ground and better understand the psychological and even spiritual condition of our time.

Fragmentation and Alienation

As already noted, all of us tend to lead "a double life." While on the surface we focus on business-as-usual, underneath there is an inchoate awareness of impending doom. As with any form of lying, this internal split produces self-doubt and cuts us off from our deep subconscious sources of creativity. Separated from our inner authority, we become more susceptible to panic and mob hysteria.

This split also begets a sense of isolation. If our deepest concerns of our world are unmentionable, if we hide them like a secret shame, they alienate us from other people. Although these concerns may seem valid on the cognitive level, their distance from the tenor of life around us makes us question them on the feeling level. A psychic dissonance is produced that can lead us to question not society's sanity, but our own. So we seal off, as in an isolation cell, an authentic part of ourselves.

Displacement Activities

Rats in the laboratory, when a threat is introduced that they cannot dispel, turn away and busy themselves in frenzied, irrelevant activities. So apparently do we. Seeking escape from the "unthinkable," our society turns increasingly to a desperate pursuit of pleasure and other short-term goals. The "new hedonism" evident in the consumption of goods, sex, and entertainment—and the cult of the pursuit of money as an end in itself—are so striking today as to suggest that they derive from more than sheer appetite. The frantic quality to it all does not convey a healthy lust for life so much as the contrary, and it suggests a profound doubt in the goodness of life and a sense of impending loss. Helen Caldicott calls this "manic denial."

Political Passivity

To allay our hidden fears about the fate of the earth, there is a tendency to take refuge in the belief that the experts know best. "There are profound, powerful and unconscious needs to see the government as powerful, protective, and wise," says Dr. Leon Balter. His report on the New York Psychiatric Association's study of psychological responses to the nuclear threat (1979) states that "people use the presence and fantasies about the government in the service of allaying anxiety. . . . Even though its efficacy to prevent war is acknowledged to be faulty, the government becomes the fantasied repository of war-preventing expertise. . . . There is (also) an emotional pay-off to have a strong, aggressive government so that the citizen does not feel aggressive."

As we saw earlier, repression of our pain for the world isolates us from others; it diminishes our sense of interconnectedness and solidarity. Therefore it serves to disempower us politically. To keep a stiff upper lip in the face of adversity is often upheld as a virtue by those in positions of power and serves as an indirect means of control. To do so as millions languish in hunger camps and detention cells, to behold impassively the destruction of our life-support system, is to relinquish a measure of our humanity—and become docile, obedient pawns.

Destructive Behaviors

"Repression is never successful," says Robert Murphy, recalling Freud's concept of the "return of the repressed." Feelings of despair over the world and the loss of our future may be pushed below conscious awareness, but they surface again in other guises. They are expressed outwardly against society in acts of violence and vandalism—acts often so senseless, so pointless, they seem motivated by nothing so much as feelings of fury and futility. And they are expressed inwardly, too, in self-destruction—as the rising rates of drug abuse and suicide among teenagers and even children attest. They cannot all be reduced to idiosyncratic disorders; to an immeasurable extent they relate to feelings about the kind of world we are living in now.

Psychological Projection

When feelings of despair and pain for our world remain unnamed and unacknowledged, the vague, free-floating sense that there is something intolerable in our situation is turned in anger against others. We seek scapegoats to blame for our inchoate sense of alarm. Carl Jung called this kind of phenomenon "the projection of the shadow." On the global scene it led us for many years to "demonize" the Russians, a term coined by historian and diplomat George Kennan (1981) in describing "the distortion and oversimplification . . . and systematic dehumanization" of the Soviet leadership and people. Brett Silverstein in chapter 6 of this volume, describes this phenomenon.

Resistance to Painful Information

To the extent that we repress feelings of despair for the world, we tend to screen out the data that provoke them. This occurs on the individual level: people admit with increasing frequency, "I don't read the paper any more . . . I tune out the news . . . I can't take it any more, it bums me out." And, what is more alarming, it occurs on the governmental level with censorship and suppression of adverse reports on oil spills, pollution, the incidence of radiation-induced cancer, and so on. It is alarming because all living systems require feedback if they are to learn, adapt, and survive. To deliberately or unconsciously block from our awareness the results of our behaviors is suicidal.

Sense of Powerlessness

The conspiracy of silence concerning our deepest feelings about the future of our species, the degree of numbing, isolation, burnout, and cognitive confusion that results from it—all converge to produce a sense of futility. Each act of denial, conscious or unconscious, is an abdication of our power to respond. "I don't think about nuclear war, because there is nothing I can do about it" is the old refrain. In such a way we choose the role of victim before attempting to organize and change the situation —even before engaging with it.

As Leon Balter (1979) has observed, "The perception of objective danger is met by a withdrawal from engagement with it. The most frequent manifestation of this mental process is the assertion of powerlessness in the face of imminent nuclear war."

There is a spillover effect to this assumption of powerlessness in the face of the nuclear threat. It is discernible in the way we tend to meet other social, political, economic, and ecological problems. Though some of these challenges are more finite and manageable, they are increasingly met with a fatalistic shrug, as if it were naive and fruitless to suppose that we could clean up our air or our water or the corruption in city hall. If, on a deep psychological level, people have difficulty confronting the most fundamental issue of our time—that of the imminent possibility of mass annihilation—they are not likely to feel either inclined or competent to address the myriad immediate issues that affect the moral and physical quality of life.

THE GENESIS OF DESPAIRWORK

We may find ourselves asking: Is there an alternative? Can we move beyond numbness without succumbing to despair? Can we acknowledge and live with our pain for the world in ways that release our vitality and our powers to act? I think we can, when we are open enough to share how we feel with one another.

In August 1978, at Notre Dame University, I chaired a week-long seminar on planetary-survival issues. College professors and administrators had prepared papers to deliver on themes ranging from the water crisis to nuclear technology. As we convened, I took time to acknowledge that the topic we were addressing was different from any other, that it touched each of us in a profoundly personal way; I suggested that we introduce ourselves by sharing an incident or image of how it had touched us. The brief introductions that followed were potent, as those present dropped their professional manner and spoke simply and poignantly of what they saw and felt happening to their world, of their children, of their fears and discouragement. That brief sharing transformed the seminar. It changed the way we related to each other and to the material, it unleashed energy and mutual caring. Sessions went overtime, laced with hilarity and punctuated with plans for future projects. Some kind of magic had happened. Late one night as a group of us talked, a name for that magic emerged, Despairwork.

Just as grief-work is a process by which bereaved persons unblock their numbed energies by acknowledging and grieving the loss of a loved one, so do we all need to unblock our feelings about our threatened planet and the possible demise of our species. Until we do, our power of creative response will be crippled.

As we struck on Despairwork, we were not being theoretical, we were groping for an explanation of what had just happened. We knew that it had to do with a willingness to acknowledge and experience pain, and that this pain for our world, like pain for the loss of a loved one, is a measure of caring. We also knew that the joint journey into the dark had changed us, bonding us in a special way, relieving us of pretense and competition. Something akin to love had occurred, an alchemy that caused us to feel less alone and bolder to face without flinching whatever challenges might lie ahead. This occasion led to the development of what I call "Despair and Empowerment Workshops." These workshops are a format for the psychological and spiritual work of dealing with our knowledge and feelings about our multiple planetary crises in ways that release energy and vision for creative response. Despair and empowerment work helps us to increase our awareness of these developments without feeling overwhelmed by the dread, grief, anger, and sense of powerlessness they arouse in us. The work overcomes patterns of avoidance and psychic numbing; it builds compassion, community, and commitment to act. The workshop will be further described in a later section of this chapter.

In designing these workshops, I drew on years of exploring the interface between spiritual growth and social change, years of adapting meditative practices to empower people as agents for peace and justice. Yet the workshops themselves taught me more than I could have imagined. The thousands of people with whom I have worked in church basements and community centers and classrooms have revealed to me, in ways I had not foreseen, the power, size, and beauty of the human heart. They have demonstrated that pain for our world touches each of us and that this pain is rooted in caring. They have demonstrated that our apparent public apathy is but a fear of experiencing and expressing this pain, and that once it is acknowledged and shared it opens the way to our power.

As I meditated on the lessons I learned from these workshops, and on the connections between pain and power, I discovered five principles that are fundamental to our response to the psychological and spiritual challenges of our time.

1. *Feelings of pain for our world are natural and healthy.* Confronted with widespread suffering and threats of global disaster, responses of anguish—of fear, anger, and grief, and even guilt—are normal. They are a measure of our humanity. And these feelings are probably what we have most in common. Just by virtue of sharing this particular planet-time, we know these feelings more than our own grandparents or any earlier generation could have known. We are in grief together. And this grief for our world cannot be reduced to private pathology. We experi-

ence it in addition to whatever personal griefs, frustrations, and neuroses we bear. Not to experience it would be a sign of intellectual and moral atrophy, but that is academic, for I have met no one who is immune to this pain.

2. *This pain is morbid only if denied.* It is when we disown our pain for the world that it becomes dysfunctional. We know what it costs us to repress it, how that cost is measured in numbness and in feelings of isolation and impotence. It is measured as well in the hatreds and suspicions that divide us. For repressed despair seeks scapegoats and turns, in anger, against other members of society. It also turns inward in depression and self-destruction, through drug abuse and suicide. We tend to fear that if we consciously acknowledge our despair we may get mired in it, incapacitated. But despair, like any emotion, is dynamic— once experienced, it flows through us. It is only our refusal to acknowledge and feel it that keeps it in place.

3. *Information alone is not enough.* To deal with the distress we feel for our world, we need more than additional data about its plight. Terrifying information about the effects of nuclear weapons or environmental pollution can drive us deeper into denial and feelings of futility, unless we can deal with the responses it arouses in us. We need to process this information on the psychological and emotional level in order to fully respond on the cognitive level. *We already know* we are in danger. The essential question is: Can we free ourselves to respond?

4. *Unblocking repressed feelings releases energy, clears the mind.* This is known as catharsis. Repression is physically, mentally, and emotionally expensive: it drains the body, dulls the mind, and muffles emotional responses. When repressed material is brought to the surface and released, energy is released as well; life comes into clearer focus. Art, ritual, and play have always played a cathartic role in our history—just as, in our time, psychotherapy does. By this process the cognitive system appropriates elements of its experience, and by integrating them gains a measure of both control and freedom.

5. *Unblocking our pain for the world reconnects us with the larger web of life.* When the repressed material that we unblock is distress for our world, catharsis occurs—and also something *more* than catharsis. That is because this distress reflects concerns that extend beyond our separate selves, beyond our individual needs and wants. It is a testimony to our interconnectedness. Therefore, as we let ourselves experience and

move through this pain, we move through to its source—reach the underlying matrix of our lives. What occurs, then, is *beyond* catharsis.

The distinction here is an important one. To present power and empowerment work as just one of catharsis would suggest that, after owning and sharing our responses to mass suffering and the prospects of mass annihilation, we could walk away purged of pain for our world. But that is neither possible nor adequate to our needs, since each day's news brings fresh cause for grief. By recognizing our capacity to suffer with our world, we dawn to wider dimensions of being. In those dimensions there is still pain, but also a lot more. There is wonder, even joy, as we come home to our mutual belonging—*and* there is a new kind of power.

To understand why this should be so—and what this kind of power is —we must look at the theoretical foundations of the work. For these principles are derived from some of the oldest and most recent insights into the nature of reality. It is important to understand the worldview in which they are rooted. Here we find the compass for our voyage and the understanding that we need to employ, in a responsible and effective fashion, the methods that are contained in Despair and Empowerment work.

THE WEB OF LIFE

What is it that allows us to feel pain for our world? And what do we discover as we move through it? What awaits us there "on the other side of despair"? To all these questions there is one answer: it is an interconnectedness with life and all other beings. It is the living web out of which our individual, separate existences have risen, and in which we are interwoven. Our lives extend beyond our skins, in radical interdependence with the rest of the world.

Contemporary science—and this is perhaps its greatest achievement —has broken through to a fresh discovery of this interrelatedness of all living phenomena. Until our century, classical Western science had proceeded on the assumption that the world could be understood and controlled by dissecting it. Breaking the world down into even smaller pieces, classical Western science divided mind from matter, organs from bodies, plants from ecosystems, and analyzed each separate part. This mechanistic approach left some questions unanswered—such as, how do these separate parts interact to sustain life and evolve?

As a result of such questions, scientists in our century, starting with the biologists, shifted their perspective. They began to look at wholes instead of parts, at processes instead of substances. What they discovered was these wholes—be they cells, bodies, ecosystems, and even the planet itself—are not just a heap of disjunct parts, but dynamic, intricately organized and balanced systems, interrelated and interdependent in every movement, every function, every exchange of energy. They saw that each element is part of a vaster pattern, a pattern that connects and evolves by discernible principles. The discernment of these principles is what is known as "general systems theory."

Ludwig von Bertalanffy, the father of general systems theory, called it a "way of seeing." And while it has spawned many derivative theories relating to particular fields and phenomena, the systems perspective has remained just that—a way of seeing, and one which is recognized by many thinkers as the greatest and farthest-reaching cognitive revolution of our time. Anthropologist Gregory Bateson called it "the biggest bite out of the Tree of Knowledge in two thousand years." For, as the systems view has spread into every domain of science from physics to psychology, it has turned the lens through which we see reality. Instead of beholding random separate entities, we became aware of interconnecting flows— flows of energy, matter, information—and see life forms as patterns in these flows.

As we saw earlier, the old mechanistic view of reality has erected dichotomies, separating substance from process, self from other, thought from feeling. But given the interweaving interactions of open systems, these dichotomies no longer hold. What had appeared to be separate self-existent entities are now seen to be so interdependent that their boundaries can only be drawn arbitrarily. What had appeared to be "other" can be equally construed as an extension of the same organism, like a fellow-cell in a larger body. What we had been taught to dismiss as "only" feelings are responses to input from our environment that are no less valid than rational constructs. Feelings and concepts condition each other; both are ways of knowing our world.

As our awareness grows, so does the image of the web, for we are the universe becoming conscious of itself. With sensibilities evolved through millennia of interaction, we can turn now and know that web as our home. It both cradles us and calls us to weave it further.

PASSAGE THROUGH DARKNESS

How, if we let ourselves feel despair, can we re-member our collective body? How can our pain for the world make us whole again? Or is it part of the re-membering?

Processes of growth and transformation are never pain-free. They require a letting-go of outmoded ways of being, of old assumptions and old defenses. As both science and religion confirm, this letting-go can be a passage through darkness, and it can be highly uncomfortable. As we open like a wound to the travail of the world, we are susceptible to new sensations and confusions. Bereft of self-confidence and hopefulness, we can feel as though our world is "falling apart." It can make some of us frantic; some of us, in desperation, become mean. That is because the system (i.e., each of us) is registering anomalies, new signals from the environment that don't match previously programmed codes and constructs. To survive, then, the system must change.

To experience pain as we register what is happening to our world is a measure of our evolution as open systems. This is not only true from the perspective of systems science but of religion as well. How many mystics in their spiritual journey have spoken of the "dark night of the soul"? Brave enough to let go of accustomed assurances, they let their old convictions and conformities dissolve into nothingness, and stood naked to the terror of the unknown. They let processes, which their minds could not encompass, work through them. It is in that darkness that birth takes place.

POWER AS PROCESS

As our pain for the world is rooted in our interconnectedness with all life, so surely is our power. But the kind of power at work in the web, in and through open systems, is quite different from our customary notions of power.

The old concept of power, in which most of us have been socialized, originated in a particular worldview. This view, as we noted, saw reality as composed of discrete and separate entities, be they rocks, plants, atoms, people. Power came to be seen as a property of these separate entities, reflected in the way they could appear to push each other around. Power became identified with domination. Look it up in the dictionary; more often than not it is still defined as having your way with other people—in other words, it is seen as power-over. In such a view power is a zero-sum game—"the more you have, the less I have," "if you win, I lose." It fosters the notion, furthermore, that power involves invulnerability. To be strong, to keep from being pushed around, defenses, armor, and rigidity are needed in order not to let oneself be influenced or changed.

From the systems perspective, this patriarchal notion of power is both inaccurate and dysfunctional, because life processes are intrinsically self-organizing and evolve through the dynamic and symbiotic interaction of open systems. Power, which is the ability to effect change, works not from the top down, but from the bottom up. It is not power-over, but power-with; this is what systems scientists call "synergy."

Life systems evolve flexibility and intelligence, not by closing off from the environment and erecting walls of defense, but by opening ever wider to the currents of matter-energy and information. It is in this interaction that life systems grow, integrating and differentiating. Here power, far from being identified with invulnerability, requires just the opposite—openness, vulnerability, and readiness to change. This indeed is the direction of evolution. As life forms evolve in intelligence, they shed their armor and reach outward to an ever wider interplay with the environment. They grow sensitive, vulnerable protuberances—ears, noses, and eyeballs, lips, tongues, fingertips—the better to feel and respond, the better to connect in the web and weave it further.

Noting this, we may well wonder why the old kind of power, as we see it enacted around us and indeed above us, seems so effective. Many who wield it seem to get what they want—money, fame, control over others' lives. But they achieve this at a cost—cost to the larger system and to themselves. Power-over is dysfunctional to the system because it inhibits diversity and feedback; it obstructs self-organizing life processes and fosters entropy—or systemic disintegration. Power-over is expensive to those of us who wield it, too. Like a suit of armor it restricts our vision and movement. Reducing our flexibility and responsiveness, it cuts us off from fuller and freer participation in life—and also from the capacity to enhance it.

What is required of us, for our survival, is an expanded sense of self-interest, where the needs of the whole, and other beings within that whole, are seen as commensurate with our own. Only then can we begin to think and act together. For this we need a "boundless heart," which I believe we have within us by virtue of our nature as open systems. If we can grieve with the griefs of others, so, by the same token, by the same openness, can we find strength in their strengths, bolstering our own individual supplies of courage, commitment, and endurance.

OPENING TO POWER

How does power as process-synergistic power—power-with rather than power-over—operate in our lives? We don't own it. We don't use it like a gun. We can't measure its quantity or size. We can't increase it at our neighbor's expense. Power is like a verb; it happens through us.

We experience it when we engage in interactions that produce value. We can experience that with loved ones and fellow citizens, with God, with music, art and literature, with seeds we plant, materials we shape. Such synergistic exchanges generate something that was not there before and that enhances the capacities and well-being of all who are involved. It involves attentive openness to the surrounding physical or mental environment and alertness to our own and others' responses. It is the capacity to act in ways that increase the sum total of one's conscious participation in life.

We can recognize this power by the extent to which it promotes conscious participation in life. To deprive someone of his or her rights is an exercise of force, not power. It diminishes the vitality, not just of that person, but cf the larger system of which we all are a part, and which is deprived now of their participation and resources. Therefore the exercise of power as process demands that we unmask and reject all exercises of force that obstruct our and others' participation in life.

The concept of synergistic power summons us to develop our capacities for nurturance and empathy. This is especially important for those who have been socialized to be competitive, especially the men in our society. But it is equally true that this notion of power presents a challenge to those who have been conditioned to please, and who have been assigned by society the more passive and nurturing roles. I am referring, of course, to women. For them, power-with can mean being assertive, taking responsibility to give feedback, and participating more fully in the body politic.

Thus we act not only for ourselves or our own group, but also on behalf of all the other "neurons in the net." At that point the myriad resources of that net are ours as well—and these include all our differences and diversities.

AWAKENING IN THE NUCLEAR AGE

Through our pain for the world we can open ourselves to power. This power is not just our own, but belongs to others as well. It relates to the very evolution of our species. It is part of a general awakening or shift toward a new level of social consciousness.

We can see that our planetary crises are impelling us toward a shift in consciousness. In that sense both the nuclear bomb and the environmental crisis are gifts to us. Confronting us with our mortality as a species, we are shown the suicidal tendency inherent in our conception of ourselves as separate and competitive beings. Given the fragility and limited resources of our planet, given our needs for flexibility and sharing, we have to think together in an integrated, synergistic fashion, rather than in the old fragmented and competitive ways—and we are beginning to do that. Once we tune into our interconnectedness, responsibility toward self and other become indistinguishable, because each thought and act affects the doer as much as the done-to.

Where, then, does despair fit in? And why is our pain for the world so important? Because these responses manifest our interconnectedness. Our feelings of social and planetary distress serve as a doorway to systemic social consciousness. To use another metaphor, they are like a "shadow limb." Just as an amputee continues to feel itches and twinges in the severed limb, so do we feel pain in those extensions of ourselves —of our larger body—of which we have yet to become fully conscious. These sensations do not belong to our past, like the severed leg or amputee, but to our future.

Through the systemic currents of knowing that interweave our world, each of us can be the catalyst or "tipping point" by which new forms of behavior can spread. There are as many different ways of being responsive as there are different gifts we possess. For some of us it can be through study or conversation, for others theater or public office, for still others civil disobedience and imprisonment. But the diversities of our gifts interweave richly when we recognize the larger web within which we act. We begin in this web and, at the same time, journey toward it. We are making it conscious.

GUIDELINES FOR DESPAIR AND EMPOWERMENT WORK

Despair and empowerment workshops, as already noted, are specifically designed to help us deal responsively and creatively with the multiple problems besetting our planet. These workshops, begun in 1979, have now been offered thousands of times by members of the Interhelp Network and by me, throughout the United States and in many other countries. The Interhelp Network, which staffs, supports, and promotes this work, articulates the purpose of despair and empowerment workshops: "To provide people the opportunity to experience and share with others their deepest responses to the dangers which threaten our planet —be they dangers of nuclear holocaust, environmental deterioration, or human oppression; and, in so doing, to enable them to know the power that comes from their interconnectedness with all life so that they can move beyond numbness and powerlessness into action" (Macy 1983).

In despair and empowerment workshops, people are drawing resourcefully from general systems theory, humanistic psychology, and spiritual teachings. By means of structured exercises, bodywork, guided meditations, rituals, and plain talk, they have broken the taboos against expressing their pain for the world, and discovered that they can use this pain in ways that affirm their distinctive gifts and common humanity. They have found that by focusing on their felt responses to the present perils, energy is released and solidarity arises. When interactions occur on the feeling level, in a setting of safety and support, mutuality arises between people of differing opinions and backgrounds. In despair and empowerment workshops, businessmen and drop-outs, military officers and peace activists, conservatives and anarchists can meet and share their anguish for the future, and find in that sharing common ground and mutual respect.

In conducting despair and empowerment workshops over a long period of time, other workshop leaders and I have found five guidelines that seem essential to the process of moving through our despair and claiming our power. Each of these guidelines is translated into a series of experiential exercises designed to create the group safety and trust required to fully explore and express our deepest emotions, fears, and images about our troubled planet. The following guidelines are the basic dynamics of despair and empowerment work, leading to a process of rediscovery and touching the truth of our pain and our shared humanity, caring, and courage.

1. *Acknowledge our pain for the world.* If it is present, we cannot deny its reality. We cannot make it go away by arguing it out of existence, or burying it inside of ourselves. We can acknowledge our pain for the world to ourselves through journal writing or prayer, and if we choose, by communicating our awareness to those around us.
2. *Validate our pain for the world.* Let us honor it in ourselves and others, by listening carefully and accepting it as healthy and normal in the present situation. To hurry in with words of cheer can trivialize its meaning and foster repression.
3. *Experience the pain.* Let us not fear its impact on ourselves and others. We will not shatter, for we are not objects that can break. Nor will we get stuck in this pain, for it is dynamic, it flows through us. Drop our defenses, let us stay present to its flow, express it—in words, movements, and sounds.
4. *Move through the pain to its source.* As we experience this pain, we learn that it is rooted in caring, not just for ourselves and our children, but for all of humanity. We rediscover our interconnectedness with all beings. Allow this sense of mutual belonging to surface in whatever words and images are meaningful and share them.
5. *Experience the power of interconnectedness.* Let us dare to translate our caring into a sense of belonging to all humanity and the web of life. Observe the trust level rise when we expose our vulnerability to pain for the world. Recognize how the realization of interconnectedness results in personal security and economy of effort.

EXAMPLES OF DESPAIR AND EMPOWERMENT WORKSHOP EXERCISES

Despair and empowerment workshops offer tools and insights to assist in our awakening, helping us lay claim to the psychological, intellectual, and spiritual resources that are within us. Since the workshops are experiential, it is recommended that the reader contact the Interhelp Network to seek out a workshop in your area. The book on which this chapter is based (Macy 1983) provides a more elaborate and detailed description of the despair and empowerment workshop format. The following exercises are suggestive of the kind of experiences provided by Interhelp facilitators at despair and empowerment workshops.

The initial stage of feeling and expressing:

As you tell your name, share a recent experience that caused you pain for the world. It can be an incident, a news item, a dream.

Working in pairs, complete sentences like: When I think of the world we are going to leave for the children . . . One of my worst fears for the future is . . . The ways that I avoid experiencing these feelings are . . .

Breaking our silence, telling our nuclear and environmental stories, bringing to the surface the ways we feel about living on an endangered planet.

A guided meditation on one's life trajectory, including the past, present, and imagined future.

The despair ritual stage:

This work of encouraging spontaneous expression is a ritual form that takes place in three concentric circles: the circle of reporting, the circle of anger and fear, the circle of sorrow. Group members move between the circles as the emotions present themselves. There is movement into the darkness and then through the darkness to affirmation. The emotions are strong, supported by the sense of commonality and shared grief.

The turning toward interconnectedness:

Spontaneous writing and sharing: "Out of this dark and painful stuff our task is to . . ."

Initial meditative quiet and then speaking that which wishes to be spoken through us.

Use of body movement work to activate the innate knowledge of our interconnectedness.

A guided meditation on the "web of life."

The stage of empowerment:

Identifying goals, resources, strengths for the tasks ahead.

Guided reflection to affirm and acknowledge our unique gifts.

Structured exercise in overcoming obstacles that keep us from following through with our commitment to heal the world.

Closure:

Final gathering, evoking the presence of all beings of past, present, and future times. It is an opportunity to practice together our extended awareness of the vast reaches of the web of life, for it can provide steadiness in the times that lie ahead.

Let us be aware that what is at work in this process is not dependent on what we know or say or do, as much as on what we allow to happen. The very process of unblocking our pain for the world releases energy, clarifies thought, breaks down isolation. The workshops offer methods for recognizing the power in our lives and for using our power to become effective agents for social change. Together, we broaden our vision of what is possible and see it clearly enough for our resolve and will to be strengthened. Together we express our care, affirm our commonality, summon our will, and return to our home communities to act as skilled and powerful agents of conscious social change.

Despair and empowerment work is consciousness-raising in the truest sense of the term. It increases our awareness not only of the perils that face us, but also of the promise inherent in the human heart. Whether we "make it" or not, whether our efforts to heal our world succeed or fail, we live then in so vivid a consciousness of our community that the most obvious and accurate word for it is love. And that seems, in and of itself, a fulfillment.

REFERENCES

Balter, Leon. (1979). Overview of Project on Attitudes toward Nuclear War by the Colloquium of Psychoanalysts and Social Scientists. Reprinted by the New York Yearly Meeting Peace Institute, Powell House, Old Chatam, N.Y.

Kennan, George F. (1981). Address at Dartmouth College. *Boston Globe.* November 29.

Lifton, Robert J. (1979). *The Broken Connection,* New York: Simon and Schuster.

Macy, J. (1983). Despair and Personal Power in the Nuclear Age. Philadelphia: New Society Publishers.

Marin, Peter. (1981). Living in Moral Pain. *Psychology Today.*

Murphy, Robert. (Unpublished). The Psychology of Despair and Empowerment. Physicians for Social Responsibility, Sheridan, Wyoming.

Robb, Christina. (1982). *Boston Globe.* January 24.

3

Psychology and Human Survival: Psychological Approaches to Contemporary Global Threats

Roger Walsh

Each of us is called on to do something that no member of any generation before ours has had to do: to assume responsibility for the continuation of our kind—to choose human survival—*Jonathan Schell*[1]

Can humankind survive? Can civilization, in any meaningful sense of the word, be assured for the majority of the world's population during our lifetime, and for our children, and their descendents? Surely these are among the most important questions of our time and raise issues and implications for all psychological disciplines, yet how rarely are they addressed in the psychological literature.

This deficiency in the literature becomes all the more remarkable when it is realized that all the major global threats to human survival and wellbeing are now primarily human caused. That is, they stem directly from our own behavior and *can therefore largely be traced to psychological origins*. This means that the current threats to human survival and wellbeing *are actually symptoms* of our individual and collective mind set. Of course, this is in no way to deny the role of social, political, and

This chapter is reprinted by permission from the *American Journal of Psychotherapy*, 43, no. 2 (April 1989).

economic factors, but simply to emphasize the much neglected psychological forces that underlie them.

These global threats can be summarized in terms of malnutrition, population explosion, resource depletion, pollution, ecology, and nuclear weapons. At the present time 15-20 million of us die each year of malnutrition-related causes, another 600 million go chronically hungry, while billions live in poverty without adequate shelter, education, or medical care.[2,3] The situation is worsened by explosive population growth, which adds another billion people every 13 years, depletes natural resources at an ever-accelerating rate, affects "virtually every aspect of the earth's ecosystems [including] perhaps the most serious environmental development . . . an accelerating deterioration and loss of the resources essential for agriculture."[4] Desertification, pollution, acid rain, and greenhouse warming are among the more obvious effects.

Despite their severity, even these problems are overshadowed by the nuclear threat with the equivalent of some 20 billion tons of TNT (compared with 3 million tons for all of World War II). These weapons are controlled by hair-trigger warning systems, create highly radioactive wastes for which no permanent storage site exists, consume over $100 billion each year in military expenditure, and threaten global suicide.[5-7]

The fact that these threats are all human caused means that to cure or at least significantly improve them may therefore demand not only symptomatic treatment, such as feeding the starving and reducing nuclear stockpiles, but also understanding and treating their psychological roots. Developing and applying such understanding may be one of the most urgent tasks facing our generation.

Mental health professionals have recently begun to respond to this challenge. However, as yet most studies have been somewhat fragmentary, usually focussing on war, particularly nuclear war, and ignoring other problems, examining only a few psychological dimensions, and employing only one psychological school or perspective. So far there has been no attempt to address contemporary global threats as a whole from multiple psychological perspectives. This article, therefore, aims to provide a brief outline of a comprehensive, multidimensional psychology of human survival by using diverse schools to analyze the psychological causes and costs of contemporary global threats and deduce principles of effective response.

PSYCHOLOGICAL CAUSES

Only on the basis of an understanding of our behavior can we hope to control it in such a why as to ensure the survival of the human race. —*Senator William Fulbright*[8]

Any psychology provides a necessarily partial and selective perspective and interpretation of the world and of ourselves, but increasing evidence suggests that different schools of psychology may be partially complementary.[9] Let us, then, attempt to ground our psychology of human survival, not in any one exclusive school or perspective, but rather within an open-minded, inclusive, integrative framework that acknowledges the possible value and complementarity of apparently divergent approaches. In doing so we model at the psychological level what we are attempting at the cultural and international; namely, to set aside traditional boundaries, conflicts, and claims for exclusivity, and to welcome for objective appraisal the potential contributions of all schools—behavioral and dynamic, individual and social, cognitive and existential, Eastern and Western.

Each of these schools provides a particular view of human nature, potential, and pathology that can be extended to an analysis of the threats to human survival. The crucial question is which of their insights may be most useful for this purpose. The criterion here is a pragmatic one and the schools and dimensions discussed here are those whose insights I personally find easiest to translate into guidelines for practical responses.

The dimensions on which I will therefore focus include cognitive factors, the behavioral factors of reinforcement and social learning, the Eastern psychologies' "three poisons" of addiction, aversion, and delusion, selected psychodynamic defense mechanisms, and the central roles of fear and immaturity. A more complete psychology of human survival might give greater attention to social factors, but since effective responses begin with individuals, it is individual psychologies I have emphasized here. Due to space limitations the following analyses are necessarily extremely brief and those wanting a fuller discussion may wish to examine a book-length analysis.[7]

Cognitive Perspectives (Beliefs/Ignorance/Presuppositions)

Within recent years there has been a growing recognition of the potent yet frequently unrecognized power of beliefs to shape experience and behavior. Beliefs tend to modify what we look for, what we recognize, how we interpret, and how we respond to these interpretations. What is absolutely crucial is that these largely unconscious processes tend to be self-fulfilling and self-prophetic.[10,11]

This is why we must identify the beliefs shaping our contemporary crises. These include beliefs about ourselves, about others and our relationship to them, and about the world, weapons, and warfare. The following are some of the beliefs that may be particularly dangerous:

The first are beliefs about ourselves and include self-limiting assumptions that reduce our sense of effectiveness: beliefs such as "there's nothing I can do," "no one will listen to me," or "it's not my responsibility."

Also dangerous are beliefs to the effect that "my beliefs/views/ideology are the truth and the only truth." Such beliefs become even more dangerous when the beliefs of others are denigrated, as in "my ideology is the only correct one, and theirs is self-serving, heretical, etc."

Beliefs about others and our relationships to them are also crucial. Particularly harmful are those that blame others, dehumanize them, or see them as fundamentally inferior to ourselves. Obvious examples here include "it's their fault, not ours, that they're hungry, that there is an arms race, etc.," "you can't trust them," or "they would never disarm," and, worst, "they're not really human."

Zero-sum "us versus them" relationship beliefs that argue that ultimately only one party can be successful or survive may be particularly dangerous. At their worst these beliefs create a Manichaean world view in which the entire world is regarded as a battlefield on which the forces of light (us) must combat the forces of darkness (them). In our time the cold war provided a tragic example in which Marxism and capitalism were frequently seen as necessarily locked in an inexorable struggle for survival and world domination. Such beliefs are both cause and effect of malignant social processes such as suspiciousness, hostility, a focus on differences and denial of commonalities, a belief that solutions can be obtained only by domination, and temptation to resort to coercion and deception.[8,12] Once set in motion, such behaviors tend to "prove" the apparent validity of the beliefs that created them as well as the "wisdom" and "foresight" of those who held them, thereby once again demonstrating the self-prophetic power of beliefs.

Then, also, there are powerful yet usually unquestioned assumptions about defense and warfare. For example, since an annual amount of less than one week's arms expenditure could eradicate world starvation[6] there is the question as to whether we really believe it is worthwhile to allow hundreds of millions of people to starve to death in order to defend ourselves. Similarly, there is also the question of whether we would really want to kill hundreds of millions of people in order to avenge ourselves in a nuclear war, especially since the vast majority of those killed would be innocent civilians.

Numerous other questionable beliefs also underlie current nuclear strategies. These include the ideas that "increased numbers of weapons provide increased security," "nuclear superiority is possible," "limited nuclear wars are containable," and "nuclear war is winnable."

Questionable beliefs about the world abound. As such, they presumably generate cognitive dissonance and support defense mechanisms preventing an accurate view of the world and appropriate responses to it. Beliefs such as "it's hopeless" and "there's nothing that can be done," though understandable in light of the enormity of our difficulties, may exacerbate feelings of apathy and despair and prove dangerously self-fulfilling. Likewise, beliefs that "there's not enough food to go around" or that "there's no way of getting the food to people" are not only patently incorrect, they are dangerous.[13]

Defense Mechanisms

"Humankind cannot bear very much reality," said T. S. Eliot, and defense mechanisms are the crutches we use to help us avoid it. Those particularly relevant to this discussion are repression, denial, projection, rationalization, and intellectualization.

Most people experience great difficulty acknowledging the true state of the world, its suffering, and its peril.[14] Repression and denial play major roles in this difficulty and spawn statements such as "I'd rather not think about it," or "it's not really so bad." Their result is an "ostrichism," which saps our motivation to respond in appropriate ways.[15]

But the effects of repression and denial extend further. We wish to deny not only the state of the world but also our role in producing it. Hence we use projection to attribute to others the unacknowledged facets of our own self-image and motives (what Jungians call the "shadow"), and thus create "the image of the enemy."[8]

This image is usually stereotypic and mirror-like. That is, no matter who "the enemy" is—Germans, Japanese, Russians, or Americans—they tend to be ascribed similar stereotypic traits and motives. These perceptions are mirror-like because enemies tend to perceive each other similarly, each ascribing hostility and untrustworthiness, for example, to the other and seeing themselves as well-intentioned and benign. The process is further exacerbated by the "mote-beam phenomenon," which allows us to recognize the faults of others with crystal clarity while somehow missing our own and by "King David's rage" that leads us to attack in others what we have denied in ourselves.[16]

"The strain to consistency" then demands that this image of the enemy be maintained through selective perception and further defenses.[8] This makes it difficult for us to attribute anything except negative intentions to "the enemy" and inclines us to view even hostility-reducing overtures as merely signs of deceit. Moreover, since we know how ethical and appropriate our own motivation is, the fact that our enemies fail to acknowledge this and even attribute their evil motivation to us only further proves their duplicity.[17]

The result is a classical paranoid relationship. What was initiated by the defense mechanisms of repression and projection is now aggravated and perpetuated by self-fulfilling negative expectations and a vicious positive feedback cycle of escalating mutual suspicion, defensiveness, and hostility. Of course there is no shortage of sometimes aggressive and dishonest governments in the world, but the situation is usually not as black and white as our defense mechanisms would have us believe.[12]

Once these distorted perceptions are established and elicit defensive and aggressive behavior, then they beg for rationalization. For now the cognitive dissonance between behavior and self-image demands explanation. Hence, the prevalence of statements to the effect that "we've got to do it," "there's no other way," "they don't think like us," and, in the extreme case, "they're not really human." Likewise, suffering may be attributed to faults in the victims ("the fair world syndrome") such as "they could solve their problems themselves if they wanted to" or "they're too lazy to work."

When the suffering we produce must be discussed, its emotional impact can be reduced by the mechanism of intellectualization. Thus, "the language of military science has always been devoid of reference to killing people or creating suffering."[8] This mechanism has reached new heights of sophistication among nuclear strategists, whose "nuke speak" is "a strange and bloodless language by which the planners of nuclear war drain the reality from their actions"[15] (227). Abstract discussions of "reentry vehicles" (missile warheads), "countervalue" (destroying cities), and "collateral damage" (killing civilians) facilitate planning for, what are in stark reality, strategic methods of producing more deaths and destruction than have occurred in all human conflicts. It seems that the ancient words of Confucius still hold true: "If names be not correct, language is not in accordance with the truth of things. If language be not in accordance with the truth of things, affairs cannot be carried on to success"[18] (264). The net result of these defense mechanisms is what Robert Lifton[19] calls "psychic numbing." This is a narcotizing of our awareness that denies the world's reality and our own, replacing them with distorted self-serving images that justify our misperceptions and deceptions, fuel our addictions and aversions, separate and alienate us from others, and further exacerbate the problems they were created to deny.

Fear

When these defenses are examined, it can be seen that they represent unskillful attempts to deal with fear. Indeed, from this perspective many international and nuclear threats can be seen as expressions of fear: fear of attack, for our survival, of losing our comforts, of alien lifestyles, of foreign ideologies, and of depletion of economic supplies. This fear then leads to perceptual distortions, stereotypic thinking, mutual defensiveness, weapons buildups, and aggressive posturing, which fuel more fear, which triggers more defensiveness. The result is a vicious positive feedback cycle demanding ever more and more powerful responses.

Reinforcers

Our individual, national, and international behaviors represent choices based on expected reinforcement. Our current difficulties should, therefore, be traceable in part to inappropriate social, economic, and political reinforcement patterns. These patterns are of course incredibly complex, but we can recognize several broad and dangerous trends.

One obvious factor involves the greater potency of immediate rather than delayed gratification. This differential potency has become increasingly important because we are now dealing with problems whose effects become identifiable only after long periods of time. Pollution, for example, can take years to accumulate to toxic levels, years more before diseases or ecological imbalances are recognized, and decades before cause-and-effect relationships are identified. It may be decades before resource depletion, desertification and deforestation reach critical levels, or before radioactive wastes outstrip temporary storage sites or result in accidents.

Yet, while we are dealing with longer-range consequences than ever before, we are simultaneously reinforcing ourselves, our political leaders, and our military for ensuring short-term gratification. Thus, for example, few politicians have been willing to support legislation to reduce consumption of nonrenewable fossil fuels. For most of them the immediate possible personal consequence of not being reelected outweighs the long-term social consequences of resource depletion, pollution, and economic disruption.

In addition decision makers are now often spatially and emotionally distanced from the consequences of their decisions. Thus, for example, leaders can merely push buttons rather than engage in hand-to-hand combat, or allow millions to starve without ever setting eyes on a hungry person, or pass legislation allowing massive pollution or ecological disturbance while living in far-removed air-conditioned comfort.

In summary, our extraordinarily large and complex hierarchical societies frequently operate to separate decision-makers from the consequences of their decisions. To use the language of sociologists, we appear to have moved in the direction of what Ruth Benedict called low-synergy cultures. The degree of synergy is determined by the extent to which an individual's decisions benefit both self and others simultaneously. The lower the synergy in the culture, the greater the conflict.

If we consider the planet as a whole and the nations as individuals in its global culture, then it is apparent that this global culture is also one of low synergy. Individual nation states function largely as laws unto themselves and are reinforced for dominating economics and resources.

Current social and economic systems also provide strong reinforcement for behaviors that enhance international tensions and arms buildups. One potent reinforcement system is the arms business, which amounts to some 25 to 35 billion dollars per year of trade,[20] and employs half the scientists and engineers in the United States and one-half million worldwide.[21] The economic and social status of millions therefore hinges on the perpetuation, and expansion, if possible, of arms production.

These factors are also closely linked to citizens' lifestyles. For example, our choice to drive our cars rather than use public transportation results in greater gasoline demands. These in turn reinforce suppliers and politicians for increasing immediate supplies even at the cost of greater pollution and more rapid depletion. In short, each of our individual lifestyle and reinforcement choices is part of a complex chain of reinforcements, which selectively supports related social and political choices.[22]

Social Learning Perspectives

Social learning theory also has much to contribute. Here I will focus synoptically on just one dimension, but one of extreme importance; namely, that of the media's role in modeling beliefs, behaviors and lifestyles that both create, and affect our responses to, global threats.

Media impact is a complex issue fraught with emotional charges and countercharges. But emotionalism aside, there seems little question that the media in general, and television in particular, exert enormous psychological and social influence. Reviews of over 3,000 research studies[23,24] point to effects of television viewing on aggressive and prosocial behavior, cognitive and affective development in children, social beliefs, relationships, and health-inducing and endangering behaviors.

Given the experimentally demonstrated power of television modeling, there is cause for deep concern with the media's preoccupation with violence and warfare, glorification of aggressive and consumptive lifestyles, reliance on sensationalism and emotionalism, and avoidance of deeper analyses of complex controversial issues. One might easily be tempted to agree with those who argue that our success in addressing the major issues of our time may well depend on the extent to which the mass media become agents of thoughtful education, analysis, and consciousness raising rather than largely of distraction and denial as they are now.[25]

Eastern Psychologies

Considerable evidence now suggests that due to paradigmatic, cultural, and language differences, as well as simple unfamiliarity, we may have significantly underestimated certain Eastern psychologies.[26-29] Certainly they suggest a wide range of mechanisms relevant to global threats and any truly eclectic and integrative global psychology must take account of them.

Buddhist psychology for example, offers sophisticated analyses of many causes of individual and social pathology. However, it claims that all these causes can be traced to three "root causes": the so-called "three poisons": addiction, aversion, and delusion.

Asian psychologies extend the scope of addiction beyond objects such as drugs and food to which Western psychologists usually limit it. Rather, they suggest that addiction can occur to practically any thing or experience, including material possessions, relationships, beliefs, ideologies, affects, and self-image. Addiction is said to fuel greed, possessiveness, anger, and frustration, to reduce flexibility and choices, and to be a basis of fear and defensiveness.

Aversion, the desire to avoid or attack unpleasant stimuli, can be regarded as addiction's mirror image and also as a source of anger, attack, fear, and defensiveness. Ancient Buddhists therefore recommended in graphic terms that it be regarded "like stale urine mixed with poison."

The person or country dominated by these forces is necessarily preoccupied with a constant quest to obtain desired situations and experiences and avoid feared ones. Yet as both Eastern and Western psychologists know well, such behavior results in only transient satisfaction and further strengthens the addictive and aversive conditioning.[30]

Thus, for example, addiction to material comforts results in lifestyles requiring heavy energy and material imports. These in turn make us dependent on foreign suppliers and willing to go to war to defend "our vital interests" there. "The world has enough for everyone's need," Gandhi is quoted as saying, "but not enough for everyone's greed."

Eastern psychologists also point to the dangers of addiction to beliefs and ideologies. We have already discussed the power of beliefs to shape perception and behavior. When to this is added the power of addiction, it is small wonder that whole cultures may live, kill, and die for their beliefs. The current superpower confrontation can therefore be traced in part to a clash between addictions to different ideologies. To the force of these addictions is added that of aversion which follows automatically and clearly lies at the root of a vast proportion of the world's hostility and aggression.

The third of the three poisons is delusion. Our usual state of mind, say Eastern psychologies, is neither clear, optimal, nor wholly rational. Our addictions, aversions, and faulty beliefs filter and distort our perception, motivation, and sense of identity in such powerful yet unrecognized ways as to constitute a form of delusion or psychosis, a form which is rarely appreciated because it is culturally shared.[29]

Such a claim is consistent with the thinking of a number of Western psychologists, such as Erich Fromm,[31] Willis Harman,[32] Fritz Perls,[33] and Charles Tart.[34] "If we had to offer the briefest explanation of all the evil that men have wreaked upon themselves and upon their world since the beginning of time . . . it would be simply in *the toll that his pretense of sanity takes* as he tries to deny his true condition," said Ernest Becker[35] (29–30). However, in general the Eastern psychologies suggest a more subtle and pervasive degree of individual and cultural psychopathology than we in the West have usually accepted.[27,28,36]

Certainly there is no denying that there is much in the world and our collective behavior that can only be regarded as insanity. "World is said to totter on 'brink of madness'," cried the headline of an American Psychological Association[37] (8) publication reporting the conclusions of the 1983 World Congress on Mental Health. The Eastern psychologies would agree and would suggest that recognizing this insanity is a necessary first step for its cure and the alleviation of the life-threatening global symptoms it has created.

Psychological and Social Immaturity

Fear, greed, aversion, ignorance, unwillingness to delay gratification, defensiveness, and unconsciousness—these are marks of psychological immaturity. They point to the fact that global crises reflect, not only the gross pathology of say a Hitler or an Amin, but even more so the myriad forms of "normal" psychological immaturity, inauthenticity, and failed actualization. This is perhaps most evident in politics, where decisions of enormous import can be shaped by personal insecurities and interpersonal jealousies.[38]

In daily life, such individual immaturities are usually regarded as unexceptional. "What we call 'normal' in psychology is really a psychopathology of the average, so undramatic and widely spread that we don't even recognize it ordinarily" said Abraham Maslow[39] (16). This claim of widespread psychological underdevelopment has since found support in studies of ego, moral, and cognitive development.[40-42]

Just as the fears, illusions, defenses, and distortions that cause our global crises reflect individual immaturity, so too do they appear to reflect cultural immaturity, distortions, and pathology. Our social goals, mores, beliefs, and norms appear to be at least partly created by, and reinforcing of, these fears, illusions, defenses, and distortions.

From this perspective culture can be seen, not only as a force for education and evolution, but also as a shared conspiracy against self-knowledge and psychological growth in which we collude together to protect one another's defenses and illusions. This sounds like an extreme statement, yet it is hardly a new one. "The effect of society is not only to funnel fictions into our consciousness, but also to prevent awareness of reality," said Erich Fromm[31] (98). For Willis Harman[32] and the Eastern psychologies culture is a shared hypnosis; for Ernest Becker[35] and Otto Rank,[43] an immortality project supporting death denial, and for Ken Wilber,[41] a system fostering substitute gratifications as much as authenticity and maturity.

Other examples could be given, but the general point should be clear. The threats to our survival can be traced to psychological and social immaturities, inauthenticities, and pathologies. These represent higher-order variables or syndromes which act through the mediation of the lower-order variables such as fear, defensiveness, etc., which we have already examined. Thus our survival may depend on our individual and collective maturation and this issue is discussed in a subsequent section.

PSYCHOLOGICAL PRINCIPLES OF SKILLFUL RESPONSES

Is it possible for us to apply our psychological understanding to our contemporary crises and become effective therapists to the world? At first thought such an idea may seem ridiculous and naive, laughable in its hubris, and Pollyanaish in the face of the enormity of our difficulties. Cynicism and despair may well seem more reasonable and realistic responses. Yet such cynicism and despair are among the causes of our difficulties and must themselves be subject to psychological exploration if we are to move beyond immobilization to contribution.[14]

Yes, it is true that we cannot know whether we will succeed and our best efforts may seem insignificant when measured against the vastness of ignorance and suffering in the world. It is also true that it may seem easier to avoid the issues entirely and to willingly succumb to what Kierkegaard called "tranquilization by the trivial," losing ourselves in the countless distractions that our culture offers us. But it is also true, as will be discussed, that such tranquilization is purchased only at great cost to personal authenticity and actualization, and, if sufficient numbers opt for this decision, perhaps also at the cost of our planet and species. Let us therefore confront the fears of both hubris and hopelessness and see how we might apply our skills at the global level. For as Erich Fromm[44] concluded in the last interview of his life, "we must not give up . . . we must try everything to avert disaster."

The following, then, are hypothesized principles intended to address aspects of the causative deficiencies, distortions, and defenses identified in the previous section

Beliefs

We are what we think
All that we are arises with our thoughts
With our thoughts we make the world. —*The Buddha*[45] (3)

Combinations of beliefs constitute images: of ourselves, of others, of the world, and of the future. Considerable evidence suggests that "the underlying images held by a culture or person have an enormous influence on the fate of the holder"[46] (214). When the dominant images of a culture are attractive and anticipatory, providing positive and uplifting yet realistic visions of what might be, then they tend to lead and direct social change. However, when traditional images lag behind cultural progress and fail to adequately address novel situations and demands then a period of social turmoil and even crisis develop. Various indicators suggest that our culture may be nearing, if not already be at, such a stage.[47,48]

In choosing our beliefs we are therefore also choosing the images that will guide, create, and pull us, along with our culture, into the future. The following, then, are beliefs that, it is hypothesized, may be beneficial for us to adopt. They can be divided into categories of beliefs about (1) the nature of beliefs; (2) ourselves; (3) others; (4) the world; and (5) nuclear weapons and warfare.

1. *Beliefs about the nature of beliefs.*

a. Beliefs operate as powerful yet usually unrecognized self-fulfilling prophecies.

This hypothesis and the evidence supporting it have already been discussed. It represents a foundation that may motivate the conscious examination and selection of individual and cultural beliefs in line with the following hypotheses.

b. Our ideologies reflect belief systems.

When we remember that our ideologies reflect beliefs, guesses, and models of the world and not "the Truth," then there may be less risk of becoming addicted to them, and killing and dying for them. Likewise, there may be less risk of denying the possible value and validity of alternate views.

c. It is possible to choose skillful beliefs.

Sidestepping the never-ending debate over free will versus determinism, this belief suggests that we can "will to believe" with William James or consciously "choose to believe."[49] We do not have to be helpless victims of our beliefs, though the exquisite paradox is that we can choose to believe we are.

2. *Beliefs about ourselves.*

a. I (and each of us) can make a useful and unique contribution.

This belief is an antidote to beliefs underlying feelings of hopelessness, inadequacy, powerlessness, and despair. Its importance is supported by evidence that our beliefs about our effectiveness function as self-fulfilling prophecies.[10]

b. Developing a psychology of human survival may be a crucial contribution that we can make.

This, of course, is the major thesis of this paper.

3. *Beliefs about others and our relationship to them.*

Skillful choices here would aim to counter beliefs that tend to degrade, dehumanize, blame, and attack other individuals and groups or separate and alienate us from them. Beliefs that heighten empathy and trust through acknowledging our shared humanity, experiences, struggles, and aspirations may therefore be helpful, as for example:

a. Despite diverse cultural and ideological backgrounds, we all share a common humanity with similar existential givens, fears, defenses and aspirations.

b. Though this common humanity exhibits diverse expressions, greater familiarity and understanding of others will result in greater empathy and recognition of commonality.

c. Our expectations (beliefs) of others tend to be self-fulfilling.

This principle, however, like the Pygmalion effect, has obvious implications for international situations where so often antagonists seem to expect, and thus elicit, the worst from each other, thereby validating Jerome Frank's[8] maxim that "enemies become what they believe each other to be."

It is important to note here the distinction between willingness to trust and gullibility. Contrary to popular belief they are not equivalent and recent studies suggest that high trusters are no more likely to be victimized than low trusters. In addition, high trusters may be happier, more likeable and psychologically healthy, and more trustworthy themselves.[50]

4. *Beliefs about the world.*

a. The global threats to human survival and wellbeing may be solvable.

Here lies the fundamental belief about the world on which are based essential beliefs about individual problems such as: we can grow enough food, alleviate poverty, limit nuclear weapons, reduce pollution, and stabilize the ecosystem. Without choosing beliefs such as these we have no motivation to even begin solving our difficulties.

Tackling these problems is among the most urgent priorities confronting us all.

So obvious as to be almost trite, but how many of us really live our lives as though it were true?

5. *Beliefs about weapons and warfare.*

It seems particularly important to question potentially omnicidal beliefs about nuclear weapons and beliefs that legitimize and glorify war by acknowledging that:

a. Nuclear superiority may not be attainable.

b. It may not be possible to limit nuclear wars once they are begun.

c. Nuclear war may not be winnable.

d. Large-scale nuclear war may result in such destruction and ecological disruption as to destroy civilization.

e. War may no longer be justifiable as a means of obtaining national goals.

These, then, are some of the beliefs that may provide a meaningful context and worldview for (a psychology of) human survival.

Education

As was described earlier, many faulty beliefs and behaviors can be traced to ignorance or defenses against recognizing the true nature of our situation. It therefore follows that:

1. Corrective education is essential.

"For the long pull, main reliance must be placed on the education and training of upcoming generations."[6] Who would disagree? Yet how many schools and universities offer adequate courses on global problems and human survival and how many psychology or psychiatry departments offer courses on their psychological roots? Here, then, is a vital role for mental health professionals.

2. To be most effective education should include information about both the state of the world around us and the psychological forces within us which create it.

3. We need to educate both ourselves and others.

As always, the ignorance of others is obvious; our own less so. Yet as so many people have pointed out, self-education is a critical first step in becoming an effective activist in this arena.

Reinforcers

1. It will be important to provide greater reinforcement for decisions that take long-term consequences into account.

2. It may be important to provide increased information, e.g., environmental impact reports and feedback on the costs and benefits, particularly long-term ones, of economic, industrial, and legislative decisions.

3. Differential reinforcement can be applied more effectively to reinforce lifestyles and consumption patterns of greater ecological appropriateness.

Both industrialists and consumers currently receive little or no reinforcement for ecologically sensitive choices.[51] For example in the United States oil, gas, and nuclear power receive billions of dollars of government subsidies each year whereas renewable resources get pennies by comparison.[52] Ecological choices could be selectively reinforced by modifying economic and social incentives and taxes, for example, by raising the price of nonrenewable resources and reducing those of renewable ones.

4. Lifestyles emphasizing voluntary simplicity may not only be essential but may also prove inherently more satisfying, particularly for the psychologically mature,[22,53] than lifestyles that emphasize high consumption.

Of course this has long been a central claim of religious sages and social activists such as Gandhi. "The fewer the necessities the greater the happiness" is the theme they echo[54] (143). Likewise at the cultural level Arnold Toynbee[55] found that mature cultures display "progressive simplification": an increasing attraction of the more subtle nonmaterial satisfactions of life. Voluntary simplicity may thus be both a means to, and an expression of, psychological maturity and satisfaction. If this is so then the combination of material necessity and conscious choice, particularly if supported by education and economic reinforcers, may encourage increasingly ecologically appropriate and voluntarily simple lifestyles.[22,56]

5. International tensions might be reduced by choosing patterns of mutual reinforcement.

Behaviorists are well aware that low rates of mutual reinforcement are both cause and effect of deterioration in marriages in particular, and relationships in general.[57] Many international tensions also can be viewed as expressions of chronic low rates of mutual reinforcement and high rates of mutual punishment. These in turn exacerbate negative mutual beliefs and expectations, distrust, paranoia, and unfavorable images of the enemy. The result is a spiral of increasing tension and animosity.

Behaviorists have had significant success with marital therapies based on education about mutual reinforcement patterns and encouragement to increase reinforcement. Of course, skillful politicians probably recognize these mechanisms intuitively, but it seems reasonable to believe that increased awareness and conscious application of them could result in improvements in international relations.

Social Learning Theory and the Media

Given the awesome psychological and social power of the media, it may be crucial to encourage them to offer more socially relevant programming and prosocial models.[25,58,59]

Mental health professionals have a great deal to contribute here. Their research has already demonstrated the multiple and frequently deleterious effects of current media programming. These contributions can be expanded by extending research and using their findings to educate the public, the media, and legislators about the psychological, social, and global implications of media content. In doing so, mental health professionals have the opportunity of becoming an invaluable advocacy group, unique in offering unbiased, experimentally based information coupled with nonpartisan concern for social and global welfare.

Skillful Actions Reduce Fear and Defensiveness

If fear and defensiveness represent two of the major psychological forces jeopardizing our survival, then it follows that one of our major tasks is to work towards lifestyles and international relations that minimize them. Our task then is to enhance a sense of mutual trust and safety. This is a familiar problem for family therapy and this model points to several useful principles.

Participants in the cold war can be seen as enmeshed in a vicious self-perpetuating cycle of mutual paranoia in which each seeks an elusive security through threatening and condemning the other.[12] The first principle of successful intervention involves assisting participants to recognize the destructive, reciprocal, and self-perpetuating nature of this process. Reducing one's threats, condemnation, and claims for self-righteous superiority must be recognized, not as signs of weakness, but rather as courageous and essential steps for reducing the antagonist's level of paranoia and belligerence, which in turn may enhance one's own sense of trust and safety. Such a process can set in train a "graduated reciprocation in tension reduction" (GRIT).[60]

For similar reasons the family-therapy model would also encourage commitments to greater communication, honesty, and ethicality, knowing that such a commitment from one partner may allow the other to feel less defensive and become in turn more honest and ethical. "Ours is a world of nuclear giants and ethical infants," said General Omar Bradley, and the costs in terms of international conflict are all about us.

Closely related to the costs of ethical infancy are the costs of poor communication. The tendencies of conflicting groups to adopt rigid, stereotyped images of one another are reinforced when adequate information is lacking. Unfortunately withholding information and spreading misinformation are frequently adopted as deliberate policy. In Iron Curtain countries censorship is routine while in the United States there existed for many years "the unwritten law that Americans remain entirely ignorant of Soviet communism. Teachers were fired for teaching about it; people lost jobs for reading about it"[61] (34). Unfortunately we tend to be particularly fearful of the unknown. The net result is that hundreds of billions of dollars are spent and nuclear war is threatened out of fear of people who exist in one another's minds largely as shadow figures constructed from misinformation and myth.

Skillful Responses Search for Areas of Commonality and Shared Purpose

Family therapists and organizational psychologists know that one of their first tasks is to help their clients recognize areas of shared purpose and commonality. As global therapists for our deeply interconnected and interdependent "global village," we would want to do the same.

So many of our contemporary difficulties are no respecters of traditional boundaries. Ecological imbalances, pollution, and radioactive contamination do not halt politely at international borders. The interconnected, holocoenetic (each part effects every other part) nature of our biosphere and of contemporary economic, social, and cultural systems is becoming more and more evident. Increasingly, what we do unto others we also do unto ourselves.

As global therapists we would therefore want to aid recognition of the shared superordinate threats such as nuclear holocaust and ecological disturbances facing us all, recognizing that superordinate threats are among the most potent forces for encouraging collaboration. Experiments suggest that cooperation on tasks that no one group can accomplish alone may be the most effective way of resolving mutual hostility.[68] We would also want to recognize the economic, social, and psychological costs of the arms race and of the ways in which poverty heightens national and international tensions, restricts trade, imposes suffering on the poor, and demands a degree of unconsciousness and "false consciousness" in the wealthy.

We would also want to acknowledge our shared humanity underlying cultural and ideological differences. Certainly we would want to recognize that we all share in the fears, misunderstandings, errors, and defenses which have created the conflicts and suffering that surround us. But we would also want to acknowledge our common human strengths; the shared hopes, ideals, and altruism that make us seek, often in foolish and unskillful ways, the happiness and well-being, love and belongingness we all desire. For in our increasingly interdependent world, it may well be that as Martin Luther King said, we will live together as brothers or die together as fools.

PSYCHOLOGICAL EFFECTS OF GLOBAL CRISES

The distinct possibility of our individual, cultural, and species extinction impacts everything in our lives in ways both obvious and subtle, immediate and far-reaching. Consequently, we face a time of great stress and challenge, risk and opportunity, and potential regression or evolution. On the one hand, we may respond defensively with an exacerbation of the fear, defensiveness, inauthentic choices, and unskillful behaviors that created our dilemma. On the other hand, we may use the situation to spur ourselves to a reconsideration of our values and choices, and of the psychological dynamics from which they spring, thereby effectively accelerating our individual and cultural maturation. Never in the course of human history have the stakes been higher.

Negative Psychological Effects

What, then, are the negative psychological effects these dangers create? Obviously the threats to human survival can constitute major stressors and presumably may create all the complications which can attend any major stress.

As yet, empirical studies of these complications are few, and largely limited to the impact of nuclear threats in developed countries. Clearly nuclear concerns have embedded themselves deeply into the psyches of both adults and children. A significant number of children, both Soviet and American, expect a nuclear war within their lifetime, doubt that they themselves will survive, and report feelings of anger, impotence, and despair.[36,69]

Presumably the massive life-threatening stresses faced by hundreds of millions in the Third World may produce severe psychological complications of all kinds and fuel not only individual psychopathology but resentment, violence, and social breakdown.

In all countries, we might expect many of the same psychological defenses, distortions, and inauthenticities that contributed to global crises also to be exacerbated by these crises. Here we may be involved in a vicious cycle in which defenses are both cause and effect. In addition, inasmuch as we fail to respond appropriately, then we might expect further reactions such as "survivor guilt" and the guilt of failed idealism.

Possible Beneficial Effects

On the other hand, these threats may also afford us great opportunities. Unprecedented challenges such as these might strip away our defenses and call us to examine our individual and collective lives with new urgency and depth. There is even the possibility of using our current dilemma to consciously cultivate our sensitivity to these existential issues. Existential and Eastern psychologies in particular emphasize using the awareness of death as a spur to fuller, more conscious and more choiceful living. In the words of Sigmund Freud[70] (299) "If you want to endure life, prepare yourself for death."

To open ourselves fully to the existential givens of life is not only one of the hallmarks of psychological maturity, but also one of its causes.[71,72] For in the light of our own mortality, of the enormity of preventable suffering in the world, of the rampant inhumanity, greed, hatred, delusion, and defensiveness, and of our precarious existence we are forced to question anew the meaning, purpose, and appropriateness of our lifestyles, work, relationships, values and social, cultural, and national goals. And to the extent we confront these questions authentically and fully, to that extent we are likely to choose to respond in helpful ways which also foster maturity and adaptation. The only alternative to nonmaturity and noncooperation may be nonexistence.

The Call to Service

Inasmuch as we respond to our current dilemma with maturing responses, then service and contribution may be among these since both research and theory indicate that psychological maturity is associated with a greater orientation toward service.[63,64,73,74] But whether significant degrees of psychological maturation occur or not, it may well be that increasing numbers of people will be moved to contribute, and one of today's more hopeful signs is the rapidly growing number of people, including psychologists, addressing global concerns.

Certainly we need contributions of all kinds, including traditional letter-writing, financial donations, educational and political activities, and more. But inasmuch as the roots of the problems are psychological, then we especially need people who are not only effective activists but also understand the underlying psychological issues.

Since many of the causes of our crises stem from normative cultural beliefs and values, then the effectiveness of the people will depend on the degree to which they can extract themselves from limiting and distorting cultural biases. This is the process of "detribalization," by which a person matures from an ethnocentric to a global worldview, develops "perspectivism" (the capacity to take other people's perspective), and become "less dependent upon tribal rewards, more questioning of tribal values, more able to look on life from a universalistic perspective."[75] Such a person no longer looks *through*, but rather looks *at* the cultural filters and hence can work *on* them.[9]

In short, we need people of wisdom and maturity who not only work to relieve suffering, but also use their work for psychological growth, learning, and awakening of themselves and others. This process of "service-learning" as it is sometimes called is of course a form of the millennia-old tradition of karma yoga, the discipline in which service and work are viewed as opportunities for learning and awakening. The aim is impeccable service that optimally relieves suffering and awakens both self and others. In doing so, it aims at inclusive treatment of both symptom and cause, self and other, psyche and world.

Mental health professionals may be in particularly strategic positions to make significant contributions. Individuals can provide public and professional education through lecturing, writing, and media, or by establishing relevant courses, can offer consultation to individuals and groups working on these issues, can do background research and study, and can counsel the growing numbers of people who are psychologically distressed by current events. Groups and organizations of mental health professionals can meet for discussion, self education, and mutual empowerment, create task forces and resource groups, organize conferences and courses, support and lobby for relevant education and research, and disseminate their conclusions. Mental health professionals can do all these and more. But in addition, in everything they do they have the unique opportunity to increase understanding of the crucially important psychological factors which must be recognized if we are to deal adequately with our current crises.

It may be, therefore, that it is time for us to create a new discipline, "a psychology of human survival": a discipline drawing on the insights of all schools of psychology, linking and facilitating all those from all nations, races, and groups who wish to apply their expertise to these, the most urgent issues of our time, unveiling the psychological forces which have brought us to this turning point in history, working to transform them into forces for our collective survival, wellbeing, and fulfillment, and thereby pointing beyond itself to a psychology, not just of survival, but of human survival and wellbeing. Such a discipline might provide not only a catalyst for work in this area, but also a context and vision for psychology as a whole. It might also serve as a model for other fields which might in their turn create, for example, a sociology, economics, or philosophy of human survival.

Perhaps Abraham Maslow[76] was not entirely hyperbolic when he said of psychologists that "the future of the human species rests more upon their shoulders than upon any groups of people now living." Never in the course of human history have the needs and opportunities for contribution in general, and psychological contribution in particular, been greater.

SUMMARY

Within recent decades, nuclear weapons, environmental deterioration, population explosion, resource depletion, and food scarcity have put human survival at ever-increasing risk. Moreover, for the first time in history, all these major global threats are human-caused and can thus be traced in large part to psychological origins. Therefore, if we are to respond appropriately to these, the most urgent issues of our time, then psychological contributions may be essential.

This paper therefore attempts to provide a framework of a psychology of human survival. A brief overview of the nature and extent of current threats is presented, followed by suggested criteria for an adequate psychology of human survival. The causes of contemporary threats are then examined from cognitive, behavioral, social learning, Eastern, psychodynamic, social, existential and developmental perspectives. Psychological principles underlying effective responses are then deduced, and the psychological effects these threats exert on us, both individually and collectively, are examined. Ways in which mental health professionals may contribute are discussed, and it is suggested that the development of a psychology of human survival may be one of the most crucial tasks facing our generation.

Acknowledgments: The author would like to thank the many people who provided assistance and feedback on earlier drafts of this paper. Those include especially B. L.'Allier, W. Andrew, W. Bridges, E. Campbell, A. Deikman, D. Elgin, D. Ellsberg, P. Ellsberg, G. Globus, E. Heim, J. Levy, R. May, F. McGuire, D. Michaels, A. Nelson, K. Ring, T. Roberts, W. Thetford, and F. Vaughan.

REFERENCES

1. Schell, J. The Abolition: Defining the Great Predicament. *The New Yorker*, No. 36, 1984.
2. Brandt, W. *North South: A Program for Survival.* MIT Press, Cambridge, MA, 1980.
3. Presidential Commission on World Hunger. *Preliminary Report of The Presidential Commission on World Hunger.* U.S. Government Printing Office, Washington, D.C., 1979.
4. Council on Environmental Quality. *The Global 2000 Report to the President.* U.S. Government Printing Office, Washington, D.C., 1979.
5. Schell, J. *The Fate of the Earth.* Knopf, New York, 1982.
6. Sivard, R. *World Military and Social Expenditures.* World Priorities, Leesburg, VA, 1986.
7. Walsh, R. *Staying Alive: The Psychology of Human Survival.* New Science Library/Shambhala, Boston, 1984.
8. Frank, J. *Sanity and Survival in the Nuclear Age: Psychological Aspects of War and Peace.* Random House, New York, 1982.
9. Wilber, K. *The Spectrum of Consciousness.* Quest, Wheaton, IL, 1977.
10. Brandura, A. Self Efficacy: Toward a Unifying Theory of Behavioral Change. *Psychol. Rev.*, 84:191–215, 1977.
11. Merton, R. *Social Theory and Social Structure.* Free Press, Glencoe, IL, 1957.

12. Deutsch, M. The Prevention of World War III: A Psychological Perspective. *Political Psychol.*, 4:3–31, 1983.
13. Brown, L. *Building a Sustainable Society.* W. W. Norton, New York, 1981.
14. Macy, J. *Despair and Personal Power in the Nuclear Age.* New Society Publishers, Philadelphia, 1983.
15. Barash, D., and Lipton, J. *Stop Nuclear War: A Handbook.* Grove, New York, 1982.
16. Laughlin, H. *The Ego and Its Defenses.* Appleton-Century-Crofts, New York, 1970.
17. Jervis, R. *Perception and Misperception in Foreign Affairs.* Princeton University Press, Princeton, NJ, 1976.
18. Legge, J., Ed. *Confucian Analects, The Great Learning and the Doctrine of the Mean.* Dover, New York, 1971.
19. Lifton, R. In a Dark Time. In *The Final Epidemic: Physicians and Scientists on Nuclear War.* Adams, R. and Cullen, S., Eds., Education Foundation for Nuclear Science, Chicago, IL, 1981, pp. 7–20.
20. Sivard, R. *World Military and Social Expenditures,* World Priorities, Leesburg, Va, 1981.
21. Caldicott, H. *Nuclear Madness: What You Can Do.* Autumn Press, Brookline, 1978.
22. Elgin, D. *Voluntary Simplicity.* William Morrow, New York, 1981.
23. Pearl, D., Bouthilet, L. and Lazar, J., Eds. *Television and Behavior: Ten Years of Sciencific Progress and Implications for the Eighties* (Vols 1 & 2). U.S. Government Printing Office, Washington, D.C., 1982.
24. Rubenstein, E. Television and Behavior: Research Conclusions of the 1982 NIMH Report and Their Policy Implications. *Am. Psychol.*, 38:820–25, 1983.
25. Elgin, D. The *"Communication Rights" Movement: A Response to National and Global Challenges.* Video-Democracy, Menlo Park, CA, 1983.
26. Walsh, R. The Consciousness Disciplines and the Behavioral Sciences: Questions of Comparison and Assessment. *Am. J. Psychiatry*, 137:663–73, 1980.
27. Walsh, R. Two Asian Psychologies and Their Implications for Western Psychotherapists. *Am. J. Psychotherapy*, 42:543–60, 1988.
38. Walsh, R. Asian Therapies. In *Current Psychotherapies*, 4th ed. Corsini, R. and Wedding, D., Eds. F. E. Peacock, Itasca, Il, 1989.
29. Walsh, R. and Vaughan, F. Eds. *Beyond Ego: Transpersonal Dimensions in Psychology.* J. P. Tarcher, Los Angeles, 1980.
30. Goldstein, J. *The Experience of Insight.* New Science Library/Shambhala, Boston, 1982.
31. Fromm, E. *Zen Buddhism and Psychoanalysis.* Harper & Row, New York, 1970.
32. Harman, W. Old Wine in New Wineskins. In *Challenges of Humanistic Psychology.* Bugenthal, J., Ed, McGraw Hill, New York, 1962.
33. Perls, F. *Gestalt Therapy Verbatim.* Real People Press, Lafayette, CA, 1969.

34. Tart, C. *States of Consciousness*. Dutton, New York, 1975.
35. Becker, E. *The Denial of Death*. Free Press, New York, 1973.
36. Shapiro, D. H. and Walsh, R., Eds. *Meditation: Classic and Contemporary Perspectives*. Aldine, New York, 1984.
37. American Psychological Association. *The Monitor*, 14:8, 1983.
38. Hersch, S. *The Price of Power*. Summit, New York, 1983.
39. Maslow, A. H. *Toward a Psychology of Being*. Van Nostrand, Princeton, NJ, 1968.
40. Kohlberg, L. *Essays on Moral Development* (Vol. I): *The Philosophy of Moral Development*. Harper & Row, New York, 1981.
41. Loevinger, J. and Knoll, E. Personality: Stages, Traits and the Self. *Psychol. Rev.*, 34:195–222, 1983.
42. Wilber, K. *The Atman Project*. Quest, Wheaton, Il, 1980.
43. Rank, O. *Beyond Psychology*. Dover, New York, 1958.
44. Fromm, E. Erich Fromm's Last Interview. *Psychiatric News*, 15:20, 1980.
45. Byrom, T. *The Dhammapada: The Sayings of the Buddha*. Vintage, New York, 1976.
46. Markley, O. Human Consciousness in Transformation. In *Evolution and Consciousness: Human Systems in Transition*, Jantsch, E. and Waddington, C., Eds. Addison-Wesley, Reading, MA, 1976, pp. 214–29.
47. Jantsch, E. and Waddington, C. Eds. *Evolution and Consciousness: Human Systems in Transition*, Addison-Wesley, Reading, MA, 1976.
48. Markley, O. and Harman, W. Eds. *Changing Images of Man*. Pergamon, New York, 1982.
49. Globus, M. and Globus, G. The Man of Knowledge. In *Beyond Health and Normality: Explorations of Exceptional Psychological Wellbeing*. Walsh, R. and Shapiro, D., Eds. Van Nostrand Reinhold, New York, 1983, pp. 294–318.
50. Rotter, J. B. Interpersonal Trust, Trustworthiness and Gullibility. *Am. Psychol.*, 35:1–7, 1980.
51. Schumacher, E. *Small is Beautiful: Economics as if People Mattered*. Harper and Row, New York, 1973.
52. Henderson, H. *The Politics of the Solar Age*. Anchor/Doubleday, Garden City, NY, 1981.
53. Mitchell, A. *The Nine American Lifestyles*. Macmillan, New York, 1983.
54. Longchenpa *Kindly Bent to Ease Us, Part I: Mind*. Dharma, Emeryville, Ca, 1975.
55. Toynbee, A. *A Study of History*. Oxford University Press, New York, 1934.
56. Elgin, D. The Tao of Personal and Social Transformation. In *Beyond Ego: Transpersonal Dimensions in Psychology*. Walsh, R. and Vaughan, F., Eds. J. P. Tarcher, Los Angeles, 1980, pp. 248–56.
57. Azrin, N., Naster, B., and Jones, R. Reciprocity Counseling: A Rapid Learning Based Procedure for Marital Counseling. *Behav. Res. and Therapy*, 11:365–82, 1973.

58. Singer, D. A Time to Reexamine the Role of Television in our Lives. *Am. Psychol.*, 38:815–16, 1983.
59. Singer, J., and Singer, D. Psychologists Look at Television: Cognitive Developmental, Personality, and Social Policy Implications. *Am. Psychol.*, 38:826–34, 1983.
60. Osgood, C. *An Alternative to War or Surrender.* University of Illinois Press, Urbana, IL, 1962.
61. Willens, H. *The Trimtab Factor: How Business Executives Can Help Solve the Nuclear Weapons Crisis.* William Morrow, New York, 1983.
62. Wahb, M. and Bridwell, L. Maslow Reconsidered: A Review of Research on the Need Hierarchy Theory. *Organiz. Behav. and Human Performance*, 15:212–40, 1976.
63. Maslow, A. H. *The Farther Reaches of Human Nature.* Viking Press, New York, 1971.
64. Walsh, R. and Vaughan, F. Towards an Integrative Psychology of Wellbeing. In *Beyond Health and Normality: Explorations of Exceptional Psychological Wellbeing.* Walsh, R. and Shapiro, D. H., Eds. Van Nostrand Reinhold, New York, 1983, pp. 388–431.
65. Bandler, R. and Grindler, J. *Frogs into Princes: Neurolinguistic Programming.* Real People Press, Moab, UT, 1979.
66. Mahoney, M. *Cognition and Behavior Modification.* Ballinger, Cambridge, MA, 1974.
67. White, R. Empathizing with the rulers of the USSR. *Polit. Psychol.*, 4:121–37, 1093.
68. Sherif, M., Harvey, O., White, E., et al. *Intergroup Conflict and Cooperation: The Robbers' Cave Experiment.* University of Oklahoma Press, Norman, OK, 1961.
69. Adams, R. and Cullen, S. *The Final Epidemic: Physicians and Scientists on Nuclear War.* Educational Foundation for Nuclear Science, Chicago, 1981.
70. Freud, S. Thoughts for the Times. In *The Standard Edition of the Complete Works of Sigmund Freud*, Vol. XIV. Strackey, J., Ed. Hogarth Press, London, 1955, p. 299.
71. Walsh, R. and Shapiro, D. H. *Beyond Health and Normality: Explorations of Exceptional Psychological Wellbeing.* Van Nostrand Reinhold, New York, 1983.
72. Yalom, I. *Existential Psychotherapy.* Basic Books, New York, 1980.
73. Heath, D. The Maturing Person. In *Beyond Health and Normality: Explorations of Exceptional Psychological Wellbeing.* Walsh, R. and Shapiro, D. H., Eds. Van Nostrand Reinhold, New York, 1983, pp. 152–205.
74. Waterman, A. Individualism and Interdependence. *Am. Psychol.*, 36:762–73, 1981.
75. Levinson, D. J. *The Seasons of a Man's Life.* Knopf, New York, 1978.
76. Maslow, A. H. *A Philosophy of Management.* Lecture presented to Cooper Union, New York, 1956.

PART TWO

AGGRESSION, CONFLICT, AND ENEMY-MAKING: SOCIAL PSYCHOLOGICAL VIEWS

The splitting of the atom has changed everything save our mode of thinking, and thus we drift toward unparalleled catastrophe. —*Albert Einstein*

The chapters in this part look at some of the important psychological forces and processes that contribute to conflict, aggression, and enmity between groups, and to the resolution of conflict, positive group relations and peace.

In chapter 4, Ervin Staub reviews research on aggression and group conflict, theories about their origins, and ways that individuals can be involved in creating nonaggressive and positive group relations. He also proposes means by which positive relations can be created among individuals and groups. In chapter 5, Jeffrey Rubin presents a psychological perspective on conflict and negotiation, reviews the study and practice of conflict-resolution approaches, and suggests roles that psychologists can play in this area in the future. Brett Silverstein, in chapter 6 presents the proposition that among the more impotant psychological barriers to peacemaking are the effects of enemy images. He reviews research on enemy-making and describes the techniques that are available and can be used to overcome the harmful exaggerations that result from enemy images.

4

The Origins of Aggression and the Creation of Positive Relations among Groups

Ervin Staub

War and other forms of violence by groups, like mass killing or genocide, have been with us for as long as human history has been recorded. The hope for peace and harmony is just as old. Widespread hope was created as the '90s began by the democratization of Eastern Europe, the turn from dictatorship to democracy in much of South America, and the turn away from apartheid in South Africa. But almost immediately the war in Iraq followed.

Is aggression innate in human beings and therefore inevitable in human relations? What are the roots of aggression on the one hand and of nonaggressive and helpful ways of relating to other human beings on the other? Might it be possible to create a world in which conflicts between groups are reduced by nonaggressive means? What can concerned citizens do to create more caring, helping, and cooperation among individuals and groups? My purpose in this chapter is to suggest some possible answers to these questions by considering what we have learned from psychology and the study of cultures about human tendencies, characteristics of individuals and groups, and life conditions that have the potential for leading to aggression and violence between groups. This will be followed by a discussion of the kinds of actions that could begin a process of social evolution toward more peaceful and cooperative relations between groups, including the positive socialization of children. Finally, we will consider how people might be mobilized to participate in and create this process.

ARE HUMANS AGGRESSIVE BY "NATURE"?

Throughout history scholars and thinkers have made assumptions and assertions about human nature, some seeing human beings as basically good, others asserting that humans are selfish and aggressive "by nature" (Staub 1978). The English philosopher Hobbes is perhaps the best known proponent of the view that humans are selfish and aggressive. In his view, without restraint imposed by the state people would use any and all means to further their own interests, resulting in a war of each against all. Among psychologists, Freud believed that human beings are only concerned with the fulfillment of their own needs, and that they are aggressive by nature. But in contrast to Hobbes, who stressed the role of external constraints in limiting aggression, Freud stressed the importance of internal constraints, the internalization of standards and values taught by our elders that constitute a conscience or superego. The ethologist Konrad Lorenz (1970) also asserted, partly generalizing from his studies of aggression in animals, that human beings are aggressive by nature.[1]

More recently, sociobiologists (Wilson 1975) have claimed a genetic basis for both aggression and altruism. Guided by their observations of animal behavior, sociobiologists look for the origins of human social behavior in the genetic makeup of humans. In their view, organisms, including humans, respond with aggression to conditions, such as scarcity, that threaten their survival and thus the transmission of their genes. But they acknowledge that human culture can overlay and modify the genetic influence.

The Effects of Assumptions about Human Nature

Assumptions about human nature themselves shape "human nature." They shape what we perceive, how we respond, and the behavior we evoke in others. Moreover, particular assumptions about human nature and human beings can become persistent characteristics of both individuals and groups.

If we assume that humans are aggressive by nature, we are more likely to perceive or interpret others' actions as hostile. We are more likely, therefore, to respond aggressively to nonaggressive or mildly hostile behavior of others. While we believe that we are simply engaged in self-defense, our actions tend to provoke hostile responses from others, which then confirm our original beliefs, and may initiate a hostile sequence of interaction.

Much psychological research indicates that beliefs about people can become self-fulfilling prophecies. For example, their belief that other people are competitive leads certain individuals to initiate competitive behavior, which results in competitive responses that confirm the original belief (Kelly and Stahlesky 1970). Aggressive boys tend to interpret others' ambiguous behavior toward themselves as hostile, which is probably one reason that they are aggressive. This aggression in turn leads others to behave aggressively toward them (Dodge 1980; Dodge and Frame 1982). Violent criminals often perceive challenge and threat in behavior that someone else may perceive as innocuous, and thus "respond" with aggression (Toch 1969).

While assumptions about the nature of individuals vary, the assumption that groups are self-seeking and aggressive seems quite common. The theologian Reinhold Niebuhr, for example, suggested that groups have no morality and are only capable of self-serving behavior (Niebuhr 1960). Such a view seems inherent also in the tradition of political realism (Morgenthau and Thompson 1984), which regards international relations as a struggle for power. In a hostile world, power is essential to give a state the capacity to protect its interests. To the extent members of groups, and their leaders, believe that other groups are self-serving and hostile, they are more likely to interpret others' actions as hostile and react with hostility or aggression. Seeing their own actions as defensive and lacking awareness of their own role in creating the hostile sequence of interaction that is likely to follow can contribute to the evolution of deep-seated antagonism.

Some Nongenetic Bases of Aggression

How can we assess the assumption that human beings are aggressive by nature? While we certainly have the potential to be aggressive, and even perhaps an inclination for it under certain conditions, there are many reasons to believe that aggression is not genetically determined, in the sense of its being an inevitable response to certain conditions. One reason is the tremendous variation among both individuals and societies in the incidence of aggressive responses to "instigating" conditions such as frustration, threat, or attack.

The extremely aggressive Mundurucu headhunters of Brazil raided and killed people in the neighboring villages. Wilson (1978), guided by his sociobiological perspective, suggests that this was in the service of survival, to reduce competition for their scarce protein source, the animals of the forest. But as Wilson himself noted, the Mundurucu had a highly aggression-generating culture: even the name for non-Mundurucu meant enemy. The adaptation that the group developed to scarcity, rather than genetic forces, may be the best explanation for their aggressiveness.

The Siriano Indians of Eastern Bolivia, in the face of severe scarcity, developed an extremely selfish mode of existence. People hid their food from others and after killing an animal might eat all the food at once, so that they would not have to share it. But certain tribes of Bushmen in Australia, faced with similar scarcity, had developed highly cooperative ways of life, sharing the available food. While some simple societies have been extremely violent even against fellow group members (e.g., the Waorani of Western Amazonia), others have been extremely nonaggressive both internally and in their relations with others (e.g., the Semai of the Malaysian rain forest).

It appears, then, that it is the way individuals and groups develop as a result of their experience that predisposes them to violence, rather than human genetic makeup. We seem to have a genetic *potential* for aggression, as well as for caring and altruism; the disposition toward one or the other evolves as a function of experience.

Individuals and groups can develop a widely differing range of characteristics as a function of conditions they have faced, the way they have dealt with these conditions, and their resulting evolution. Research findings show that the way children are socialized and their experiences with people strongly shape their values and determine whether their orientation to other people becomes caring or hostile. These issues will be discussed in later sections.

MOTIVES FOR AGGRESSION

The characteristics of individuals and of groups and the conditions they face at particular times jointly affect their psychological states, including their motives for aggressive behavior. The history of an individual's or group's relations to others can also affect the ease with which aggression-generating motives arise. If we want to understand and control aggression, we must come to understand what motives it serves, what environmental conditions give rise to these motives, and what characteristics of individuals and groups, and of their relations, make the arousal of these motives, and aggression as the mode of their fulfillment, probable. To reduce aggression, the "activation" of these motives must be reduced, and alternative avenues for their satisfaction must be found.

One of the earlier hypotheses in psychology about the causes of aggression is the "frustration-aggression" hypothesis (Dollard et al. 1939). This still-influential hypothesis stated that frustration, or the blocking of goal-directed behavior, leads to aggression. But now we know that this is not always true. For example, prior training can lead children to respond to frustration with renewed efforts at reaching a goal rather than with aggression (Davitz 1952).

The originators of the frustration-aggression hypothesis would have regarded threat or attack—either on the physical self or on the psychological self—as simply different types of frustration. But it is worthwhile to differentiate among these as instigators of aggression. Attacks on the self or the self-concept may be especially potent sources of aggression-generating motives. This would explain why in laboratory research an attack on a person's competence or other aspects of his or her self-concept has usually brought about more aggressive behavior than the frustration of their goal-directed behavior, such as the completion of a task (Baron 1977).[2]

Frequently, difficult conditions of life in a society are the starting point for violence by groups. These conditions include economic problems like inflation, depression, or unemployment; political conflict; and rapid or profound social change. Such conditions are likely to give rise to feelings of threat, or they are experienced as an attack on one's physical self or one's self-concept, values, and way of life. They can also frustrate the fulfillment of needs and desires of the whole group or of large subgroups of it. Conflict with another group, or disorder in international relations, can also give rise to feelings of threat, attack, or frustration. Frustration, attack, or threat, in turn, tend to give rise to the following aggression-generating motives (see Staub 1989b):

1. *Anger and hostility, which are the most basic and purest sources of aggression.* The resulting aggression has been called "hostile aggression," because the motive or desire is to cause suffering. It is most likely to arise when one perceives the other as having intentionally harmed oneself or one's group (Pastore 1952; Mallick and McCandless 1966), and probably also when threat, attack, or frustrating actions by others are intense. Certain personal and group characteristics (see below) also make hostile aggression more likely.

2. *Self-defense, the defense of the physical self, including the satisfaction of basic needs.* This motive can arise without direct attack on the self. Economic problems or political violence can create insecurity, vulnerability and fear, and the *experience* of threat and attack. A past history of antagonism with another group can lead to a constant feeling of threat, and the interpretation of even its neutral actions as an attack on the self.

3. *Defense of the psychological self—of one's self concept, worldview, and way of life.* The inability to fulfill basic security and material needs of oneself and one's family, and chaos and disorganization in society, can result in feelings of powerlessness, helplessness, and diminished sense of self-worth and of the worth of one's group. Aggression has an impact; it involves the use of power over others, and can provide a feeling of strength and power. Scapegoating, identifying a specific cause of one's problems, can reduce the feeling of responsibility for those problems and enhance self-esteem.

4. *The need for a comprehension of reality, for a coherent and "usable" worldview.* Difficult life conditions in a society (or in an individual's life) can lead to the experience of chaos and upheaval. One's comprehension of reality, of the world and one's place in it, can become untenable. A usable understanding of reality is a profound human need (Epstein 1980; Janoff-Bulman 1985; Staub 1989b), and people will turn to any possible means to fulfill this need. Here also, scapegoating comes into play: it "explains" the reasons for life problems by identifying a cause and implies that "dealing with" the scapegoat might be the solution for them.

Adopting new ideologies can provide a new comprehension of the world, but many ideologies include the identification of enemies who supposedly interfere with the fulfillment of the ideology. Ideologies usually present a vision of a better way of life. Sometimes such ideologies stress nationalist goals. Such was the case of Turkey just prior to the genocide of the Armenians (in 1915), when a pan-Turkish ideology offered a vision of national greatness, power, and purity. At other times ideologies are universalistic, in that they promise a better world for all. Communism is one example. Paradoxically even Nazism had "better world" implications: by killing off racially "inferior" human beings, the Nazis promised to improve all of remaining humanity (Staub 1989b).

Additional motives for aggression are inherent in instrumental aggression, which refers to promoting self-interest or gaining material advantage by aggressive means. Conquest motivated purely by the desire to gain territory or wealth may be regarded as instrumental aggression. Aggression can also be the result of obedience to authority, of submitting the self to the wishes of leaders or of a group.

BASIC HUMAN TENDENCIES AS SOURCES OF ANTAGONISM AND AGGRESSION

There are many basic human psychological tendencies that contain the potential for leading to antagonism, and to aggression. We will consider only three of them here—"us-them differentiation," "moral exclusion," and "just-world thinking."

Us-them Differentiation

There seems to be a human tendency to devalue people who are seen as outside the boundaries of one's own group, which makes aggression against them more likely. How does a negative view of human beings in general, or devaluation of specific groups of people, develop?

There is a basic human tendency to differentiate between "us," members of an ingroup, and "them," members of outgroups. This tendency appears to have roots in the human genetic makeup. For example, the human infant normally develops a strong affectional tie, or attachment, to primary caretakers. The overt manifestation of attachment and a negative reaction to strangers, or "stranger anxiety," both appear at about six months of age. While both of these phenomena appear to have a genetic source, their nature and intensity are shaped by the infant's experience.

For example, infants who spend time with a greater variety of people tend to show less stranger anxiety (Shaffer 1988). Stranger anxiety seems to be an early manifestation of a tendency to react with fear and anxiety to the strange and unfamiliar.

Fear of the unknown, or perhaps of what is merely different from the known, seems to characterize both animals and human beings. In the relationship between human groups, such discomfort or fear is often enhanced. Members of groups whose behavior, habits, beliefs, and values are different from our own are often feared, disliked, and devalued. Devaluation is especially likely if the other's way of life and values raise questions about the goodness of our own. Frequently, over time, us-them differentiations, stereotypic images, and the devaluation of specific groups become deeply embedded in cultures, as expressed in their literature, folklore, art, and societal institutions and practices. Children are then told, and shown by the example of adults, and through exposure to the culture, whom to like and dislike, trust or mistrust. Over time they develop the habit of differentiation, of the creation of ingroups and outgroups.

Piaget and Weil (1951) have shown that by the age of nine or ten, Swiss children have developed very clear stereotypes—i.e., strong and exaggerated beliefs about members of other groups (Allport 1954). The same is certainly true of children in other nations. Many of these stereotypes are devaluative in nature; for instance, one ten-year-old Swiss boy believed that "the French are not very serious, they don't worry about anything, and it is dirty there," and the Russians "are bad, they're always wanting to make war."

There is evidence from a substantial body of recent research that such stereotypes result in selective remembering, selective attention to and biased interpretation of the behavior of members of stereotyped groups, and that they foster behavior toward outgroups that elicit stereotypical responses (Brewer and Kramer 1985; Hamilton and Trolier 1984; Rothbart 1981). Cultural devaluation of groups, which is coded into devaluative stereotypes or negative images, is likely to lead to negative interpretations of the actions of those groups or their individual members and to antagonism and hostility toward them.

Research in the last several decades has also shown that people create us-them differentiations on the basis of minimal information they receive about themselves and others; for example, information that shows differences in preference for certain modern painters, or in the perception of clusters of dots on a page (Brewer 1978; Tajfel et al. 1971). Such information leads to a more favorable evaluation of members of the ingroup and less favorable evaluation, or devaluation, of outgroup members. A further consequence is discrimination: in distributing rewards, people come to favor others who have been defined as "us" (even though on very trivial bases) in comparison to those defined as "them" (Brewer 1978; Tajfel et al. 1971).

Differentiating the ingroup from an outgroup and devaluing the outgroup is a precursor to many forms of group violence. In the Holocaust, in the killing of Armenians in Turkey, in the "autogenocide" in Cambodia, and in the "disappearances" in Argentina, profound devaluation preceded the killings (Staub 1989b). In war, as for example in the Indian-Pakistani wars, there is often mutual devaluation rooted in the cultures of opposing parties, or in religious or other differences (Stoessinger 1982). Similarly, in raids in Lebanon by Christian militias on Palestinian camps there was frequently widespread killing, but Palestinians who were identified as Christian were repeatedly spared (Kuper 1981). Research evidence also shows that people who are devalued will be harmed more, while those who are positively valued will be harmed less (Bandura et al. 1975).

In summary, the tendency to differentiate ingroup and outgroup and to devalue outgroups and their members enhances the potential for aggression toward other human groups. Once devaluation or the tendency to create it become embedded in the culture, economic, social, and political problems within a group are likely to result in turning against a devalued group, and conflict with a devalued group is less likely to be resolved in nonaggressive ways.

Another human tendency that carries the potential for antagonism is *moral exclusion* (Staub 1990), which is an extreme consequence of intense devaluation of a group. In moral exclusion the group and its members are regarded as less than human and are excluded from the moral universe. Moral values and standards become inapplicable to them. While this makes extreme violence against them possible, moral exclusion is itself usually the result of increasingly harmful acts against the group.

Increasing discrimination and violence against a victim group, a progression of "steps" along what I have called a *continuum of destruction*, have characterized many mass killings and genocide (Staub 1989b). Both research findings (Buss 1966; Goldstein et al. 1975) and the evidence of these real life events indicate that perpetrators of violence change as a result of their own actions. The changes in the perpetrators, which make it possible for them to inflict even greater violence on their victims, include the development of moral exclusion.

Just-world thinking (Lerner 1980) refers to the tendency to believe that the world is just and, therefore, people who suffer must deserve their suffering, due either to their actions or to their character. This is a self-protective tendency, helping people to maintain the belief that as long as they do no wrong, no harm will befall them. This belief leads bystanders to devalue innocent victims and can lead perpetrators to devalue their own victims, and thereby to justify their violent actions.

GROUP CHARACTERISTICS AND AGGRESSION

There are several aspects of ethnic and national group identity that can contribute to a group's use of aggression. These include a culture's *worldview*, its *self-concept*, its *orientation toward aggression*, and its *orientation toward authority*.

A *worldview* includes a group's basic assumptions about human nature as either negative or positive. A worldview predominant in a group can represent human beings in general, or people who are not part of the group, as untrustworthy, dangerous, or evil. Thus the tendency to devalue "them" has become a shared characteristic of the members of the group. Another important characteristic is group or societal *self-concept*. An aspect of the self-concept is qualitative, the evaluation of the self, or what is referred to as self-esteem. As in individuals (Loban 1953), so in groups, moderately positive self-esteem can make aggression less likely and positive behavior more likely.

But a group's belief in its superiority or specialness frequently leads to a belief in its right to dominate others. Pride in one's strength and power, and valuing an image of strength and power, can lead to what Ralph White (1984) described as "macho pride," an unwillingness to compromise with others and a need to save face. This frequently contributes to the occurrence of war. It probably contributed to the behavior of both parties leading up to the United States attack on Iraq. Valuing strength and power and seeing oneself as strong, powerful, and superior makes the chaos, upheaval, and feelings of powerlessness that frequently arise from difficult life conditions especially difficult to tolerate and the need for self-defense especially great (Staub 1989b). Using military power against Iraq may have helped both George Bush and the American people to reduce the psychological impact of the frustrations of recession, relative loss of economic power, and a range of domestic problems, including homelessness, violent crime, drug abuse, and the Savings and Loan crisis.

In addition to its quality, the content of the self-concept can be important. The self-definition of ethnic or national groups often includes the possession of certain territories. Conflict over territories that are part of the self-definition or identity of two different groups is a frequent source of long-term hostility. Intense conflict can arise even when materially, in terms of its population or resources, the territory is of little value. This was the case, for example, in the Falklands war between Argentina and England. Conflict over territory that is part of each group's identity is one source of the ethnic conflicts that have reemerged in Eastern Europe and the Soviet Union when communist oppression lifted.

The *values* of a society are important in determining how self-interest is defined and what goals are set. Values that stress the importance of wealth and power are likely to increase aggression, both because they make instrumental aggression probable, and difficult life conditions that entail economic problems and loss of power will be more frustrating.

The society's *orientation toward aggression* is important in two ways. In some societies there is a history of aggressiveness between subgroups or with other nations, and aggression has customarily been used to resolve conflict, which makes aggression normal, acceptable, even "right." For example, the United States use of force in Grenada, and in Panama, its air attack on Libya, its support of the Contras in Nicaragua, and other involvements in overthrowing governments was probably a factor in facilitating the relatively speedy turn to war in the face of Iraqi aggression against Kuwait. Groups also develop ideologies that idealize aggression. The Nazis idealized aggression, and the early Bolsheviks regarded it as an important tool of the revolution. Alternatively, aggression may be inhibited by certain predominant values and further discouraged by a history of nonaggression. The Semai of Malaysia, for example, strongly value peace and avoid aggression, both as individuals and as a group (Gregor and Robarcheck 1990).

A strong *orientation toward authority and a monolithic culture,* that is, a limited number of predominant values and limited freedom to express contrary views, also contribute to a predisposition toward aggression. These make it more likely that members of the group will submit themselves to the decisions of their leaders. When hardship or conflict with another group creates fear and uncertainty, members of groups that are accustomed to strong leadership may find it especially difficult to think independently about events. They will be more likely to seek solutions from leaders and less likely to oppose or resist actions by the group that may be contrary to their personal values. For example, they will be more likely to remain passive bystanders to progressively increasing hostility and aggression toward members of an outgroup. A broad range of values and views in the society and the habit of independent judgment by citizens make it more likely that opposing views or disagreement about policies and actions will be expressed in the public domain and inhibit such an evolution toward aggression.

Another important factor in the development of aggression is the *history of relationship* between the group and other groups. Historic differentiations develop between ingroups and specific outgroups. A history of *cultural devaluation* of minorities, for example of Jews in Germany or Armenians in Turkey, "preselects" these minorities for the role of scapegoat, or as the group identified as a hindrance to the fulfillment of a nationalistic or better world ideology. In contrast, what I have called an *ideology of antagonism* is the deep-seated devaluation of an *external* group and the perception of it as hostile, as an enemy bent on harming one's group (Staub 1989b). It leads groups to believe that they need to possess superior strength to reduce their vulnerability, or that they must strive to actively dominate their enemy.

Ideologies of antagonism are at the root of the enduring hostility between groups that reemerged in Eastern Europe and the Soviet Union as communist repression lifted. They tend to lead to a "conflict mode" of relating where the aim is to gain *relative* advantage over the other even if it diminishes one's own welfare. Until recently such a conflict mode seems to have characterized U.S.-Soviet relations; one of its examples was the U.S. policy of engaging in a costly arms race, partially aimed at ruining the Soviet economy, which damaged the U.S. economy as well.

Ideologies of antagonism are resistant to change, partly because they have become deeply embedded in the groups' cultures. As the reemergence of ethnic conflicts in the Soviet Union indicates, they do not vanish simply with the passage of time. They require the healing of historic wounds or the evolution of positive relations in ways to be described below.

THE ROLE OF BYSTANDERS IN AGGRESSION

Increasing violence by a majority against a minority, or by one group against another, is also affected by the behavior of bystanders, both internal bystanders who are members of a society and external bystanders such as other nations. There are many actions that can be taken by bystanders. They can speak out against the violence; they can threaten perpetrators with a variety of consequences; they can stop trade with the aggressors; or they can employ boycotts and sanctions. By all of these means, they call public attention to the violations being committed. These nonviolent reactions can change the perpetrators' perception of their actions. For example, they can make perpetrators aware that other nations regard their victims as human beings to whom moral rules apply. They can create fear of the consequences of their aggression for themselves. There are many important historical examples of the impact of the behavior of bystanders on perpetrators (Staub 1989b). A contemporary example may be the changes in the policy of apartheid in South Africa. It is unlikely that the change in government policy would have occurred without the international boycott.

Unfortunately, however, bystanders frequently remain passive, confirming the perpetrators in their actions. Since passivity in the face of others' suffering is painful, it will change the bystanders themselves, who can use just-world thinking and other mechanisms to distance themselves from the victims. Bystanders can themselves become supporters of the perpetrators, or even join as perpetrators. For example, a group of Berlin psychoanalysts during World War II started out as passive bystanders, but over a period of time some of them developed into perpetrators by participating in the euthanasia program, and in other ways (Staub 1989a).

The Iraqi invasion of Kuwait would most likely have been averted if bystanders, that is, other nations including the United States, had clearly opposed prior Iraqi aggression. Instead, many nations supported Iraq after it invaded Iran, and continued to support it even after it had used chemical weapons against Iran and engaged in the mass killing of Kurds in Iraq.

I have considered in this section a range of forces—psychological, cultural, and historical—that contribute to intergroup hostility and aggression. In the next section I shall consider some of the means by which more peaceful, cooperative, and constructive intergroup processes might be set into motion.

TURNING THE TIDE: FROM AGGRESSION TO POSITIVE GROUP RELATIONS

What principles can we derive from psychological theory and research that may point the way toward building more positive, cooperative relations between groups, which may make intense conflict less likely and nonviolent resolution of conflict more likely?

Healing Past Wounds

When a past history of antagonism exists, the healing of past wounds is the best starting point. Psychological research has shown that following aggression, if the offending party is willing to acknowledge responsibility for the harm caused and asks for forgiveness, or offers restitution, the victim's anger and hostility, which fuels reciprocal aggression, is likely to diminish. Such actions by perpetrators indicate that they have no future intention to cause harm, and restores balance in the relationship of perpetrator and victim (Berscheid et al. 1968; Staub 1971).

However, harmdoers are not easily inclined to ask for forgiveness. History suggests that asking for forgiveness is even more difficult for groups than for individuals. Partly this is due to their perception of victims, who are devalued, blamed, scapegoated, or identified as enemies, all of which fuels aggression and makes it seem justified. In addition, pride, which resides in the nature of group self-concept and creates a need to maintain an image of strength and power, adds to the unwillingness of groups to acknowledge any wrongdoing. To make aggressors assume responsibility for the harm they caused and to lead them to ask for forgiveness and make reparations often requires the active role of "bystanders." When the aggressor is a group or a nation, it is other nations who must play the role of active bystanders.

A recent approach to resolve deep-seated hostility between groups is the use of "dialogue" groups. Members of antagonistic groups who are open to working on resolving the hostility and improving relations are brought together for several days. In one approach, the participants are first guided to mourn the pain and loss their groups have suffered, then to acknowledge a share of responsibility and their own group's role in the conflict and in causing the other's suffering. Finally, they are to ask each other's forgiveness (Montville 1987; Volkan 1988). (Conflict resolution techniques are further discussed in chapter 5 by Jeffrey Rubin.) For such an approach to be effective, either influential members of each group must be involved, or the experience of these groups must be brought to the larger group—perhaps in television programs or in other ways. The sensitive use of the more general approach described below can also provide the starting point for building positive group relations.

Building Positive Group Relations

As suggested above, both individuals and groups learn by doing. If they engage in behavior that benefits or harms another, they change in their perception of and orientation to the victims or beneficiaries of their acts, as well as in their self-concept. Harmful acts prepare the way for more intense harm-doing. Experimental research with the teacher-learner paradigm shows that when teachers are told to administer shocks to "learners" when the latter make mistakes on a task, and then it is left to them to determine the shock level they will give, they administer increasingly intense shocks over time (Goldstein et al. 1975; Buss 1966). Real life examples of the behavior of perpetrators of torture, mass killing, and genocide also show such "learning by doing" (Staub 1989b). That is, the act of engaging in cruel and destructive behavior makes it increasingly easier to engage in such behavior.

But evolution also takes place in a positive direction. My research has shown that children who make toys for poor hospitalized children or teach skills to younger children are subsequently more helpful (Staub 1975, 1979). In another study, adults who had helped others earlier (Harris 1972) or were induced to express the intention to help (Freeman and Frazer 1966) were later more helpful. People who during World War II endangered their lives to save persecuted Jews in Nazi Europe often started out helping in a more limited way, often on the basis of personal

acquaintance, but then continued to devote themselves to helping anyone they could (Oliner and Oliner 1988; Tec 1986). Helpful acts presumably bring about more positive evaluation of the beneficiaries of one's
behavior and a perception of oneself as more helpful and more willing to
help others. The way is thereby prepared for later helpful behavior
(Staub 1975, 1979, 1989b).

There is also evidence of reciprocity in behavior (Gouldner 1960;
Staub 1978). People tend to harm those who have harmed them and help
those who have helped them. But the intention attributed to the actor is
also important. Some studies have shown that believing that another
intends to harm us, we are likely to harm the other (Epstein and Taylor
1967). Believing that another has helped us for selfish reasons, in order
to gain benefit for himself or herself, for example by inducing us to
reciprocate, diminishes positive reciprocity (Staub 1978). Especially when
long-lasting hostility exists, initiating positive behavior may be greeted
with the suspicion that it serves self-interest. The U.S. government
responded with suspicion, for example, when the Soviet Union stopped
underground nuclear testing in the mid-1980s, claiming that it did so
after a long series of tests had given it an advantage over the United
States. Overcoming suspicion may require either acts that are difficult to
interpret as completely self-serving, or a consistent pattern of positive
behavior. Over time, a system of positive reciprocity can be built, each
party acting in ways that benefit the other.

Joint projects between members or institutions of different groups can
further develop ties and connections. Research findings with children
show that when groups have developed antagonistic relations, joint efforts for shared goals can resolve feelings of antagonism and build positive
connection (Sherif et al. 1961). Research on cooperation between children shows that cooperation builds positive feelings not only toward
those engaged in the cooperative effort, but even toward outsiders (Heber and Heber 1957) and that cooperation builds positive attitudes and
behavior across group lines (Aronson et al. 1978; Johnson et al. 1981). It
is important that each party benefits from joint projects, and that each
party feels it can make valuable contributions. Within societies, members
of different groups can join in community efforts like cleaning up the
environment, building playgrounds for schools, or renovating buildings
and neighborhoods. Between societies, joint projects can range from

cultural events, to manufacturing, to space exploration, to research on health problems, to joint action to save the environment.

These efforts can begin something that is essential to create on a broad scale: cross-cutting relations between groups (Deutsch 1973), that is, members of groups working and playing together, so that genuine connections can develop (Staub 1989b). For successful cross-cutting relations and engagement in joint projects, it is important that groups learn about each other's habits, customs, and ways of life. Without such preparation cultural differences, even simple but basic ones like styles of emotional expression or individual tempo in everyday life, can create walls that separate people.

Joint projects can start with and further develop shared goals, some of which can become superordinate goals (Sherif 1958) that are dominant over individual and potentially conflicting goals. Ultimately, connection and cooperation can become superordinate goals in their own right.

For positive relations to withstand the vicissitudes of difficult life conditions and the conflicts that are inevitable in human relationships, it is essential to build institutions that can maintain these positive relations in the face of conflict. Binational and international institutions can provide a framework to discuss and resolve conflicting interests, and engage in mediation and, if necessary, arbitration. The deeper the system of connections, including institutional ties, that develops among nations, the more effectively can such institutions function.

Holding a vision about the possibility of positive relations between groups can motivate efforts to fulfill the vision. Some of the ideas in this section offer such a vision: the possibilities inherent in initiating positive actions, joint projects, cross-cutting relations, and the like. The vision of peaceful, cooperative relations between groups and of ways of fulfilling it should not become abstract, but should maintain its focus on the concrete well-being of individuals. Social activism is usually the result of a combination of the experience of threat (e.g., the nuclear threat, or threat to the environment) and a feeling of empowerment (see chapter 16 by Douglas McKenzie-Mohr in this book). But response to threat can be very slow. A positive vision can motivate people to work for creating caring societies—and positive relations between them—and thereby reduce the likelihood of conflict and aggression and the disregard of human needs.

THE ROLE OF PARENTING

A variety of personality traits in individuals have been identified in psychological research that appear to be related to a tendency to behave in positive, nonaggressive ways toward others. For example, a "prosocial value orientation," which consists of a positive evaluation of people and feelings of personal responsibility for their welfare, makes it more likely that people will help others in physical or psychological distress (Feinberg 1978; Grodman 1979; Staub 1974, 1978). Other research has shown that feelings of empathy or sympathy—reacting to other people as if their need or distress were one's own (Hoffman 1982), or with caring and concern (Batson 1990)—also contribute to people helping others (Eisenberg 1986). Empathy also tends to reduce aggression (Feshbach and Feshbach 1969; Staub 1971), as do a prosocial value orientation and certain other personal characteristics, such as advanced moral reasoning (Kohlberg and Candee 1984) and "aggression anxiety" (Baron 1977).

While the relationship between these personal characteristics and the overall level of aggression and violent conflict engaged in by a group needs to be further explored, analyses of group violence using historical, cultural, and individual information suggest that they make such violence less probable (Staub 1989b). Are there ways through which these traits can be fostered and developed in a culture? A variety of research studies done in the past four decades suggest such characteristics can be promoted through socialization by parents and schools and by various types of childhood experiences. Moreover, the child-rearing practices that contribute to children's kindness, helpfulness, and generosity seem exactly the opposite of those that lead to aggressiveness.

A pattern of parental practices is required for these positive outcomes (Eisenberg 1986; Grusec 1981; Staub 1979, 1981, 1986). Parental *love, warmth, and nurturance* appear essential both in their own right and as a background to other practices. *Reasoning* with the child, explaining the reasons for rules and prohibitions, and especially pointing out to the child the consequences of his or her behavior on other people *(induction)*, whether positive or negative, are important. So is *effective guidance or control*, in which parents maintain at least minimal standards that they regard as important, and are firm in leading the child to act according to these standards. Parents serving as *models* of positive behavior, acting positively in relating to their own child and to other people, are also important in leading children to acquire positive values and the tendency for positive action.

Another critical ingredient is guiding children to *act* positively toward other people, so that they learn by participation. As noted earlier, a number of studies have shown that children who are repeatedly led to help others—for example, to make toys for poor hospitalized children or to teach younger children—are subsequently more helpful and generous (Staub 1975, 1979, 1986).

A variety of desirable consequences are likely to follow from the positive socialization and parenting practices just described. The child comes to perceive and evaluate other people as benevolent and trustworthy; value people and develop a feeling of responsibility for their welfare; experience himself or herself as a worthy person. Positive self-esteem is also associated with people helping others (Karylowski 1976; Rosenhan et al. 1981) And the positive identity and feelings of self efficacy that result also enable people to pursue self-related goals more effectively (Staub 1978).

In contrast to the preceding positive socialization practices, parents who use highly forceful discipline, who deprive children of rights and privileges, and especially those who use frequent or severe physical punishment or who are critical and rejecting, will tend to have aggressive children (Eron 1982; Huesmann, Lagerspetz, and Eron 1984; Huesmann, Eron et al. 1984; Zahn-Waxler 1986). Parental example and the general mode of interaction within the family are also important contributors to children's aggression. In some families, aggressive coercion is a dominant mode of relating among members, so that children learn to regard aggression as normal and even as necessary for self-defense and for influencing others (Patterson 1982).

This brief review suggests ways of raising children that make the development of aggression less likely and caring and helpfulness more likely. How can these ways of raising children be promoted?

Parent Training and Education

Training parents in specific skills of child rearing can be a highly effective way to promote positive socialization. The state of Missouri, for example, initiated a demonstration project, starting with prospective parents and continuing until the children reached age three. Participants were taught simple skills, such as setting clear limits for their children as early as their first year, and shaping their children's experience by providing them with environmental and social stimulation (Meyerhoff and White 1986). There was formal evidence that the training advanced the intellectual functioning of children in comparison to others in a control group, and informal evidence of their better social functioning. If the value of such "positive parenting" programs is clearly demonstrated over time, it is reasonable to hope that parents will increasingly use them to reduce their uncertainties about how to be effective in raising their children.

Certain beliefs about the nature of children are preconditions for parental interest in and effective use of positive socialization practices. In pre-twentieth century Germany and England, there was a widespread belief that the child is innately willful—that the child's will had to be broken, usually by forceful means, if he or she was to be capable of goodness and obedience (Miller 1983; Stone 1977). Such beliefs and values still linger; for instance, physical punishment remains a widely respected method of disciplining children (Straus et al. 1980). We must become aware of, and work to change, societal and parental beliefs that lead to harsh, punitive parenting. This can be done partly in the context of training in parenting skills. It is my experience in working with parents and teachers in workshops on positive socialization that, as they realize that positive methods of discipline can be effective in guiding children and gaining their cooperation, they acquire both a sense of power and an increased feeling of benevolence.

Psychologists and other social scientists interested in promoting a peaceful world have an essential role in communicating information to the public about research on the effectiveness of positive socialization practices. For example, love and responsiveness to the infant's needs are essential for the development of a positive, "secure" attachment between the infant and its primary caretakers. Securely attached infants, in turn, are responsive and cooperative, and they have positive relations with their peers in the early school years (Sroufe 1979; Waters et al. 1979).

Beyond specific socialization practices, various aspects of a family's structure, rules, and expectations affect the development of children's personalities. For example, in authoritarian families, where rules are laid down for the child without explanation, justification, or discussion, children are less likely to acquire the capacity for independent judgment

(Miller 1983). This may make it less likely that, as adults, they would resist leaders who create hostility toward and confrontation with other groups. In many families, explicit and implicit rules prohibit the expression of varied emotions and desires. Not only anger and hostility, but also the expression of anxiety, even positive feelings such as joy, and feelings of sexuality may be prohibited. Restrictions on the feelings, thoughts, and judgments of the evolving child prevent the development of a full, positive identity, thereby perhaps preventing the development of respect for and acceptance of the identity of others.[3]

It is only during the past decade that public attention has finally begun to turn toward a consideration of the harmful and lasting effects of the various forms of abusive and exploitative treatment of children within their families. A vast clinical literature in psychology, psychiatry, and social work has developed in the '80s which demonstrates the tragic and destructive consequences to children of physical, sexual, and emotional abuse by parents and other family members. Victimization seems to be "a strong factor for the development of . . . lifetime mental health problems" (Kilpatrick et al. 1987, 65). Although its degree is a matter of dispute, these forms of abuse tend to be perpetrated across generations. And a high percentage of individuals convicted of violent crime have a history of sexual and/or physical abuse in childhood. The broader social implications of this knowledge must be considered in any serious exploration of group violence and aggression, and of broad-based educational efforts aimed at parent training and education. Widespread mistreatment of children is an expression of cultural characteristics, and further shapes cultural characteristics, including those that make group violence more likely. In contrast, the positive socialization practices described above are inherently benevolent and are likely to generate benevolence.

The life conditions of parents and their resulting psychological states affect both their inclination and capacity for positive socialization of their children. Difficult conditions that produce chaos and disorder, great poverty, uncertainty about means of livelihood, and feelings of relative deprivation and injustice are important sources of frustration, stress, and of a poor self-concept. Even minimally supportive social conditions and the fulfillment of basic human needs make positive child-rearing practices more likely. Thus it is important to work for social legislation that would help families live under conditions conducive to positive socialization of their children. These might include paid parental leave, adequate day care for young children, birth control education, adequate support for single parents, and programs of parent education (Staub, in press).

Concern with these problems has long existed, but I suggest that they must be remedied not only for humanitarian reasons—not only to improve the quality of life for many and create greater social justice—but also to contribute to positive socialization on a societal scale, which is essential for the evolution of human connection, caring, and nonaggression.

SOCIALIZATION IN SCHOOLS

Schools play an important role in shaping children's characteristics in four respects. First, positive disciplinary practices by teachers, in contrast to power-assertive or physically aggressive methods that diminish the child, will have the same kinds of beneficial consequences as in the case of parents. This was recently demonstrated in a longitudinal study in which a number of practices and programs were introduced into schools to promote children's prosocial behaviors and values, social skills, and role taking. The use of positive discipline practices by teachers was found important in promoting such characteristics (Solomon et al. 1986).

Second, the mode of operation of schools—that is, how democratic or autocratic they are, and to what extent they stress cooperation versus competition—strongly affects the developing personality of children and adolescents. Democratic schools will promote the evolution of psychological independence and independent moral judgment and decision making, and thereby a feeling of responsibility for judgment and action (Lippitt and White 1943).

Third, by the content they teach, schools affect children's knowledge, awareness, perceptions, and understanding of the world. Fourth, by special activities, such as guiding children to engage in behavior that benefits others, schools provide opportunities for learning by participation.

These different influences combine to shape students' relationship to authority. People are constantly influenced by leaders, experts, and other authorities. For instance, after Nixon's visit to China, the former Chinese communist hordes became viewed as friendly ping-pong players. Negative views and feelings are perhaps even more easily shaped.

Through both the content of education and students' experience in the school setting, we must strive to help every student evolve a *critical consciousness*—that is, the tendency to evaluate events independently and to bring multiple perspectives to events, rather than simply accepting the word of "experts" or those in authority.

Schools must also contribute to children's learning about the shared humanity of all persons. This can happen in many interconnected ways. In the educational realm, students can learn about differences in customs, beliefs, and values of different groups of individuals, while coming to appreciate commonalities in desires, in feelings of joy and sorrow, and in physical and other needs. In *Homage to Catalonia,* George Orwell described a profound change in his attitude toward his "enemy" and war in general while fighting as a volunteer in the Spanish Civil War; he had a sudden feeling of shared humanity when, about to shoot, he saw an enemy soldier pull down his pants and relieve himself. By concretizing and particularizing human beings (Tversky and Kahneman 1974), through such examples and in other ways, rather than perpetuating abstractions and stereotypes, we can enhance empathic responsiveness to a wide range of people and diminish the tendency for us-them differentiation and devaluation.

The schools have a special opportunity to engage students in behavior that benefits others and thereby to promote helpful, responsible behavior through learning by participation. They can guide them to community service. Or, as some high schools already do, they can require students to spend a certain number of hours in community service in order to graduate. Their experience in these service activities and their gain in understanding the lives of others is described by many students with great enthusiasm (Boyer 1983). Within the schools themselves there are many opportunities to help others: students can tutor younger children or each other, or they can assume responsibility for tasks that maintain or improve the functioning of their classroom or school.

How can we convince schools to adopt practices that will contribute to prosocial goals and behaviors? We must stress that the school experience inevitably affects children's personality, values, and social behaviors (Staub 1981). Since the consequences are inevitable, the question is which values, characteristics, and behaviors schools should promote. We must advocate the values and goals of interconnectedness and cooperation. (See chapter 17 by Phyllis La Farge.)

Currently, most schools promote *competitiveness* in learning and performance, which is a likely source of negative orientation toward other people. In contradiction to the usual justification for promoting it, competition diminishes rather than enhances achievement in varied settings (Johnson et al. 1981; Kohn 1986). *Cooperative learning procedures* are at least as effective as traditional ones in teaching academically advanced children, and they are more effective with disadvantaged, underachieving, minority children. In addition, they contribute to participants' positive self-esteem, positive interpersonal behaviors that extend across group lines, and the capacity to listen and to communicate with others (Aronson et al. 1978; Hertz-Lazarowitz and Sharan 1984; Johnson et al. 1981). In such procedures, the status of children and the recognition or rewards they receive are usually equalized. Such procedures can create effective cross-cutting relations across group lines. As noted earlier, cooperation contributes to a positive orientation to, or liking for, not only one's partners in the cooperative activity, but also other people in general (Heber and Heber 1957; Staub 1978).

Even less directly positive activities, such as general participation in the school community, can be important in promoting responsibility. A study on the effects of small versus large schools on students has shown that in the smaller schools, students participated more in varied school activities (music, drama, sports, clubs, etc.). In large schools, a much larger proportion of students constituted the audience for, rather than the participants in, such activities (Gump and Friesen 1964). Being a participant helps develop a students' capacity for action. The feeling of responsibility to oneself and one's community that participation helps promote may be essential for children to become socially responsible adults.

An important task for social scientists, concerned educators, or people concerned with human welfare is to demonstrate to school administrators and policymakers that positive socialization and related practices contribute to a positive orientation toward people and to helpful behavior and thereby benefit both the students and the community. They probably also enhance the effectiveness of academic instruction.

On the basis of information currently available, specific socially constructive methods for school instruction need to be developed, disseminated, and advanced. For example, in the still ongoing longitudinal study of Solomon et al. (1986), three schools have employed a set of practices that stress cooperative learning, opportunities for prosocial action as a basis for learning by doing, teachers' use of positive discipline techniques, and related procedures. The initial findings after three years of the five-year program are promising. They show, in comparison to children in control schools, an increase in the participating children's social skills, including their capacity for resolving conflict peacefully, as well as their prosocial classroom behaviors and peer interactions. Even simpler procedures, which lend themselves more easily to adaptation and use in regular school curricula, may prove effective (Staub 1991).

MOBILIZING CITIZENS FOR SOCIALLY RESPONSIBLE ACTION

For change to occur in a society and for one's nation to contribute to change in the world, many members of society must become active participants in working for the social good and human welfare.

First, creating awareness in people is important. One kind of awareness is that of the psychological processes in individuals—like the devaluation of "them" and just world thinking—that lead them to turn against others, or allow them to distance themselves both from people who suffer and from events and conditions that endanger people or, as in the case of environmental pollution, their own future. Another kind of awareness is of the characteristics of one's own culture and the institutions in one's society that can lead the group to turn against others or promote discrimination and injustice (Staub 1989b).

A third kind of awareness is of the potential power of bystanders—of individuals and groups—to influence events. Research findings (Latane and Darley 1970; Staub 1974) as well as real life examples of people taking action (Hallie 1979; see also Lifton 1986, on the termination of the euthanasia program in Nazi Germany as a result of the reactions of the population) show the tremendous potential of individuals and nations to influence each other's actions. Passive bystanders and perpetrators can be changed by the words and actions of individuals and groups (see Staub 1989b).

Workshops, seminars, television, and the other media, as well as literature and the words and actions of political leaders and other public persons, can all contribute to create these different kinds of awareness. To get influential individuals and the media involved, social activists need to develop channels to such people, need to create an ongoing dialogue with them about societal and human issues.

For people to engage in social action, they must also become aware of their own potential to influence events. They must identify the realms in which their actions can make a difference; and they need to identify both less ambitious intermediate goals and long-term goals. As people begin to act, they will learn by doing, and an evolution can follow with an increase in caring and social responsibility. This is especially likely to happen if people join together and support each other. Over time, social action will tend to enhance commitment to the values that underlie action and to the principle of action itself (Locatelli and Holt 1986).

NOTES

1. It is informative to consider what leads scientists and social thinkers to make the assumption that "human nature" is aggressive. Lorenz, who was sympathetic to the Nazis and made statements advocating the elimination of "morally inferior human beings" (Lorenz 1940; see also Staub 1989b), may have been also influenced in his belief that human aggression was genetically based by Nazi views that elevated and glorified aggression. Freud was apparently influenced by the tremendous destructiveness of World War I to assume that human beings were aggressive "by nature."
2. Alternatively, the intensities of frustration and attack may not have been adequately equated in these experiments.
3. While information that promotes positive socialization, training in methods of child rearing, and family system diagnoses may be highly effective in bringing about positive socialization, the parents' own personality can place a limitation on their effectiveness. For example, some parents, who as children experienced nonnurturant, cold, or punitive parenting, may find it extremely difficult to be warm and nurturant in their interactions with their own children. For some parents, their children may become the objects of displaced anger. In-depth procedures, such as therapy, may enable many but not all such parents to adopt positive socialization practices.

REFERENCES

Allport, G. (1954). *The nature of prejudice.* Reading, Mass.: Addison-Wesley.

Aronson, E., Stephan, C., Sikes, J., Blaney, N., and Snapp, M. (1978). *The Jigsaw Classroom.* Beverly Hills, Calif.: Sage Publications.

Bandura, A., Underwood, B., and Fromson, M. E. (1975). Disinhibition of aggression through diffusion of responsibility and dehumanization of victims. *Journal of Research in Personality, 9,* 253–269.

Baron, R. A. (1977). *Human Aggression.* New York: Plenum Press.

Batson, C. D. (1990). How social an animal? The human capacity for caring. *American Psychologist, 45,* 336–347.

Batson, C. D., Duncan, B., Ackerman, P., Buckley, T,, and Birch, K. (1981). Is empathic emotion a source of altruistic motivation? *Journal of Personality and Social Psychology, 40,* 290–302.

Berscheid, E., Boye, D., and Walster, E. (1968). Retaliation as a means of restoring equity. *Journal of Personality and Social Psychology, 10,* 370–376.

Boyer, E. (1983). *High School: A Report on Secondary Education in America.* New York: Harper and Row.

Brewer, M. B. (1978). Ingroup bias in the minimal intergroup situation: A cognitive-motivational analysis. *Psychological Bulletin, 86,* 307–324.

Brewer, M. B., and Kramer, R. M. (1985). The psychology of intergroup attitude and behavior. *Annual Review of Psychology, 36,* 219–243.

Buss, A. H. (1966). The effect of harm on subsequent aggression. *Journal of Experimental Research in Personality, 1,* 249–255.

Davitz, J. R. (1952). The effects of previous training on post-frustration behavior. *Journal of Abnormal and Social Psychology, 47,* 309–315.

Deutsch, M. (1973). *The Resolution of Conflict: Constructive and Destructive Processes.* New Haven: Yale University Press.

Dodge, K. A. (1980). Social cognition and children's aggressive behavior. *Child Development, 51,* 162–170.

Dodge, K. A., and Frame, C. L. (1982). Social cognitive biases and deficits in aggressive boys. *Child Development, 53,* 620–635.

Dollard, J., Doob, L., Miller, N. Mowrer, O., and Sears, R. (1939). *Frustration and Aggression.* New Haven: Yale University Press.

Eisenberg, N. (1986). *Altruistic Emotion, Cognition and Behavior.* Hillsdale, N.J.: Lawrence Erlbaum Associates.

Epstein, S. (1980). The self-concept: A review and the proposal of an integrated theory of personality. In E. Staub, ed., *Personality: Basic Aspects and Current Research.* Englewood Cliffs, N.J.: Prentice-Hall.

Epstein, S., and Taylor, S. (1967). Instigation to aggression as a function of degree of defeat and perceived aggressive intent of the opponent. *Journal of Personality, 35,* 265–289.

Eron, L. D. (1982). Parent-child interaction, television violence, and aggression in children. *American Psychologist, 37,* 197–211.

Feinberg, J. K. (1978). Anatomy of a helping situation: Some personality and situational determinants of helping in a conflict situation involving another's psychological distress. Ph.D. diss., University of Massachusetts, Amherst.

Feshbach, N. D., and Feshbach, S. (1969). The relationship between empathy and aggression in two age groups. *Developmental Psychology, 1,* 102–107.

Freedman, J. L., and Fraser, S. C. (1966). Compliance without pressure: The foot-in-the-door technique. *Journal of Personality and Social Psychology, 4,* 195–202.

Goldstein, J. H., Davis, R. W., and Herman, D. (1975). Escalation of aggression: Experimental studies. *Journal of Personality and Social Psychology, 31,* 162–170.

Gouldner, A. W. (1960). The norm of reciprocity: A preliminary statement. *American Sociological Review, 25,* 161–179.

Gregor, T., and Robarcheck, C. A. (1990). Two paths to peace: Semai and Meinahu. Paper presented at the conference: "What we know about peace." Charleston, S.C.

Grodman, S. M. (1979). The role of personality and situational variables in responding to and helping an individual in psychological distress. Ph.D. diss., University of Massachusetts, Amherst.

Grusec, J. (1981). Socialization processes and the development of altruism. In J. P. Rushton and R. M. Sorrentino, eds., *Altruism and Helping Behavior.* Hillsdale, N.J.: Lawrence Erlbaum Associates.

Gump, P. V., and Friesen, W. V. (1964). Participation in nonclass settings. In R. G. Barker and P. V. Gump, eds., *Big School, Small School: High School Size and Student Behavior,* pp. 75–93. Stanford: Stanford University Press.

Hallie, P. P. (1979). *Lest innocent blood be shed. The story of the village of Le Chambon, and how goodness happened there.* New York: Harper and Row.

Hamilton, D. L., and Trolier, T. K. (1984). Stereotypes and stereotyping: An overview of the cognitive approach. In J. Dovidio and S. L. Gaertner, eds., *Prejudice, Discrimination, and Racism: Theory and Research.* New York: Academic Press.

Harris, M. B. (1972). The effects of performing one altruistic act on the likelihood of performing another. *Journal of Social Psychology, 88,* 65–73.

Heber, R. F., and Heber, M. E. (1957). The effect of group failure and success on social status. *Journal of Educational Psychology, 48,* 129–134.

Hertz-Lazarowitz, R. and Sharan, S. (1984). Enhancing prosocial behavior through cooperative learning in the classroom. In E. Staub, D. Bar-Tal, J. Karylowski, and J. Reykowski, eds., *Development and Maintenance of Prosocial Behavior.* New York: Plenum.

Hoffman, M. L. (1982). Development of prosocial motivation: Empathy and guilt. In N. Eisenberg, ed., *The Development of Prosocial Behavior.* New York: Academic Press.

Huesmann, L. R., Eron, L. D., Lefkowitz, M. M., and Walder, L. O. (1984). Stability of aggression over time and generations. *Developmental Psychology, 20,* 6, 1120–1134.

Huesmann, L. R. Lagerspetz, K., and Eron, L. D. (1984). Intervening variables in the television violence-aggression relation: Evidence from two countries. *Developmental Psychology, 20,* 746–775.

Janoff-Bulman, R. (1985). The aftermath of victimization: Rebuilding shattered assumptions. In C. R. Figley, ed., *Trauma and Its Wake*. New York: Bruner/ Mazel.

Johnson, D. W., Maruyama, G., Johnson, R., Nelson, D., and Skon, L. (1981). The effects of cooperative, competitive and individualistic goal structures on achievement: A meta analysis. *Psychological Bulletin, 89,* 47–62.

Karylowski, J. (1976). Self-esteem, similarity, liking and helping. *Personality and Social Psychology Bulletin, 2,* 71–74.

Kelley, H. H., and Stahleski, A. J. (1970). Social interaction basis of cooperators' and competitors' beliefs about others. *Journal of Personality and Social Psychology, 16,* 66–91.

Kilpatrick, D. G., Saunders, B. E., Beronen, L. J., Best, L. L., and Von, J. M. (1987). Criminal victimization: Lifetime prevalence, reporting to police and psychological impact. *Crime Delinquency, 33,* 479–489.

Kohlberg, L., and Candee, L. (1984). The relationship of moral judgment to moral action. In W. M. Kurtines and J. L. Gewirtz, eds., *Morality, Moral Behavior, and Moral Development,* 52–73. New York: Wiley.

Kohn, A. (1986). *No Contest: The Case against Competition.* Boston: Houghton Mifflin.

Kuper, L. (1981). *Genocide: Its Political Use in the Twentieth Century.* New Haven: Yale University Press.

Latane, B., and Darley, J. (1970). *The unresponsive bystander: Why doesn't he help?* New York: Appleton-Crofts.

Lerner, M. (1980). *The Belief in a Just World: A Fundamental Delusion.* New York: Plenum Press.

Lifton, R. J. (1986). *The Nazi doctors: Medical killing and the psychology of genocide.* New York: Basic Books.

Lippitt, R., and White, R. K. (1943). The "social climate" of children's groups. In R. G. Barker, J. S. Kounin, and H. F. Wright, eds., *Child Behavior and Development,* 485–508. New York: McGraw-Hill.

Loban, W. (1953). A study of social sensitivity (sympathy) among adolescents. *Journal of Educational Psychology, 44,* 102–112.

Locatelli, M. G., and Holt, R. R. (1986). Antinuclear activism, psychic numbing and mental health. In M. Schwebel ed., Mental health implications of life in the nuclear age. *International Journal of Mental Health, 15,* 143–162.

Lorenz, K. (1940). Durch Domestikation verursachte Störungen arteigenen Verhaltens. *Zeitschrift für angewandte Psycholgie un der Charakterkunde* (Journal of Applied Psychology and the Science of Character), *59,* 66, 71.

Lorenz, K. (1970). *On Aggression.* New York: Bantam Books.

Mallick, S. K., and McCandless, B. R. (1966). A study of catharsis of aggression. *Journal of Personality and Social Psychology, 4,* 591–596.

Meyerhoff, M. K., and White, B. L. (1986). Making the grade as parents. *Psychology Today, 20,* (September), 38–45.

Miller, A. (1983). *For Your Own Good: Hidden Cruelty in Child-Rearing and the Roots of Violence*. New York: Farrar, Straus, and Giroux.

Montville, J. V. (1987). Psychoanalytic enlightenment and the greening of diplomacy. *Journal of the American Psychoanalytic Association, 37,* 297–318.

Morgenthau, H. J., and Thompson, K. (1984). *Politics among Nations: The Struggle for Power and Peace*. New York: Alfred A. Knopf.

Moynihan, D. P. (1986). *Family and Nation*. New York: Harcourt Brace Jovanovich.

Niebuhr, R. (1960). *Moral Man and Immoral Society: A Study in Ethics and Politics*. New York: Charles Scribner's Sons [Originally published in 1932]

Oliner, S. B., and Oliner, P. (1988). *The Altruistic Personality: Rescuers of Jews in Nazi Europe*. New York: Free Press.

Pastore, N. (1952). The role of arbitrariness in the frustration-aggression hypothesis. *Journal of Abnormal and Social Psychology, 47,* 728–731.

Patterson, G. R. (1982). *Coercive Family Processes*. Eugene, Oreg.: Castilia Press.

Piaget, J., and Weil, A. (1951). The development in children of the idea of the homeland and of relations with other countries. *International Social Science Bulletin, 3,* 570.

Rosenhan, D. L., Salovey, P., Karylowski, J., and Hargis, K. (1981). Emotion and altruism. In J. P. Rushton and R. M. Sorrentino, eds., *Altruism and Helping Behavior*. Hillsdale, N.J.: Lawrence Erlbaum Associates.

Rothbart, M. (1981). Memory processes and social beliefs. In D. L. Hamilton, ed., *Cognitive Processes in Stereotyping and Intergroup Behavior*. Hillsdale, N.J.: Lawrence Erlbaum Associates.

Shaffer, D. R. (1988). *Social and Personality Development*. Monterey, Calif.: Brooks-Cole.

Sherif, M. (1958). Superordinate goals in the reduction of intergroup conflict. *American Journal of Sociology, 63,* 349–358.

Sherif, M., Harvey, D. J., White, B. J., Hood, W. K., and Sherif, C. W. (1961). *Intergroup Conflict and Cooperation: The Robber's Cave Experiment*. Norman, Okla.: University of Oklahoma Book Exchange.

Solomon, D., Watson, M., Battistich, V., and Schaps, E. (1986). Promoting prosocial behavior in schools: An interim report on a five-year longitudinal intervention program. Paper presented at the annual meetings of the American Education Research Association, San Francisco, April.

Sroufe, L. A. (1979). The coherence of individual development: Early care, attachment, and subsequent developmental issues. *American Psychologist, 34,* 834–842.

Staub, E. (1971). The learning and unlearning of aggression: The role of anxiety, empathy, efficacy and prosocial values. In J. Singer, ed., *The Control of Aggression and Violence: Cognitive and Physiological Factors*. New York: Academic Press.

Staub, E. (1974). Helping a distressed person: Social, personality and stimulus determinants. In L. Berkowitz, ed., *Advances in Experimental Social Psychology*, vol. 7. New York: Academic Press.

Staub, E. (1975). To rear a prosocial child: Reasoning, learning by doing, and learning by teaching others. In D. DePalma and J. Folley, eds., *Moral Development: Current Theory and Research*. Hillsdale, N.J.: Lawrence Erlbaum Associates.

Staub, E. (1978). *Positive Social Behavior and Morality: Social and Personal Influences*, vol. 1. New York: Academic Press.

Staub, E. (1979). *Positive Social Behavior and Morality: Socialization and Development*, vol. 2. New York: Academic Press.

Staub, E. (1981). Promoting positive behavior in schools, in other educational settings, and in the home. In J. P. Rushton and R. M. Sorrentino, eds., *Altruism and Helping Behavior*. Hillsdale, N.J.: Lawrence Erlbaum Associates.

Staub, E. (1986). A conception of the determinants and development of altruism and aggression: Motives, the self, the environment. In C. Zahn-Waxler, ed., *Altruism and Aggression: Social and Biological Origins*. New York: Cambridge University Press.

Staub, E. (1989a). Steps along the continuum of destruction: The evolution of bystanders, German psychoanalysts and lessons for today. *Political Psychology, 10*, 39–53.

Staub, E. (1989b). *The Roots of Evil: The Origins of Genocide and Other Group Violence*. New York: Cambridge University Press.

Staub, E. (1990). Moral exclusion, personal goal theory and extreme destructiveness. In S. Opawa, ed., Moral exclusion and injustice. *Journal of Social Issues, 46*, 47–65.

Staub. E. (1991). A proposal to develop caring and helpful behavior, positive self-esteem and positive behavior across group lines through socialization in the schools. Unpublished manuscript, University of Massachusetts.

Staub, E. (in press). The origins of caring, helping and nonaggression: Parental socialization, the family system, schools, and cultural influence. In S. Oliner and P. Oliner et al., eds., *Embracing the Other: Philosophical, Psychological and Historical Perspectives on Altruism*. New York: New York University Press.

Stoessinger, J. G. (1982). *Why Nations Go to War*. New York: St. Martin's Press.

Stone, L. (1977). *The Family, Sex and Marriage in England, 1500–1800*. New York: Harper and Row.

Straus, M. A., Gelles, R. J., Steinmetz, S. K. (1980). *Behind Closed Doors: Violence in the American Family*. Garden City, N.Y.: Anchor Press/Doubleday.

Tajfel, H., Flamant, C., Billig, M. Y., and Bundy, R. P. (1971). Societal categorization and intergroup behavior. *European Journal of Social Psychology, 1*, 149–177.

Tec, N. (1986). *When Light Pierced the Darkness: Christian Rescue of Jews in Nazi-occupied Poland*. New York: Oxford University Press.

Toch, H. (1969). *Violent Men*. Chicago: Aldine.

Tversky, A., and Kahneman, D. (1974). Judgement under uncertainty: Heuristics and biases. *Science, 185*, 1124–1131.

Volkan, V. D. (1988). *The Need to Have Enemies and Allies*. Northvale, N.Y.: Jason Aronson.

Waters, E., Wippmann, J., and Sroufe, L. A. (1979). Attachment, positive affect, and competence in the peer group: Two studies in construct validation. *Child Development, 50*, 821–829.

White, R. K. (1984). *Fearful warriors: A psychological profile of U.S.-Soviet relations*. New York: The Free Press.

Wilson, E. O. (1975). *Sociobiology: The New Synthesis*. Cambridge: Belknap Press of Harvard University Press.

Wilson, E. O. (1978). *On Human Nature*. New York: Bantam Books.

Zahn-Waxler, C., ed., (1986). *Altruism and Aggression: Social and Biological Origins*. New York: Cambridge University Press.

5

Conflict, Negotiation, and Peace: Psychological Perspectives and Roles

Jeffrey Z. Rubin

We live in a truly amazing time. As we approach the end not only of this century but also of this millennium, we appear to be standing at the margins of new and remarkable opportunities: opportunities for a peace that never could have been imagined in the throes of two world wars, or the bipolar cold war universe that has preoccupied us for the last forty years. Despite the unexpected trauma of the Persian Gulf crisis, beginning in the summer of 1990, it is clear that dramatic changes are taking place with almost daily frequency, changes that are transforming the world map and creating new political and economic realities.

In this chapter, I wish to do several things: first, to indicate what I believe to be the distinguishing characteristics of a so-called psychological perspective on conflict and negotiation; second, to briefly trace the

This chapter was first presented, with only a few minor differences, as the G. Stanley Hall Lecture at the Annual Convention of the American Psychological Association, Boston, August 10, 1990. A number of the ideas presented in that address in turn first saw light in some other format, including: the keynote address to the Peace Bridge Conference, Buffalo, N.Y., September 15, 1989; a presentation at the Stanford Center on Conflict and Negotiation, February 20, 1990; a chapter on psychological issues in international negotiation (to appear in a volume edited by Victor Kremenyuk, *International negotiation: Analysis, approaches, issues;* and Program on Negotiation Working Paper 86-5, "Opportunities for international dispute settlement."

rapidly changing history of interest in the study and practice of conflict resolution approaches; and finally, to indicate how psychologists will both need and want to create a role for themselves in the changing arena ahead.

I wish to begin more personally, however, by observing the now distant origins of my own interest in conflict. One of the things that binds psychologists together is their shared interest in the world of experience. External reality may be the province of the physical and natural sciences, but it is the *experience* of this reality by the human organism that is the special province of psychology and philosophy. And since psychologists are often the very object of our own inquiry, it seems reasonable to ask how the very questions we pose, and the topics we find of interest, have been influenced by our own experiences as people. In my own case, I am convinced that my interest in conflict and its possible resolution had their origins in my early experiences.

I was born in January 1941, after the war in Europe had already begun and shortly before Pearl Harbor and American entry into the Second World War. When I was about one year old, my father (a physician who until recently practiced in New York City, where I grew up) was inducted into the army. He returned home in November 1945.

Some personal, nonrandom memories of that period come to mind. For example, there was a hook outside our house in Astoria, New York (used for hanging a clothes line) which I was convinced was really a hook from which prisoners of war were to be hanged by the neck until dead. There were the blackouts in New York City during the war, in preparation for the possibility of a German bomber attack, when no light whatsoever, including a lit cigarette, was permissible. The reasoning apparently was that the Nazis would be able to spot this light from miles away (as far as Europe, I wondered, in my childish imagination), and a light would be a tip-off on where to drop their bombs. And then there was the sound of a truck backfiring in the street one night, which I was sure, in my three-year-old mind, was the sound of a bomb exploding.

The war's end was followed immediately by the onset of the Cold War, an era that has continued, largely without interruption, until the last few months of dramatic change in U.S.-Soviet relations. Some scattered memories of this period: The dog tags issued to the kids in my school; the air raid sirens that went off at unexpected moments during the school day, leading to drills in which we either sat beneath our desks or had time to march off to the stairwell, where we sat until the siren stopped its shrill scream; New York's governor, Nelson Rockefeller advocating that all New Yorkers build fallout shelters for themselves, so they could survive the nuclear devastation that might be upon them at any moment; photos of assiduous citizens who had built these very fallout shelters—bunkers beneath the ground containing cans of Campbell soup, candles, weapons, portable potties, books and magazines, checker games, and all the other sundries that would be necessary to endure the weeks of radiation that would follow a nuclear attack, except a television since there would be no one around to broadcast anything. And finally, years later, in October 1962, there was the Cuban Missile Crisis and the moment—everything seemed to come to a standstill then—when John Kennedy and Nikita Khrushchev confronted each other, through their respective navies off the coast of Cuba, and it was not clear if a nuclear exchange was imminent.

Such scattered memories may seem unreal or irrelevant. But multiplied by the number of people of my generation who knew such a world, experienced in their own idiosyncratic ways, our shared understanding of the world was shaped in distinct ways. Those of us who grew up in the years of World War II and beyond knew a world of Black Hat versus White Hat, Cowboy versus Indian, the open world of democracy versus the dark dungeon of totalitarianism, truth versus falsehood, good versus evil. We believed in the untold opportunities of technology, free enterprise, democracy; but even as we did so, so too did we look over our shoulders at the menace of genocide, enslavement, nuclear holocaust, the threat of technology run amok. Can anyone be surprised, in light of this shared history, that so much attention by psychologists has been given to topics such as stereotyping, cognitive biases, groupthink, conformity, obedience to authority, dissonance, incongruity? And is it a surprise that social psychologists such as I came to have an abiding interest in the topics of conflict and negotiation?

Psychological interest in the study of conflict dates back at least to the work of social psychologist Kurt Lewin, a German immigrant who in the 1930s and 1940s examined the factors affecting group decision-making under conditions of conflict. It is long way, of course, from the study of interpersonal conflict to international conflict. And it is also a long way from conflict to negotiation. Serious interest in international conflict dates to the pioneering work by social psychologist Herbert C. Kelman who, in 1965, edited perhaps the first important collection on the subject, *International Behavior: A Social-Psychological Analysis*. Subsequent work by Dean Pruitt and Richard Snyder, *Theory and Research on the Causes of War*, in 1969, and most recently the outstanding 1986 collection edited by Ralph White, *Psychology and the Prevention of Nuclear War*, have continued the tradition begun by Kelman.

The transition from the psychological study of conflict to a focus on the important topic of negotiation has occurred gradually over the last two decades. Partly responsible for this transition has been the growing awareness of the important role played by *enlightened self-interest* in the management of conflict. While some researchers and theorists have long argued for the importance of cooperation (and the attitude change that accompanies cooperation) in the resolution of conflict, more recent writings by scholars and practitioners have made clear that people in conflict are often able to do well simply by focusing on the attainment of their own objectives—in ways that also make it possible for others to do well. Instead of trying to develop a cooperative relationship, characterized by attitude change and the *resolution of conflict*, a focus of enlightened self-interest opens the door to behavior change through negotiation, and the simpler, more modest attainment of conflict *settlement*. Negotiation is not a tool that can easily be used in the resolution of conflict (with its concomitant change in underlying attitudes). But it *is* the right tool if one's objective is to change behavior, to bring about a settlement of a dispute where none seemed possible before.

Thus, while social psychologists have had a long-standing interest in conflict, it is only more recently—perhaps within the last several decades—that attention has shifted from interpersonal and intergroup conflict to international conflict and negotiation; and even now, it is fair to say that psychology has had relatively little to contribute to the international domain. The field has been more productive over the years in the study and application of findings on the negotiation process, per se.

An impressive number of books have reviewed the empirical and theoretical psychological literature on conflict and negotiation in domestic and international settings.[1] On the basis of this work, as well as other writings by political scientists and lawyers with a particularly "psychological" bent, it is possible to characterize a distinctly "psychological" approach to the study of negotiation.

1. *A focus on interaction.* Social psychologists in particular have understood that negotiation is an act that requires two or more participants. It is no more sensible to attempt to understand the nature of negotiation processes through analysis of a single actor than it is to create the sound of applause with a single hand. Negotiation is a quintessential illustration of interaction; and while this understanding is universally shared, it is psychologists who—through their research and theory—have attempted to incorporate this insight into their work in an explicit and self-conscious way.

Two implications of an interactive focus are worthy of special mention. First, any serious attempt to understand negotiation in terms of the exchange or interaction among the protagonists necessarily increases the complexity of the analytic task. To understand an exchange of negotiation offers among two players, for example, requires that one not only examine an offer by Party A and the response it generates from Party B, but also consider the extent to which A's offer has been provoked by previous offers (by both A and B) and/or may be an offer made in the context of some anticipated future offer by either side. As decision analysts have been quick to point out, careful evaluation of the decisions made by a single decision maker is a woefully difficult task. Once a second player is added to the loop, and the focus shifts as well to decision-making under conditions of uncertainty (as is necessarily the case in negotiation), the job of interpreting the moves made by both sides in their interactive *pas-de-deux*—as well as acting on one's interpretation—becomes all but impossible.

The writings of social psychologist Harold Kelley (1966) nicely illustrate a research and conceptual approach that is attentive to the complexity of the negotiation process. He writes, for example, about the inherent tension in negotiation between obtaining and disclosing information. Even as one proceeds to ask questions of the other party—questions that enable one to do a better job of ascertaining what offers the other is likely to proffer and which he or she is likely to accept—the act of questioning in and of itself discloses information that may be used by the other side. Because the two players in negotiation are inextricably bound together through their joint commitment to explore solutions that are mutually acceptable, it is virtually impossible to disentangle the dynamic nature of the exchange that takes place. More recently, statistician David Lax and economist James Sebenius (1986) have developed a similar distinction in their writings, in describing the tension between "creating" value and "claiming" it.

If a first implication of an interactive focus, then, is that the interpretive, theoretical task becomes terribly complex, a second implication is that this opens the door to examination of relationships between not only two protagonists but among and between the members of groupings larger than the dyad. Indeed, psychologists have had a long-standing interest in group behavior, as reflected in writings on topics ranging from leadership, group cohesiveness, intergroup conflict, and group decision-making. Writing in each of these areas has found its way, sooner or later, into thinking about negotiation.

By way of broad illustration, consider the writings on "groupthink" by social psychologist Irving Janis (1972). This is the phenomenon by which highly cohesive groups tend to make unwise decisions, precisely because their high degree of cohesiveness leads individual members, who may be harboring private reservations about the wisdom of some recommended course of action, to keep these reservations to themselves. The result is often a group decision in favor of some risky course of action (e.g., the U.S. decision to support an invasion of Cuba at the Bay of Pigs in 1961) that belies the private views of dissenting group members. When foreign policy decision-making bodies of different countries are engaged in a "groupthink" mode of analysis and decision-making (e.g., the United States and the Soviet Union during parts of the 1962 Cuban Missile Crisis, or perhaps the Iranian and American governments during the so-called Iranian hostage crisis of 1980, or maybe even the American and Iraqi leaders during the Persian Gulf Crisis that began in 1990), the result may be international conflict and negotiation played out under the shadow of a dangerous form of group behavior.

Or consider the "conflict workshop" approach to the study of international conflict, as developed by Kelman (1979) who, in turn, built on the work of other scholars (i.e., Burton 1969; Doob 1974). Applying the findings of many dozens of laboratory experiments on leadership and group decision-making to his interest in intergroup and international conflict, Kelman convenes small group meetings of parties to real, ongoing international conflicts, and gives the participants an opportunity to work toward some modest increment in their ability to settle their conflict. A conflict of particular interest to Kelman has been that between

Palestinians and Israelis, and he has run dozens of conflict workshops in which middle-level Israeli and Palestinian leaders have been brought together under special "laboratory" conditions, and have been tutored in more effective communication, have been gently helped to understand and modify their interpersonal perceptions, and so forth. While the effectiveness of this work by Kelman (as well as others) does not easily lend itself to quantification, it is important work nevertheless, and constitutes a clear illustration of the kind of interactive analysis and intervention that psychologists are capable of bringing to the world of international conflict.

As one final illustration of a psychological approach to the complexities of interaction, consider the classic studies of intergroup conflict by Muzafer and Carolyn Sherif (1953). In a series of field experiments, the Sherifs brought preadolescent boys to summer camps in the American Midwest and, through a series of competitive activities, induced conditions of intergroup conflict between the different cabins. Having created intergroup conflict, the researchers then set out to evaluate the effectiveness of various means for reducing such conflict. Among the techniques they tried, without success, included simply bringing the group leaders together for a face-to-face exchange (given the fact that the cabins were not ready to "make peace," this "summit" idea proved to be of no avail), and bringing the cabins together for feasts and other occasions in which they might enjoy each other's presence (again, given the continuing animosity between the cabins, such moves only created additional opportunities to hurl food and insults at the rival cabin). What *did* work was the introduction of "superordinate goals"—that is, goals that managed to supersede or transcend the existing bases of conflict. Thus, the Sherifs arranged for a truck that was taking the two rival cabins on a camping trip to run out of gasoline. Since no gas cans were available, the only way the truck could be refueled was by towing it to a nearby gasoline station, and the only way to do that was by requiring all the boys in both cabins to jointly pull on a rope that was tied to the truck (a rope, incidentally, that had previously been used for tug-of-war matches between the rival cabins). Thus, it was only when new group tasks were introduced, requiring the collaboration of the groups in conflict, that a new, higher order of cooperation could be devised.

As the above examples are meant to suggest, psychologists have done a great deal of field and laboratory research on decision-making within and between groups, and much of this work lends itself readily to extrapolation into the complex realm of international negotiation processes.

2. *A focus on perceived, rather than actual, conflict.* Whereas economic theorists are likely to study the effect on conflict settlement and negotiation of actual divergence of interest, psychologists tend to focus on divergence of interest as it is subjectively experienced. Thus it is not *actual* differences that typically drive parties to behave in particular ways, but *perceived* differences, the *belief* that such differences exist. Two people, groups, or nations may have little by way of objective conflict dividing them, but may nevertheless act as if such conflict exists. Similarly, parties to a conflict may be divided by deep objective differences, but may nevertheless believe that no such differences exist, and may act upon their (illusory) views of reality and avoid overt conflict or confrontation.

What ultimately matters in negotiation, this psychological view argues, are the perceptions, beliefs, and assumptions that protagonists bring with them into the fray, rather than any objective measure of difference. It is beliefs that determine how people are inclined to act— whether it is in the spirit of escalating conflict or moving more resourcefully toward its settlement. And it is the realm of beliefs and perceptions that therefore warrant the full and complete attention of scholars and practitioners alike.

This point of view is reflected both in book-length treatments of social conflict and negotiation (e.g., Deutsch 1973; Druckman 1977; Kelman 1965; Pruitt and Rubin 1986), and in much of the research. To offer but one example, consider once again the conflict workshop approach developed by Kelman. The primary focus of these workshops is not behavioral change, but modification of perceptions of, and attitudes toward, the conflict. Thus, Kelman (1979) writes: "The unique claim of the approach is precisely that it is capable of promoting system-level changes by producing changes in individuals—that is, changes in policy by way of changes in individual perceptions and attitudes." It is especially perceived and not only actual conflict that is of interest to Kelman, and it is here that virtually all of his attention has been directed.

Is this an appropriate analytic decision to be made by psychologists? In my judgment, the answer is clearly "yes." Conflict that derives from real and objective resource discrepancies is important, of course. Of equal or greater importance, ultimately, is how the conflict is regarded by the decision-makers and others charged with influencing public opinion. There may be objective bases for serious divergence of interest among the member nations of the European Economic Community; however, given a mentality of collaborative problem solving, characterized by a view that calls for a new outlook that bridges traditional national boundaries, any objective basis of disagreement among the members of the EEC hardly matters at all.

3. *A focus on cognitive biases.* A psychological focus on perceptions extends beyond the conflict per se to views of the other side. People—and negotiators in particular—bring with them in the field of conflict a host of biases that may overdetermine their characteristic ways of evaluating the conflict, the other negotiator, and themselves. These biases have been extensively studied by psychologists as cognitive processes that are at play in a great many situations. Among those studied over the last several decades are such processes as the phenomenon of *selective perception,* by which decision-makers attend to certain features of their cognitive environment rather than others. For example, in the research on intergroup conflict described above, Sherif and Sherif (1953) demonstrated the role of selective perception in the following way: The campers in two rival cabins were invited to take part in a jelly-bean hunt to see which cabin could collect the largest number in a fixed period of time. After the hunt was over, the researchers showed the boys a photograph of a jar of jelly beans, telling some boys that this contained the jelly beans collected by the boys in their cabin, and telling others that the jar contained the collection of the boys in the other, rival cabin. Interestingly, the Sherifs found that, when asked to evaluate the results of their own group's effort, the boys systematically overestimated the group's productivity. But when asked to evaluate the work of the outgroup, the number of jelly beans was systematically underestimated. In fact, the identical photograph was shown to both groups, so any differences were purely a matter of selective perception, a tendency to see a half full glass as half empty. A special form of selective perception is *distorted hypothesis testing,* by which people in conflict go out of their way to pose interpersonal hypotheses about their adversary that are guaranteed to generate confirming data. For example, to follow up the hypothesis that one's adversary is an unduly defensive person by asking the question "Why, exactly, are you so defensive?" is to guarantee a response that will confirm the hypothesis.[2]

Also included among the cognitive biases of interest to psychologists is the general and important topic of *stereotypic distortion*, the tendency to simplify a truly complex cognitive environment in ways that make it easier to sort information into extreme categories: good versus bad, black versus white, with us versus against us, and so on. Several important contributions to an understanding of international conflict have been made by social psychologists with an interest in stereotypic distortion. Thus, developmental psychologist Uri Bronfenbrenner (1961), in a classic essay on Soviet-American relations, described the role of the "mirror image" in understanding the kinds of stereotyping that each side used to characterize the other during the height of the Cold War. He argued that five major themes characterized each side's (parallel) view of the other nation: "They are the aggressors"; "their government exploits and deludes the people"; "the mass of their people are not really sympathetic to the regime"; "they cannot be trusted"; "their policy verges on madness." Each side, he argued persuasively, has managed to develop information in support of the identical stereotypic views of the other.

In his 1984 book, *Fearful Warriors: A Psychological Profile of U.S.-Soviet Relations*, social psychologist Ralph White similarly describes the role of what he calls a "diabolical enemy image" (according to which Satan is always on the side of the enemy) and a "moral self-image" (God is on one's own side).

Attributional distortion is yet another cognitive bias that people in conflict typically bring with them into the fray. Kind acts by one's adversary are attributed to manipulative intent, while uncharitable acts are attributed to an undesirable, untrustworthy disposition. One's own kind acts, in turn, are attributed to one's being a truly nice, kind person, while one's less wonderful behavior is attributed to circumstance or to behavior by the other person that has necessitated an unkind response. Research demonstrating the important contribution of attributional bias has been conducted by social psychologists Regan, Straus, and Fazio (1974) and Hayden and Mischel (1976), among others.

A final illustration of the kind of cognitive bias that has been the object of study by psychologists is the *self-fulfilling prophecy*, whereby Party A expects Party B to behave in some way (e.g., aggressively), hence A protects itself by raising a hand in defense—and this move is regarded by B as an aggressive assault, and leads B to respond to raising its own hand (in defense), an act that confirms A's expectation; in this way, A's prophecy is fulfilled. Laboratory research, documenting the significance and ubiquity of the self-fulfilling prophecy, has been conducted by Rosenthal and Jacobson (1968), Word, Zanna, and Cooper (1974), and Jones and Panitch (1971), among others.

The above examples are illustrative of a growing movement in the field of psychology, a movement that has increasingly turned to understanding individual behavior in terms of cognitive processes. And as the above listing is meant to suggest, much of this work has play in the more specific realm of conflict and negotiation.

This work on cognitive biases is potentially of great importance in its application to the realm of international negotiation. Foreign policy decision-makers are frequently placed in the position of having to make judgments about a set of issues, the nature of a conflict, and the negotiators on the other side of the table before sitting down to engage in the work of negotiation. The burgeoning area of research on cognitive biases has made eminently clear that the kinds of judgments such policy-makers are likely to make may well be affected—often adversely—by the baggage they carry along with them in the form of various biases and perceptual predispositions.

4. *A focus on learning and change over time.* Psychologists have had a historic interest in the processes by which individuals *learn*. Learning entails the incorporation of new information or insights, new ways of seeing the world, and this process of necessity involves *change over time*. Things that individuals once did not know or do are now part of their repertoire.

To be sure, other disciplines (economics and game theory, in particular) share psychology's interest in change over time. Still, psychology has brought special enthusiasm and perspective to this area, and this has manifested itself in two distinct ways: (1) a focus on conflict spirals and escalation; and (2) a focus on strategies for settling or resolving conflict.

While political scientists have been interested in conflict spirals, psychologists have focused on the *dynamics* of these escalatory exchanges in far greater detail. For example, the research on the social psychology of "entrapment" has examined the process by which people overcommit themselves to a course of action; in pursuit of some objective, decision-makers often find themselves incurring costs that they subsequently feel compelled to justify by incurring even greater cost.[3] The importance of this social psychological work, based on extensive laboratory research, is that it bears directly on a great many of the decisions that negotiators are called upon to make in international affairs. To the extent that negotiators find themselves locked into particular points of view, lines of argument, or positions during negotiations, or that they find themselves developing a particular style of negotiating (tough and ruthless, for example) from which they feel they cannot easily budge without incurring significant loss, they may well be entrapped. As a result of entrapment, they may see things differently in the midst of an escalating conflict than they would at the outset. Caught up in the "investment" that has already been made in some course of action, foreign policy decision-makers may find themselves unable to bring to bear the kind of rational, dispassionate analysis that is necessary to make wise decisions in the throes of international crises. Needless to say, the consequences for international negotiation could be profound.

In general, while relatively little is yet known about the exact circumstances that surround the escalation of conflict, it is psychologists who have paid particular attention to this important process. As another illustration of the kind of psychological contribution that has been made in this regard, consider the writings of Morton Deutsch (1973) who has attempted to characterize a "malignant (spiral) process of hostile interaction" in international affairs. Among the characteristics of such a process, Deutsch identifies a win-lose competitive orientation, inner conflicts within each of the parties, cognitive rigidity, misjudgments and misperceptions, unwitting commitments, vicious escalating spirals, and a gamesmanship orientation.

A final example of the kind of psychological research on escalation that may have applications for international negotiation is Philip Tetlock's (1985) work. He has conducted extensive research into the relationship between policymakers' "cognitive complexity" (as measured by the complexity of the arguments they develop in their written and spoken rhetoric) and the escalation of conflict. Tetlock finds that as conflict escalates in intensity, moving the parties closer to a confrontation, the arguments advanced by each side become *less* cognitively complex. There is a tendency, in other words, for increasing conflict intensity to predispose decision-makers to develop relatively simplistic, stereotypic views of the other side and the issues under discussion; and this tendency, in turn, makes it all the more difficult to disconfirm each side's "pet hypotheses" about the other.

The second implication of psychological interest in learning and change over time, as mentioned above, has been represented by continuing research on strategies for settling or resolving conflict. This tradition has had a long and distinguished history, as exemplified by the laboratory experimentation by Deutsch and his students (see, for example, Deutsch 1973). This body of research has examined the strategies that can be used to convert an adversary into an ally. Among the strategic maneuvers examined in this work are a "reactive defensive" strategy, in which cooperation is responded to in kind, but attack is reciprocated with defensive maneuvering; a strategy that "reactive aggressive," again responding to cooperation with cooperation, but reacting to attack with counterattack; a Christian-like "turn the other cheek" strategy; as well as several strategies that first create a sense of intimidation, then shift to one of the above more conciliatory strategies.

Political scientist Robert Axelrod (1984) has summarized the extensive writings on strategies for inducing cooperation in an adversary—notably the so-called tit-for-tat strategy, by which kindness is responded to with kindness, and aggression with aggression. In his book, *The Evolution of Cooperation,* Axelrod argues that the tit-for-tat strategy is the single most important and effective way of changing a competitor into a cooperator. Roger Fisher and Scott Brown (1988) take issue with this position in their book on relationships, arguing that the major problem with such a tit-for-tat strategy is that it is *reactive,* waiting for an adversary to make the first move before responding in kind; needed is an "initiating" strategy, one that is willing to make the first move rather than wait for the other side.

Underlying this extensive body of laboratory and conceptual work is the assumption that negotiation and conflict management are learning processes, according to which protagonists acquire new behavior and beliefs as adjustments to changing realities and changing perceptions of an adversary. This is a potentially important body of work, with many potentially practical implications for the realm of international negotiation. Like the psychological focus on interaction, a learning emphasis correctly acknowledges the changing and complex nature of negotiation processes, and invites interventions that are responsive.

5. *A focus on relationships.* As I indicated earlier, psychologists have had an abiding interest in the nature of interaction. A related but distinct arena of psychological concern involves the *relational* aspects of negotiation. More than scholars in other disciplines, psychologists have tended

to analyze the implications of reaching agreement, or failing to do so, for an emerging relationship between protagonists. While much of the research and writing on negotiation processes has focused on the "bottom line," that is, the tangible outcome or payoff that is yielded as a result of agreement, many negotiations have, as their focus, considerations other than economic ones. Thus, while many negotiations would appear to take place as one-time-only exchanges, far more actually occur on an ongoing basis. Even in what we believe to be one-time-only negotiations, our reputation has a way of surviving us and transforming even these exchanges into ones with the properties of ongoing relationships.

A focus on relationships, psychologists believe, is thus an important one in negotiations. It has also been largely neglected in the literature. Perhaps in keeping with the cultural traditions of the United States and Western Europe—rather than cultures such as those of the Middle East, South and East Asia, and Africa, where ongoing relationships among parties to a negotiation are the norm rather than the exception—the emphasis in negotiation writings has been placed largely on economic considerations. Clearly, more writing is needed by negotiation scholars, researchers, and practitioners on the relational aspects and implications of negotiation.

A related need, also largely neglected to date in the literature, is for more thoughtful and extensive writing on the relationship between culture and/or nationality and negotiation. So much of what has been written has assumed an economic focus of negotiation, whereas many, many cultures are likely to have a far more relational focus. While numerous books and manuals *do* exist that prescribe the right and wrong ways for decision-makers to negotiate with representatives from other nations, these contributions have done little to identify the underlying processes that are at work when one negotiates with others from a background different than one's own.

In some sense, the work that is needed here—work that psychologists should be centrally positioned to contribute, given our disciplinary interest in individual and group differences—resembles the work needed on the personality attributes of an effective negotiator. Thus it can be argued that negotiation differences that are attributable to culture are closely akin to the differences that can be traced to individual differences of personality. Cultural or national differences are individual personality differences writ large, carrying over to an entire population, and characterizing general national or cultural tendencies to behave in negotiations in particular ways.

6. *A focus on multiple research approaches.* A final distinctive marking of psychological approaches to the study of negotiation concerns the plethora of research techniques that psychologists typically resort to. The reason for this is perhaps self-evident: individual and group behavior are often so complex and difficult to study systematically that what is typically required is a rich mixture of different research approaches—each of which brings a somewhat different lens to bear on the problem at hand. Only when multiple lenses (in the form of a combination of research approaches—laboratory experimentation, archival study, field experimentation, field study, simulation research, etc.) lead to convergent findings can the psychological researcher begin to have the confidence that the findings generated through this research are valid and reliable.

In his influential and important 1976 book, *Perception and Misperception in International Politics,* political scientist Robert Jervis wrote a scathing, if somewhat overstated, critique of psychological contributions to international relations. Among the litany of faults he has laid at the doorstep of psychology are the following: "more attention . . . paid to emotional than to cognitive factors" (3), almost exclusive reliance on data derived from laboratory experiments; and research attention given to relatively simple beliefs and decisions, at the exclusion of more complex and realistic matters (4).

While some of Jervis's critical comments seem justified, others do not. Thus the last criticism does appear to be warranted, at least in part. Psychologists *have* tended to focus on relatively simple decision-making tasks and arrangements, because these are the ones that lend themselves most readily to empirical study. Clearly, more work does have to be addressed in the future to complex social arrangements in which the dynamics of interaction are difficult to trace but important nevertheless. On the other hand, researchers should not lose sight of the potential elegance of simplicity. The fact that a phenomenon is capable of analysis in terms of a relatively small number of conceptually moving parts may be a strength rather than a liability—if the result is a more elegant theory.

Jervis's criticisms certainly seem outdated and unjustified when it comes to the first and second comments above. As I have tried to indicate psychologists have turned their attention increasingly to the role of cognitive factors in international conflict and negotiation—and they have done so without neglecting the contributing role of affective (emotional) considerations. And it is also true that far less research is being done by psychologists exclusively in the laboratory, as the profession has moved increasingly toward the use of other research methods.

The sad reality is that the profession of psychology has moved to the margins of research and writing about conflict negotiation over the last decade or so. What was once a boom industry has now—judging by the *frequency* of empirical studies in major psychology research journals— fallen on hard times. Psychology, it might appear at first blush, no longer has much to contribute to the study and practice of negotiation.

The reasons for the decline in the volume of psychological research are not entirely obvious, although several factors appear to have played a part. First, experimental social psychology for a long time relied on a relatively small number of experimental paradigms, notably the Prisoner's Dilemma game. As this paradigm lost favor, after having been examined from every possible angle, with an eye to every possible independent and dependent variable, interest in the conflict/negotiation domain faded as well. Second, the study of conflict and negotiation has always had an applied flavor, and this emphasis runs counter to a prevailing interest among many research psychologists in more general, conceptual approaches. Third, and perhaps most important, many psychologists *are,* in fact, still hard at work looking at conflict and negotiation processes; instead of publishing in the traditional research psychology journals, however, these scholars are increasingly finding their voice in the journals of other professions; international diplomacy, community relations environmental management, communications, business, and law, to name but a few.

But if psychological contributions appear to have declined over the last several decades, the field of conflict and negotiation has become a boom industry—despite our absence on the scene. Only five years ago, the field of negotiation and conflict management studies and practice was, if not exactly in its infancy, a young juvenile. For example, the Program on Negotiation at Harvard Law School—a consortium of schools in the Boston area, consisting of faculty from a dozen or so disciplines— was just getting under way; few if any other university-based applied research centers like this existed back then in the mid-'80s. While some professional organizations had already been in existence for a number of years (the American Arbitration Association, for example), others such as SPIDR (the Society of Professionals in Dispute Resolution) were still relatively young. SPIDR had a membership five years ago of less than one thousand, half of its present number and largely limited to specialists in labor relations. Today the organization has dispute resolution professionals across a far broader spectrum. NIDR (the National Institute of Dispute Resolution), a funding agency in Washington, D.C., that supports a variety of creative initiatives and analyses concerned with domestic conflict and its resolution, was just then beginning its important work.

Only a few years ago, the conversations that took place between scholars and practitioners were sometimes strained and difficult. The former group did their research and wrote their theoretical tracts, often in ignorance of the world of practice and application. In turn, the latter group tended to regard the work of the "ivy tower crowd" as largely irrelevant, and certainly not useful, to the concerns of practitioners dealing with real and immediate problems.

Meanwhile, the kinds of conversations that were taking place among the various scholars and researchers in negotiation and conflict studies were characterized by a certain amount of joyful enthusiasm and perhaps a bit of naiveté. Having spent years thinking about conflict, negotiation, and the third-party intervention, in the private world of their respective disciplines, these scholars began to emerge from their individual ivory towers to converse with one another. Common themes and concerns took shape as mathematicians, lawyers, economists, psychologists, urban planners, anthropologists, international diplomats, sociologists, and political scientists, among others, participated in these refreshing exchanges. It was exciting to find so very many people, operating is so many of the corridors of academic life, discovering for the first time that they were not alone.

To move to the world of today, it is clear that the field of negotiation and conflict studies is in full bloom. The William and Flora Hewlett Foundation in Menlo Park, California, has funded more than a dozen applied research centers for the study of negotiation, mediation, and other forms of conflict settlement or resolution. These centers extend from the University of Hawaii in the West to George Mason, Rutgers, Syracuse, and Penn State in the East; from Michigan, Wisconsin, Northwestern, and Minnesota in the North to Georgia in the South.

The field has also gained enough recognition and numbers to warrant special inclusion in professional meetings, and the formation of new professional organizations. For example, the 1989 program theme of the American Bar Association meetings in Honolulu was "Dispute Resolution in Pacific Ways." The American Management Association has its own special interest group that focuses on negotiation and other forms of conflict settlement. Ombudsmen and women around the country have now formed themselves into a special association, designed to address matters of joint interest and concern. And NCPCR (The National Conference on Peacemaking and Conflict Resolution) has sponsored a series of biennial meetings for third parties that attract thousands of participants. Even the United States government has joined the party, through its recently formed and very effective United States Institute of Peace.

There is now hardly a state of the United States where conflict and/or negotiation is not formally studied or practiced. Community mediation programs are to be found all across the country, as are various outreach, family counseling, and divorce mediation programs.

Perhaps as many as fifty new books on negotiation and third-party intervention—as these play out in international relations, environmental affairs, community conflict, labor relations, and in countless other settings—have seen the light of day in the last five years or so. *Negotiation Journal* is now completing its sixth year of publication, and nearly 250 articles have appeared during this period. *Mediation Quarterly* has also begun its publication during this general time frame, while other journals —such as *Conflict Resolution, Industrial and Labor Relations Review,* and *Journal of Peace Research*—continue to publish papers on conflict and negotiation on a regular basis.

But if psychologists appear to have disappeared from this bustling scene, then the question is: How can they find their way back into the center of a psychologically rich domain? What are some of the roles that psychologists might reasonably occupy in the months and years ahead? The American Psychological Association has recently approved the formation of Division 48: The Division of Peace Psychology. What sorts of research questions should members of this division, and other divisions, attempt to answer?

Clearly, a psychological perspective remains as germane today as ever, characterized by its distinctive focus on interaction, on perceived rather than actual conflict, cognitive biases, learning and change over time, relationships, and a tolerance of multiple research approaches. However, lest the reader conclude that these are the distinctive contributions likely to be made by social psychologists in particular, rather than by Psychology with a capital P, permit me to point out a few of the many questions that are in need of answers.

What is the biological basis of aggression? Under what conditions are frustration and aggression causally related, and when do they merely co-vary? What are the biological accompaniments of escalating conflict? Are there—biologically speaking—better times than others to intervene in a conflict in order to help bring it to resolution or settlement?

How, exactly, do children learn norms of cooperation and competition, and how do these vary from one culture to the next? What regimens can be devised for early education into the ways of conflict resolution? Stated most generally, and grandly, if one could establish a learning environment that would be optimal for teaching productive ways of settling conflict, what would this learning environment have to consist of? Do any models of such an environment currently exist anywhere in the world? (For a discussion of some of these issues, see chapter 4 by Ervin Staub.)

In the study of social movements, activism, and social change, we psychologists are still primitives at best. What are the psychological conditions that predispose groups and organizations to change the way in which they function—and in particular, the way in which they address conflict? Similarly, what are the necessity preconditions that make individual citizens more likely to take a position in opposition to, or in support of, official views? (That is, when are people likely to decide in favor of "standing up and being counted," rather than continuing in more typical, if passive, compliance with existing institutional arrangements? Again, see chapter 4.) At an even more micro level, following in the tradition of some European psychologists, when are minority group members likely to stand up in opposition to the tyranny of the majority —and to persist in their opposition until the majority has been persuaded to change its attitude?

At the level of personality and individual differences, we need to know more about the kinds of people who are likely to experience stress in the midst of conflict, and those who are likely to respond to such stress in very different ways. Why, for example, do some respond to conflict with greater empathy, while others respond with an increased need for control and domination? What kinds of people, and under what conditions, are likely to respond to conflict through defenses such as denial, displacement, rationalization, projection, or—to use Robert J. Lifton's term—"psychic numbing?"

The list of research questions that psychologists can and should continue to address in the period ahead is close to endless, and the above smattering is meant to be suggestive only. In addition, let us not forget the possible role of psychologists as policy analysts. When you stop to think about it, *who* is it, exactly, who has the expertise necessary to set and evaluate policy for a group, organization, or nation? What disciplines do these political/analytic types come from? Law? Economics? Physics? Political Science? Psychologists are just as good and are often likely to be far better, at analyzing policy through the prism of our own distinctive discipline, and at evaluating the merits and drawbacks of any given approach. Stated most grandly, I would hope that there will eventually come a time when psychologists will find their way into the inner "corridors of power" as readily as others, and no government cabinet will be quite complete without the sage counsel of someone trained in psychology. But don't hold your breath . . .

By way of concluding this chapter, permit me to return to the point at which I began. When I was growing up, the world was a bipolar place, dominated by two superpowers, each capable of destroying much of the human race in a nuclear exchange. The United States for much of this period was like the biggest elephant in the jungle who, in answer to the question, "Where does the biggest elephant sit?" sits exactly where it wants. We didn't have to do much negotiating with other countries; rather, as the biggest elephant around, we simply called the shots, announced our decisions, and were able (most of the time) to impose our views on those around us.

The world has changed, and changed dramatically. The United States is still the most powerful military machine in the world, but the world has, the Persian Gulf Crisis notwithstanding, mercifully become a place that is a bit less likely to rely on or resort to military solutions. Economically, the United States has declined in importance, even as the economies of the two grand losers of World War II—Germany and Japan—have grown dramatically. The map of Europe is being redrawn before our very eyes, and it is a map of a unified, highly interdependent Europe in which political, cultural, even national boundaries are likely to be superseded by a complex web of economic ties and relations. Thanks to modern telecommunication and transportation technology, and the emergence of multinational corporations, geographical boundaries now have far less meaning than ever before; more importantly, no individual nation—no matter how powerful or wealthy—is likely to be able to impose its views unilaterally; witness, in this regard, the Persian Gulf conflict in which neither the United States, the Soviet Union, or even the United Nations was easily able to impose a unilateral solution on Saddam Hussein and Iraq. Germany is part of a European community that will shortly, after the 1992 meetings, be one of the largest and most important economic arenas anywhere in the world; and someday the Soviet Union, as well as the nations of Eastern Europe, may well be part of this community too. Japan will be part of an emerging partnership with other nations of East and Southeast Asia, and perhaps someday China will be part of that condominium of nation-states. Even here, in the United States, we are at last joining with our neighbors to the north and south to form an economic community of our own. Interdependence, then, is a more powerful organizing concept than ever, and it is precisely because of such growing interdependence that the nations of the world will find it in their enlightened self-interest to work to settle their conflicts in productive, mutually acceptable ways. Interdependence is the engine that will drive the machine forward in the years ahead.

The preceding mention of the world's nations and how they fit together contains some glaring omissions, of course. It is the developing nations, those of the so-called Third World, largely located in the Southern Hemisphere, that have been left out of the mix, even as the more developed states find ways of working together. And yet the future cannot be a bright one without these developing nations, for it is here that many of the world's richest resources are located, it is here that the population is exploding at the highest rate, and it is also here that the problems of poverty, malnutrition, disease, and despair run most rampant. If we truly are a global commons, as I believe, then the problems and opportunities of the developing South are also the problems and opportunities of the developed North.

Where, then, does this leave those psychologists with an interest in conflict, negotiation, and the quest for global peace? Earlier models of conflict and negotiation, designed to mimic the external reality that people of my generation grew up with, were portraits of two-party, equal-power relationships, characterized by often adversarial exchanges.

In contrast, the models of the next generation, the one that is now upon us, will have to capture the essence of relationships among multiple, interdependent parties, possessing resources that are distributed asymmetrically, where no one is able to *impose* its will—but must negotiate solutions instead.

The conflict and negotiation problem will thus be one not of equal but unequal power, where the research and conceptual challenge will require understanding the nature of such power asymmetry, and the things that the so-called weaker side can do to augment its power or persuade its stronger counterpart to take its interests into account. And in a world that is a global commons, it will be more necessary than ever to understand from a psychological perspective the role of cultural similarity and difference in the conflict resolution process; we can no longer afford to use simplistic labels and stereotypes as a way of organizing our perceptions of people different than ourselves—not when we will be relying on these very people in order to negotiate an agreement that we need.

We live in remarkable and wonderful times. The field of psychology stands to make a signal contribution to the world of opportunities before us. The Persian Gulf Crisis aside it is a world that has shifted from the convenient characterization of people as ally versus enemy, white hat versus black hat, to a place where—because of our vastly increased interdependence—it is no longer so easy to sort people into neat little categories or take what one wants, when one wants it. The continuum of psychological complexity and conflict-resolving opportunity is richer than ever before.

An old Chinese blessing/curse is alleged to say, "May you live in interesting times." These *are* interesting times, a perfect occasion for psychology, once again, to get involved—and stay involved.

NOTES

1. See for example, Rubin and Brown 1975, Pruitt 1981, Druckman 1977, and Austin and Worchel 1979.
2. See the essay by Joel Cooper and Russell Fazio, "The formation and persistence of attitudes that support intergroup conflict," in Austin and Worchel's *The social psychology of intergroup relations* (1979) for an excellent review of the research mentioned in this section on cognitive biases. Also, see Dean

Pruitt and Jeffrey Rubin's *Social conflict: Escalation stalemate, and settlement* (1986) for additional discussion.
3. See, in particular, the writings of Teger (1980) and Brockner and Rubin (1985).

REFERENCES

Austin, W. G. and Worchel, S. *The social psychology of intergroup relations.* Monterey, Calif.: Brooks/Cole, 1979.

Axelrod, R. *The evolution of cooperation.* New York: Basic Books, 1984.

Brockner, J., and Rubin, J. Z. *Entrapment in escalating conflicts: A social psychological analysis.* New York: Springer-Verlag, 1985.

Bronfenbrenner, U. "The mirror-image in Soviet-American relations." *Journal of Social Issues* (1961), *16*, 45–56.

Burton, J. W. *Conflict and communication: The use of controlled communication in international relations.* London: Macmillan, 1969.

Chapman, L. J., and Chapman, J. P. "Illusory correlation as an obstacle to the use of valid psychodiagnostic signs," *Journal of Abnormal Psychology* (1969), *7*, 271–280.

Cooper, J., and Fazio, R. H. "The formation and persistence of attitudes that support intergroup conflict." In W. G. Austin and S. Worchel, eds., *The social psychology of intergroup relations*, Monterey, Calif.: Brooks/Cole, 1979.

Deutsch, M. *The resolution of conflict: Constructive and destructive processes.* New Haven, Conn.: Yale University Press, 1973.

Doob, L. W. "A Cyprus workshop: An exercise in intervention methodology." *Journal of social psychology* (1974), *94*, 161–178.

Druckman, D. *Negotiations: Social-psychological perspectives.* Beverly Hills, Calif.: Sage Publications, 1977.

Fisher, R., and Brown, S. *Getting together: Building relationships that get to YES.* Boston: Houghton Mifflin, 1988.

Fisher, R., and Ury, W. L. *Getting to YES: Negotiating agreement without giving in.* Boston: Houghton Mifflin, 1981.

Hamilton, D. L., and Gifford, R. K. "Illusory correlation in interpersonal perception: A cognitive basis of stereotypic judgments." *Journal of Experimental Social Psychology* (1976), *12*, 392–407.

Hayden, T., and Mischel, W. "Maintaining trait consistency in the resolution of behavioral inconsistency: The wolf in sheep's clothing?" *Journal of Personality* (1976), *44*, 109–132.

Janis, I. L. *Victims of groupthink: Psychological studies of policy decisions and fiascoes.* Boston: Houghton Mifflin, 1972.

Jervis, R. *Perception and misperception in international politics.* Princeton, N.J.: Princeton University Press, 1976.

Jones, S. C., and Panitch, D. "The self-fulfilling prophecy and interpersonal attraction." *Journal of Experimental Social Psychology* (1971), 7, 356–366.

Kelley, H. H. "A classroom study of the dilemmas in interpersonal negotiations." In K. Archibald, ed., *Strategic interaction and conflict: Original papers and discussion.* Berkeley, Calif.: Institute of International Studies, 1966.

Kelman, H. C., ed. *International behavior: A social-psychological analysis.* New York: Holt, Rinehart and Winston, 1965.

Kelman, H. C. "Reduction of international conflict: An interactional approach." In W. G. Austin and S. Worchel, eds., *The social psychology of intergroup relations,* Monterey, Calif.: Brooks/Cole, 1979.

Kremenyuk, V. *International negotiation: Analysis, approaches, issues.* San Francisco: Jossey-Bass, 1991 (in press).

Lax, D., and Sebenius, J. *The manager as negotiator.* New York: Free Press, 1986.

Lifton, R. J., and Falk, R. *Indefensible weapons.* New York: Basic Books, 1982.

Pruitt, D. G. *Negotiation behavior.* New York: Basic Books, 1981.

Pruitt, D. G., and Rubin, J. Z. *Social conflict: Escalation, stalemate, and settlement.* New York: Random House, 1986.

Pruitt, D. G., and Snyder, R. C. *Theory and research on the causes of war.* Englewood Cliffs, N.J.: Prentice-Hall, 1969.

Raiffa, H. *The art and science of negotiation.* Cambridge, Mass.: Harvard University Press, 1982.

Regan, D. T., Straus, E., and Fazio, R. "Liking and the attribution process." *Journal of Experimental Social Psychology* (1974), *10,* 385–397.

Rosenthal, R., and Jacobson, L. *Pygmalion in the classroom: Teacher expectation and pupils' intellectual development.* New York: Holt, Rinehart and Winston, 1968.

Rubin, J. Z. Some wise and mistaken assumptions about conflict and negotiation. Working paper #88-4, Program on Negotiation at Harvard Law School. Cambridge, Mass., 1988.

Rubin, J. Z., and Brown, B. R. *The social psychology of bargaining and negotiation.* New York: Academic Press, 1975.

Sherif, M., and Sherif, C. W. *Groups in harmony and tension.* New York: Harper Brothers, 1953.

Teger, A. I. *Too much invested to quit.* New York: Pergamon Press, 1980.

Tetlock, P. E. "Cognitive perspectives on foreign policy." *Political Behavior Annual.* Boulder, Colo.: Westview Press, 1985.

White, R. K. *Fearful warriors: A psychological profile of U.S.-Soviet relations.* New York: The Free Press, 1984.

White, R. K., ed., *Psychology and the prevention of nuclear war.* New York: New York University Press, 1986.

Word, C. O., Zanna, M. P., and Cooper J. "The nonverbal mediation of self-fulfilling prophecies in interracial interaction." *Journal of Experimental Social Psychology* (1974), *10,* 109–120.

6

The Psychology of Enemy Images

Brett Silverstein

A former president of the United States had the following to say about a foreign country:

> We concur in considering [its] government as totally without morality, insolent beyond bearing, inflated with vanity and ambition, aiming at the exclusive domination of the [world], lost in corruption, of deep-rooted hatred towards us, hostile to liberty wherever it endeavors to show its head, and the eternal disturber of the peace of the world. (Ford 1848, 519)

The year of writing was 1815 (when the passions of the war of 1812 had not yet subsided), the ex-president was Thomas Jefferson, and the country he was excoriating was England. Even a leader renowned for learning, sophistication, and humanitarianism fell prey to what has been called "the psychology of enemy images."

We might define an "enemy" as any group, whether it is a racial or ethnic group or a nation, that is viewed by someone with hostility or as a threat. The psychology of enemy images describes the process wherein people exaggerate the negative or threatening characteristics of such a group. Sometimes, such as when a prejudiced person insults members of a racial group, enemy images affect the attitudes or behaviors of individuals. At other times, enemy images may exert important influences on large groups of people, fueling destructive arms races between nations and even leading to war.

Psychologists have done a great deal of research on the causes and effects of enemy images. One conclusion that strongly emerges from this research is that people's reactions to information they receive about the actions of groups that they consider to be "enemies" are open to biases. That is, when people read or hear about something an enemy has done, they tend to interpret the information in very negative ways. As a result, the original negative attitudes are reinforced or become even more negative.

In some cases, particularly when the enemy is a foreign nation, most people do not experience directly the actions of enemies. Instead, they receive their information about the enemy from other people, by word of mouth or through the mass media. This leaves open the possibility for biases to affect not only people's responses to the reports they receive of enemy actions but also to distort the reports themselves. For example, in 1947, Allport and Postman published a classic study in which they asked white college students to play an experimental game of telephone —one student describing what he or she had seen to the next, who passed on the description to the next, and so on—using as the message a picture of a white man threatening a black man with a razor. In the course of passing on the message, over half of the chains of students who participated in the study transferred the razor from the white man to the black man. If we assume that the subjects in this study did not intentionally lie to each other, we may hypothesize that the hostility, distrust, and fear felt by some of the white students toward black people, which might be described as an "enemy image," influenced their perceptions and communications strongly enough to lead the majority of groups to transform the victim in a dangerous situation into the aggressor.

Thus, the psychology of enemy images works on a social as well as an individual level and can be demonstrated in experimental and survey studies done on average people, in the words and actions of political leaders, and in analyses of the mass media. Here I will focus on how this process has affected the image of many groups, with particular emphasis on U.S. images of the Soviet Union. We can take advantage of the relaxation of tensions between the two nuclear superpowers to understand the processes that turned a serious, possibly hostile, competition into a Cold War and a wasteful, dangerous nuclear arms race.

ATTENTION AND MEMORY

One of the simplest effects of an enemy image found by psychologists is that it leads people to focus attention on and to remember the negative and threatening characteristics of an enemy rather than its positive and peaceful characteristics. This tendency works to reinforce stereotypes. For example, one study found that when English Canadian subjects chosen for their unfavorable attitudes toward French Canadians were asked to recall a series of pleasant and unpleasant adjectives, they remembered more pleasant adjectives when used to describe English Canadians but more unpleasant ones when used to describe French Canadians. Results for French Canadian subjects were reversed (Dutta, Kanungo, and Freiberg 1972; see also Hastorf and Cantril 1954).

The media may also exhibit some biases in the attention given to enemies. In a 1946 study, the news items dealing with the Soviet Union that appeared in the *New York Times* between 1917 and 1946 were sampled. Each item was rated as either favorable or unfavorable to the Soviet Union. The study found that the more negative the news about the Soviet Union, the more attention it was given (Kriesberg 1946). Herman (1982) tallied the coverage given by the *New York Times* to dissidents in various nations. Between January 1975 and July 1981, Soviet dissidents Alexander Ginzburg, Anatoly Scharansky, and Andrei Sakharov were mentioned in the *Times* 68, 138, and 223 times, respectively, whereas Archbishop Camara, a church leader from Brazil, Jose Luis Massara, a noted mathematician from Uruguay, and Heri Akhmadi, a student leader in Indonesia, all of whom are major dissident figures in nations allied with the United States, were mentioned 4, 5, and 0 times, respectively. One labor leader, Lech Walesa of Poland, was mentioned 81 times, whereas another important leader of a labor movement, Luis Silva of Brazil, was mentioned 3 times. These differences may result from biases on the part of the reporters or editors of the *Times* or from their belief that the American public has no interest in Brazilian or Indonesian dissidents. (As interest on the part of the public often results from media attention, however, the process may be circular.) In either case, Americans were often exposed to messages from people who were criticizing the Soviet Union and other communist nations. Think back to all the news items you read or watched on television about Ayatollah Khomeini of Iran or Saddam Hussein of Iraq. How many of these even attempted to discuss seriously the points of view of these leaders of "enemy" nations? How can we make informed decisions if we do not even hear the other side of important issues facing the United States?

CREDIBILITY

Such communications not only receive much exposure, they are accorded credibility. Some sources of information are accorded more credibility than others, that is, they are treated as more expert and trustworthy. Psychologists have found that messages emanating from sources accorded high credibility have more influence on people's opinion than those coming from low-credibility sources, even when the messages are identical and a number of studies appear to demonstrate that more credibility is accorded to statements attacking enemies than to those defending enemies. Thus, given equally strong evidence, people are more likely to be influenced by statements attacking enemies than by those defending enemies.

Zanna, Klosson, and Darley (1976) showed newscasts to students who were either pro-student or pro-police in which either students or police were blamed for initiating a violent confrontation. They found that compared to the subjects for whom the conclusion of the newscast was consistent with their beliefs, those who did not agree with the point of view of the newscast rated it as less objective, rated the newscaster as less credible and more intending to persuade, and attributed to the newscast and newscaster more extreme political positions consistent with the newscast's conclusion. Similar results were found in a study of the response of students who were either pro-Israel or pro-Arab to a newscast describing the 1982 Beirut massacre (Vallone, Ross, and Lepper 1985).

Along with Catherine Flamenbaum, I did a study (Silverstein and Flamenbaum 1989) in which we asked college students to read a selection they thought came from a textbook dealing with international events. The selection contained descriptions of hostile and peaceful actions ascribed to a target nation. Half of the subjects read a selection that supposedly dealt with recent relations between the Soviet Union and China. The other subjects read the exact same selection except for the substitution of Australia for the Soviet Union. Australia was chosen because it is near enough to China to fit the events described in the selection and because pretests for another study had found that students were neutral to moderately positive about Australia but knew little enough about it so that the information included in the selection was plausible. Thus both groups of students read descriptions of the same actions, but one group thought the actions were performed by the Soviet Union, which was definitely considered to be an enemy when the study was done in 1986, while the other students thought the actions were performed by a nonenemy. While they were reading the selections, the students did not know that they would be asked fifteen minutes later to write down everything they could remember from the selection.

Two items in this study tell us something about the credibility accorded to statements attacking or defending enemies. One item alleged that the target nation *may* have performed an aggressive act: "More recently, the Soviet Union (for half of the students the word 'Australia' was substituted) has provided assistance and training, perhaps some of it military, to nations bordering on China." Notice that the statement includes the word "perhaps," signifying that the target nation may or may not have provided military assistance. We measured the number of students who recalled this item without mentioning the modifier "perhaps," counting the people who reported that the target nation had definitely supplied military assistance to China's neighbors. Of the students who read the selection dealing with Australia, fewer than one in ten (7 percent) reported that the nation had actually provided military assistance to China's neighbors, compared to almost one third (30 percent) of the students who read the identical selection dealing with the Soviet Union.

Another item in the study extended the analysis of credibility to include a statement attributed to the non-Chinese nation: "The Soviet Union/Australia, on the other hand, denies the Chinese countercharges concerning the beaming of radio broadcasts into China." Twenty-six percent of the subjects in the Soviet group recalled this item as saying that the Soviet Union did beam radio broadcasts into China, compared to 7 percent of the students in the Australia group. Thus, over one quarter of the subjects treated an accusation against a supposed enemy as a fact while completely ignoring that country's denial of wrongdoing.

Based upon their official statements, several U.S. government officials have been willing to accord credibility to charges against the Soviet Union that were based on little evidence. For example, on January 30,

1981, Secretary of State Alexander Haig received front-page coverage in the *New York Times* with his accusation that the Soviet Union was responsible for promoting international terrorism. On February 9 of that year, the *Times* reported (not the front page) that U.S. intelligence had little evidence to back Haig's accusations. On March 19, Secretary of State Haig again received front-page coverage for the same accusation. On April 25, the *Times* reported on its front page yet another speech by the secretary accusing the Soviet Union of promoting international terrorism. On April 27, the *Times* reported (again not on the front page) that the director of the F.B.I, said that he had no evidence linking the Soviet Union with terrorism, and two days later the C.I.A. reported that it had insufficient evidence to substantiate the accusations. Yet these accusations, made by American leaders based on little evidence, continued, including a speech by Secretary Haig's successor, George Shultz. On June 25, 1984 (p. 1), the *New York Times* reported that Secretary Shultz "said the Soviet Union and its allies provided 'financial, logistic, and training support for terrorists worldwide.' The Russians, he said, 'use terrorist groups for their own purposes, and their goal is always the same: to weaken liberal democracy and undermine world stability.' " And on January 23, 1986, William Casey, director of Central Intelligence, presented no new evidence but continued the accusations in a speech in which he charged that "these causes [of terrorism] are to be found . . . in the activities of those states that find it in their interest to support international terrorism—the Soviet Union, . . ." (*New York Times*, p. 1). The American public, like that of most other nations, attends and believes statements made by their own leaders, even if they are based in little evidence, more than statements from nations labeled as enemies.

ATTRIBUTION

Attribution is the name given by psychologists to the process wherein people infer the causes of behavior. One of the most important questions that people focus on when they try to make sense of the actions of others is why those actions were performed. For example, your response to being hit on the back by someone will be quite different if you think the intent was to mug you than if you think it was to swat a mosquito.

Psychologists have found that enemy images distort the process of attributing the motivation of actions in three ways: (1) When nations that are assumed to be enemies perform actions that might be considered hostile, people tend to underemphasize or ignore the situational pressures experienced by the "enemy"; as a result, the actions are viewed simply as proof that the enemy is hostile or barbaric. (2) When nations that are assumed to be enemies perform actions that might be considered peaceful, people tend to overemphasize the situational pressures experienced by the enemy; as a result, the actions are viewed as being forced upon the enemy by circumstances and not as evidence that the enemy truly wants peace. Thus, apparently hostile acts do more to strengthen enemy images than apparently peaceful acts do to dispel time. (3) When enemy images are powerful enough, apparently peaceful actions of nations that are assumed to be enemies may even be attributed to hostile motives; thus, a proferred peace treaty may be viewed as crass propaganda, an attempt to increase tensions among allies, or a trick to allow enemies to maintain or increase military superiority.

One study conducted in India (Taylor and Jaggi 1974) provided evidence regarding the first two of these processes. The investigators gave short descriptions to Hindu office clerks in southern India of either a Moslem or a Hindu behaving in friendly or unfriendly ways in various situations, and asked the subjects to choose the major reason that the person in the description behaved as he or she did. The Hindu subjects in the study ascribed the friendly behaviors of the Hindu characters in the story to their personalities and the unfriendly behaviors to circumstances. For the Moslem characters the results were reversed: their unfriendly behaviors were ascribed to personality dispositions and their friendly behaviors were ascribed to the situation. When a psychologist in the United States showed white undergraduates a videotape depicting either a black or white person ambiguously shoving another person, the subjects tended to attribute the shove to personal, dispositional causes (i.e., it was seen as intentional) when the harm-doer was black, but to situational causes (i.e., it was seen as an accident) when the harm-doer was white (Duncan 1976).

Several studies have demonstrated that all three of these processes may have affected U.S. interpretations of Soviet actions. In one (Burn and Oskamp 1989), U.S. college students were provided with a list of Soviet actions, including an apparently peaceful action, the 1985 moratorium on nuclear testing, as well as apparently hostile actions, such as the downing of Korean Airlines flight 007. The study found that when asked to attribute motivations for the actions listed, about 60 percent of the subjects tended to choose the most negative motivations, whether the actions appeared to be peaceful or not.

A similar study was done using fictional situations such as the shipment of arms, in one case, and the sending of aid, in another, to an African nation (Sande et al. 1989). Although the actions were fictional, the student subjects thought that they had actually occurred. The use of the fictional situations allowed the investigators to determine that in attributing motivations for the actions, U.S. students chose more negative motives when the actions were supposedly performed by the Soviet Union than when the actions were supposedly performed by the United States or by France. This demonstrates that biases did affect U.S. attributions of both positive and negative Soviet actions, and that the biases were more anti-Soviet than pro-United States. Furthermore, Canadian students did not attribute more negative motivations to the Soviet Union than to the United States.

These processes may also affect governmental leaders. One political scientist, for example, analyzed all of the public statements dealing with the Soviet Union made by U.S. Secretary of State John Foster Dulles between 1953 and 1959 (Holsti 1986). He coded these statements into 3,584 assertions that were placed into one of four categories: (1) assessments of the friendship or hostility exemplified by Soviet actions; (2) evaluations of the Soviet Union on a good-bad dimension; (3) assessments of the strength or weakness of Soviet capabilities; (4) assessments of the success or failure of Soviet foreign policy. He divided the data into twelve six-month periods. He found no relationship between the assessments of the hostility exemplified by Soviet actions and the evaluations of the Soviet Union, whereas the relationships between these hostility assessments and the assessments of Soviet weakness and failure were strong. That is, during those periods when Dulles perceived Soviet actions as not very hostile, he did not change his overall evaluation of the Soviet Union, but he did perceive the Soviet Union as weaker and less successful.

Koopman et al. (1989) asked a sample of subscribers to the journal *International Security*, which included academic experts as well as government advisors, to respond to scenarios describing hypothetical situations in which the Soviet Union sent military forces into Iran. Varying the circumstances of the scenarios, such as the balance of conventional or nuclear forces or—more relevant to this chapter—the likelihood that the Soviets were acting in response to a perceived threat had very little effect on the policy recommendations made by the respondents in the study; that is, the elite respondents surveyed in this study essentially ignored the evidence regarding possible situational pressures leading the Soviet Union to act in an apparently hostile manner. What did predict the recommendations were the initial beliefs held by the respondents regarding the Soviet Union and U.S.-Soviet relations.

All three of the processes discussed here have influenced U.S. responses to the actions of "enemies." The first process, wherein the situational pressures motivating apparently hostile acts are ignored, played a major role in U.S. responses to two similar incidents that occurred seventy years apart. In 1915, when the Germans sank the British liner *Lusitania*, resulting in the loss of some American lives, the United States treated the event as proof of German inhumanity. It ignored the fact that the *Lusitania* was listed as part of the British navy, that Germany had warned it would destroy British ships in the war zone, just as the British were preventing ships from reaching Germany, and most important of all, that much of the *Lusitania*'s cargo was munitions (Zinn 1980). The situation faced by the German U-boat commander, sighting an enemy ship carrying ammunition to Britain to be used to kill Germans, was downplayed, and U.S. sentiment to enter World War I on the side of Britain grew.

Similarly, in 1983 the Soviet air force shot down a civilian Korean airliner. While American leaders and the American press treated the event as evidence of Soviet barbarism, they paid little attention to several facts that eventually surfaced: at the outset of World War II, the Nazis destroyed nearly half of the Soviet air force on the ground, an accomplishment due in part to earlier reconnaissance made from the air. The United States had a history of using spy planes for reconnaissance over the Soviet Union. A U.S. RC-135 spy plane had been spotted in the area earlier that day, and, contrary to early U.S. allegations, pilots have concluded that it is quite possible to mistake an airliner like the KAL for for an RC-135. The Soviet pilot shot down the plane only after following recognized international procedures in trying to warn the plane that it must land.

These facts do not justify the downing of the airliner, but they are important aspects of the situational pressures experienced by the Soviets when they decided to shoot down the plane. Ignoring such pressures or underestimating their importance may originate from an enemy image and probably helps to reinforce that image.

The second process, whereby apparently peaceful acts are viewed as being forced by circumstances upon the enemy, was exemplified in a *New York Times* 1982 response to Soviet actions. On September 27, 1982, the *Times*, one of the most respected newspapers in the United States, quoted the analysis of recent Soviet international activity made by a "State Department expert." Here is what the expert said:

> There's a lot of talk here that the Soviets won't stand in the way of getting the Cubans out of Angola. They could have been much more obstreperous in Lebanon. They've shown restraint in their arms shipments to Central America. They could have done more in Poland. And they haven't escalated in Afghanistan, and Afghanistan no longer looks like the first step in a grand strategic drive.

In analyzing the cause of such behavior, the article did not mention the possibility that the Soviet Union might have been trying to be peaceful. Instead, the newspaper attributed the apparently pacific behavior of the Soviet Union to "a kind of creeping paralysis in Soviet decision-making that has led to an essentially passive world posture."

The third process, whereby apparently peaceful acts are attributed to hostile motivations, was evident in 1956, when the Soviet Union offered to follow a plan suggested by the British and French and limit its troops to 1.5 million if the United States would do the same. The Soviet offer of March 28, 1956, to cut its troops would appear to have been a move toward peace. But the response made by U.S. Secretary of State John Foster Dulles appeared in the *Times* on May 16: "Mr. Dulles went on, however, to point out that by releasing uniformed soldiers and airmen into industry and agriculture the Soviet Union might increase its war-making power." When asked if he would have preferred that the Soviets keep the men in the armed forces, Dulles replied: "Well, it's a fair conclusion that I would rather have them standing around doing guard duty than making atomic bombs."

The U.S. response to these incidents points up the relationship between the processes discussed earlier and the attribution process. If processes of perception and communication lead people to be ignorant of many of the positive actions taken by enemies and of the hardships experienced by enemies, attributions of apparently hostile enemy actions to feelings of defensiveness or reactions to situational pressures will be unlikely. Ignorance of the munitions that were carried by the *Lusitania*, of the large number of casualties suffered by the Soviet Union as a result of invasions by other nations, or of the attempts made by the Soviet pilots who shot down the KAL to contact what they thought was a U.S. spy plane greatly reduced the probability of perceiving an apparently hostile action as a response to situational pressures.

In the next few years, U.S. leaders and the American press will probably be treating other nations as enemies. A psychological theory called "realistic group conflict theory" predicts that conflicts occur between groups when those groups compete over scarce resources. Given that the coming years are likely to see increased economic competition between Japan and the United States, Japan may be pictured increasingly in terms of enemy images. Because of conflicts over Israel and over control of oil, several Middle Eastern nations will be viewed as enemies, as will some Latin American leaders who attempt to decrease the dominant role played by the United States in their economies. The attributional biases described above will affect descriptions of how these nations act. When we read or hear these descriptions, it is important that we think of how they would differ if the nation described were perceived as an ally. As soon as one realizes that the reports deal with an assumed enemy, one should ask oneself: Why might they have performed those actions?

HOW DO ENEMY IMAGES DEVELOP?

One question of importance to psychologists is how these biases develop. Assuming people are not born with enemy images, where do they come from? Several studies of the developmental psychology of enemy images have been undertaken. Based on their interviews with Swiss children, Piaget and Weil (1951) concluded that children first develop the ability to locate themselves geographically and to understand the concept of their nation, and then they develop reciprocity, or the ability to understand that people from other nations have their own point of view and pride in country or ethnicity. At the same time, however, children increasingly come to accept the biases of their societies. One group of studies found that although the ability to understand foreigners' point of view did develop with age among the English children being studied, the children had most difficulty empathizing with people from nations their government disliked (Middleton et al. 1970).

Studies of Australian children (Connell 1971) demonstrated that unlike many other cognitive structures, children do not develop their cognitive structures regarding other nations based upon direct experience. The studies found that at early ages images of enemies took the form of fantasy figures that present threats to the warm and safe places in the children's lives, but that with age they became increasingly political—first against the Vietnamese, whom the Australians were fighting at the time, then of communists in general. Studies conducted in the 1960s found that as American children became older, they increasingly named Russians as the people they most disliked. American children's information about most nationalities came, at age six, from the media and, to a lesser extent, from their parents; at age ten from the media and, to some extent, from school; and at age fourteen from school and from the media. With regard to Russians, however, school never became an important source of information (Lambert and Klineberg 1967).

One clue as to the illogical nature of the development of enemy images comes from a study of children who reported that they did not like particular nations even before they were able to answer any questions about them (Johnson 1973). In other words, distrust develops before children know anything about enemy nations.

Motivations Underlying Enemy Images

Several psychological theories may help to explain why people have such a strong tendency to look for and hate enemies. Let me mention but a few.

Realistic group conflict theory was developed by social psychologist Muzafer Sherif. He found that young boys attending a summer camp who were organized into teams competing in a color war for special prizes came to view the boys on the other teams very negatively. The more often the boys were placed in situations where, in order to gain something—such as pocket knives, special snacks, interesting outings— for their own group, the other group had to lose, the more conflict developed between the groups and the more negatively the members of each group came to view one another (Sherif et al. 1961). The implication is that enemy images are particularly likely to develop between groups that are in conflict over scarce resources.

Social identity theory postulates that people want to see themselves in as positive a light as possible, and that one way to do that is to identify with the groups one belongs to and to perceive members of these groups as superior to members of other groups. According to this theory, it is not enough simply to take pride in one's own group; there is a strong tendency to want to see other groups as worse. The tendency is so strong that rather than have the two groups both do as well as possible, people will sometimes prefer to have their own group sacrifice something as long as the other group loses more. Rather than striving to obtain as many resources as they can, as postulated by realistic group conflict theory, people may have an even stronger need to feel superior (Tajfel and Turner 1986).

Finally, psychoanalytic theorists discuss the means used by people to ward off the anxiety inherent in the human condition. According to this theory, the human infant develops in a context in which he or she feels quite powerless to control the environment, to obtain the love of apparently omnipotent adults, and to be protected from a world seen as threatening. To avoid being overwhelmed by the anxiety caused by this powerlessness, the human mind develops defenses. Some people may not be able to deal comfortably with the natural hostility that is mingled with the love they feel for those adults, such as their parents, who are seen as all-powerful but who, even in the best of circumstances, will inevitably sometimes frustrate and enrage the child. These people may feel less conflicted if they project that hostility by labeling it as hatred toward some external group such as an ethnic or religious group or an "enemy" nation. Children also tend to see the world in fairly simple, primitive terms. Sometimes they see the people who provide love and protection, often their mother or father, as all good, loving, and unrealistically perfect and, at other times, when those same people are angry, inattentive, or punishing, they see them as totally bad, threatening, or even evil. They have trouble integrating these conflicting perceptions, and so they resort to "splitting" to divide them into separate entities, constructing in their minds two distinct individuals rather than realizing that the same person can be sometimes good and sometimes bad. This model of people as either Dr. Jekyll or Mr. Hyde, but not both simultaneously, may later be built upon in viewing the world as composed of one's own "all good" nations versus other "all bad" nations (cf. Volkan 1988).

The Mass Media

Along with parents, the mass media play a role in the development of enemy images. They often create products that are popular because they take advantage of the cognitive biases and irrational human motivations that underlie such images. Recent studies have shown that children's cartoon shows often depict people who look or speak differently than Americans as totally evil, with no positive qualities (Hesse and Mack 1991). When they become somewhat older, children stop watching cartoons, but they continue to be exposed to enemy images. Analyses of U.S. textbooks conducted thirty years apart have found inaccuracies and sketchy information not only about the Soviet Union, but about many Third World nations and even about minority groups in the United States (Burkhardt 1947–1948; Danilov and Sharifzhanov 1981). Thus schoolchildren are often exposed to biased information.

Perhaps the most extreme enemy images to which children are exposed occur in motion pictures, so I will devote some attention here to enemy images on film. Almost since their beginnings, motion pictures became an important medium of enemy portrayals. In the words of George Creel, head of the U.S. government's Committee on Public Information, organized to promote support for American participation in World War I: "I believe in the motion picture just as I believe in the press, and in my work it plays just as powerful a part in the production of an aroused and enlightened war sentiment."

During the First World War, actor Eric von Stroheim rose to fame playing cruel, mean-looking German officers who pushed around old women and pulled the hair out of children's heads. In a scene from one film, *The Heart of Humanity*, he plays a German officer attempting to rape a sweet-looking Red Cross nurse who is holding a baby. He yanks the baby away from her, she struggles, while he rips and bites the clothing from her body. Meanwhile, downstairs, German soldiers ignore her cries as they guzzle beer. The baby starts to cry, disturbing von Stroheim in the middle of his rape, so he rushes over to the window and tosses the baby out.

While evil Russians appeared in a number of Cold War films of the

1970s and '80s (notably several of the James Bond series), the enemy image is most evident in four: *Rambo* and *Rocky IV*, both starring Sylvester Stallone; *Invasion U.S.A.*; and *Red Dawn*. In *Rambo*, Stallone, in the title role, singlehandedly locates and frees several American P.O.W.s who are imprisoned by the Vietnamese, who are clearly under the command of Soviet officers. *Rocky IV* pits Stallone as the champion boxer against a mighty Russian challenger. *Invasion U.S.A.* portrays Chuck Norris (who in *"Missing in Action"* also frees P.O.W.'s from Vietnamese imprisonment) as the one American who can prevent two agents named Nikko and Mikhail Rostov from using terrorism to push the United States into mass anarchy. *Red Dawn* depicts the effects of a Soviet invasion of the United States on a Mid-Western town.

In these films, costumes, makeup, lighting, and acting are combined to make the actors portraying the Russians appear savage and fierce. The gigantic, steely-jawed Russian boxer in *Rocky IV*, who is often shown wearing a Soviet military uniform, is so animalistic that he barely speaks through the film, other than to utter threats in a deep, spooky voice reminiscent of the character "Lurch" on the old television program, "The Addams Family."

All of the horrible behaviors of enemies past is exhibited by the Soviets in these films. Electric shock torture administered by a Russian is graphically depicted in *Rambo*. Perhaps even more horrifying is the way in which the Russians in the films are portrayed as enjoying killing and inflicting pain. In *Invasion U.S.A.*, one of the Russian agents murders, in cold blood, two American teenagers who are necking on a beach while watching a portable television; immediately after the murder he smiles as he stops to watch a talk show. In *Rocky IV*, immediately after he pulverizes a Muhammed Ali-like character called "Apollo Creed" in an exhibition match, the Russian boxer comments, "If he dies, he dies." Civilians are massacred in *Invasion U.S.A.* and *Red Dawn* and in both films the Russians deliberately gun down young children. *Red Dawn* actually portrays the Soviets as beginning their invasion of the United States by slaughtering most of the students and teachers of a Mid West high school. *Invasion U.S.A.* even includes a touching holiday scene in which the evil Mikhail Rostov smiles as he blows up a suburban home along with the family residing there—just after a little girl places an angel atop her Christmas tree. It is one thing to portray competition with or even danger from another nation, but only in a full-fledged "enemy portrayal" are groups of people shown as being totally evil, enjoying murder for murder's sake, and expending massive resources at great risk to themselves in order to hurt or destroy harmless civilians. In the next decade, we can expect Arab terrorists, Latin American drug dealers, and "inscrutable Orientals" to become the heavies in such popular adventure films.

CONCLUSION

Now is a good time to focus on the workings of enemy images. With the easing of international tensions between the United States and the Soviet Union, we can look back on the processes that for almost five decades greatly exaggerated hostilities between the two nations. By understanding the psychology of enemy images, we may be better able to avoid being controlled by the process in the future. The Soviet Union may once more become the focus of enemy images, or it may be replaced with Japan, China, Cuba, a reunited Germany, or any nation whose aspirations seem to be in conflict with our own. On the domestic level, attitudes toward racial and ethnic groups will continue to be affected by the process.

While real competition and hostilities will continue to exist in this world, necessitating caution, people living in a nuclear age can no longer afford to let themselves be irrationally pushed around by psychological forces that we are increasingly able to understand. Each of us must learn to recognize and resist these forces when they enter our own lives. We must work to educate others as to the dangers of the process. We must pressure our friends, our teachers, our leaders, and the mass media when we see them falling prey to enemy images.

This is no easy task. When the whole society begins to treat a particular group as an enemy, it is difficult to recognize that that group may not be quite as evil as it appears, and even more difficult to stand up to social pressure and say so. Psychologists may play an important role in fostering resistance to future enemy imaging. Developmental psychologists will continue to research the process wherein children learn to hate enemies, and they may act as consultants to schools attempting to reform their curricula and to community groups working to put pressure on the mass media to moderate their use of enemy images. Other psychologists will further our understanding of the cognitive processes that lead to biases in people's interpretation of the actions of supposed enemies, and of the emotional processes that lead people to externalize their dissatisfaction with their own lives by blaming the world's problems on a particular enemy nation or on an ethnic or religious group. Activist psychologists will work to educate the public about these processes. Psychologists for Social Responsibility, for example, has compiled a Speaker's Manual on the Psychology of Enemy Images that can be used by people who want to learn about, and to teach others about, these processes.

The hope is that through research and education, we can come to understand fully the workings of enemy images and to help the educated people living in a modern democracy learn to resist insidious processes that have afflicted humankind for centuries. As I write this, it appears that we may have squeezed through the Cold War without a nuclear hot war. If we do not learn from science and from our past, however, we may not be so fortunate the next time around.

REFERENCES

Allport, G., and Postman, L. (1947). *The psychology of rumor.* New York: Holt.

Burkhardt, R. W. (1947–1948). The Soviet Union in American school textbooks. *Public Opinion Quarterly, 11*(1), 567–571.

Burn, S. M., and Oskamp, S. (1989). Ingroup biases and the U.S.-Soviet conflict. In R. Holt and B. Silverstein, eds., The psychology of enemy images. *Journal of Social Issues, 45*(2), 73–90.

Connell, R. W. (1971). *The child's construction of politics.* Carlton, Victoria: Melbourne University Press.

Danilov, A. I., and Sharifzhanov, I. L. (1981). The history of the USSR according to school textbooks of the USA. *Social Education* (April), 239–244.

Duncan, B. L. (1976). Differential social perception and the attribution of intergroup violence: Testing the lower limits of stereotyping of blacks. *Journal of Personality and Social Psychology, 34*(4), 590–598.

Dutta, S., Kanungo, R. N., and Freiberg, V. (1972). Retention of affective material: Effects of intensity of affect on retrieval. *Journal of Personality and Social Psychology, 23*(1), 64–80.

Ford, P. L., ed. (1848). *The writings of Thomas Jefferson,* vol. IX. New York: Putnam.

Hastorf, A. H., and Cantril, H. (1954). They saw a game: A case study. *Journal of Abnormal and Social Psychology, 49*, 129–134.

Herman, E. S. (1982). *The real terror network.* Boston: South End.

Hesse, P., and Mack, J. (1991). The world is a dangerous place: Images of the enemy in children's television. In R. W. Rieber, ed., *The psychology of war and peace: The image of the enemy.* New York: Plenum.

Holsti, O. R. (1986). The belief system and national images: John Foster Dulles. In R. K. White, ed., *Psychology and the prevention of nuclear war.* New York: New York University Press.

Johnson, N. (1973). The development of English children's concept of Germany. *Journal of Social Psychology, 90,* 259–267.

Koopman, C., Snyder, J., and Jervis, R. (1989). American elite views of relations with the Soviet Union. In R. Holt and B. Silverstein, eds., The psychology of enemy images. *Journal of Social Issues, 45*(2), 119–138.

Kriesberg, M. (1946). Soviet news in the "New York Times." *Public Opinion Quarterly,* 540–562.

Lambert, W. E., and Klineberg, O. (1967). *Children's views of foreign peoples: A cross-national study.* New York: Appleton-Century-Crofts.

Middleton, M. R., Tajfel, H., and Johnson, N. B. (1970). Cognitive and affective aspects of children's national attitudes. *British Journal of Social and Clinical Psychology, 9,* 122–134.

Piaget, J., and Weil, A. M. (1951). The development in children of the idea of the homeland and of relations with other countries. *International Social Science Bulletin, 3,* 561–578.

Sande, G. N., Goethals, G. R., Ferrari, L., and Worth, L. T. (1989). Value-guided attributions: Maintaining the moral self-image and the diabolical enemy image. In R. Holt and B. Silverstein, eds., The psychology of enemy images. *Journal of Social Issues, 45*(2), 91–118.

Sherif, M., Harvey, O. J., White, B. J., Hood, W. R., and Sherif, C. W. (1961). *Intergroup cooperation and competition: The Robbers Cave experiment.* Norman, Okla.: University Book Exchange.

Silverstein, B., and Flamenbaum, C. (1989). Biases in the perception and cognition of the actions of enemies. In R. Holt and B. Silverstein, eds., The psychology of enemy images. *Journal of Social Issues, 45*(2), 51–72.

Tajfel, H., and Turner, J. C. (1986). The social identity theory of intergroup behavior. In S. Worchel and W. G. Austin, eds., *Psychology of intergroup relations.* Chicago: Nelson-Hall.

Taylor, D. M., and Jaggi, V. (1974). Ethnocentrism and causal attribution in a South Indian context. *Journal of Cross-Cultural Psychology, 5* (2), 162–171.

Vallone, R. P., Ross, L., and Lepper, M. R. (1985). The hostile media phenomenon: Biased perception and perceptions of media bias in coverage of the Beirut massacre. *Journal of Personality and Social Psychology, 49,* 577–585.

Volkan, V. D. (1988). *The need to have enemies and allies.* Livingston, N.J.: Jason Aronson.

Zanna, M. P., Klossen, E. C., and Darley, J. M. (1976). How television news viewers deal with facts that contradict their beliefs: A consistency and attribution analysis. *Journal of Applied Social Psychology, 6,* 159–176.

Zinn, H. (1980). *A people's history of the United States.* New York: Harper.

PART THREE

MENTAL HEALTH AND PSYCHOTHERAPY IN A GLOBAL CONTEXT

The proper consideration for therapists is the recognition that whatever we do or do not do in our encounters, whatever we forget or remember, whatever truths we keep alive or lies we fabricate will help form a world inhabited by others. Our actions will play a significant part in defining not only the social and political life of our own people, but the future of countless and distant others as well, whose names we will not know and whose faces we will not see. The responsibility of the therapist, then, neither begins nor ends with the individual client, and the client's responsibility neither begins nor ends with him/herself. Both extend far outward from the past into the future, to countless other lives. —*Peter Marin*

The authors in this part describe their approaches to broadening the perspectives of the mental health professions to include the social, political, and economic contexts of clients' lives. Lane Gerber, in chapter 7, examines the reasons for the pervasive silence in the therapy room about social and political issues and presents a rationale and some techniques for bringing these issues into the practice of psychotherapy. Bianca Cody Murphy and Jonathan Reusser, in chapter 8, describe ways in which concern about nuclear weapons has been addressed in family therapy and discuss the application of family systems theories to the field of international relations. In chapter 9, George Albee, writing from a community psychology perspective, presents his views on the relationship between oppression, powerlessness, and psychopathology and the need for psychology to work toward bringing about a more just social order. In chapter 10, Richard Sherman writes about the opportunities that mental health professionals have to integrate their social and political concerns with their professional work, thereby becoming agents of social change.

7

Integrating Political-Societal Concerns in Psychotherapy

Lane A. Gerber

Living in the shadows of nuclear, societal, and environmental disasters affects us all, whether we are therapists or patients. While these horrors outside of our office doors continue to grow, they are rarely admitted into our psychotherapy hours. Should what we see and hear of the world outside of our therapy offices influence what we do as therapists? Could it be that the psychic numbing that we may decry in society at large also affects what we hear and what we attend to in our work with patients? What is our responsibility as people who are also psychotherapists?

Although a large majority of psychologists support a nuclear weapons freeze (Polyson 1986; Parker 1989) and are very concerned about nuclear war, and although the literature on attitudes and meanings of the threat of nuclear war in society is extensive, there is very little published on how political-societal issues might be integrated into the clinical setting. The recent works of Porter, Rinzler, and Olsen (1987) and of Levine, Jacobs, and Rubin (1988) are some of the exceptions.

One wonders why more psychotherapists do not incorporate their attitudes toward nuclear freeze or toward other political and social issues into their work. Is it because of ethical concerns and trying to maintain "value-free" work (Robinson 1984), or because of psychological factors

This chapter is adapted from an article of the same title which appeared in the *American Journal of Psychotherapy*, 44, no. 4 (October 1990). Reprinted by permission.

such as denial and helplessness (Gilbert 1988; Lifton and Falk 1982; Mack 1984)? Have we become part of what Prilleltensky (1989) calls "maintainers of the status quo?" Or do we attribute "the trend toward increasing violence in our nation . . . to defective individual superegos, and therefore . . . ignore the systemic context in which this trend toward increasing violence is occurring" (Marmor 1988)?

Keeping one's beliefs about political and social issues separate from one's professional role was a code reinforced during my clinical training in graduate school, which was delimited by John Kennedy's assassination near the beginning of my training and Robert Kennedy's just as I completed my dissertation. These events and the accompanying feelings were on everybody's lips yet were seldom mentioned in our classrooms or consultation sessions. When the patients that I saw during this time talked about the assassinations, civil rights issues, or simply the politics of everyday life, my supervisors regarded the material as sometimes "interesting," but "not therapy material."

I would like to explore some possible reasons for the relative paucity of clinical literature in this area, and also why most psychotherapists do not hear much about nuclear, societal, and environmental concerns from their patients. Then I will describe an approach I used to integrate this material into the psychotherapy situation and discuss the results.

DIFFICULTIES OF DEALING WITH THE ISSUES IN THE CLINICAL SETTING

Do Patients Talk about These Issues?

How can we understand the fact that most psychotherapists claim that their patients do not discuss nuclear, societal, and environmental issues within the therapy hour? If these concerns are shown daily on television and reported daily in the newspapers, and if we believe our scientists that the continuation of life as we know it on this planet is in peril, how is it that our patients never mention these factors in their psychotherapy? Although Mack and a few others report that their patients do talk about "external" concerns, certainly there are many patients who believe that global matters are not "what people come to a psychiatrist about" (Mack 1988). As a patient of mine stated, "I have all the rest of the week to think about other things. Being here I want to use my two hours a week to concentrate just on me." Another patient asked, "Therapy isn't supposed to deal with external problems, is it?" Rubin (1988) has suggested that perhaps some of the reasons that more patients do not talk more about these issues have to do with the passivity and depression in the general population in the face of nuclear threat, and that the lack of conversation about these issues in therapy hours is an expression of this depression and numbing. Rubin stated that what is required in order to recognize and face the problems and anguish of the world is a capacity in our patients to mourn, and that without this capacity they are unable to work through these difficult issues. In chapter 3, Walsh has suggested that societal denial prevents an awareness of threatening and difficult issues that happen in the everyday real world, and that our patients reflect this greater societal denial by not talking about issues that are too painful and that make them feel too helpless. Walsh has further argued that it is the responsibility of educators and mental health professionals to point out, teach, and do whatever is appropriate to remove the blinders of societal denial so that people can more fully see and hear the world.

Another viewpoint on why patients do not talk about the fears and horrors of nuclear war, environmental threats, and societal disruption is offered by Lifton (1979). Lifton states that "psychological theory has tended either to neglect death or render it as a kind of foreign body, to separate death from the general motivations of life." He argues very convincingly that not only do atomic annihilation and environmental pollution raise the possibility of our own death, but they also destroy the very possibility of our symbolic survival. Or as Segal (1988) writes, "The existence of nuclear weapons and the prospect of nuclear weapons and the prospect of nuclear war makes impossible either acceptance of death or symbolic survival. The prospect of death in atomic warfare leaves an unimaginable void and produces terror of a different kind." Lifton's extensive work with survivors of Hiroshima and the victims and perpetrators of other extreme situations has convinced him that "we are haunted by the image of exterminating ourselves as a species by means of our own technology." Further, he states that "we require symbolization of continuity—imaginative forms of transcending death—in order to confront genuinely the fact that we die" (Lifton 1979).

The presence of nuclear weapons and an increasingly threatening environment obliterate the likelihood of our living on via our children, our creative works, or the world of nature around us. That is, the possibility of the death of all life on earth now and in the future makes contemplating our own deaths impossible. Thus, if death has always been among the most difficult of all issues to talk about, whether in or out of therapy, the fact that we have the means to carry out our own death and the death of all life on this planet makes the possibility for awareness of these issues and conversation and exploration of them in the psychother-apy hour extremely difficult. "Given the fact that the fear of our own death must exist in all," Parens (1988) has said, "it is impressive how little we encounter it as a constant source of anxiety in our analytic patients. Indeed, analysts have long held that we do not dream about our own death, and I have never encountered such dreams in any of my analysands, child or adult." Strozier (1990) has added,

> We erect such enormous defenses against death that neither images of individual death nor the mega-death of nuclear holocaust can enter into psychoanalysis in any meaningful way. . . . Death is the issue. Psychoanalysts are asking the wrong question. It is not a matter of whether nuclear threat exists and whether they see its direct expression in clinical psychoanalysis. It is rather how nuclear threat, as a remote and abstract threat to existence, changes everything else.

It is as though there is now a shadow over the way we see everything, including our own notions of our self in this world. Perhaps we have been looking for isolated dark spots on the horizon rather than realizing that the lens with which we look at ourselves and the world around us has itself become gray and clouded.

Factors in the Therapist and in the Nature of Therapy

An important factor in trying to understand the lack of a clinical literature in this area has to do with the political nature of the subject and "the reluctance of psychotherapists to pursue with patients areas that raise questions of social and political values, and potential pressures for deci-sion and action. We worry, not without justification, that we may risk imposing our points of view upon our patients; to escape this hazard we may avoid the topic all together" (Mack 1988). Indeed, all psychothera-pists worry about "contaminating" the therapeutic situation or using the context of therapy to influence or direct the patient to areas that are not of his or her concern. At the same time, Segal (1988) and Staub (1989) remind us of the silence of the psychoanalytic community inside as well as outside of Germany during the Nazi regime. Segal states that "we psychoanalysts who believe in the power of words and the therapeutic effect of verbalizing truth must not be silent." Staub suggests that bystanders in Germany under the Nazi regime, and perhaps bystanders in other situations, too, who accept a particular status quo will begin passively to change and undergo a resocialization to values and beliefs that are more akin to those they may have initially disliked but to which they did not object. While writers such as Mack, Segal, and Staub emphasize the caution that clinicians must exercise in the treatment situation, they seem to argue against the complete separation of one's professional life from one's personal life—a separation that is so prevalent in our culture.

A number of psychotherapists argue that patients do indeed talk about global concerns in the therapy hour and that it is the therapist who does not hear these concerns. Segal has stated that "as analysts, in this, as in other situations, we must look into ourselves and be aware of turning a blind eye to reality. . . . We are prone to the same denials, and, moreover, we can hide behind the shield of psychoanalytic neutrality" (Segal 1988).

Mack has suggested a "kind of tradition in psychoanalysis or psychodynamic psychotherapy, a tacit agreement between analyst and patient, that broad social problems at the national or global level, especially political ones, are not appropriate subjects for treatment" (Mack 1988). This seems to mean either that patients don't talk about these areas, therapists don't hear these concerns, or that therapists hear them only as fears tied to "private, symbolically represented memories and structural conflicts derived from relationships with the family" (Mack 1988). It would seem that rarely is nuclear content or the content of other "external" concerns heard as reflecting a menacing reality in its own right, as opposed to or in addition to the ways it affects the early conflicts and meaning of the patient's inner world. Rubin (1988) adds, "In my opinion, the fears and anxieties do come up; they are simply not being heard. If analysts were sensitized to the issue and listened with this in mind, they would begin to hear the material . . . despite a general attitude of free-floating attention. We, like archaeologists, must have some idea of what we are looking for in order to see what we have in front of us."

Whether or not psychotherapists hear material as important is related in large measure to the nature of the psychotherapy theory and practice they use. Thus Rubin states that "analysts are not thinking about the latent material in terms of a reality-oriented stimulus. Our bias is to focus in terms of earlier experience, family dynamics, and transference meanings, rather than to attend to ongoing, current reality fears." In addition, in the analytic situation and in many psychotherapy situations the patient regresses and increasingly looks toward the analyst or therapist for gratification of needs. "Attention is shifted away from the outside world toward the internal world, from outside concerns to concerns about the past or the relationship to the analyst" (Rubin 1988). When this regressive transference is at least partially resolved, Jacobs (1988) believes that the emerging sense of the patient within the context of the larger human community might then be explored; however, this rarely if ever happens.

In discussing how psychotherapy theory and practice may have helped to prevent political and societal issues from being talked about and explored in the psychotherapy situation, Jacobs has wondered whether our patients even at the end of their therapeutic work still suffer from a particular form of narcissism. His claim is that we therapists have "not paid sufficient attention to the ways in which our patients, by pursuing through love and work their own happiness, have failed to identify themselves with the larger community, now seriously at risk" (1988). The current nuclear age, with its advanced technology as well as its escalating international concerns about warfare and pollution, has forced upon us a kind of interconnectedness not previously experienced. This interconnectedness must now cause us to change the way in which we think about mental health and perhaps the way we listen and even interact with our patients. Sampson (1989) also argues that the world is undergoing a major historical transformation to a globally linked world system, and that this has transformed the basic unit of the social system from the isolated individual to a more globally interconnected form.

The Relevance of Context

When Jacobs, Sampson, and others talk about the transformation of the world into a globally linked society, they are emphasizing the importance that context has for our notions of being a person in this postmodern world. Statements about the relevance and importance of context typically seem to come from discussions of extreme situations—that is, situations of war, torture, and so on, in which the stress from the environment is so extreme that it must be considered in order to understand and treat those individuals affected by it. Wachtel (1989) has suggested that psychotherapists who tend to focus intensely on early repressed experiences often give much less credence to the present context of the people they see in therapy. That is, for these psychotherapists, context almost exclusively means their patients' memories of early experiences and how these are played out with the therapist. Wachtel adds, "A basic structure of Freudian thought . . . is to view desire itself as a kind of prime mover, emerging from within one person rather than from transactions with others . . . concerns for the welfare of others or the pleasure of joining with others in common purpose are secondary or derivative in nature." In contrast to this understanding of context, phenomenology "stresses that human existence is fundamentally relational. To be a person is to be open to, in relation to, concerned about, a world" (Valle and Halling 1989). This more inclusive emphasis on context, of course, was emphasized in the work of Sullivan (1954) and Horney (1937) as they viewed the person within the context of a particular society and culture whose values and attitudes at a given historical period impacted the person living in it. Skinner (1974), of course, has argued that all behavior is related to the environment in which it occurs.

Psychotherapy and Individualism

Sampson (1989) dates the modern era as beginning in the fifteenth and sixteenth centuries and as being the birthplace of our notion of the self-contained individual. In its vision, modernism changed the meaning of both individuals and of community. Persons were now viewed as detached from the social and historical contexts that had previously constituted their very being. Furthermore, since psychology grew up within this liberal individualist tradition, we should expect it to reveal a central feature of the tradition in its own theories of the person. Bellah (1985) described contemporary psychotherapy's Horatio Alger notion of change as concentrating on the individual rising above his or her context, as opposed to being limited by it or interacting with it. This notion of individualism conveys a sense of an autonomous self mainly concerned with issues of separation and individuation. Within this view, leaving home and starting one's life in a separated independent fashion is what we emphasize as a basic definition of health. Bellah notes that associated with individualism, especially in this country, is a division of one's life into separate functional sectors so that interrelationships in society between one's public and private self, between one's work and one's personal life, and between the external world and one's inner feelings are separated from each other.

Wachtel (1989) continues this theme of American individualism, noting that "individualistic thinking, particularly of a sort that stresses the separate responsibility of each person for himself and minimizes our interdependence, is a central feature of our society and shapes our assumptions about political and moral issues as it does our assumptions about psychotherapy." He goes on to state that "we have tended not to balance this attention to autonomy with a sufficient appreciation of the fact and the necessity of interdependence. A conceptual framework that most psychotherapy shares with the society at large makes it easy to conceive of our ethical responsibility to the patient as requiring that we ignore almost totally the needs of those around him." Jacobs (1988) more recently continues this discussion of Western, especially American, notions of individualism and the connection of these cultural values to psychotherapy in the following comments:

Psychoanalytic thought in America . . . may too often stress autonomy and self-reliance. The American view of ego psychology may subtly portray patients as psychological cowboys pushing back the frontiers of their own mental habitation, courageous settlers clearing the psychic landscape of obstacles so as to live in increasing domestic comfort and with greater financial personal reward. . . . As long as the language and conceptualization of psychoanalysis is weighted toward a language of radical autonomy and a one-person psychology, we will tend to think of ourselves and our patients as arbitrary centers of volition. We may be inadvertently locking ourselves and our patients into a cocoon of therapeutic narcissism that contributes to our own and our patients' growing sense of historical isolation and helplessness.

Thus our consideration of the rise of individualism and its influence on the theory and practice of psychotherapy enables us to understand how individual patients in psychotherapy or psychoanalysis would ignore more systemic roots of their problems and not discuss "external" political-social issues within their treatment hours, and how many therapists might not be able to hear such information as "therapy material."

ASKING ABOUT NUCLEAR-SOCIETAL-ENVIRONMENTAL
ISSUES IN THERAPY

I have discussed the above issues with a number of my colleagues. I have also done considerable therapy work on myself—exploring my motivations for avoiding such issues as a therapist as well as examining my motivations for wanting not to exclude such material in the therapy work I do with others. Through these efforts I became satisfied that any personal problems of my own were not major motivating forces in my interest in including the political-social self in psychotherapy. Rather, I did feel that I was practicing denial by not hearing and including such issues in my professional work.

Accordingly, I began considering asking all my new patients during one of their first sessions about whether they had any reactions or feelings about the issues of nuclear weapons, ecology, or the various social problems, including poverty and homelessness, that were periodically described and discussed by the media. My aim was not to proselytize my patients, but to make sure that any concerns they had about the state of the world and their own position could be stated during a session if they so chose. I was concerned, of course, that by introducing this material into therapy I would lead a patient to a particular direction that might not have been his or her own and thereby disturb the psychotherapy situation or transform it into one where the patient was acting in a way to please. I was also concerned about what might happen if I inquired as to whether nuclear or societal issues were concerns for the patient and then got a positive response from the patient. If my patients did begin talking about some of these issues, how would we use it in their psychotherapies?

I decided to ask all patients sometime during their first several "intake" sessions to tell me about how they saw the state of the world around them and any feelings they might have about this. I decided to ask this at this time because I use the first several sessions with a new patient to get acquainted and to help confirm or change decisions to work together in psychotherapy. So if a patient felt uneasy about my questions, he or she could choose not to continue to work with me. I would follow this initial question by saying that there has been coverage in newspapers and on the television news about nuclear issues, economic and social issues, and environmental issues, and asked if the patients had special feelings about any of these issues. What was it like for them to see or hear this? I did this within the context of getting some information from them at the beginning of therapy about their background, family of origin, relationships, job, and so forth.

I will present here brief summaries of my work on these issues with two particular patients and some general observations on this work with the total group.

Patient A

The first patient when I asked these questions said that he had thought about "all those issues"—alternately felt guilty, yet helpless about them —then paused to say that guilty and helpless were the ways he felt about a lot of things in this life. It turned out as his therapy progressed that this 35-year-old male professional who came in with feelings of depression and meaninglessness grew up in a physically abusive family. He described his parents as "good at looking good to others," but tightly controlling of their children's behavior and given to fits of anger during which they often beat the children seemingly with little or no provocation. He felt that it was crucial for his survival not to talk, not to think, and especially not to feel. He previously had never told anyone about his home situation. At the same time he had a younger sibling who did try to defend himself verbally and received even more severe punishment. As a youngster the patient witnessed his parents severely beating his younger brother on a number of occasions and was told if he misbehaved or talked about what he saw he would get the same treatment. He described the guilt at seeing his brother hurt but not trying to help him.

He talked about the world being a frightening and lonely place where one could do little more than hide from its blows. He described how he turned off the news on television and never read the front pages of the newspaper because they were too upsetting to him (although with friends he simply said it was because it was all too boring). He described feelings of helplessness and guilt when he would catch glimpses of the news before he turned it off. As treatment went on, he went back and forth between talking about the fears and guilt and helplessness he experienced while growing up (and his attempt to blot out this period from his memory), and the fears, guilt, and helplessness he felt on hearing the media today (and his attempts to blot out these feelings).

As treatment progressed, he allowed himself to recall more of the difficult early material *and* to allow himself to read more of the newspaper. He became involved in working for some social issues (especially those concerning child abuse) "to help those who may feel helpless themselves" as well as because he felt that he needed to do this for himself—part of his work at regaining his self-respect. This patient continues to work on his issues of trust and guilt in his treatment. He does this as he explores his inner memories that were long blocked off, as well as when he involves himself now with his brother and with societal problems about which he feels strongly.

I am sure that therapy with him would have been meaningful and helpful if I had not asked about nuclear and societal issues at the start. His fears, guilt, and helplessness have been themes throughout his life. But his talking about his societal concerns was important, as it offered him access to related feelings about his past, which had been too difficult to talk about before. In addition, talking in this way also has opened opportunities for him to try grappling with these issues in the wider world of others in addition to his inner explorations. One of the feelings he is beginning to report now is more of a feeling of "living in the world" as opposed to hiding in himself.

Patient B

I have found that references to death and destruction appear more frequently with this group of patients than in the therapy I had done previously. One of the first patients who made reference to issues of death was surprised by my asking him at the beginning of therapy about any feelings and reactions he might have had about how he perceived the state of the world. He, a 42-year-old physician who was married and the father of three children, said that he hadn't expected that kind of question. Being asked "that kind of question" scared him, although he did not know why it did.

In the early spring approximately one year later, as he and I talked of his work-driven style despite chronic feelings of exhaustion and depression, he referred back to my original questions. He commented, "You were really asking about death. The questions about nuclear and environmental stuff were really about death, about the fact that we all may have no future. It's almost beyond my imagining and yet it could happen. I feel overwhelmed by it and yet I think about it."

These thoughts had come to him as he, having decided to start a small garden, went into his yard to plant some vegetable seeds. As he began preparing the earth, he also was calculating the time until he would be able to enjoy the results of his labors. His next image was a scene out of one of the "Mad Max" videos he had seen at home with his son. The thought that followed was: "How do I know if these plants would survive a nuclear holocaust? Would I or anything survive? It could happen."

The image and the accompanying thoughts stayed with him. He found himself mourning the possible destruction of all life on this planet. He then recalled going through a serious illness and surgery that was almost fatal when he was about twelve. He said that he remembered overhearing his parents talking about death and suddenly realized that it was the possibility of his death that they were talking about. He recalled picturing his own death in a dream that occurred shortly after overhearing the conversation. He dreamed that he saw his dead body on a hospital bed surrounded by his family while he, the dreamer, tried to shout to his parents that he was still alive.

As we talked about the dream and then the scene from the video and then the ritual of preparing the earth for new growth, he said that he felt that he had always been living his life to avoid death. He felt that if he worked hard trying to help others, "death wouldn't come for me." He said that my early therapy questions seemed associated with the scenes from the video. They reminded him that death would come, and he was no longer able to deny or avoid it by working hard and avoiding the world around him.

As time went by he realized "as if for the first time" that he was alive; he had made it through that surgery. The dreamer who had shouted that he was alive was correct. This realization seemed to end his mourning and depression. He said that he felt as if he woke up from a coma "with a picture of death" that made him want to use his life despite the risks of living. He continues in therapy and recently said, "I feel as though I went through a sickness, a kind of death, and I think I am different now. I don't have to act as though I were dead. I must use my life for life. . . . We are all in debt to life for our lives and the only way to repay is to face our lives and this world." With this patient, mourning the possible death of the planet has led him to remember his own fear of death from when he was younger and then to a realization of the gift and the responsibility of and for life.

General Observations

I talked about these issues with a total of eighteen new patients over a period of thirty months. There have been patients who did not seem to react to my initial questions except to say that there were indeed big problems in the world and they hoped that the issues could be solved. Some said, "I hope the politicians in government get their acts together to do something about that." Others just shook their heads in recognition of the difficulties but said nothing. Some stated, "Things aren't always as bad as the media portray, and besides I have enough to worry about in my own life. I don't have time to worry about that, too." When I received responses such as these I generally did not comment, but as with any statement wondered what it might be indicating about the nature of the person sitting with me. Sometimes what has seemed to be a denial of nuclear and other dangers was simply one manifestation of a more general character structure of not facing difficult material from whatever source, but this has not always been the case. And often, but not always, a comment that referred societal problems to our government leaders for solution has been a more general statement about the patient's feeling of powerlessness and the giving up of responsibility to others.

There also have been a couple of patients who responded to my early question about social and global issues by spending a great deal of time talking about the possibility of the destruction of the planet and the amount of pain there is in the world, without facing their own personal pain. In these situations I simply would listen, acknowledge the scariness of the events, and also ask if they ever experienced similar feelings that seemed to originate from within themselves. As children both patients were caretakers to their parents. They seemed to have little sense of the legitimacy of their own needs. Part of my task in these cases was to call their attention to the many times they lapsed back into talking about nuclear, peace, and justice concerns as a way of avoiding their own dynamic issues. This is not to say that I ignored the importance of their concerns or their pain about events going on in the larger world. Integrating political-societal concerns into psychotherapy must mean, of course, that these issues *and* psychodynamic issues are both important in the composition of the self and in therapy.

Overall, my experience asking patients as they have begun therapy about any thoughts and reactions they might have about the state of the world has been quite positive and therapeutically productive. Out of this group of eighteen new patients, only one has decided not to continue to do therapy with me and in that case the patient was offered a promotion, which meant relocation. No patient has terminated therapy because of this approach. Several patients have begun working or volunteering within local nuclear, social justice, environmental, or political groups. At this point, thirteen of the eighteen patients have reported dreams involving death. Death is not only in their dreams, but it also surfaces as they report their reactions to newspaper articles, conversations with friends, television programs, and so on. With most of the patients there is a sense of helplessness and aloneness that goes with the themes of death and destruction. Yet as the talk continues, most often the depression yields to an anger and a conviction to use what energies they have to act for what they believe in—and this in turn seems to be leading them to increased connections to other people with similar commitments.

Approximately three-fourths of this group has spontaneously brought up, at some time over the course of their therapy, comments or showed reactions to something of the political-social world around them (e.g., a particular presidential action, encountering a homeless person on the street, votes on Contra aid, discussion of test bans, etc.). My response has been to listen carefully, acknowledge what I hear, and then to ask if the patient has any more thoughts or feelings about the matter. When I do listen, acknowledge, and ask about the comments, I find there is much that results. Often the patients will talk about their feelings of helplessness when dealing with these issues, or of feelings of being overwhelmed by the magnitude of the problems, or often of a grandiose sense of responsibility that drives them to feel that it is up to them to make the crucial difference in bringing peace to the world, and that anything less that results from their actions means they are a failure. Such conversations can continue into a deeper exploration of their more general feelings of helplessness (at least in part a reflection of their psychodynamic issues), or a sense of their needing to act on their beliefs in the world of others. It also may offer, as a number of patients have said, "one of the few places in my world where I can talk about these things and also have someone who really listens and doesn't tell me that I'm 'so depressing.' " One of these patients continued: "I usually feel when I talk about these things with people like I am a child at a party of grown-ups—all of whom shake their fingers at me and tell me that nice people don't talk about such things and that I had better learn that or no one will ever want to talk to me." (This is perhaps a clear example of an individual describing what Mack has called "collective resistance" and "the fear of a kind of tribal ostracism.")

With many of these patients I have the sense that in their therapy they are talking about themselves both in terms of their inner personal issues and as people connected to the world of others around them. As I compare therapy with these patients with my previous therapy, I am struck by the additional amount of therapy work we are doing that is concerned with connectedness and involvement with others in the world. Relationships with others of course are always a central part of the therapy conversation; however, earlier the focus was on establishing a strong sense of self and the capacity to love and be loved within a more circumscribed context. It is my sense that now the context is larger. There is a broader awareness, caring, and concern for the life of the community as well as a greater sense of connectedness to events in the larger national and even international context.

Overall, these questions seem to have played an important and positive part in patients' personal therapeutic work, and to have offered a place where "worldly" concerns can be expressed and acknowledged, where individuals can make clearer the links (in thoughts and in action) between their inner processes and the social and political world in which they live.

To quote Becker (in Porter et al. 1987), "We would err as clinicians if we did not look to the evocative material of our time and how it affects and intrudes on us." This is neither a denial of our patients' inner dynamics nor a denial of the world in which we live. If "the self is affected by powerful social and historical currents . . . we must assume that important things are happening to the contemporary self" (Lifton 1989). Let us make the most of these opportunities for our patients and ourselves.

REFERENCES

Becker, E. Addressing the Nuclear Issue in the Psychotherapy Hour: A Clinical and Personal Perspective. In *Heal or Die*, ed. by K. Porter, D. Rinzler, and P. Olsen. Psychohistory Press, New York, 1987.

Bellah, R., Madsen, R., Sullivan, W., Swidler, A., and Tipton, S. *Habits of the Heart*. University of California Press, Berkeley, 1985.

Gilbert, R. The Dynamics of Inaction: Psychological Factors Inhibiting Arms Control Activism. *Amer. Psychol.*, 43:755–764, 1988.

Horney, K. *The Neurotic Personality of Our Time*. Norton, New York, 1937.

Jacobs, D. Love, Work, and Survival. In *Psychoanalysis and the Nuclear Threat*, ed. by H. Levine, D. Jacobs, and L. Rubin. The Analytic Press, Hillsdale, N.J., 1988.

Levine, H., Jacobs, D., and Rubin, L. *Psychoanalysis and the Nuclear Threat*. The Analytic Press, Hillsdale, N.J., 1988.

Lifton, R. *The Broken Connection*. Basic Books, New York, 1979.

Lifton, R. *The Future of Immortality*. Basic Books, New York, 1989.

Lifton, R., and Falk, R. *Indefensible Weapons*. Basic Books, New York, 1982.

Mack, J. Resistance to Knowing in the Nuclear Age. *Harvard Ed. Rev.*, 54:260–270, 1984.

Mack, J. The Threat of Nuclear War in Clinical Work. In *Psychoanalysis and the Nuclear Threat*, ed. by H. Levine, D. Jacobs, and L. Rubin. The Analytic Press, Hillsdale, N.J., 1988.

Marmor, J. Psychiatry in a Troubled World: The Relation of Clinical Practice and Social Reality. *Am. J. Psychother.*, 58:484–491, 1988.

Parens, H. Psychoanalytic Explorations of the Impact of the Threat of Nuclear Disaster on the Young. In *Psychoanalysis and the Nuclear Threat*, ed. by H. Levine, D. Jacobs, and L. Rubin. The Analytic Press, Hillsdale, N.J., 1988.

Parker, R. Anti-Nuclear Weapons Advocacy: A Survey of American Psychological Association Members. Ph.D. diss., Texas A & M University, College Station, 1989.

Polyson, J., Stein, D., and Sholley, B. Psychologists and Nuclear War: A Survey. *Amer. Psychol.*, 41:724–725, 1986.

Porter, K., Rinzler, D., and Olsen, P. *Heal or Die*. Psychohistory Press, New York, 1987.

Prilleltensky, I. Psychology and the Status Quo. *Amer. Psychol.*, 44:795–802, 1989.

Robinson, D. Ethics and Advocacy. *Amer. Psychol.*, 39:787–793, 1984.

Rubin, L. Melancholia, Mourning, and the Nuclear Threat. In *Psychoanalysis and the Nuclear Threat*, ed. by H. Levine, D. Jacobs, and L. Rubin. The Analytic Press, Hillsdale, N.J., 1988.

Sampson, E. The Challenge of Social Change for Psychology. *Amer. Psychol.*, 44:914–921, 1989.

Segal, H. Silence Is the Real Crime. In *Psychoanalysis and The Nuclear Threat*, ed. by H. Levine, D. Jacobs, and L. Rubin. The Analytic Press, Hillsdale, N.J., 1988.

Skinner, B. *About Behaviorism.* Vintage, New York, 1974.

Staub, E. The Evolution of Bystanders, German Psychoanalysts, and Lessons for Today. *Pol. Psychol.*, 10:39–51, 1989.

Strozier, C. On Psychoanalysis and the Nuclear Threat. *Psychohistory Rev.*, 18:137, 1990.

Sullivan, H. *The Interpersonal Theory of Psychiatry.* Norton, New York, 1954.

Valle, R., and Halling, S. *Existential-Phenomenological Perspectives in Psychology.* Plenum, New York, 1989.

Wachtel, P. *The Poverty of Affluence.* New Society Publishers, Philadelphia, 1989.

Wachtel, E., and Wachtel, P. *Family Dynamics in Individual Psychotherapy.* The Guilford Press, New York, 1983.

Walsh, R. Toward a Psychology of Human Survival: Psychological Approaches to Contemporary Global Threats. This volume, chap. 3.

8

Family Therapy, Systems Theory, and Nuclear Issues

Bianca Cody Murphy and Jonathan W. Reusser

Family therapy is not only a clinical orientation to human problems but also represents a minority ideology . . . (which) challenges us to move beyond only clinical interpretations of our role. —*Liddle 1985, 6*

The field of family therapy has grown over the past thirty years to include numerous approaches and schools of thought. Among these are psychoanalytic family therapy (Ackerman 1966; Boszormenyi-Nagy and Sparks 1973), structural family therapy (Minuchin 1974), intergenerational family therapy (Bowen 1978), strategic family therapy (Haley 1976), and systemic family therapy (Selvini-Palazzoli, Boscolo, Cecchin, and Prata 1978), to name a few. Despite this diversity, most family therapists share a common set of assumptions that underlie their understanding of human behavior. They believe that individuals can best be understood within the context of the relationships in their lives. Family therapists maintain that there is more to a family than the sum of its constituent parts; that in addition to their individual members and subgroups of members, families (and other complex living systems) are also characterized by important patterns and processes that are not located within any particu-

This chapter is an expanded and updated version of J. Reusser and B. C. Murphy (1990), Family therapy in the nuclear age: From clinical to global. In M. Mirkin, ed., *The social and political contexts of family therapy*, pp. 395–407. Boston: Allyn & Bacon.

The authors wish to thank Margaret Herzig for her helpful comments on this chapter.

lar member. Family systems thinkers share a particular view of the nature of cause and effect. They believe that events that occur in families are not adequately described by viewing one particular action as a "cause" and another as an "effect." Rather, events in families and other complex systems mutually, simultaneously affect each other, both as cause and effect. Change or movement in one arena reverberates throughout multiply-embedded systems.

Therefore, family therapists recognize the importance of attending to the interactions between the interlocking systems within which the family is embedded—from the smaller ones like the extended family to the larger social and political contexts of racism, sexism, and poverty (Imber-Black 1986; Mirkin 1990; Schwartzman 1985). Recently, some family therapists, using their skills as family therapists and the lens provided by systemic thinking, have attempted to directly address these broader social issues.

One of the most pressing social issues confronting us today is the threat of nuclear holocaust. With the advent of nuclear arsenals, we have acquired the ability to destroy the world as we know it. Never before have humans been capable of such destruction. As Jonathan Schell (1982) has eloquently expressed it, today "the fate of the earth" lies in the balance. "Nuclear weapons radically alter our existence. Nothing we do or feel in working, playing and living, and in our private, family and public lives is free of this influence. The threat they pose has become the context of our lives, a shadow that persistently intrudes upon our mental ecology" (Lifton and Falk 1982, 3). Although there has been a warming of relations between the Soviet Union and the United States since Lifton and Falk's statement, the danger of nuclear weapons and international conflict remains a pressing concern. Ongoing fighting in the Middle East, continued outbreaks of regional conflicts, and the potential of nuclear proliferation maintain the shadow of nuclear threat.

Recently, family therapists have become involved in applying their theoretical and clinical skills to the challenges of the nuclear threat. Over the last ten years, a small but growing body of literature has developed in which family therapists discuss the impact of the nuclear threat on families and children. More recently, a handful of family therapists have attempted to address the impact family therapists might have on the social and political context in which the threat is embedded, both on the national and the international level. In this chapter, we undertake to describe some of the work currently being done by family therapists to address the nuclear threat, ranging from interventions made in the clinical setting to those made in the international/global arena.

PSYCHOLOGY IN THE NUCLEAR AGE

The broader field of psychology has long been committed to applying psychological concepts to issues in the nuclear age (Morawski and Goldstein 1985). In the late '50s and early '60s such eminent psychologists as Urie Bronfenbrenner (1961); Morton Deutsch (1963); Jerome Frank (1960, 1967); Herbert Kelman (1966); and Charles Osgood (1959, 1962) wrote about international relations in the nuclear age. Psychological concepts such as aggression, attribution, cognition, conflict resolution, game theory, group psychology, mirror image, negotiation, perception, personality theory, and psychoanalysis were applied to understanding nuclear strategy and international relations.

There was a decline in interest in nuclear issues on the part of psychologists in the 1970s, perhaps reflecting the decreased interest on the part of the public as a whole after the trauma of the Cuban Missile Crisis, the ensuing test ban treaty of 1963, and the upsurge of interest in other social issues such as poverty, racism, and the like (Morawski and Goldstein 1985).

However, the 1980s saw a resurgence on the part of the psychological community in both research and writing on the nuclear threat. Psychologists have continued their writings about international relations (Blight 1987, 1988; Deutsch 1983; Frank 1987; Jervis, Lebow, and Stein 1985; Kelman 1986; Lifton and Falk 1982; Mack 1985; White 1984, 1986). Psychologists have also focused attention on the psychological effects of living in the nuclear age. Many researchers (Beardslee and Mack 1982; Escalona 1982; Goodman, Mack, Beardslee, and Snow 1983; Schwebel 1982, 1986) have studied the impact of the nuclear threat on children in particular. Others have examined attitudes toward nuclear issues and the connection between attitudes and activism (Fiske 1987; Kramer, Kalick, and Milburn 1983; Tyler and McGraw 1983). Psychologists have also begun to introduce war, peace, international relations, and nuclear issues into the psychology classroom (Moyer 1987; Murphy and Polyson, 1991; Wagner and Bronzaft 1987). In 1989 the American Psychological Association approved its newest division, Division 48—The Division of Peace

Psychology. The division encourages psychological research on peace, nonviolent conflict resolution and reconciliation, as well as the application of psychological knowledge and methods to these issues.

FAMILY THERAPY AND NUCLEAR ISSUES

As family therapists we are faced with the dilemma of the nuclear threat in dual roles: as clinicians and as citizens. How are we to help families discover affirmative ways to face a situation so overwhelming and unthinkable? How can we use our skills as creators of context to foster meaningful and novel dialogue in the global arena? Compared to their colleagues in individual psychology, who have been active in nuclear issues since the 1940s, family therapists have only recently begun to address themselves to this topic.

In 1982, the American Family Therapy Association (AFTA) established the Nuclear Issues Task Force. The goal of the task force has been to lend support to family therapists addressing nuclear issues in their professional roles. AFTA is in the process of publishing its first book, entitled *Family Systems Thinking and Global Security* (Berger Gould and DeMeuth, in press).

It was also in 1982 that Don Bloch and Peggy Penn of the Ackerman Family Institute organized a session at the Annual Meeting of the other major family therapy organization, the American Association of Marriage and Family Therapists (AAMFT), to explore the role family therapists could play in preventing nuclear holocaust. During discussions that took place at that meeting, it was pointed out that "family therapy concepts like reframing, paradox, symmetrical escalation, and systems and cybernetics theory . . . [might be] valuable tools for understanding the nuclear threat, and thus somehow could be our contribution toward finding a solution" (Fine 1984, 69).

Family therapists have also been active in the Nuclear Issues Study Group of the American Orthopsychiatric Association (ORTHO). The annual meetings of ORTHO have had nuclear issues as a focus in plenary sessions since the beginning of the '80s. The annual ORTHO program contains workshops, papers, and panels addressing nuclear concerns from a family therapy perspective.

The work in which family therapists are engaged to meet the challenge of the nuclear threat can be divided into three types: those that focus on

family/clinical approaches; those that attempt to make community/edu-
cational interventions; and those that explore how family systems concepts can be applied to the international/global arena.

Family/Clinical Approaches

Many family systems therapists who have addressed nuclear issues have
been working in the context of the clinical setting. In their clinical work,
they have helped clients focus on the effects of living in the nuclear age
—anxiety, fear, depression, numbness, a sense of powerlessness and
isolation. Some approaches to this work are *responsive;* others are *evocative.*

Some family therapists have responded to clients' nuclear worries as
they appear in the clinical setting. For example, it is not uncommon for
the adolescent engaged in a struggle with her parents over her school
performance to announce that there is no point to studying, since the
world could blow up any day. While it is tempting to treat this as an
evasive maneuver on her part, the alert family therapist can also see it as
an opportunity for dialogue about very real fears shared by the entire
family. A sensitive inquiry about the impact of such a statement on the
rest of the family can assist all the family members to draw upon their
collective strength in facing serious obstacles to productive living. Nuclear concerns often surface in the form of sardonic humor about the end
of the world, or in allusions to unnerving dreams of global disaster. The
family therapist concerned with responding to these worries will ask how
much the clients worry about nuclear war, to whom they talk about it,
and how it affects their vision of their future.

While some families are coping with fears of nuclear radiation, others
are coping with the actuality of nuclear exposure. In their work with
families of atomic veterans—veterans who were exposed to ionizing
radiation as part of the above-ground nuclear testing between 1944 and
1963—Murphy, Ellis, and Greenberg (1990) note that the veteran's
exposure to low level ionizing radiation had powerful psychological effects on all members of the family. They describe the themes common to
the families attempting to cope with the reality of radiation and exposure
and, in a subsequent paper (Ellis, Greenberg, Murphy, and Reusser, in

press), they discuss implications for clinicians working with families concerned with nuclear and other environmental contaminants.

Other family therapists have initiated discussions with clients about nuclear concerns. Wetzel and Winawer (1986) have said:

The threat of global nuclear extinction constitutes a danger to the survival of every family, couple, or individual who comes into our practice. The consequences of this danger for the physical and mental health, for the general well-being, of our clients, particularly the children and young adults, are becoming increasingly evident. This threat is therefore of immediate therapeutic concern and should be part of our professional responsibilities. (305)

Some family therapists agree with their view that it is, therefore, appropriate for the family therapist to initiate discussion of the nuclear threat with clients, just as the therapist inquires about issues such as money, sex, or religion. These issues are often of pressing concern to family members although they may at first be reluctant to discuss them. The therapist's willingness to speak openly about the nuclear threat can offer the family the opportunity for enhanced dialogue in a previously taboo area.

DeMeuth (1990) discusses the ways in which nuclear stress affects family coping patterns, and offers a model for effective family functioning vis-á-vis nuclear issues. She argues that families should have open communication about their concerns. Discussion of these concerns, DeMeuth believes, should lead to family action in world affairs, which would lead to a greater sense of mastery and connection with others. Parents should assume leadership and facilitate this action in ways that are appropriate to the developmental stage of the family.

Nuclear issues can evoke powerful reactions—outrage, fear, helplessness, despair—not only in clients but also in therapists. Therapists themselves need to find supportive places to deal with the feelings that nuclear issues evoke. Ellis et al. (1992) note that it is important that family therapists receive supervision to monitor their feelings and to prevent their own values from interfering with the clients' ability to come to terms with these issues.

We should also be aware that clients may undergo changes in their political views during therapy. Clients may want to take political action themselves at different times. But clinicians must avoid pushing them into action or condemning them for inaction even if the clinicians believe in the importance of taking action themselves (1992).

Community/Educational Interventions

Many family therapists believe we have a responsibility that extends beyond therapy into the larger community. An increasing number of projects are being undertaken by family therapists that address the impact of the nuclear threat on our daily lives in a nonclinical, educational context (Berger Gould 1986; Eisenbud, Van Hoorn, and Berger Gould 1986; Greenwald and Forman 1987; Reusser 1987; Simon 1984; Zeitlin 1984). Many educational workshops, seminars, and family interviews have been designed in a wide variety of formats; some of these are described in more detail below for the purpose of illustration.

In gathering data for their research, Greenwald and Zeitlin (1987) asked families to have a conversation about their feelings and thoughts about the possibility of nuclear war. These conversations were themselves powerful educational interventions, frequently resulting in parents and children talking with each other in a new way. In follow-up interviews, some of the families studied had the opportunity to view the videotapes of their interview. These interviews were even more exciting, in some ways, than the initial ones. Family members now had the opportunity to see themselves as they appeared to others and, more importantly, to share their reactions to their own statements and behavior. These interviews usually led to both an enhanced acknowledgment of shared feelings of vulnerability and an affirmation of the family's caring for each other. (See Zeitlin's discussion of these issues in chapter 19 of this volume.)

Another approach taken by many family therapists involves direct work with parents on the difficulties they face in dealing with their children about the nuclear threat. A wide variety of educational seminars and parenting workshops have been developed for use with school, community, and religious groups. A typical example of this type of workshop has been described by Reusser (1987). In these workshops, groups of parents met without their children, comparing their own experiences as they became aware of the nuclear threat and the beliefs they developed in response. The parents role-played conversations with their children about the nuclear threat, providing them with the opportunity both to play out the question they dreaded being asked by their own children, and to compare their fears with those of other parents. The dialogue generated in such workshops usually had the effect of alleviating the sense of isolation felt by many parents around this issue, clarifying the areas in which some parents felt blocked, and affirming many parents' resolve to face squarely their own feelings and those of their families about the nuclear threat.

Berger Gould and her colleagues have developed a series of multigenerational family workshops in which they bring together four or five families with children of various ages "to facilitate communications between family members of different generations about the nuclear threat and to redefine nuclear anxiety as a normal shared feeling" (Berger Gould 1986, 115). They found that it was easier for children to talk to parents other than their own. As a result of their experiences, they developed a series of guidelines entitled "How to Talk to Your Children About Nuclear War" (Berger Gould, Eden, and Gould 1984).

The educational efforts of these and other family therapists are founded on the belief that increased dialogue about thoughts and feelings about the nuclear threat will deepen the participants' relationships and open the door to an increased sense of social connectedness and responsibility.

International/Global Arena

What are family systems therapists doing in the international sphere, not only to deal with the effects of living with the nuclear dilemma but also to explore the underlying international conflicts and the belief systems which perpetuate them? In reviewing the literature and conducting interviews with family therapists involved in nuclear issues, we have found two broad categories in which family therapists are attempting to have an impact in the international/global arena: international community building and the application of systems thinking on a global level.

1. *International community building.* Many family therapists have become involved in international exchanges with other family therapists, creating opportunities for personal contact and dialogue between citizens of different countries beyond the bounds of traditional diplomatic channels. Family therapist Berger Gould (1985) explains the rationale for these exchanges with reference to Bateson's (1971) ideas on differ-

ence: "If new information and energy proceed from the study of differences, it is logical to conclude that information taken in from visiting another culture will change our way of thinking about that culture" (68).

Family therapists believe that changes at any point in the system reverberate throughout the system. Meaningful contact between people of different countries and cultures, and resultant changes in beliefs about each other, will effect changes in the beliefs held in the wider cultures of each country about the other. Concurrently, changes in popular beliefs and cultural attitudes will be felt at the level of international policy and decision making. For example, it can be argued that the numerous Soviet-American citizen exchanges in the 1980s helped to produce the dramatic changes in popular American imagery about Soviet culture and people and contributed to the changing political relations between the two countries.

Within the family therapy community, family therapists have been working with their colleagues in international professional organizations to address the roles that family therapists can take in response to the nuclear threat. At the International Family Therapy Conference entitled "The Pattern Which Connects," held in Prague in May 1987, an entire half day was devoted to nuclear issues. One panel, composed of participants from both East and West, discussed nuclear issues and their psychological impact on the family. A number of papers were presented and participants were able to meet in small international groups (Winawer, pers. comm., September 10, 1987). Two subsequent international family therapy conferences, one in Budapest in 1989 and the other in Krakow in 1990, have helped the development of an active international community of family therapists.

Bloch (pers. comm., September 18, 1990) noted a shift during the course of these conferences from a preoccupation with issues of the Cold War to discussions of the changing political realities and governmental structures that resulted from the lessening of tensions between the Soviet Union and the United States and the political upheaval of Eastern Europe in the late 1980s. In the later conferences, family therapists addressed the important role of the family in the face of a decline of governmental structures. Bloch suggests that the family therapy community can help develop a vision of the centrality of the human family in dealing with the hardship of transition.

2. *Systems thinking on a global level.* Over the past decade, a few family therapists have begun to apply family systems concepts to the sphere of international relations. Early efforts drew parallels between the superpowers and conflicted marital systems (Berger Gould 1986) or tried to construct a meta-position from which to be a "family therapist to the world" (Fine 1984).

Chasin and Herzig (1987) offer a thoughtful application of family systems theory to the patterns of geopolitical conflict and the belief systems that underlie this conflict. The notion of "circular causality" is a pivotal family systems concept with clear application to the nuclear threat. Circular causality refers to the belief that events which occur in complex systems, such as the global community, reciprocally influence each other, with each event existing both as cause and effect of the others. An example of this principle familiar to most family therapists is that of the couple in which one member showers his or her partner with affection, wishing to become more intimate. The partner, feeling smothered and invaded, becomes unresponsive and withdrawn. The first partner, alarmed at this distancing, redoubles his or her attentions. And so on, indefinitely. Each partner sees the other as "causing" the problem. A similar pattern of thought and behavior can be seen in relationships between nations and other groups with differing ideologies.

Chasin and Herzig (1987) highlight two related notions. One is the idea that "action patterns and belief systems have a circular relationship to each other: actions are justified by beliefs and beliefs rationalize actions" (2). For example, the American belief that the Soviets seek nuclear superiority justifies American initiatives in building a new generation of space weapons. These actions reinforce Soviet beliefs that Americans seek nuclear superiority. These beliefs in turn justify Soviet initiatives in space weaponry. These Soviet actions in turn reinforce the American beliefs with which we began. In this way we can see that the belief systems and action patterns of both parties have a reciprocal influence on each other.

A related concept is that of "punctuation," the way in which people construct complex circular realities into simple linear causes and effects. In trying to make sense out of a set of complex related behaviors, such as the arms race, people tend to see the behavior as having starting points ("causes") and stopping points ("effects"). However, the choice of a specific event as a starting or a stopping point is an arbitrary one. Chasin and Herzig (1987) point out that the way in which we designate certain events as causes and others as effects, that is, the way in which we punctuate events, flows from our belief systems and also tends to support them. The process of punctuation has profound significance on our understanding of conflict, and on our attempts to move beyond it. On the global level, each nation sees their own hostile actions as responses to provocations by an adversary, both supported by and reinforcing beliefs that the other country embodies dangerous and untrustworthy attributes.

Another family therapy concept applied by Chasin and Herzig to the international/global arena is that of "symmetrical escalation." In work with families, therapists often see relationships as either complementary or symmetrical. In complementary relationships, the participants occupy significantly different positions: typically, one is more powerful than the other. Some examples of this type of relationship are the boss-underling system, the pursuer-distancer system, and the persecutor-victim system. In symmetrical relationships, however, the participants hold roughly equivalent power, and behave toward each other in a similar manner. In families, we see this manifested, for example, in a blamer-blamer interaction. When one partner finds fault with the other, the second is likely to respond with a counteraccusation, to which the first will react with intensified blaming, and so on. This illustrates symmetrical escalation, which Chasin and Herzig point out "has the potential for great destructiveness" (4). On the international level, this process is all too familiar. Chasin and Herzig suggest that not only the actions of nations, but also the belief systems they hold about each other, can be involved in symmetrical escalation.

Chasin and Herzig (1987) make a final point: just as the family therapist "explores the negative consequences of apparently positive change, . . . we must make that inquiry, also, in our study of obstacles to true international security" (5). They give as an example the possibility that if there were no nuclear standoff between the United States and the Soviet Union the then stable NATO and Warsaw Pact alliances might destabilize. Events since that time have borne out their hypothesis.

A different application of family therapy concepts to the international level was made by Wetzel and Winawer (1986). They point out that families can collectively exhibit self-destructive behavior that does not reside in a single family member. In a similar manner, the global community appears to have self-destructive elements that are not inherent in particular nations, or in particular decision-making bodies. They note that change can originate and flow from anywhere in the system, not just from the governing group. Wetzel and Winawer are hopeful that changes that family therapists are able to effect in smaller systems will ultimately bear fruit in the international arena.

Other family therapists are interested in the usefulness of family therapy concepts to nuclear strategists. Bloch has proposed setting up a context within which systems thinkers could join with nuclear policymakers and strategists, hopefully creating the opportunity for unexpected solutions to emerge. He imagines that the knowledge held by systems thinkers that would be appealing to strategists would be precisely in the area of the unanticipated or counterintuitive behavior of complex human systems—that its, how to understand why, and predict when, elaborate strategies produce unpredictable kinds of change (Bloch, pers. comm. August 15, 1987).

Although most of what has been written about the application of family therapy concepts to the global arena is theoretical in nature, Chasin, Herzig, and Gutlove, of the Center for Psychological Studies in the Nuclear Age at Harvard Medical School, have developed and implemented international workshops that make use of family systems theory and tools. The goal of these workshops is to facilitate dialogue and "to unearth and to help transform destructive assumptions and perceptions in an atmosphere of openness and curiosity" (*Center Review*, Spring, 1988, 10). Their work is one of the few examples of the active application of systems techniques to the global level.

The first workshop was conducted in Moscow with a Soviet colleague at the 1987 International Physicians for the Prevention of Nuclear War (IPPNW) Congress (Chasin and Herzig 1988a). The workshop was designed to elicit the assumptions that members of national groups make about one another, assumptions which may contribute to the arms race and international conflict. The workshop employed a form of circular questioning called "mind reading," often used by family therapists in couples work. This type of questioning is used to stimulate a variety of beliefs in areas where there has been a fair amount of rigid thinking. In the workshop, participants were divided into groups of allies and asked to list assumptions they believed other groups held about their own country's cultural characteristics and political objectives. These assumptions had to have the additional characteristic of contributing to international tension and danger. Members of each group were then given an opportunity to identify some of the assumptions as less accurate than others and to attempt "to refute the mistaken assumption that aroused in him/her the strongest negative feeling" (95).

For example, the Soviets and their allies listed as an assumption they felt others held of them that they seek to dominate the world by force. One Soviet woman said: "My generation can still feel the war pain (from World War II). There may be people dissatisfied with the socialist order but you won't find a single person for war." The Americans and their allies felt others presumed that they believe a nuclear war can be won. They strongly disavowed this assumption (Herzig, pers. comm., January 8, 1991).

When dealing with people who are stuck in rigid belief systems, one approach used by family therapists is to flood them with information which does not directly contradict their belief systems, but which does not support those beliefs either. This induces a sort of "benign confusion" (Chasin, pers. comm., June 24, 1987). Because it is nonconfrontational, this approach evokes a thoughtful or curious response rather than a defensive one. This is one of the principles applied in the Chasin workshop. The participants are exposed to an array of new information, presented in a format that avoids accusation and direct contradiction of beliefs. Furthermore, participants can learn about the sensitivities and concerns of their counterparts. When stereotypes are disavowed with emotion, "hot" areas in the relationship are identified. When stereotypes are listed but not disavowed, participants implicitly own up to their contribution to hostilities. Workshop participants report that they learn a lot about each other and themselves. Authentic expressions of concern and good-humored self-criticism were found to engender warmth and enhance empathy (Chasin and Herzig 1988c, 5).

Variations of this workshop have been implemented in Canada, Australia, Japan, and Stockholm.

In another workshop setting, Chasin invited family systems therapist Michael White to interview a group of defense analysts and "nuclear psychologists" (psychologists active in applying psychological concepts and theories to nuclear issues), all of whom were concerned with avoiding nuclear war, albeit from widely divergent perspectives (Chasin and Herzig 1988b). White applied principles he would use in a clinical family therapy interview: helping the participants to become aware of how they were oppressed by a shared problem and to notice exceptions to the "problem saturated" description of their situation. This opens the possibility for new descriptions and new ideas about themselves and their future. The problem, in this context, was the unproductive and ritualized debate between the two factions. White made use of a reflecting team, another common systemic therapy tool. Members of the reflecting team observed behind a one-way mirror, then reversed roles with the participants. While behind the mirror, the two groups of nuclear psychologists and defense intellectuals were united as one group in relation to the reflecting team. Through the course of the interview, participants found that they were able to disassemble their previously ritualistic debates and engage in new forms of dialogue.

Chasin, Gutlove, and Herzig are currently working at the Center for Psychological Studies in the Nuclear Age at Harvard University Medical School on their project: Promoting Effective Dialogue Across Ideologies. In April 1990 the project convened a two-day workshop for leaders in the field of dialogue facilitation (Herzig, Gutlove, and Chasin 1990). Gutlove collaborated in a meeting of arms control experts in Geneva, Switzerland in June 1990 (Gutlove 1990). The project members continue to use systems concepts to help facilitate dialogue among groups whose perceptions of each other may be distorted by hostility, and to promote collaboration among individuals whose pursuit of common goals may be hampered by ideological and/or institutional differences.

The work of Chasin, Herzig, and Gutlove demonstrates the effectiveness of applying family systems concepts on the global level. It is important that their work and the thinking of other family therapists like Bloch, Berger Gould, Wetzel, and Winawer stimulate still others to apply their skills to the global arena.

CONCLUSIONS

Although family therapists are working in widely varied arenas to address the challenge posed by the nuclear dilemma, their work shares common themes.

Whether their focus is in the clinical, the educational, or the international sphere, family therapists working on nuclear issues share a belief that in seeking new responses to the nuclear threat it is crucial that we direct attention into arenas that have previously been unexplored or unnoticed. This is clearly seen in the efforts of those family therapists who are attempting to enable families to move beyond the taboo against acknowledging their reactions to the nuclear threat. It can also be observed in the efforts of family therapists who, in the international sphere, are exploring the ways in which our belief systems evolve and are maintained, and how they might be transformed.

A second shared belief is in the creative potential of dialogue. It is through true dialogue, the juxtaposition of multiple perspectives and descriptions, that we can move beyond the limitations of linear beliefs in which the nuclear dilemma is embedded. Family therapists are often specialists in the creation of contexts in which dialogue can take place in novel ways between people with differing, and sometimes conflicting, experiences and beliefs. Whether the context involves parents and children, Arab and Israeli citizens, or the policymakers that shape our nuclear policy, the interventions we have discussed all suggest the importance of true conversations and dialogue.

Finally, most family therapists recognize that intervention in any part of a system will have reverberations in the entire system. The work of family therapists in nuclear issues shares the idea that whether one is working with individual clients, with parents, or with national leaders, all are working to impact the global arena, that is, to prevent nuclear destruction. The work in all these areas is important and mutually reinforcing.

We have attempted to present an overview of the variety of ways in which family therapists are using their skills to address the nuclear threat in many arenas: the clinical, community, and international/global. The challenge presented to us by the nuclear threat is overwhelming; it raises extremely high levels of anxiety and often results in apathy and despair. Linear approaches to problem solving tend to reinforce despair, since so many steps seem necessary to be taken in a sequential fashion before one reaches a solution. Family therapy concepts, which are often circular and ecological, highlight the interconnections between elements in complex systems. Family therapists, therefore, recognize that transformations can take place in a large system by an effective intervention in any of its subsystems. This can help empower those of us who might otherwise be overwhelmed and incapacitated by the magnitude of the nuclear challenge.

REFERENCES

Ackerman, N. W. (1966). *Treating the troubled family.* New York: Basic Books.

Bateson, G. (1971). The cybernectics of "self": A theory of alcoholism. *Psychiatry, 34,* 1–8.

Beardslee, W., and Mack, J. (1982). The impact on children and adolescents of nuclear developments. In American Psychiatric Task Force Report, No. 20. *Psychosocial aspects of nuclear development* (pp. 64–93). Washington, D.C.: American Psychiatric Association.

Berger Gould, B. (1985). Large systems and peace. *Journal of Strategic and Systemic Therapies, 4*(2), 64–69.

Berger Gould, B. (1986). Siblings in the same race: Family therapists and the nuclear issue. In M. Ault-Riche, ed., *Women and family therapy,* 112–116. Rockville, Md.: Aspen.

Berger Gould, B., and DeMeuth, D. H., eds. (In press). *Family systems thinking and global security.* Boston: Allyn and Bacon.

Berger Gould, B., Eden, E., and Gould, J. B. (1984, Summer). How to talk to your children about nuclear war. *Therapy Now.*

Blight, J. (1987). Toward a policy-relevant psychology of avoiding nuclear war: Lessons for psychologists from the Cuban missile crisis. *American Psychologist, 4,* 12–29.

Blight, J. (1988). Can psychology help reduce the risk of nuclear war? Reflections of a "little drummer boy" of nuclear psychology. *Journal of Humanistic Psychology, 28*(2), 7–58.

Boszormenyi-Nagy, I., and Sparks, G. (1973). *Invisible loyalties: Reciprocity in intergenerational family therapy.* New York: Harper and Row.

Bowen, M. (1978). *Family therapy in clinical practice.* New York: Jason Aronson.

Bronfenbrenner, U. (1961). The mirror image in Soviet-American relations: A social-psychologist's report. *Journal of Social Issues, 16*(3), 45–56.

Center Review (Spring, 1988, p. 10). (Available from the Center for Psychological Studies in the Nuclear Age, 1493 Cambridge Street, Cambridge, MA 02139.)

Chasin, R., and Herzig, M. (1987). A systems theory approach to US/Soviet relations. A working paper of the Project on Assumptions and Perceptions that Fuel the Nuclear Arms Race. (Available from the Center for Psychological Studies in the Nuclear Age, 1493 Cambridge Street, Cambridge, MA 02139.)

Chasin, R., and Herzig, M. (1988a). Correcting misperceptions in Soviet-American relations. *Journal of Humanistic Psychology, 28*(3), 88–97.

Chasin, R., and Herzig, M. (1988b). Traversing the American "peace activist-defense analyst" impasse. *Family Therapy Case Studies, 3*(2), 35–39.

Chasin, R., and Herzig, M. (1988c). Mind-reading in Soviet-American dialogue. *Center Review, 2*(1), 1,5.

DeMeuth, D. H. (1990). Some implications of the threat of nuclear war for families and family therapists. In M. Mirkin, ed., *The social and political contexts of family therapy,* 335–381. Boston: Allyn and Bacon.

Deutsch, M. (1963). On changing an adversary. *American Journal of Orthopsychiatry, 33,* 244–246.

Deutsch, M. (1983). The prevention of World War III: A psychological perspective. *Political Psychology, 4,* 3–31.

Eisenbud, M. M., Van Hoorn, J. L., and Berger Gould, B. (1986). Children, adolescents, and the threat of nuclear war: An international perspective. In D. Jelliffee, ed., *Advances in international maternal and child health,* vol. 6. Fairlawn, N.J.: Oxford University Press.

Ellis, P., Greenberg, S., Murphy, B. C., and Reusser, J. W. (1992). Environmentally contaminated families: Therapeutic considerations. *American Journal of Orthopsychiatry, 62.*

Escalona, S. K. (1982). Growing up with the threat of nuclear war: Some indirect effects on personality development. *American Journal of Orthopsychiatry, 52,* 600–607.

Fine, M. (1984). Family therapists and symmetrical nuclear escalation. *Journal of Strategic and Systemic Therapies, 3*(1), 66–71.

Fiske, S. (1987). People's reactions to nuclear war: Implications for psychologists. *American Psychologist, 42,* 207–217.

Frank, J. (1960). Breaking the thought barrier: Psychological challenge in the nuclear age. *Psychiatry, 23,* 245–266.

Frank, J. (1967). *Sanity and survival: Psychological aspects of war and peace.* New York: Vintage Books.

Frank, J. (1987). The drive for power and the nuclear arms race. *American Psychologist, 42,* 337–344.

Goodman, L. A., Mack, J. E., Beardslee, W. R., and Snow, R. M. (1983). The threat of nuclear war and the nuclear arms race: Adolescent experience and perceptions. *Political Psychology, 4,* 501–530.

Greenwald, D., and Forman, W. (1987). Families communicating about the nuclear threat. Paper presented at the Annual Meeting of the American Orthopsychiatric Association, Washington, D.C.

Greenwald, D., and Zeitlin, S. (1987). *No reason to talk about it: Families confront the nuclear taboo.* New York: Norton.

Gutlove, P. (1990). Adding new dimensions to the disarmament debate: Dialogue among international arms control experts. *Center Review, 4*(2), 9. (Available from the Center for Psychological Studies in the Nuclear Age, 1493 Cambridge Street, Cambridge, MA 02139.)

Haley, J. (1976). *Problem solving therapy.* San Francisco: Jossey-Bass.

Herzig, M., Gutlove, P., and Chasin, R. (1990). Facilitating the facilitators: Defining and advancing the field of dialogue facilitation. *Center Review, 4* (2), 8–10. (Available from the Center for Psychological Studies in the Nuclear Age, 1493 Cambridge Street, Cambridge, MA 02139.)

Imber-Black, E. (1986). *Families and larger systems: A therapist's guide through the labyrinth.* New York: Guilford.

Jervis, R., Lebow, R. N., and Stein, J. G. (1985). *Psychology and deterrence.* Baltimore, Md.: Johns Hopkins University Press.

Kelman, H., ed. (1966). *International behavior: A sociological analysis.* New York: Holt, Rinehart and Winston.

Kelman, H. (1986). An interactional approach to conflict resolution. In R. White, ed., *Psychology and the prevention of nuclear war,* 171–193. New York: New York University Press.

Kramer, B. M., Kalick, S. M., and Milburn, M. A. (1983). Attitudes toward nuclear weapons and nuclear war: 1945–1982. *Journal of Social Issues, 39*(1), 7–24.

Liddle, H. (1985). Beyond family therapy: Challenging the boundaries, roles, and mission of a field. *Journal of Strategic and Systemic Therapy, 4*(2), 6.

Lifton, J., and Falk, R. (1982). *Indefensible weapons; The political and psychological case against nuclearism.* New York: Basic Books.

Mack, J. (1985). Toward a collective psychopathology of the nuclear arms competition. *Political Psychology, 6,* 291–321.

Minuchin, S. (1974). *Families and family therapy.* Cambridge, Mass.: Harvard University Press.

Mirkin, M., ed. (1990). *The social and political contexts of family therapy.* Boston; Allyn and Bacon.

Morawski, J. G., and Goldstein, S. C. (1985). Psychology and nuclear war: A chapter in our legacy of social responsibility. *American Psychologist, 40,* 276–284.

Moyer, R. S. (1987). Teaching psychology courses on the nuclear arms race. *Contemporary Psychology, 12,* 101–110.

Murphy, B. C., and Polyson, J. A. (1991). Peace, war, and nuclear issues in the psychology classroom. *Teaching of Psychology, 18,* 153–157.

Murphy, B. C., Ellis, P., and Greenberg, S. (1990). Atomic veterans and their families: Responses to radiation exposure. *American Journal of Orthopsychiatry, 60,* 418–427.

Osgood, C. (1959). Suggestions for winning the real war with communism. *Journal of Conflict Resolution, 3,* 295–325.

Osgood, C. (1962). *An alternative to war or surrender.* Urbana, Ill.: University of Illinois Press.

Reusser, J. W. (1987). Working with parents around nuclear threat. Paper presented at the Annual Meeting of the American Orthopsychiatric Association, Washington, D.C.

Schell, J. (1982). *The fate of the earth.* New York: Avon.

Schwartzman, J., ed. (1985). *Families and other systems: The macrosystemic context of family therapy.* New York: Guilford.

Schwebel, M. (1982). The effects of nuclear war threat on children and teenagers: Implications for professionals. *American Journal of Orthopsychiatry, 52,* 608–618.

Schwebel, M. (1986). *Mental health implications of life in the nuclear age.* Armonk, N.Y.: Sharpe.

Selvini-Palazzoli, M., Boscolo, L., Cecchin, G., and Prata, G. (1978). *Paradox and counterparadox.* New York: Jason Aronson.

Simon, R. (1984). The nuclear family. *The Family Therapy Networker, 8*(2), 22.

Tyler, T. R., and McGraw, K. M. (1983). The treat of nuclear war: Risk interpretation and behavioral response. *Journal of Social Issues, 42*(3), 207–217.

Wagner, R. V., and Bronzaft, A. L. (1987). Sprinkling psychology courses with peace. *Teaching of Psychology, 14,* 75–81.

Wetzel, N., and Winawer, H. (1986). The psychological consequences of the nuclear threat from a family systems perspective. *International Journal of Mental Health, 15* (1–3), 298–313.

White, R. K. (1984). *Fearful warriors: A psychological profile of US-Soviet relations.* New York: Free Press.

White, R. K., ed. (1986). *Psychology and the prevention of nuclear war.* New York: New York University Press.

Zeitlin, S. (1984). What do we tell mom and dad? *Family Therapy Networker, 31,* 38–39.

9

Powerlessness, Politics, and Prevention: The Community Mental Health Approach

George W. Albee

INTRODUCTION

I would like to begin this presentation with a parable. About four years ago I was invited to give a talk at Grand Rounds in Psychiatry at the Downstate Medical Center in Brooklyn, New York. Psychiatry there is housed in one of a cluster of high-rise expensive hospitals sitting right in the middle of the Bedford-Stuyvesant district, one of the worst slums in North America. But because the hospitals cannot be moved, and the investment in them is enormous, they function, but with a very tight security system.

I flew down from Vermont to LaGuardia Airport early one morning. When I got into the New York taxicab outside the LaGuardia air terminal and told the driver where I wanted to go, he said, "You don't want to go there!"

I said, "Yes, I do."

He said, "Well, *I* don't want to go there!" I reminded him that he was obligated by law to take any sober person to any destination in the five boroughs of New York and so he grudgingly slammed his cab into gear, told me to lock my doors, and we were off.

We drove through long stretches of Bedford-Stuyvesant, which looked a lot like a post-World War II bombed-out city. Buildings were boarded up, or scorched from fires; able-bodied men were passing around bottles in brown paper bags, teenagers who should have been in school were rapping on our cab windows and asking for quarters, teenage prostitutes shared the littered sidewalks with teenage mothers and teenage muggers. In short, we saw the pathology that characterizes this urban monument to an economic system which encourages discrimination, prejudice, involuntary uenmployment, and that results in every form of social pathology.

When I got to the high-rise hospital that houses psychiatry, I went inside and sat in the lobby because I was more than an hour early for my talk. Almost immediately a guard appeared and told me that I could not sit there unless I had a badge, which, I learned, I could only obtain if I went to the security office some blocks away. So I elected, instead, to go out and sit on the hospital steps in the sunshine of a March day. There I noticed a strange phenomenon. Chauffeur-driven limousines—Cadillacs, BMWs, Mercedes-Benzs, Lincolns, etc., drove up and double-parked near the hospital entrance. Well-dressed women (it was now 11:00 A.M.) got out of the back seats of the cars and entered the hospital. Other women were leaving the hospital and were departing in their own chauffeur-driven limousines. I could not figure out what was going on. Finally, my curiosity aroused, I could stand it no longer, and I went out to the street and asked one of the chauffeurs what was happening, who were these well-dressed people leaving and entering their chauffeur-driven cars?

"Psychoanalysis," my informant replied. "Every day we bring our employers here for their hour-long psychoanalytic session."

A light bulb flashed above my head. Here was, in prototypical form, an illustration of one of the wrongs in our U.S. mental health system. A department of psychiatry, surrounded by many square miles of human suffering, personal misery, drug abuse, child abuse, child and adult psychopathology in every form, was offering nothing for the local community, but was doing intensive one-to-one daily therapy with the affluent, who lived miles away in safe suburban enclaves.

Let me hasten to say that I have no particular bias against psychoanalysis. I prefer it to many other forms of individual therapy, like drugs, electric shock, and lobotomy. I believe we have learned a great deal about the human psyche from psychoanalytic investigations. But is there not a place for a community mental health training program in Bedford-Stuyvesant? Could not something be done to prepare young psychiatric trainees to deal with children and adolescents at high risk for neglect, abuse, and exploitation? Or for work with the bag ladies and the lonely men who have been discharged from the public hospitals and who curl up under newspapers in doorways? Could there not be programs that try to help all of those people damaged by an economic system that talks about unemployment in percentage points rather than in human terms? And could there be a psychology that uses its skills on behalf of the prevention of such vast human degradation and suffering as is seen in Bedford-Stuyvesant and other inner-city neighborhoods?

THE GAP CANNOT BE BRIDGED

The analogy is equally applicable to psychology and education. We learn from a major epidemiological study (Regier et al. 1984) that there are 37 million disturbed adults in U.S. society, *not* including those in mental institutions and prisons, nor the homeless, those with sexual problems, and also not including disturbed children and adolescents. If we add all these latter groups to the 37 million, we have more than 60 million emotional casualties in our U.S. society. Yet the current near-exclusive preoccupation of psychology, and psychology training programs, is with one-to-one psychotherapy for those with health insurance that pays the therapist. And the major lobbying effort by psychological associations is to secure more coverage for our psychotherapy, not to try to remedy the injustices of our exploitative society. Let me make clear the fact that the *incidence* of any condition (the number of new cases) is not affected in the slightest by the treatment, intervention and/or cure of affected cases. This fact is critical to our understanding of the role, especially, of community psychology, but also of child guidance programs focused on the individual child or adolescent. Interventions that *help* groups of people that are already damaged (neglected or abused children, black males, the disabled, the sexually abused adolescent, etc.)—while humane and desirable—do nothing to affect *incidence*. And if our goal is to prevent or reduce these pathologies, then our intervention programs should be preventive, not palliative. Only successful prevention efforts reduce incidence.

For twenty-five years Amnesty International has been pursuing justice for political prisoners subjected to torture and human rights violations. Amnesty International has worked for all prisoners of conscience, for prompt trials for political prisoners, and for an end to torture in countries around the world. The organization has helped thousands of prisoners, has gained freedom or reduction in sentences, or an end to torture, in innumerable cases by putting the spotlight of publicity on barbarisms that thrive under the cover of secrecy. Members of Amnesty International provide funds for this extremely important work. I am happy to be a contributing member of Amnesty International. Most of us who send money feel strong empathy for political and other prisoners subject to torture and imprisonment for their political beliefs.

But, and this point is crucial, the effects of Amnesty International alone, focused as they are on individual cases of injustice, are not going to bring about a significant reduction in the *incidence* of oppression, torture, and injustice. Let's be clear. The work that this organization is doing is critically important in the lives of the people affected. But the only hope for reduction in *future* barbarisms is effective action to ensure that primary prevention efforts are successful. Primary prevention means *proactive* efforts to halt torture and injustice against future prisoners of conscience and future political prisoners. Only through successful efforts at primary prevention will there be a reduction in the number of new cases.

Similarly, successful efforts at individual therapy—whether by educators and psychologists, or by pediatricians, heart surgeons, or dentists —are helpful to the individuals who are suffering. But let us not misunderstand: such efforts do not change the rate of future pathologies.

There are some other lessons that need to be learned from these observations. We must face squarely the fact that psychologists and educators can never reach the vast majority of children who have been damaged by an uncaring society with our attempts at one-to-one psychological treatment by high-priced professionals. Nearly three decades ago, I demonstrated with great statistical clarity (Albee 1959) that the human resources available for one-to-one intervention in the mental health field were so scanty as to be almost nonexistent, and more recently (Albee 1979) that the situation has not improved, but has only gotten worse. (If one is interested in the mechanism of *denial,* one need only consider the exclusive preoccupation with individual treatment by both the leaders and members of the U.S., Canadian, and possibly British and German mental health establishments.)

The field of cancer research, after all these years of being involved in a "War on Cancer," has finally seen the light. In spite of billions of dollars sunk into research seeking the causes and cure of cancer, that field has finally awakened to the reality that the war is being lost, that there are more cancer victims now than there were when the war on cancer was declared, and that a shift to efforts at cancer prevention is necessary and long overdue (though costly to profits). A similar insight has not yet reached the leaders of psychiatry who control our U.S. National Institute of Mental Health. They are still looking for biological causes and cures of "mental illness" and rejecting prevention efforts that involve social change. We need to understand that political conservatives usually oppose prevention efforts because social change and threats to profits are often required as prevention.

Unfortunately the field of psychology itself is becoming increasingly conservative. Fifteen years ago there was more interest in social action and political change among psychologists than there is today. As psychologists become more affluent and successful, we become more conservative. Fifteen years ago psychologists were active supporters of the anti-Vietnam War movement. I marched with a large group of psychologists down Connecticut Avenue in Washington, D.C., during the APA Convention in 1971. The march ended at Lafayette Park where I. F. Stone and I made impassioned speeches against the war to the assembled psychologists-activists. Psychologists for Social Action was a viable group and the APA Convention was occasionally disrupted by groups seeking to make our discipline more relevant. Today our political efforts are more likely to be directed at improving psychology's economic position with respect to psychiatry, at securing our broader eligibility for health care Medicare payments, and at getting recognition for our independent practitioners' status. Like many of my friends, I yearn nostalgically for the exciting days of the late '60s and early '70s when we joined forces with the student radicals and civil rights leaders in the belief that we might change society in the direction of a more even distribution of power. Now as we attract more neophytes who are interested in building a private practice like TV's Dr. Hartley, our radical quotient declines steadily.

THE ASCENDENCY OF THE THERAPIST

The field of psychology in the United States is being taken over and dominated by the individual psychotherapists. I need not spend much time defending the accuracy of this statement. The struggle for control of our Association is rapidly becoming a rout. Any academician can attest to the disproportionate interest in psychotherapy careers among undergraduates, graduate school applicants, and graduate students. The new professional schools of psychology are flourishing, in part by accepting large numbers of unqualified applicants for their doctoral programs—applicants whose backgrounds are in social work, counseling, and even more distantly related fields. Indeed, it is now possible to get a doctorate in psychology without having had a single course in the field before the Master's degree! For this reason, short crash programs in basic psychology flourish because they help professional graduates, with little or no preparation in basic psychology, to pass the national licensing exam.

And what of community psychology? Our graduate programs have not prospered because we are a threat—albeit only a small but troubling voice—to the system. Community psychologists have the disturbing habit of suggesting that there are serious faults with our larger society. The diverse programs all speak to empowerment—of women, minorities, the aged, the disabled—as well as concern with the violent family, the chronically mentally disordered; many are seekers of peaceful coexistence. Empowerment means redistribution of power—and those that control training funds in any society are not going to pay to disrupt the system!

All of these groups we focus on are powerless because they have been deprived of power by the system. I want to do the unforgivable: to name the enemy! *It is the exploitative economic system.* Personally, I long ago tired of doing psychoanalysis in the middle of Bedford-Stuyvesant.

And I am tired of hearing community psychologists' voices urging caution, voices that suggest a *priori* needs-assessment to see what are the real human problems of the Bedford-Stuyvesants in the U.S.A. and around the world; I am too old to want to wait for the traditional liberal approaches of educational reform, persuasion, and attitude change.

If we are unwilling to work actively for major social change, for *democratic socialism based on scientific humanism,* then we are simply dilettantes. (I am not so irrational as to think we can change society overnight—but we can, as the Quakers say, "Speak truth to power"; we can advocate for major social changes and give support and courage to the groups we focus on. We can join with others to try to redistribute power.)

THE POWER OF IDEOLOGY

Before we can start, it is necessary to disavow many shameful errors of our predecessors in the field of psychology: those who provided "scientific" support and comfort to those "leaders" who believed in genetic determinants of social class position, "scientific" evidence of the inferiority of the brunette races and of women, and of the constitutional and genetic determinants of poverty and mental disorder. In an article in the *American Psychologist* (Albee 1986) I spell out in some detail the reasons why racists and sexists *must* view their targets as possessing defects that are inborn, genetic, and unchangeable. And frighteningly, these racists and sexists are in charge of many governments in the world and have been, in the past, (and are sometimes now), responsible for colonialism, injustice, imperialism, and exploitation.

Our own society is characterized by hierarchical power relations of all kinds, but especially between men and "their women and children." It has been argued that all social oppressions in a society ultimately are reflections of the power relations that exist between men and women. From the ancient Greeks, when slaves and women were considered irrational species, to modern religious androlatry (male God worship), social violence preserves and sustains hierarchical relations emphasizing male power. When an agency of the U.S. federal government recently classified jobs according to social desirability, nuclear physics was at the top and child care was at the bottom. Changes in the nation's economic power structure further advance the process of "feminization of poverty" and the masculinization of war and medicine. The U.S. federal government now proposes that it retain responsibility for war, weapons, and medical care, and that it relinquish to the individual states responsibility for inadequate block grants that involve a reduced level of support for welfare programs which most heavily involve women and children.

According to Yale University historian Catherine Ross (1980) one of the many consequences of the decentralization of welfare programs— pushing them back to the states and local communities by the federal government—will be the decreasing effectiveness of child advocacy groups. In the past, when the federal government was largely responsible for support programs for children, families, and the poor; groups advocating for these populations could focus their efforts on members of Congress and on the executive agencies in Washington. By fragmenting advocacy groups' efforts, pushing them back to each state, effective lobbying is lost.

Five years ago, Justin Joffe and I wrote: "There is a strong tendency in our society to separate and isolate social problems. We have a social problem labeled violence against children in the family, and other problems labeled battered wives, sexism, racism, abuse of elderly persons, family disruption, poverty and unemployment, the incarceration and decarceration of persons we call mentally ill, the neglect of the mentally retarded, and the isolation of the physically handicapped, to name just a few" (see Joffe and Albee 1981, 322).

What do all these problems involving different groups have in common? We suggested the best answer we could come up with. It is their *powerlessness*. People without power are commonly exploited by powerful economic groups who explain the resulting psychopathology by pointing to the inborn defects in the victims. The rest of us do not rush to the defense of the victims because we are caught up in the prevailing ideology that puts "justice" in the hands of those with power. We join the groups "blaming the victims."

The French philosopher Pascal (see Hutchins 1952) put it well: "Justice is subject to dispute; might is easily recognized and is not disputed. So we cannot give might to justice, because might has gainsaid justice and has declared that it is she herself who is just. And thus, being unable to make what is just strong, we have made what is strong just" (Hutchins 1952, 227).

If the foregoing analysis is accurate, it makes little sense to try to develop separate and independent programs for the prevention of child abuse, spouse abuse, elder abuse, the exploitation of women, minority group members like unemployed black males, migrant farm workers, the handicapped and disabled, the homeless mentally disturbed, and the mentally retarded. If we see all these groups as powerless because of the operation of exploitative socioeconomic forces then the logical approach would be to determine ways to achieve an equitable redistribution of economic power. One of the slogans of the '60s was "Power to the people." Another piece of conventional wisdom holds that "Money is power." Without meaning to be simplistic, we might suggest that we examine the argument for a redistribution of power through a redistribution of wealth in our society. This means organizing for political action.

APPROACHES TO EMPOWERMENT

When confronted with the issues of powerlessness, many psychologists tend to approach it as a question of individual aberration, as personal misperception of reality. The simplicity of such a view is commendable, but the resulting attempt to alter people's perceptions of their ability to affect their own lives is often not only misguided but counter-productive and ultimately damaging. Joffe and I (Joffe and Albee 1981) edited a volume on *Prevention through political action and social change.* The papers therein documented the fact that a great many people in our society, in many situations, are personally powerless. If they believe that they cannot do much to affect their personal circumstances, alleviate their misery, or build a better world for their children, it is not because they perceive contingencies incorrectly, but because their perceptions are accurate. They see themselves as powerless because they have no power. No doubt this perception itself further exacerbates their feelings of hopelessness and further reduces the likelihood of their making the necessary effort on those few occasions in their lives when they might be able to act effectively. If so, something might be said in favor of "therapy" to make them feel less powerless. But therapists are in short supply and rarely available to those powerless groups who concern us—and anyway the therapists have a different agenda.

In any case, what do we know about the effects of feeling that one is in control in a world where, in fact, one is not? It seems that either our "therapy" has to create a very powerful delusional system so that the powerless never notice that their actions are not efficacious, or we have to run the risk that those who acquire *feelings* of control will be even more frustrated when they encounter reality. To prevent psychopathology we should not alleviate feelings of powerlessness by altering perceptions, but by encouraging efforts at altering reality. This is not as straightforward as it may sound. A key question—to which there is no easy answer—is how to make those who feel powerless take action to alter the maldistribution of power? Perhaps one answer is to be found in the process of helping people understand why they feel powerless and helping them to attribute that feeling to the socioeconomic system rather than to personal inadequacy. This approach obviously harks back to the condemnation of the "defect model" of psychopathology and to Ryan's (1971) demonstration of the social process of "blaming the victim." The problem of powerlessness is exacerbated by the fact that the victims blame themselves, as they accept the dominant society's assessment of their plight. The social rationalization at once excuses the rest of us from working for social change (instead we can do individual therapy, with chemicals or couches), and it keeps the victims from blaming anyone but themselves. The message we see in all this is that our role is to assure those who feel helpless that their feeling is due in fact to being powerless —perhaps only then will they seek to change the system that has made them so. But the attack on the system must be a joint effort of all powerless groups.

Binstock (1981) suggested that we will not have significant social changes until a national political crisis has been precipitated by *"coalitions of the severely deprived."* He suggested that we must "undertake direct militant action in our local communities." The tactics of Saul Alinsky and of Martin Luther King, Jr., were effective, he notes, in provoking social change. Indeed, during the early history of unionization, effective organizing of strikes, sit-ins, welfare demonstrations by coalitions of have-not groups and more recently the civil rights movement and the anti-war movement, were effective in bringing about political change.

It is often said that power is not given up voluntarily. Indeed, it often appears that those persons who hold power are protected by laws, by elected officials, by the police, by folkways, and, perhaps most importantly, by the beliefs and attitudes of the powerless! We are all encouraged to accept the superior wisdom of leaders and gurus, probably transferring our childhood reverence for parental authority onto these other parentlike figures. Rebellion against the patriarchy does not come easily. But when it does come it often comes with a violence and turbulence that is shocking in its intensity. Once some authority is challenged successfully other potential challengers take courage and continue the pressure.

THE YOGI AND THE COMMISSAR

In an oft-quoted essay, Arthur Koestler (1942) described two separate and distinct approaches to affecting people in ways that lead to political change. At one extreme are those approaches using the methods of the Yogi, and at the opposite pole are those using the methods of the Commissar.

The Yogi approach seeks to promote change *from within*, physical or psychological change, whereby each individual gains new control or new insights through attempts at personal reconstruction; each comes to seek a new perception or interpretation of external reality. Most Yogi approaches focus on individuals or small groups, on effecting more widespread social improvement through one-by-one personal efforts at change.

A variant of the Yogi approach is to be found in the teachings of Gandhi, who sought to encourage or inspire in his followers nonviolent resistance to oppression, personal civil disobedience, and renunciation of power-seeking Western values and Western ways. Gandhi, however, sought to expand the Yogi realm by influencing the mind and heart of the oppressor as well as the oppressed through the use of Satyagraha, "truth force," as the medium for exposing injustice. With meticulous discipline and intentionality, Gandhi organized mass public demonstrations that focused on the great injustices of society, and that called forth the best in individual courage and commitment. Gandhi acted always with a vision of simultaneous change for both the individual and the socio-political culture that frames an individual life. He paid strict attention to the nonviolent means that would result in the desired harmonious ends, and he sought nothing less than a completely revitalized community. Gandhi's success in leading India to independence attests to the effectiveness of the ways of the Yogi, although it is likely that Indian independence was inevitable, perhaps through more violent means.

Many spiritual leaders throughout history, such as Jesus and the Buddha, have adopted a Yogi approach. Closer to home was the philosophy of Dr. Martin Luther King, Jr., who sought to encourage his followers to seek freedom for blacks through personal commitment to nonviolence and civil disobedience tempered with love and Christian forgiveness. King, like his mentor Gandhi, was concerned for the spiritual welfare of the white oppressor as well as for his own flock. His goal was to lead the entire society into the process of self-reflection, growth, and change, and to bring about the Beloved Community of the Christian faith.

In direct contrast to the Yogi, the Commissar seeks to force change from without—through externally imposed structured resistance, compulsory rules, laws, and social manipulation. The Commissar seeks to organize masses of people by training effective leaders who can then change systems: by organizing unions fomenting class struggle and political conflict, and by undermining the structure of existing economic power. Marx and Lenin stand out as examples of this approach, though it clearly is not limited to a socialist system. B. F. Skinner clearly is Commissar-like in his writings (like *Walden Two*). Leaders of many political persuasions have sought to change social relationships by reorganizing their societies, by imposing their rules on the populace. Leaders of many third world nations today cannot wait to educate the masses—so they impose a social structure that includes new economic and social organization.

According to Koestler, these two opposite approaches to social change appear and reappear throughout history. He argued that middle-ground compromise efforts are relatively less effective than either extreme, that a successful middle position between these two extremes is uncommon.

Koestler's arresting dichotomy is also attractive when seeking to order efforts at changing the distribution of psychological power. Yogi approaches clearly include efforts focused on helping individuals effect personal changes whether through teaching or encouraging attitudinal change, behavioral change, psychotherapy, or physical and mental reorganization. Commissar approaches *impose* change in the form of laws and regulations—modest examples include ERA, affirmative action, and progressive taxes.

Narrowing our focus still further, we can begin to develop an heuristic model of interventions in the field called community mental health by contrasting the methods of the Yogi and the Commissar as they are applied to reduce psychopathology. But first one additional set of conceptually polar alternatives will be useful. There has been developing, among those interested in explaining human behavior, another bipolar set of models which we can label the organic-molecular approach at one extreme, and the social-environmental approach at the other.

ORGANIC AND SOCIAL MODELS

One major current explanatory model for many forms of human "inferiority" emphasizes a biochemical and *organic defect model* with genetic vulnerability or genetic pathology—in short, a position which insists that there can be "no twisted behavior without a twisted molecule," and that emphasizes the necessity of an underlying organic defect as a cause of poverty, crime and delinquency, life failure, and pathological emotional reactions and behavior. At the opposite extreme, we find a *social environmental learning model* which explains pathology in terms of missed or distorted early environmental opportunities, poor interpersonal relationships, often traceable to the experience of pathological parenting early in life, to disturbed conditioning experiences both originating in and resulting in a poor social environment. These two polar opposite explanatory models lead often to bitter debates about both causation and remediation efforts, and also to sharp disagreements about the distribution of funding for interventions. The group favoring an explanation emphasizing defective organic origins of psychopathology and human inequality stresses the importance of *fate:* individual change is difficult and requires drugs and other physical approaches to counter underlying biological imbalances; they often stress the need to find the underlying organic causes of delinquency or the major mental illnesses, and they deny, or minimize, the contribution of social conditions like poverty and social discrimination in producing emotional disturbances.

Those favoring a social environmental learning view as explaining psychopathology, on the other hand, want to help people change by corrective social learning experiences, and they may argue that to prevent future disturbances it is necessary to work to establish social justice and social equality.

When we put our two dichotomies together, the Yogi and the Commissar approaches, and the organic and the social environmental approaches, we find four interesting quadrants (see Fig. 1). On one side of the *vertical* axis, we find an emphasis on individual change, and on the other side an emphasis on group prevention. This distinction does not hold perfectly, as we shall see, but it clearly differentiates the preferences for approaches of the two groups. If we look at the two sides of the *horizontal* axis, we see that nearly every effort above the line is biological/physical and nearly everything below the line is social/educational.

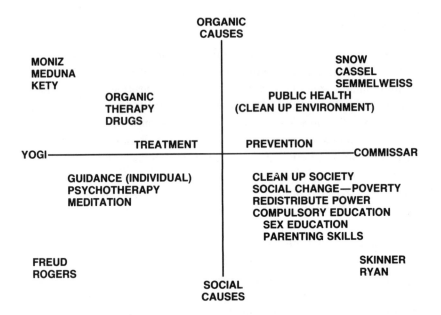

Meduna (1955), the first to use convulsive therapy to treat schizophrenics, sounds the theme of the biological-medical model: "After half a century of mummery came the reaction and the Society of Biological Psychiatry was founded by a few men, good and true. Our main tenet is that the Thing is what it is—that mental disturbances are disturbances of the brain. All mental disturbances, therefore, have to be expressed and defined, not in terms sociological or religious, or in symbols philosophic and magic-phallic, but in terms physiological and biological. We uphold the truth of the Judaic thinkers of old: *God is that he is,* and a thing is what it is, and a symbol is only a means of communication; and finally, that in the human brain there are no symbols, there are only the cells and they are magnificent but silent biochemical and physiological processes. A nerve cell can be stimulated by no symbol, but only by another nerve cell" (Meduna 1955, 4).

By way of contrast Watson (1924) presents the social-environmental models as follows: "Give me a dozen healthy infants, well formed, and my own specified world to bring them up in, and I'll guarantee to take any one at random and train him to become any type of specialist I might select—doctor, lawyer, artist, merchant chief, and yes, even beggarman and thief, regardless of his talents, penchants, tendencies, abilities, vocations and race of his ancestors" (Watson 1924, 201).

Wiggin (1985) sounds another Yogi-environmental theme based on clinical experience: "Children learn how to love and nurture from being touched, held, and talked to during their earliest moments and throughout their childhood. They learn their sense of self-worth from the way they are treated by parents and others close to them, especially day-care providers, preschool and elementary teachers. Parents are constantly teaching many aspects of sexuality without ever saying a word" Wiggin 1985, 1).

Looking at the upper left quadrant, we find the Yogi approach combined with the organic-biological approach. This clearly is the major focus of contemporary American psychiatry and medicine, and also characterizes the model that stresses genetic and organic causation of inequality. The model is pessimistic about change and about prevention. Individuals are inferior, and powerless, because they are genetically, physically and/or constitutionally doomed. We hear echoes of Social Darwinism here. The emphasis is on individual treatment, on quarantine and on repression—helping the individual involves using physical and biological interventions or incarceration; children are given prescriptions for tranquilizing or energizing drugs, mega-vitamin therapy; even electro-shock therapy and lobotomy clearly belong to this quadrant. The focus here is on specific treatment or incarceration of individuals within identifiable diagnostic disease categories. The search of the mental health system continues for better diagnostic methods and more specific, effective, organic therapies. Research aims at proving a genetic defect in many disorders, and at finding specific organic pathology in the affected individual.

Now, looking below the horizontal line, we find in the lower left quadrant, the focus is on a more Yogi-like approach, emphasizing individual social learning. We find here, particularly, the large and growing field of psychotherapy. Clearly this is an individual treatment that pays special attention to correcting the lingering effects of poor early social learning (psychoanalysis, for example, or compensatory early education) or altering current unfortunate social learning (the behavioral or cognitive rehabilitation approaches). In this quadrant we find a broad range of different learning or relearning approaches: what they have in common is the effort to help the individual change by offering something that has consequences inside his or her skin. These may be efforts at the development of insight, or personal relaxation through meditation, or the extinguishing of a conditioned response such as a phobia, or the acquisition of new sets of operant responses, such as learning assertiveness. Again, it must be emphasized, these are individual approaches that do not change incidence.

In the upper right quadrant, we find the combination of the Commissar approach and the biological approaches. Clearly this is a domain associated with the field of public health. It is on the prevention side of the dichotomy, as are most Commissar approaches. So examples here would include improved maternal diet programs, public housing, immunization, elimination of environmental pollution, programs to reduce the amount of lead and other heavy metals in the environment, etc.

Finally, in the lower right quadrant, we find the combination of the Commissar and the social environmental approaches. Here, clearly, are many of those community mental health approaches termed primary prevention of psychopathology. While there are some preventive approaches to mental disorder and programs for improvement in the quadrants directly adjacent, this lower right-hand corner clearly is the place of the largest number of efforts at reducing avoidable stress, building social coping skills into groups, improving the self-esteem of large numbers including the elderly, minorities, and other discriminated-against groups; clearly this is the major preventive area. I argue this is where most community prevention efforts belong.

Kenneth Clark (1974) asked social science to find ways to help control human exploitation and intergroup hostility, and at the same time to study ways to foster love and human empathy. Clark wants us to do research to determine the effects of institutions and social arrangements, issues of status and hierarchical distinctions—as these relate to injustice and cruelty. He says: "If social scientists do not directly address themselves to the problems of social justice and social responsibility, assuming all of the risks involved, this failure will not be a passive act but an active one. Social science will have become an accessory to our society's defeat by irrationality, to its victimization by uncontrolled passions and prejudices and cruelties. . . . the most serious threat to the survival of mankind is not now ignorance in the traditional sense, but a morally neutral, that is, an insensitive or inhibited human intelligence" (Clark 1974, 147–148).

Some of the work, some of the thinking, has already been done for us. There are many examples of effective efforts at the redistribution of power. Gandhi's success, and the success of others in defeating colonialism; the success of Martin Luther King, Jr., and the civil rights movement, the women's movement; the inspiration of Danilo Dolci—we can all name our own heroines and heroes who "speak truth to power." But we must understand the structure of power. Our first task is to identify, and then to openly challenge, the enemies of justice.

Johan Galtung (1971), a Norwegian social philosopher, has developed an insightful theory of imperialistic power between and among nations that also provides insight into power relations within a society, among social classes, and between the sexes as well. Galtung accounts for the continuing inequality that exists between nations, within a single nation, between social classes and between sexes with the argument that power elites within a "Central Industrial Society" form a community of self-interest that relates to the self-interests of those elites in power in a "Peripheral Society." This alliance results in exploitation of a majority of the people in the peripheral countries' social classes. In other words, powerful groups in powerful Central Industrial nations support and reward peripheral power elites who, in turn, exploit and oppress their own people in the interest of the alliance and their own self-interest. As a consequence, there is great economic and psychological benefit to the modern Central Industrial nations and great suffering among the exploited in the poor Third World, or other oppressed groups, with lowered self-esteem and early death common.

The pattern of exploitation is similar *within* the modern industrial society. A small powerful elite group maintains its authority by forming alliances with special groups that are enlisted to help in the continuing oppression of large numbers of exploited people. How is this exploitation perpetuated? By selecting and rewarding small numbers of talented persons from these exploited groups, people who become policemen, school teachers, politicians, and officials in the bureaucracy and in the factory. These "indigenous" leaders are rewarded to the degree that they accept the myths and models of the ruling classes and participate in the exploitation of their own groups.

In a ten-year follow-up to his original article, Galtung (1981) extends his analysis to consider what happens when both nature and groups of people are exploited beyond their regenerative capacity. Self-centered elites do not take the long view. They show little concern about the damaging consequences of their exploitation and about the depletion of natural and human resources so long as these bolster and increase their own power. In many ways, in many parts of the world, nature is currently in danger of being exploited beyond any possibility of regeneration: the rain forests are being destroyed in Central and South America; the whales are killed; the top soil washes away; and so are groups of human beings destroyed; particularly vulnerable to excessive stress is their capacity for reproduction, which falls victim to excessive exploitation. In the United States, the group with the highest rate of every kind of disease and infant mortality, early death, and psychopathology, is the army of five million migrant farmworkers and their families. The exploitation of this group is so enormous in terms of resulting physical and mental pathology that their very capacity for reproduction is curtailed. But because there is a seemingly endless supply of new migrant farmworkers, there is little concern about the "superexploitation" of this group.

Galtung also describes the exploitation of members of the individual family, especially women and children; also the individual worker, in Third World countries, and among the impoverished within industrial societies. The same analysis applies to the elderly, the handicapped, the unskilled, and the mentally disturbed in all societies.

What does all of this abstract discussion about imperialism and exploitation have to do with our more specific concerns about community psychology? I am sure the parallel is obvious. Small elite groups shape and influence the social order between and within industrial societies by controlling the mass media, the politicians, and the ruling myth system. And the existing social order involves perpetuating a maldistribution of power. And, I believe, the core result of powerlessness and psychopathology is the feeling of oppression in the absence of hope.

What is the role of community intervention efforts to reduce imperialism among patriarchal social class structures and exploitative societies? How do we help foster a just society? Let me list a few suggestions.

We must recognize, state openly, and teach our students:

1. Individual treatment has no effect on incidence. It patches up the casualties of the system, but it does not change the system.
2. Programs aimed at helping groups of the already-afflicted have no

effect on incidence. Only primary prevention programs can reduce incidence. Until we understand this we are dancing in the dark.

3. We do not live in a Just World and there is no external Divine Plan that will set things right. Justice will be achieved only through our own human efforts at forcing change, in cooperation with political alliances with the powerless and the disadvantaged.

4. Psychology has supported, historically, the forces of privilege, exploitation, and reaction. We have provided "scientific" support for the argument that social classes are based on genetic differences, that the poor and exploited are naturally inferior. We must disavow these errors and help undo the damage that our errors have caused.

I urge Community Psychology to formulate a basic manifesto, a statement of principles, that will announce our alliance with the exploited and offer our assistance to all those who struggle for a redistribution of power.

REFERENCES

Albee, G. W. (1959). Mental health manpower trends. New York: Basic Books.

Albee, G. W. (1979). Psychiatry's human resources: 20 years later. Hospital and Community Psychiatry 30, 11, 783–786.

Albee, G. W. (1986). Toward a just society: Lessons from observations on the primary prevention of psychopathology. American Psychologist 41, 891–898.

Binstock, R. H. (1981). The politics of aging: Dilemmas and opportunitive. In: Joffe, J. M., and Albee, G. W. (Eds.): Prevention through political action and social change. Hanover, N.H.: The University Press of New England, 57–74.

Clark, K. B. (1974). The pathos of power. New York: Harper and Row.

Galtung, J. (1971). A structural theory of imperialism. Journal of Peace Research 13, 81–94.

Galtung, J. (1981). Fourth Annual Chase Millenium Lecture, London School of Economics.

Hutchins, R. M., Ed. (1952). Great books of the Western World: Vol. 33. Pascal. Chicago: University of Chicago Press.

Joffe, J. M., and Albee, G. W. (Eds.) (1981). Prevention through political action and social change. Hanover, N.H.: University Press of New England.

Koestler, A. (1942). The Yogi and the Commissar. London: Horizon.

Meduna, L. J. (1955). The place of biological psychiatry in the evolution of human thought. Journal of Nervous and Mental Disease 121, 1–4.

Regier, D. A., Myers, J. K., Kramer, M., Robins, L. N., Blazer, D. G., Hough, R. L., Eaton, W. W., and Locke, B. Z. (1984). The NIMH epidemiologic catchment area program. Archives of General Psychiatry 41, 934–941.

Ross, C. J. (1980). The lessons of the past. In: Gerbner, G., Ross, C. J., and Zigler, E. (Eds.): Child abuse. An agenda for action. New York: Oxford University Press.
Ryan, W. (1971). Blaming the victim. New York: Random House.
Watson, J. B. (1924). Behaviorism. New York: People's Institute.
Wiggin, S. J. (1985). Enhancing family communication. Edsource 1, 2.

10

Mental Health Practice in a Global Context

Richard C. Sherman

For many years, I have been interested in the interrelationship between sociopolitical developments and mental health training and practice. I specifically have been concerned with how mental health work has been viewed as distinctly separate from the world of national and global developments.

My path began while growing up as a child of a politically aware social worker and later as a student who was shaped by the 1960s' preoccupation with "relevance," the tying of our learning to the here and now. It continued during graduate study in history which substantiated beyond any doubt that a person's work is an integral part of his cultural context. The prevailing orientation of the culture determines the lens through which historians view events, and shapes how a person perceives and interprets his or her place in the everyday world.

Yet in my years as a clinical social worker, I have been struck by how this societal-professional connection has been regularly ignored, how there has been little focus on the ways our political-cultural context affects both mental health work and mental health itself. It seems as if the helping professions struggle to keep the external world at a safe distance. For example, during my graduate study in social work, President Nixon and Vice-President Agnew resigned and the controversial Vietnam War ended. Yet, my school and the social work profession largely failed to acknowledge the impact these events had on clients and practitioners. Outside the classroom, students, like other Americans, were preoccupied with these developments and what they would mean. Yet in the classroom the events and how we felt about them were ignored. This oversight was especially noteworthy since social work has always been the helping profession most centered in the political world, a field so rich in social activism that initially "social work" and "social reform" were terms that were used interchangeably.

Indeed, most mental health practitioners seem to live out this basic disconnection between their professional role and the political world. It is the rare helping professional who is able to integrate cultural, national, and global realities within the customary professional scope—the individual and the family. As I hope to demonstrate in this chapter, achieving a better understanding of the connection between the political and professional worlds can enrich mental health practice and can reveal the potential for helping professionals to make a significant contribution in the political realm.

IMPEDIMENTS TO INTEGRATION: OUR CONTEXT

We have underestimated how profoundly our lives have been shaped by social, cultural, and political forces, that is, by the context in which we live. The psychotherapist and client alike are affected by society's views on a broad range of matters such as class, race, sex, and technology. We can only appreciate our clients' struggles if we consider the effect of our society's attitudes and values on certain aspects of their personal experience.

Nancy, a 28-year-old computer programmer, was confounded by her inability to form and sustain nurturing relationships. She initially attributed her isolation to her noncommunicative parents who served as poor role models. She saw her problem as intergenerational and formidable. The therapist urged her to consider her surroundings, her context. Nancy noted that her colleagues too were working long hours in isolation from one another and similarly had minimal social lives. The discussion then included the cultural emphasis on, as Nancy put it, "me, myself, and I," which led her to note, "Maybe we're all very alone; I guess I can't blame my parents for everything."

This context determines the nature of our relationship to society, and it shapes the philosophies of the mental health professions as well. It thus provides the framework for our psychotherapeutic training and practice.

An array of powerful societal forces that comprise our context have served to inhibit integration of sociopolitical concerns with our mental health study and practice. Indeed, these elements have placed obstacles before us which encourage us to live a life of fragments.

Our society's emphasis on the individual is one such impediment. Our society views life as an individual struggle for survival and thus values independence over interdependence, competitiveness over connectedness. As a result, knowledge, educational institutions, social planning, and so much else are segmented into specialties or subsystems. This subdividing contributes to the fragmenting of our society where social and political realities discourage relatedness and connectedness and pull people apart (Auerswald 1990). We see ourselves as independent of society's support systems as well as its major governmental structures. We are thus prone to feeling unsupported and unempowered, uninvolved, and disconnected.

Separation and fragmentation are also fostered by the stresses of our times. The rush of events, the technological breakthroughs, the threats to our planet have preoccupied, if not numbed, the population. Whether we view the public as suffering from "future shock," selective inattention, or psychic numbing, we are tempted to compartmentalize (Toffler 1970; Jacobs 1989; Lifton 1979). We are hesitant to "put it all together," to integrate. Allowing our many concerns about the world to pervade our everyday life can be fatiguing, even overwhelming. Such a process would break through our denial. Thus, despite complaining of feeling fragmented, we may welcome a life of fragments.

The political culture of the Untied States is also a barrier to integration as it discourages citizen involvement in political concerns. In reality, our political culture has always been an apolitical one, featuring shallow and episodic participation in the political process (Piven and Cloward 1989). In addition, in recent years respect for our political leaders as well as our major institutions has declined. The political world is increasingly seen as ineffectual and inhabited by scoundrels. Indeed, the public distances, if not recoils, from the political realm.

This context makes it understandable why mental health practitioners would be tempted not to respond when clients refer to sociopolitical developments. With varying degrees of self-awareness, therapists "choose" to ignore these foreign and threatening external realities. As therapy is viewed as an already intense, complicated matter, these "external" concerns are felt as complicating the treatment. Mental health professionals thus appear to function in a self-protective manner. They commonly view their clinical practice as an enthralling entry into the mind of the client, as an enlivening, yet comforting dyadic or group exchange that is quite apart from the external world. This need for safety encourages therapists to unwittingly see it in their own "best" interest not to hear, let alone address, the full meaning of a client's material in its cultural context. For example, when a client refers to nuclear destruction or environmental decay, such material is seen as simply reflecting some aspect of the client's inner world. It is viewed as a mere derivative of intrapsychic conflict. These harsh external realities indeed often mirror and reinforce a client's view of the world as dangerous and depressing. By refusing to validate these concerns, the therapist fails to legitimize a significant part of the client's reality. Furthermore, when a therapist acknowledges the connection between the client's inner and outer worlds, it comforts and clarifies and thus enhances the treatment.

It is hardly surprising that this cultural context has inhibited the development of useful theories for our practice. We have predictably been forced to rely on intrapsychic and interpersonal theories that do not connect individual experience with the external world. These theories show how family histories and troubled relationships affect an individual's well-being. However, they do not help us understand how a state budget squeeze or a failing business climate impacts an individual or family.

In addition, the mental health professions have at best sporadically involved themselves in social issues. It has been difficult for them to sustain this interest, as psychological organizations and institutions, after all, are very much part of the culture. They are tied to a large network of interactions with other systems. The professions depend on sanctions and approval from institutions and from state and national bodies for securing of grants, training, or approval of ethical standards and credentials.

The professions thus are bound to reflect society's apolitical nature, specifically the minimal involvement of people in national and world affairs. For example, during World War II, members of the psychological professions participated in government and focused more on government and international affairs. The discipline of psychology especially sought to bring its expertise to the study and implementation of United States foreign policy (Jacobs 1989). Yet, in the postwar world the federal government and foundations reduced funds for psychology's study of international relations.

Similarly, social work has been unable to remain connected to its social activist roots. As it developed its clinical methodologies between the two world wars, it emulated other mental health disciplines, principally clinical psychiatry. Individual therapy—"social casework"—became the preeminent methodology. As a result, a long-standing split was spawned between the social reform and the clinical practice traditions of social work, a split that continues to haunt the profession.

Instead of believing that sociopolitical developments shape our practice, mental health practitioners have generally thought that such issues divert us from our goal. Our central mission has been commonly viewed as providing psychological services that should be aimed "to reduce pain and discomfort and to increase the capacity of the individual to adjust satisfactorily. . . . any attempt to dilute or divert the activity. . . . into a political instrument is extremely detrimental to achieving the primary objective of providing adequate psychiatric services for all citizens" (Halleck 1971, 11–12).

WHAT NEEDS TO BE DONE: MOBILIZING THE PROFESSIONS

The task of integrating concerns about global and national affairs with professional practice can seem Herculean. The mental health practitioner faces a societal and professional homeostasis that is exceedingly difficult to alter. But the obstacles at hand are not insurmountable. Mental health professionals can draw on models, trends, and supports that encourage integration of our socio-political context with our professional work. The groundwork is being laid by numerous theoreticians and practitioners who are wrestling with these issues.

Redefining Our Worldview: Politics and Values in Psychotherapy

One initial step toward achieving integration is to understand that since we live in a political world, we need to define ourselves as political beings. But first we need to be clear about what constitutes "politics," and how intensely political our professional work is.

For example, during the 1980s when I was making numerous presentations to clinic staffs regarding the threat of nuclear war, some mental health centers overtly warned that such talks were unacceptable if my content were "political." If one utilizes a standard definition of the term, politics as "the science and art of political government," then one is relegating politics to a separate sphere. Other definitions, however, place the professional squarely in the political world. Webster noted it to be also "factional scheming for power and status within a group," while Key states that "politics deal with human relationships . . . of dominance and submission, of the governors and the governed" (Key in Halleck 1971, 34).

With this fuller understanding of the term, we can begin to consider how mental health practitioners are assuredly political. Heretofore we believed that therapists who referred to socio-cultural issues were "political," while those who did not refer to such matters were not political. We must now acknowledge that whether by our action or by our inaction, we are always making a political statement. Our interventions either reinforce or alter the current condition of the client. Thus, if mental health treatment does not include discussion of the client's environment, if it discourages addressing that part of the world that is adversely affecting the client, then treatment encourages or at least accepts the status quo. Conversely, if the therapist addresses that part of the system that needs to change, then treatment has served to challenge the status quo. This is true in regard both to the family system and the larger social system. Halleck summarizes this position thus: "There is no way in which the psychiatrist can deal with behavior that is partly generated by a social system without either strengthening or altering that system. Every encounter with a psychiatrist, therefore, has political implications" (Halleck, 36).

In the everyday addressing of a client's interaction with the greater environment, we are always making political choices. For example:

Mrs. A., a single mother, sadly noted that she had been cut off from medicaid, leaving her without health insurance for her and her three children. She struggled to determine why this had happened to her, wondering how she had somehow erred and what she had done to deserve this fate. The therapist extensively sympathized with Mrs. A.'s plight, then began a discussion about how she could provide for her family, specifically addressing the subject of health insurance.

The mental health professional here made no less a political move than if he had also asked the client if she knew why she had been dropped from the Medicaid rolls. When the client learns that her family was one of tens of thousands who lost benefits from a Reagan Administration policy decision, she also learns about being one of many victims of our society. Her new vision is therapeutic as it will surely diminish any self-blame, the responsibility that the client shouldered for this development.

Mr. P. bemoaned his feeling of inadequacy, his sense of failure. He cited his difficulty paying for his house and car, noting that he "should" be able to be financially successful. When the therapist asked Mr. P. to clarify, Mr. P. replied that he had worked hard yet was a failure since he could not achieve "the American Dream." His therapist empathized with Mr. P., then added that perhaps Mr. P. wasn't alone in struggling to attain the American Dream, that the economy of the late twentieth century put the Dream out of reach for many people. Client and therapist discussed how many people could not afford to buy houses or required two incomes to make ends meet (Mrs. P. did not work outside the home). With unusual animation, Mr. P. wondered aloud how he could act to improve his situation. "If part of my problem is the system, maybe I should do something about the economy, taxes . . . something!"

The objection to therapy that incorporates sociopolitical developments, so-called politicized therapy, is sometimes expressed as an insistence that we must not impose our "values" on our clients, that we must practice "value-free" psychotherapy. Invariably, however, the therapist brings a set of values to treatment which impact the encounter. Our every statement, our choice of waiting-room materials, our fee structure, our wall decorations reveal our values. Part of the developing therapeutic assessment is observing how our clients come to mirror some of our beliefs, interests, even our personal habits. In any ongoing treatment, our clients are very aware of and partially integrate our value system. For example, they learn how we cherish identifying feelings, personal growth, self-determination, empowerment, democracy and justice. Mental health practitioners are increasingly acknowledging that therapists indeed are "value-loaded," that our actions reflect the dominant social and economic forces of society (Prilleltensky 1989).

Helping professionals also must be able to bear the feelings that accompany this politicization. Integration of sociopolitical topics can only occur if therapists can also confront their own fears and anxieties about these issues. Essentially, mental health practitioners are able to fully hear their clients when they have the ability to tolerate their own feelings about the issues. Only then can therapists expand their scope of inquiry and, inevitably, their effectiveness.

Even those with an intellectual understanding of the need for a broader scope may avoid the larger context. These professionals too can feel overwhelmed and thus need to retreat from the upsetting external world.

Cheryl B. returned to her patients after a week's absence. She had been participating in an extended civil disobedience protest and had found the experience enthralling and exhausting. When clients inquired about her absence, she merely cited "family obligations." She later explained to her supervision group that she had scrupulously avoided the topic because she thought "therapy is intense enough as it is; I don't want that stuff in treatment."

In nonpoliticized therapy our clients' fears of world destruction, for example, are commonly ignored. While therapists may see these remarks as displacements of their clients' issues of rage and vulnerability, since they are "political" comments, they are not viewed as appropriate material for therapy. When they do respond to this content in a politicized orientation, helping professionals validate client concerns and they discover additional opportunities for addressing rage, vulnerability, helplessness, and autonomy-separation issues (Mack and Redmont 1989; Sherman 1988).

Ten-year-old Brian and his parents had expressed through words and actions their considerable ambivalence about their therapy. In individual treatment Brian employed prodigious use of activity as a defense as he ceaselessly played a board game. In one session, however, Brian suddenly referred to President Reagan and the fact that "the whole world is coming to an end." When these remarks were shared with his parents, Mr. and Mrs. R. eventually recalled hearing him say similar things at home. This sharing led to a fruitful discussion of the parents' chronic inability to hear and contain their son's anxiety, specifically Brian's fears of paternal rejection and parental separation.

In my observations, therapists who believed that treatment should be shielded from national and world developments usually insisted that their clients never referred to fears about nuclear war, ecological devastation, political events, or their children's economic future. Further exploration, however, revealed that their patients had occasionally made comments, especially at the beginning of sessions, such as, "Did you see that nuclear television program?" or, "Some election, huh?" Yet, these therapists chose to treat these remarks as throw-away chit-chat, often bringing the comments to a conclusion with the statement, "OK, now, how was your week?," thus "beginning" the session. Their disinclination to join their clients, their inability to integrate these external events into the therapeutic work thwarted an assortment of potential interventions and discouraged the client from further reference to such matters. In contrast, there were a small number of therapists who cited their clients' regular references to current event. These individuals conveyed a developed understanding, a sophistication as to their relationship to the world. They acknowledged that frightening national and global realities impacted on their own and their clients' lives.

Mr. W., age 40, had long insisted that the chronic upset within his marriage was caused by his cramped housing. At the outset of one session, in the nerve-wracking days preceding the U.N. deadline for Iraq's withdrawal from Kuwait, he alluded to the therapist's anti-war bumper sticker and remarked, "Looks like they'll just go in and make Iraq a parking lot." In the context of having just discussed Mr. W.'s explosive encounter with his mother, the therapist explored this comment. Mr. W. soon noted that "maybe there's a connection between my family and my politics: I treat my mother like the U.S. military would treat Iraq, I enter destructively and leave without a productive result." This was followed by a discussion that focused on his difficulty letting go of his fury with his mother for her alleged lifelong favoring of his siblings and how a Persian Gulf war could affect his job security as well as his housing.

New Directions in Integration

Practitioners who aspire to integrate their practice can find comfort and inspiration by some new directions in society and in the mental health professions. Economic and environmental problems have stimulated nations to increasingly adopt an interdependent, global perspective. As a result, pressure is building in the United States to shift from fragmented, isolated ways of living toward an emphasis on interdependence and connectedness. This change will undoubtedly be resisted, as individuals and vested interests struggle to harmonize corporate, national, and global needs. One can be cautiously optimistic, however, that this change is inexorable, since more and more of us are convinced that to survive we must alter our ways of thinking.

In the mental health professions there has been a surge of interest in past and current thinkers and practitioners who stress the importance of a wider scope of psychotherapeutic inquiry. Several disciples of Freudian psychiatry broke, to varying degrees, from mainstream psychoanalysis and introduced broad social factors into their theories. Alfred Adler differed with his teacher by highlighting the social roots of mental disorders (Adler 1927). Harry Stack Sullivan expanded Freud's vision by viewing psychiatry as a study of interpersonal relations and interactions (Sullivan 1953). C. J. Jung is often seen as the first Freudian to move toward a more interdependent psychiatry that views people as in constant interaction with larger sociocultural systems (Jung 1965). A number of early social workers recognized the connections between the clinical and the social activist traditions of the profession. One of these, Bertha Reynolds, is championed as a role model. Today, a progressive social work society bears her name (Reynolds 1951). Among psychologists are the humanistic and transpersonal psychologies of Abraham Maslow, which emphasize social interdependence (Maslow 1962). The recent work of psychologist Ken Wilber, which highlights a "biosocial" level of consciousness, is one of several that emphasizes the impact of the social environment on the individual (Wilber 1977).

Systems theory is another major influence in countering our society's tendency toward fragmentation. A popular approach to psychotherapy, systems theory views the world as composed of separate components which are constantly reshaped by interaction with other interdependent components. A growing chorus calls for the helping professions to use and extend systems theory. The development of family therapy based on systems theory enabled us to understand families as interdependent systems. Previously we tended to limit our scope of inquiry by targeting family scapegoats such as the "schizophrenogenic mother." In applying systems theory we do not have to limit our analysis to the family or even the community network. When we apply a "macrosystemic" level of assessment we learn what larger systems interact with our clients and the nature of the larger context that contains these systems (Imber-Black 1990).

Accordingly, we now hear of a number of broad-based theories. "Biopsychosocial theory," for example, explains our increasingly violent society as a consequence of a growing disparity in wealth distribution, not as a function of brain or family pathology (Marmor 1988). Theorists urge us to replace the "specialization and culture bound lenses" of social workers and substitute a "global model for social work" (Ramsay 1989). thus, mental health may be defined a being successful at love, work, and caring for the planet (Conn 1990).

The Mental Health Professional as Advocate and Activist

There are many ways in which mental health workers can begin to learn to integrate these issues into their professional work. Beginning with professional training, the importance of the political and social context needs to be stressed. Mental health trainees have not been adequately exposed to the many ways larger systems like state agencies, the state legislatures, or Congress affect their daily lives. Our state legislatures determine whether we get adequate mandated mental health reimbursement. These same legislatures have cut human services in the inevitable fiscal squeeze following a decade of federal cutbacks to the states. Our exercise of power, through phone calls, meetings, and other lobbying efforts can affect the adoption and maintenance of these mandated benefits and whether or not mental health services will be revamped or dismantled.

Trainees must also learn the points at which interventions in these systems are possible and most effective so that they can perform these interventions themselves and so that they can model for their clients. Mental health training programs thus should not only include a caseload of clients, but also an analysis of the institutions themselves.

We can also apply this vision in the course of our clinical activities in administrative meetings, in-service training, and clinical supervision. For example:

The professional staff of a mental health center felt isolated from one another and powerless to cope with clinic budget problems. In an effort to improve morale, one therapist suggested forming a support group, a "political action committee." Ongoing meetings led to a discussion of the state's mental health policies and their impact on the center as well as what clinicians could do to protect themselves. Subsequently, the group secured permission to display a bulletin board with voter registration material accessible to both staff and clients. Speakers were invited to address the staff on various public policy questions. Debates ensued in meetings and in clinical supervision regarding the appropriateness of addressing political material in clinical treatment. The group also felt bold enough to question several administrative policies of the agency's director.

Even though we may adopt a new understanding of how we define our clients' problems, some mental health professionals will find it difficult to involve themselves directly in political life. Often, we suspect we are ill-suited to having any involvement in the mysterious "political process." We picture an "old-boy network" making deals in smoke-filled rooms at State Houses or in Congress. We cannot imagine what skills we may have that could sway public officials. Yet we are experts about which conditions and services contribute to people's and families' well-being, and which detract from it. We hold a wealth of information about how real people are affected by the government's decisions regarding which services and benefits are available and which are not.

Few of us realize that we can easily and effectively transfer many of our clinical skills to working with public officials (Stein 1989). Our training equips us to be skilled at establishing relationships and making a differential, purposeful use of self. We understand environmental manipulation and how to link people with community resources. We know the utility of reframing issues. We are trained to attune to powerful, overwhelming affect and to appreciate the interplay of forces that determine the functioning of the individual and of the family. These and other skills are part of our clinical repertoire and can be effective in the legislative and public policy arena.

Mental health professionals have already made significant contributions as activist-professionals. In the past decade, the helping professions have been leaders in the peace and justice field. Physicians for Social Responsibility, Social Workers for Peace, and Psychologists for Social Responsibility have demonstrated leadership in educating the general public on issues relating to our military and economic policies. Through local, national, and international forums, members of these groups have simultaneously lobbied their professions to more adequately address the issues that influence clients, colleagues, and themselves.

Our commitment as mental health professionals has long been to the well-being of our clients. We can only fulfill these responsibilities if our practice addresses the role of the political-cultural context in the lives of our clients and ourselves. To do any less would be to shortchange the people we have pledged ourselves to help.

REFERENCES

Adler, Alfred. *The Practice and Theory of Individual Psychology.* New York: Harcourt, 1927.

Albee, George W. "Politics, Power, Prevention, and Social Change." In Justin M. Joffee and George W. Albee, eds., *Prevention through Political Action and Social Change,* 3–19. Hanover, N.H.: University Press of New England, 1981.

Auerswald, E. H. "Toward Epistemological Transformation in the Education and Training of Family Therapists." In Marsha Pravder Mirkin, ed., *The Social and Political Contexts of Family Therapy,* 19–50. Boston: Allyn and Bacon, 1990.

Capra, Fritjof. *The Turning Point.* Toronto: Bantam Books, 1982.

Conn, Sarah. "Protest and Thrive: The Relationship Between Global Responsibility and Personal Empowerment." *New England Journal of Public Policy,* vol. 6, #1 (Spring/Summer 1990).

Halleck, Seymour L. *The Politics of Therapy.* New York: Science House, Inc., 1971.

Imber-Black, Evan. *Multiple Embedded Systems.* In Mirkin 1990, 3–18.

Inclan, Jaime, and Ferran, Ernesto. "Poverty, Politics and Family Therapy: A Role for Systems Theory." in Mirkin 1990, 193–213.

Jacobs, Marilyn S. *American Psychology and the Quest for Nuclear Peace.* New York: Praeger, 1989.

Jung, C. G. *Memories, Dreams, Reflections.* New York: Random House/Vintage, 1965.

Lifton, Robert J. *The Broken Connections.* New York: Basic Books, 1979.

Mack, John E., and Redmont, Janice C. "On Being a Psychoanalyst in the Nuclear Age." *Journal of Humanistic Psychology*, vol. 29, #3 (Summer 1989), 338–355.

Marmor, Judd. "Psychiatry in a Troubled World: The Relation of Clinical Practice and Social Reality." *American Journal of Orthopsychiatry*, vol. 58, #4 (October 1988), 484–491.

Maslow, Abraham. *Toward a Psychology of Being*. Princeton: Van Nostrand Reinhold, 1962.

Mirkin, Marsha Pravder, ed. *The Social and Political Contexts of Family Therapy*. Boston: Allyn and Bacon, 1990.

Murphy, Gardner, and Kovach, Joseph. *Historical Introduction to Modern Psychology*. New York: Harcourt Brace Jovanovich, 1972.

O'Connor, Terrance. "Psychotherapy for a Dying Planet." *Family Therapy Networker* (September–October, 1989), 69–72.

Piven, Frances Fox, and Cloward, Richard. *Why Americans Don't Vote*. New York: Pantheon Press, 1989.

Porter, Kenneth. "The Psychotherapist in the Nuclear Age." In K. Porter, D. Rinzler, P. Olsen, eds., *Heal or Die*, 6–19. New York: Psychohistory Publishers, 1986.

Prilleltensky, Issac. "Psychology and the Status Quo." *American Psychologist*, vol. 44, #5 (May, 1989), 795–802.

Ramsay, Richard, et al. "A Global Model for Social Work." Unpublished manuscript, 1989.

Reynolds, Bertha. *Social Work and Social Living*. New York: Citadel Press, 1951.

Sherman, Richard C. "Psychotherapy While Rome Burns: Integrating Our Personal Politics with our Professional Lives." Unpublished manuscript, 1988.

Stein, Miriam. "Using Our Clinical Skills for Social Change." Unpublished manuscript, 1989.

Sullivan, Harry Stack. *The Interpersonal Theory of Psychiatry*. New York: Norton, 1953.

Toffler, Alvin. *Future Shock*. New York: Bantam Books, 1970.

Wilber, Ken. *The Spectrum of Consciousness*. Wheaton, Ill.: Theosophical Publishing House, 1977.

Wilkeson, Adlea. "Psychotherapy, Countertransference and the Nuclear Arms Race." In Porter 1986, 60–83.

PART FOUR

PSYCHOLOGY AND THE ENVIRONMENT

If we do not speak for earth, who will? If we are not committed to our own survival, who will be?—*Carl Sagan*

Treat the earth well. It was not given to you by your parents; it was lent to you by your children. —*Kenyan proverb*

The two authors in this part address, each from a different perspective, the question: How is psychology relevant to the serious environmental problems that we face today?

In chapter 11, John Mack proposes that we need to invent a new psychology of our relationship to the Earth, a psychology that would explore our feelings, impulses and desires in relation to the physical world, and how and why we have created institutions that are so destructive to it. This new psychology would need to be "comprehensive, holistic, and systemic," enabling us to experience deeply our rootedness in and dependence on the earth. In chapter 12, Scott Geller discusses the relevance of a behavior change approach to environmental problems and summarizes a number of intervention programs that have been used by environmental psychologists for the protection of the environment. He believes that behavioral and social scientists have an important role to play in increasing environmentally protective behavior on the part of citizens, corporations, and governments.

11

Inventing a Psychology of Our Relationship to the Earth

John E. Mack

In April 1990 I was in Japan for a United Nations conference, held in the industrial city of Sendai, on the relationship of science and technology to international peace and security. On the night before returning to the United States, which happened to be Earth Day (April 22) while sleeping in a typical old-style Japanese inn in Kyoto, I had a dream that reflected my experience of coming back to a country that had been changed drastically from the place I had once known. Thirty years ago my wife and infant son and I had lived for two years in Japan near Tokyo in an old house with shoji screens and tatami mats in a country of exquisite beauty. I returned to a polluted land desecrated by the mindless excesses of industrialization. On every small hill was a tower for power lines, which draped themselves ungracefully across the countryside, dominating the landscape of miniature rises and subtle contours.

In my dream I am on a hillside just across the Hudson River, perhaps in New Jersey, through which I had driven so often with my parents in my childhood on the way to the seashore. Someone is lecturing to a group of us, as if we were at the United Nations conference for which I have come to Kyoto, telling us that there is still much beauty in the New York City environs. Then, with others from the conference, I take a kind of quick aerial and ground tour of these hills but see no beauty, for on each field of straw-colored New Jersey swamp grass there is at least one rectangular industrial or commercial building. Furthermore, there is an unmistakable chemical stench that pervades the scene, which is only partially acknowledged by the group.

The scene shifts to a meeting around a conference table where people are sharing their experiences, and what is bothering them. I say that what troubles me most, beyond what we have witnessed, is when someone, or a policy, or some enterprise, contradicts or denies, or pretends that reality is different than what my own experience tells me it is, that is, it invalidates my direct experience. Then a man sitting across the table from me—a kind of combination of an energetic representative of the British scientific establishment who was at the conference and of a younger person more eager for change—reacts intensely positively to my sentiment and I feel very much supported.

I will return shortly to certain of the dream's meanings.

We sense now a need for a new psychology of the environment in order to understand what we have done, and continue to do, individually and collectively, to the earth that is our home, so that we may change our behavior, locally and globally, in order to save its life. But how is this to be done? How do we invent a new psychology of our relationship to the Earth? I use the word invent, because of its implication of creating something new, an entity, a combination that has not been put together before.

Without a human problem there is no psychology, or at least not a clinical or dynamic one, so we start by identifying the problem, one that might have existed before, but which has gained preeminance as a result of new historical and cultural circumstances. Freud and his followers to a degree *invented* psychoanalysis in response to the fact that the extreme, deceitful ordering of men and women's sexual lives by a rigidified bourgeois society was becoming emotionally intolerable and producing behavioral and physiological manifestations that could not be understood or treated by the medicine or neuropsychiatry of their day. We confront now a new kind of problem, global in scope, namely, the agonizing murder of the life systems of the earth, the home on which we depend for everything, which affects each of us in profound personal ways, no matter how intensely we may deny it.

This new psychology must include not only the development of a body of theory that would understand or interpret our relationship to the environment, but also ways of working with clients and patients that will bring forth direct or disguised thoughts and feelings in relation to the environment and empower constructive initiatives. At the very least, this must mean that when we hear expressions of distress about pollution or other forms of environmental destruction in dreams and other communications, we not hear or interpret these simply as displacements from some other, inner source (Gerber, chapter 7, this volume). For example, a young woman in a human growth workshop that I co-led in Manhattan complained that she could not do all of the work, which involved exercises using rapid deep breathing, because the air was too foul. "I can't breathe," she said repeatedly. "It's just too toxic. Are there chemicals stored here?" (There were not. The room we used was a dance hall on the lower West Side.) Others in the workshop resonated with this woman's complaint, and acknowledged the foulness of the city's air. But they were able to complete this part of the workshop. Although her complaints could have been connected to early childhood experiences of disgust or intrauterine distress ("toxic planetary influences or insufficient nourishment"; Grof 1988), there was no opportunity to explore this possibility. Yet the acknowledgment of the validity of her complaint enhanced positively her further participation and experience in the workshop.

But what kind of psychology is relevant to a problem of this scope? What would a psychology of the earth be like? It would need to be comprehensive, holistic, systemic—I am not sure what the correct terms would be except that they must convey the fact of wholeness, connection, interrelatedness and complexity. It would have to be a dynamic psychology in the sense that it would need to explore profound, largely ignored conscious and unconscious feelings, impulses, and desires in relation to the physical world, rather than one of the variations of neurophysiology or biochemistry that now dominate the American psychiatric establishment. In addition to recognizing the systemic nature of the problem, the practitioners of this dynamic psychology of the environment would need to tell unpleasant or unwelcome truths about ourselves—here is one of the meanings of my dream—as we have learned to do from psychoanalysis, but now in an altogether new arena. We would need to explore our relationship with the Earth and understand how and why we have created institutions that are so destructive to it. Even in Freud's time, dynamic psychology was relational, initially describing the forces connecting the agencies of the psyche (id, ego, and superego), and between and among individuals in dyadic relationships, families, and small groups. But a relational psychology of the earth would be much broader, including our connectedness to peoples and other creatures all over the planet and with the earth itself as a living entity.

Actually we (by "we" I mean, by and large, citizens of Western and other industrialized nations, for many native cultures experience and avow a very different relationship to their environment) do have a psychology, or at least a prevailing attitude, conscious and unconscious, toward the earth. We regard it as a thing, a big thing, an object to be owned, mined, fenced, guarded, stripped, built upon, dammed, ploughed, burned, blasted, bulldozed, and melted to serve the material needs and desires of the human species at the expense, if necessary, of all other species, which we feel at liberty to kill, paralyze, or domesticate for our own use. Among the many forms of egoism that have come to be the focus of psychodynamically oriented psychologists in an age of self-criticism about our narcissism, this form of species arrogance has received little scrutiny. This attitude contrasts dramatically with the pragmatic, live-and-let-live and reverential relationship with nature that is reflected in the words of native American leaders such as Chief Seattle and Sioux Medicine Man John (Fire) Lame Deer, who recognize our complete interdependence with the earth and the need to live in balance and harmony with nature. "This we know," Chief Seattle told a Pacific Northwest Assembly in 1854,

the earth does not belong to man; man belongs to the earth. This we know. All things are connected like the blood which unites one family. All things are connected. Whatever befalls the earth befalls the sons of the earth. Man does not weave the web of life, he is merely a strand in it. Whatever he does to the web, he does to himself. (Chief Seattle 1988)

More than a century later Lame Deer wrote:

To come to nature, feel its power, let it help you, one needs time and patience for that. Time to think, to figure it all out. You have so little time for contemplation; it's always rush, rush, rush with you. It lessens a person's life, all that grind, that hurrying and scurrying about. (Lame Deer 1972)

The seemingly mindless destruction of the natural landscape by the Japanese, a people who have been known for their delicate appreciation of nature, attests to the degree to which disciplined industrialization and accretion of wealth can overwhelm such sensitivities and separate us from the earth itself. This cutting off of consciousness from a connection with nature, and the spirit that most peoples throughout human history have experienced as inherent in it (and in us, of course, as part of nature), is one of the supreme negative achievements of modern, industrially developed man. This separation is painfully demonstrated in modern Japan, and is reflected in my dream. One must wonder how or why we have done it, how we have so overdeveloped the use of reason at the expense of feeling, in the service of a fear-driven need to conquer other peoples and the material world on a planet with a growing population that is perceived as yielding finite, diminishing resources. Chief Seattle shared this bewilderment. "In your perishing you will shine brightly," he warned, "fired by the strength of the God who brought you to this land for some special purpose [and] gave [you] dominion over this land and over the red man. That destiny is a mystery for us" (Chief Seattle 1988, 72).

So a psychology of the environment would be an expanded psychology of relationship, a conversation or experiencing in the deepest parts of our being, of our connection with the earth as sacred. I say sacred because I do not believe that a mere threat to survival will be sufficient to create this new relationship without a fundamental shift in the nature of our being, as Vaclav Havel—who surely must have been personally revolted to discover the environmental catastrophe which his communist predecessors left him and which I witnessed from a train traveling from Prague to Berlin—so eloquently told the U.S. Congress: "Without a global revolution in the sphere of human consciousness, nothing will change for the better in the sphere of our being as humans, and the catastrophe toward which this world is headed—be it ecological, social, demographic or a general breakdown of civilization—will be unavoidable." (Havel 1990)

But here we encounter a problem in developing the new psychology. For it must, by virtue of the very nature of the task, be a psychology that includes a powerful spiritual element. This will mean, for example, a reanimation of the forests and of nature, which we have so systematically and proudly denuded of their spiritual meaning. As a recent article in the newsletter of the International Research Center for Japanese Studies (Nichibunken), entitled "Animism Renaissance" (Yoshinori 1990), which acknowledges Japan's "responsibility for a great deal of destruction of tropical rain forests" (2) points out, "severe natural destruction started at a point parallel with that of the disappearance of Animism" (4).

Here then is the problem. By and large we in the West have rejected the language and experience of the sacred, the divine, and the animation of nature. Our psychology is predominantly a psychology of mechanisms, parts, and linear relationships. We have grown suspicious of experiences, no matter how powerful, that cannot be quantified, and we distrust the language of reverence, spirit, and mystical connection, recalling perhaps with fear the superstitiousness and holy wars of earlier periods. Academic psychology, embodying now a reverence of numbers, tight reasoning, and linear thinking in opposition to intuition, direct knowing, and subjective experience is likely to look askance at efforts to reinfuse its body with the imprecise notions of spirituality and philosophy, from which it has so vigorously and proudly struggled to free itself in an effort to be granted scientific status in our universities, laboratories, and consulting rooms.

But this cannot be helped. For the route to a new psychology of the environment, which might contribute to our protecting it, probably cannot be achieved by measuring our reactions or talking about the problem. Only experiences that profoundly alter our view of nature and reconnect us with the divinity in ourselves and in the environment can empower people to commit themselves to the prodigious task before them. The therapeutic methods must be powerful enough to shift the ground of our being so that we experience the earth in its living reality. This is why people like Walter Christie (1984, 1985) and his wife Ellen, Joanna Macy (1983 and in this volume, chapter 2), and Stanislav and Christina Grof (1988), who have been pioneers in creating methods of reconnecting us with the earth and with ourselves in nature, rely on experiential, imaginal, and consciousness altering or opening approaches. Interestingly, people who open themselves to this connection, discovering their "ecological selves," seem often now to encounter disturbing images, bad smells, and other psychological experiences suggesting the earth's desecration in their dreams, fantasies, and deeper consciousness. This can become intolerably painful but also seems to empower people, impelling them to take action on behalf of the deteriorating environment. I have been struck by the fact that powerful images of the earth's polluted landscape are appearing with increasing frequency on the covers of leading magazines and in a proliferation of articles in newspapers, magazines, and books, and there are more and more television and radio programs about how we can save the earth. It is also possible that these images are now significantly penetrating our cultural consciousness and may contribute to fundamental changes in behavior and policy.

What I have described so far is, in a sense, the easy part of the problem. Deepening our conscious awareness, reanimating our connection with the earth, is important and can lead to responsible intitiatives by individuals. But the stench of my condensed Japanese–New Jersey dream landscape, the pollution of our world, and the destruction of its resources by the earth's expanding population are the problems of humankind as a whole, acting collectively through institutions, especially business corporations, often with direct or indirect governmental support. For a psychology of the environment to be meaningful, it must address these powerful institutional, structural, or systemic realities. Social institutions are, in a sense, the expressions of our collective psyches. But we come so much to take their existence and modes of operating for granted that to consider openly that we have the power to modify, transform, or dismantle them will, inevitably, encounter intense resistance because of the political, economic, and psychological vested interests with which they are associated. To bring about structural changes of this kind, psychologists will need to work closely with policymakers, corporate leaders, economists, and many people representing other related disciplines and groups committed to social change.

The political and personal resistance to environmental transformation can be flagrant. When I was in Japan, I read that industrial pollution in Korea had become so severe that, among other things, the water in the public water system in Seoul was condemned as unsafe to drink. A professor at Seoul University who documented the severity of the industrial pollution problem was fired from his position, and people who supported environmental change were accused by the government of being communist sympathizers. I had a similar experience in Paris in 1988 upon returning from a conference in Findhorn, Scotland, on "Politics as if the Whole Earth Mattered." Fresh from hearing moving talks about the pollution problem and the Green movement in Britain and elsewhere in Europe, I shared my experience and concern with a French psychologist, who dismissed these environmental concerns as communist propaganda, despite the fact that her own senses—just breathing the air in Paris—could confirm their truth.

Resistance to facing the costs of environmental transformation may extend beyond top management to the shareholders themselves. Initiatives proposed by shareholders from various environmental groups were overwhelmingly rejected by the vastly greater numbers of the company's supporters at Exxon's annual shareholders meeting in April 1990. Pleas about wildlife destruction, poisoning of children by toxic chemicals, and other dangers from hazardous waste were ignored, presumably because reparative or healing actions might reduce shareholders' profit margins and dividends. One Exxon spokesperson suggested to the environmentalists that they should, "store your car, stop flying airplanes and walk or ride a horse in the winter snow or summer heat" (Hayes 1990). Over and above the speaker's insensitivity, the remark is interesting for its implication, which is not so far off the mark—that what is at stake is the way we live in a developed society and the fact or extent of industrialization itself.

It is not realistic to expect that the environmental crisis will be solved simply by deindustrialization. But the unwelcome news the new psychology for the environment will need to communicate is that the unbridled license given in the West to free-market forces, and the irresponsible overbuilding of heavy industries in the socialist systems, have both led to the same disastrous result—a planet dying in the excesses of human waste. As my barber put it, "Johnny, we are drowning in our industrial feces." The greatest challenge we now face in this rapidly changing world is to create political institutions that use the resources of power and responsibility in conjunction with economic structures that are accountable to future generations of human beings, to other species, and to the earth itself. Psychologists of the environment, while enabling increasing numbers of people to connect with the earth and its transcendent meaning, must also participate with committed citizens and community and corporate groups in a broad-based movement that must aim at nothing less than the transformation of our political and economic institutions. Ultimately this means joining with others in a search for alternatives to the material values that now dominate the spirit in the United States and much of the world.

An environmental movement on the scale necessary to bring about the changes that are essential for protecting the earth, a process to which psychology has a useful contribution to make, must be authentically international and cross-cultural in two senses. First, we in the West or developed countries must be aware how powerfully precedent-setting is our example. When we destroy our own forests, pollute our air, and poison our streams with our industrial and personal garbage, it little avails us to admonish developing countries for unhygienic industrialization. Often-heard arguments, such as the fact that we cut down our timber in a more orderly manner than the developing countries that are destroying their rain forests, become trivial in relation to the psychological and economic forces involved. Second, we need to be aware of the economic priorities and vital needs of the peoples of developing countries. Campaigns to save natural resources, such as trees and animals, upon which impoverished peoples depend for their livelihoods, without addressing the material needs of those societies, cannot be effective.

In sum, a psychology of the environment to be comprehensive must include at least the following elements:

1. An appreciation that we do, in fact, have *a relationship with the earth* itself, and the degree to which that relationship has become inimicable to the sustaining of human lives and those of countless other species.
2. *An analysis of traditional attitudes toward the earth* in our own and in other cultures that may facilitate or interfere with the maintenance of life. The dominant attitude to the earth in the industrially developed countries has been one of unchecked exploitation.
3. *The application of methods of exploring and changing our relationship to the earth's environment* that can reanimate our connection with it. These approaches must be emotionally powerful, experiential, and consciousness-expanding, opening us to ourselves in relation to nature.
4. An *examination of politics and economics from an ecopsychological perspective*. Political and economic systems, institutions, and forces embody collective attitudes toward the earth and its living forms but have a compelling life of their own. Psychologists committed to environmental change must, therefore, work with professional environmentalists, policymakers, population experts, corporate leaders, economists, and representatives of relevant other disciplines to make these

structures compatible with an environment that can support the continuation of human life and well-being.

5. This will mean, even more than in the case of the nuclear threat, that, to be effective, psychologists will need *to become professionally and personally committed and involved outside of their offices and laboratories.* We must discover new forms of personal empowerment for ourselves and our clients that integrate exploration and activism, becoming—men and women together—archetypal warriors in the battle to protect our planet.

Kurt Vonnegut has recently captured the monumental seriousness of the environmental problem. It is too serious, he says, to be dealt with through humor. "Jokesters" he writes,

are all through when they find themselves talking about challenges so real and immediate and appalling to their listeners that no amount of laughter can make the listeners feel safe and perfectly well again. I found myself doing that on a speaking tour of campuses in the spring of 1989, and canceled all future engagements. . . . I said that the whole world faced a problem far worse than the rise of another Hitler, which was our destruction of the planet as a life-supporting apparatus of delicate and beautiful complexity.

I said that one day fairly soon we would all go belly up like guppies in a neglected fishbowl. I suggested an epitaph for the whole planet, which was: "We could have saved it, but we were too darn cheap and lazy." (Vonnegut 1990)

REFERENCES

Chief Seattle. (1988). In *Thinking Like a Mountain: Towards a Council of All Beings*, ed. J. Seed, J. Macy, P. Fleming, and A. Naess, 67–73, 71. Philadelphia: New Society Publishers.

Christie, W. (1984–1985). A Series of Six Articles in 1984 and 1985 on "Human Ecology" in *Habitat*, Journal of the Maine Audubon Society.

Gerber, L. in this volume.

Grof, S. (1988). *The Adventures of Self-Discovery: Dimensions of Consciousness and New Perspectives in Psychotherapy and Inner Exploration*, 12. Albany: State University of New York Press.

Havel, V. (1990). Address to the United States Congress, February 21, 1990. *Washington Post*, February 22.

Hayes, T. C. (1990). "Exxon Voters Reject Environment Plans." *New York Times*, April 26, p. A22.

Lame Deer, J. (Fire), and Erdoes, R. (1972). *Lame Deer, Seeker of Visions*, 116. New York: Pocket Books.

Macy, J. (1983). *Despair and Personal Power in the Nuclear Age.* Philadelphia: New Society Publishers.

Vonnegut, K. (1990). "Notes from My Bed of Gloom: Or, Why the Joking Had to Stop." *New York Times Book Review,* April 22, p. 14.

Yoshinori, Y. (1990). Animism Renaissance, *Nichibunken Newsletter.* The International Research Center for Japanese Studies (Nichibunken), January 1990, no. 5, pp. 2–4.

12

Solving Environmental Problems: A Behavior Change Perspective

E. Scott Geller

Most thoughtful people agree that the world is in serious trouble . . . fossil fuels will not last forever, and many other critical resources are nearing exhaustion; the earth grows steadily less habitable; and all this is exacerbated by a burgeoning population that resists control. The timetable may not be clear, but the threat is real. That many people have begun to find a recital of these dangers tiresome is perhaps an even greater threat. —*Skinner 1987, 1*

The above quote by the most eminent behavioral scientist of our time defines the crisis addressed in this chapter, and sets the stage for finding solutions to critical environmental problems. Many people deny our environmental exigencies, including acid rain, damage to the earth's ozone layer, ocean pollution, the loss of tropical forests, and the worldwide misuse of land and water (Goleman 1988); whereas others claim some environmental crises have reached dimensions beyond repair (e.g., Ehrlich, Ehrlich, and Holdren 1977; Rifkin 1980). Many people maintain a relentless optimism regarding planetary concerns, some adopting a "business as usual" stance (as if environmental problems will correct themselves naturally) and others assuming that high technology engineering will find sufficient answers (Robertson 1986). While a number of technological advances have mitigated environmental problems and we can hope for more of these in the future, we cannot count on "quick-fix" engineering technology alone to solve the environmental crisis. In fact,

248

human behavior contributes most significantly to the degradation of Planet Earth. In other words, as Pogo has said, "We have met the enemy and he is us." Thus the role of the human element in contributing to environmental problems or in helping to alleviate the crisis is undeniable. Understanding and changing individuals' behaviors and attitudes in order to solve problems is a prime focus of psychology, and applying this information to solve environmental problems is one aspect of a relatively new subdiscipline of psychology—environmental psychology.

ENVIRONMENTAL PSYCHOLOGY AND APPLIED BEHAVIOR ANALYSIS

As a forum of research and teaching, the field of environmental psychology is less than twenty-five years old, with the first college textbooks in this domain having appeared in the mid-1970s (e.g., Ittelson et al. 1974; Proshansky, Ittelson, and Rivlin 1976). Two basic research questions are addressed by environmental psychologists: (1) How does the physical and natural environment affect people? and (2) How do people affect the environment? Although the second question is more pertinent to the theme of this chapter, the vast majority of research in environmental psychology relates to the first question. In other words, environmental variables have been investigated most often for their effect on behavior rather than vice versa (cf. Stokols and Altman 1987). Cone and Hayes (1980) referred to this research as "reactive" (as opposed to "active") because it "examines reactions or responses *to* environmental problems rather than [examining] the problems themselves" (12). However, recent textbooks in environmental psychology (e.g., Bell et al. 1990; Gifford 1987) have given substantial attention to the second question raised above, and in fact, have addressed a third related question, most relevant to the theme of this chapter: How can human behavior be changed to benefit the environment? To review answers to this question, the textbooks refer to another subdiscipline of psychology—applied behavior analysis.

Applied behavior analysis is founded on the approach to behavioral science developed by B. F. Skinner (1938). In his experimental analysis of behavior (or operant learning paradigm), Skinner rejected unobservable inferred constructs such as drives, needs, motives, cognitions, and so on; and he studied only overt behavior and its observable environmental, social, and physiological determinants. Therefore, behavior analysts usually identify overt behavior as their dependent variable (i.e., the target to measure and change), and environmental stimuli or contingencies (i.e., relationships between designated target behaviors and their consequences) as independent variables (i.e., the aspects of the situation manipulated to change a target behavior). Thus, behavior analysts have addressed environmental problems by first defining the problem in terms of relevant overt behavior, and then designing and implementing intervention programs to decrease behaviors that cause the problem and/or increase behaviors that can alleviate the problem.

Before discussing behavior change interventions for environmental preservation, it is instructive to consider a critical perspective of the behavior analysis approach which is contrary to numerous intervention strategies used currently to attempt an increase in environmental responsiveness among the public. A common notion among social scientists (including psychologists) is that individuals change their behaviors as a result of information or advice, and that attitude change is the necessary mediating variable (e.g., Dennis et al. 1990; Fishbein and Ajzen 1975). In other words, information (e.g., about environmental protection) should focus on changing people's attitudes (e.g., about the environment), and then, after appropriate attitude change, individuals will change their behaviors (e.g., to be more protective of the environment). Behavior analysts do not deny that attitude change can lead to behavior change, but claim (on the basis of empirical evidence) it is usually more cost effective to target behaviors directly and then expect desirable attitude change to occur as a result of behavior change (cf. Geller 1986, 1989).

B. F. Skinner (1987) maintained that human behavior is selected (or determined) by its consequences, and we should not expect many people to change their behavior as a result of information or advice alone, especially when the information is about a distant future, as is the case with most environmental problems. People may follow advice when the advice-giver's information has led to beneficial consequences in the past, but this situation requires people to experience the reinforcing consequences of prior compliance with similar advice-givers or similar rules. Such operant learning or response selection by reinforcing consequences is quite difficult (perhaps impossible in some cases) when the future reinforcing or punishing consequences are unclear, vague, or remote (and all three of these characteristics are relevant in the domain of environmental protection). Collecting recyclables, for example, has typically not become common practice until individuals have experienced the consequences of excess solid waste (e.g., the problems of finding suitable landfill space or a port to dock a garbage barge); and petroleum or water conservation behavior have not been practiced widely until the punishing consequences (e.g., inconveniences) of gas or water shortages were experienced.

Although individuals are more inclined to follow advice (e.g., regarding resource conservation) after experiencing consequences related to such advice (e.g., the displeasures or inconveniences of resource shortages), there are often ongoing response-consequence contingencies supporting behaviors incompatible with the advice. For example, the excessive use of environmental resources and the pollution of air and water is maintained by varieties of reinforcing consequences, including convenience, comfort, money, and everything money can buy. Thus, effective behavior change for environmental protection may require the modification or removal of contingencies currently supporting behaviors detrimental to the environment, as well as establishing new response-consequence contingencies to motivate the occurrence of behaviors beneficial to the environment. Most of the applied behavior analysis research for environmental protection has focused on the second challenge, and we turn now to an overview of that research.

DESIGNING INTERVENTION PROGRAMS TO PROTECT THE ENVIRONMENT

A simple Activator-Behavior-Consequence framework, or ABC model, defines the basic behavior analysis approach to intervention development. In other words, conditions or events preceding (i.e., activators) or following (e.g., consequences) designated target behaviors are arranged systematically to increase or decrease the target behavior's frequency of occurrence. Therefore, the first step in designing an intervention program is to define a target behavior to change. Behavior analysts attempt to define the target behavior so precisely (i.e., operationally) that its frequency or rate of occurrence can be observed and tallied reliably. This enables the behavior analyst or intervention agent to obtain an objective record of the target behavior before and after the intervention program, thereby evaluating the behavior change impact of the intervention. Ideally, some behavioral recordings are taken long after the intervention program has ended in order to assess the long-term effects or durability of the behavior change procedures. This entire process can be readily remembered by the acronym "DO RITE" representing the sequence of: (1) *Define* the target behavior to be changed; (2) *Observe* the target behavior; (3) *Record* occurrences of the target behavior; (4) *Intervene* with a program to change the target behavior; (5) *Test* the impact of the behavior change intervention by comparing records of behavior *before* and *after* the intervention; and (6) *Evaluate* whether the program was cost effective, whether a more potent intervention program is needed, whether the program should be implemented on a larger scale, or whether it's advisable to start the DO RITE process all over again (Geller, Lehman, and Kalsher 1989). To do this process right for optimal environmental protection is not as straightforward as it seems, as we realize by considering only the first step of DO RITE—defining a target behavior to change.

Defining Target Behaviors for Environmental Protection

The variety of human behaviors related to environmental protection are numerous, occurring daily in almost every setting (e.g., at home, at work, at school, at commercial locations, and in transition between settings). However, defining responses detrimental and beneficial to the planet and prioritizing recommendations regarding desirable change usually requires interdisciplinary input (Geller, Winett, and Everett 1982). For example, engineering data are required to advise which appliance or vehicle is most energy-efficient or environment-polluting; architectural data are often helpful in defining optimal insulation techniques and landscape designs for conserving energy in heating and cooling residences; biological data are essential to prescribe optimal procedures for composting and for disposing of hazardous waste; and information from physics and human-factors engineering is relevant for defining the most environment-preserving ways to use appliances, vehicles, industrial machinery, conservation devices, and systems for heating, cooling, recycling, or water treatment (Geller 1986).

To categorize the potential target behaviors of a comprehensive plan for environmental protection, Geller et al. (1982) proposed a $2 \times 3 \times 5$ factorial array (or three-dimensional matrix), with the following variables: (1) two basic intervention *approaches* (physical versus behavioral technology); (2) three community *sectors* requiring direct intervention (residential/consumer sector, governmental/institutional sector, and commercial/industrial sector); and (3) five *targets* or domains for intervention within each sector (i.e., heating/cooling, solid waste management, transportation, equipment efficiency, and water). It is noteworthy that these five targets do not cover the entire environmental crisis. For instance, problems related to population explosion, air pollution, land misuse, hazardous waste, and mineral depletion were not addressed by Geller et al., and have not been researched by environmental psychologists or behavior analysts. Cone and Hayes (1980) covered two more environmental targets (population control and noise pollution) in their text on behavioral approaches to the prevention of environmental problems, but the behavior change research in these additional areas has been minimal. In addition, almost all of the behavior change research has targeted behaviors in the residential/consumer sector rather than the governmental/institutional or commercial/industrial sectors, where the potential for large-scale change for environmental protection is greatest. However, the principles and intervention strategies derived from demonstration projects in the residential/consumer sector are relevant for developing behavior change programs and policy in the corporate and governmental sectors of society. The point is that intervention change researchers have clearly only cracked the surface with regard to making a significant contribution to the human element aspect of environmental problems.

1. *One-shot vs. repetitive behaviors.* Some strategies for preventing environmental problems require only one occurrence of a particular target intervention or a one-time behavior change (e.g., installing a thermostat that automatically changes room temperature settings to preprogrammed levels; undergoing surgical sterilization for birth control; purchasing an energy-efficient vehicle with optimal emission controls; wrapping insulation around a water heater; inserting a shower-flow restrictor in a showerhead; installing a solar heating system; adding insulation to a building; purchasing longer-lasting equipment; applying appropriate irrigation technology and constructing a high-technology waste separation system). On the other hand, other behavioral approaches to solving environmental problems require repetitive action in order to effect significant environmental protection (such as setting back room thermostats each night; using contraceptives consistently; following anti-pollution guidelines regularly; driving 55 mph or less; taking shorter and

cooler showers; purchasing low-phosphate detergents, white toilet paper, and returnable bottles; using separate containers for recyclable paper, metal, glass and biodegradable trash; maintaining a compost pile for food and yard wastes; and wearing more clothes indoors in order to withstand lower room temperatures).

For "one-shot" behaviors, the user usually pays a one-time, relatively high cost in time and/or money for the subsequent convenience of not having to make continued response input. However, several strategies for environmental responsiveness involve both a one-shot investment and repeated actions. For example, a window fan can be purchased to substitute for an air conditioner, or a moped acquired to substitute for an automobile, but energy conservation does not occur unless the consumer makes repeated decisions to use the more energy-efficient equipment. Likewise, energy-saving or antipollution settings on new energy-efficient and environment-protective appliances are not worth much unless they are used regularly. Furthermore, innovative equipment for separating, transporting, and reprocessing recyclable trash are not protecting the environment until they are used appropriately each day by numerous individuals (e.g., from residents who initiate the process by collecting recyclables to retailers who promote the purchase of recyclable and recycled commodities).

2. *Peak shift behaviors.* In the realm of energy conservation, there is an additional class of target behaviors for environmental protection. These are "peak shift behaviors," which refer to changing the time when residents (and corporations and governments) emit certain energy consumptive behaviors. Reducing peak demands for energy decreases the need for power companies to build or borrow supplementary generators or other energy sources (e.g., nuclear reactors). In fact, electricity suppliers have been willing to vary their rates according to peak demand (i.e., peak-load pricing), but residents have found it difficult to shift various energy-consuming tasks (Kohlenberg, Phillips, and Proctor 1976). And, apparently this strategy has not been seriously considered by industries, institutions, or governments.

Peak shifting is usually associated with residential energy use (e.g., changing showering, cooking, laundering, and sleeping times), but this class of behaviors may be even more feasible as a large-scale conservation strategy for the corporate and municipal sectors of a community. Consider, for example, the peak-shift advantages of altering the scheduling and/or length of work shifts at industrial complexes and government agencies (e.g., through the adoption of flexible work schedules or a four-day work week). Large-scale changes in work schedules could result in peak shifts (and energy savings) at the work setting, at home, and during commuting. The major function of urban transit systems, for example, is to serve individuals traveling to and from work; and since most of this commuting occurs during only two short rush periods per weekday, numerous bus drivers make nonproductive runs or actually sit idle much of the day (Zerega 1981). Before instituting large-scale shifts in work schedules, however, it is necessary to conduct comprehensive, multifaceted pilot testing to define the most energy-efficient plan without disrupting family life, leisure activity, and other functions of a "healthy" community (Winett and Neale 1981).

Activators for Environment Preservation

Activators (often referred to as stimulus control, prompting, response priming, or antecedent techniques) are environmental manipulations occurring before an opportunity for the target behavior, in an attempt to increase the frequency of desired target behaviors or decrease occurrences of undesired target responses. Activators can take the form of (1) verbal or written messages; (2) awareness or education sessions; (3) modeling or demonstrations; (4) goal setting or commitment strategies; and (5) engineering or design procedures.

1. *Verbal and written messages.* Messages designed to promote environment preservation have been presented in television commercials, pamphlets, films, verbal instructions, and demonstrations (e.g., from peers, parents, teachers, or public officials) and on environmental displays (such as speed limit signs, feedback meters, beautified trash receptacles, and "energy saving" settings on appliance controls). Behavior change researchers have studied the impact of various antecedent messages on energy conservation, litter control, and resource recovery (see review by Geller et al. 1982) and have defined some basic characteristics of effective behavior change messages, including (1) messages should refer to specific behaviors (desirable or undesirable); (2) when the avoidance of undesirable behaviors is prompted (e.g., antilittering), an alternative desirable behavior should be specified that is relatively convenient; (3) messages should be stated in polite language that does not

threaten an individual's perceived freedom; (4) to be most effective, behavior change messages should occur in close proximity to opportunities to emit the desired or undesired target behavior; and (5) messages announcing a certain consequence following the target behavior are more effective than those that do not specify a response consequence. The announcement of a pleasant consequence following the desired behavior (e.g., 10 cents per returnable bottle) is termed an *incentive;* whereas a *disincentive* is the announcement of a penalty if a certain undesirable behavior occurs (e.g., $100 fine for littering).

Delprata (1977) and Winett (1978) were successful in prompting occupants of public buildings to turn off room lights when they placed messages at light switches that specified the lights should be turned out when leaving the room; and Geller, Witmer, and Orebaugh (1976) found 20 percent to 30 percent compliance with antilitter messages on handbills when the prompt politely requested that the handbill be deposited for recycling in a conveniently located (and obtrusive) trash receptacle.

2. *Awareness and education.* Before attempting to change intervention, it is often important to offer potential participants a sound rationale for the behavior change program. A reasonable rationale can facilitate a participant's acceptance of attempts to motivate behavior change, and increase the probability that the person will develop a personal (or intrinsic) justification for the desired behavior and continue this behavior in the absence of extrinsic motivators (i.e., incentives or disincentives).

Applied psychologists (e.g., Lewin 1958) have shown that education directed toward behavior change is more effective in small (i.e., ten to fifteen participants) rather than large groups, and that the education should include interactive demonstrations, discussion, and perhaps consensus building, rather than lecturing or showing films to a passive audience. In this regard, a well-known but not frequently practiced educational principle is relevant: *Tell them and they'll forget—demonstrate and they'll remember—involve them and they'll understand.* Education/awareness sessions and informational packages that did not promote participatory involvement nor provide extrinsic incentives or disincentives were not successful in motivating newspaper recycling, residential energy conservation, or water saving (e.g., see reviews by Geller 1986, 1989; Geller et al. 1982).

3. *Modeling and demonstrations.* Modeling refers to the demonstra-

tion of specific behaviors for a target audience, and sometimes includes the display of a response-consequence relationship (or contingency) by presenting a pleasant or unpleasant consequence following a model's desirable or undesirable behavior (Bandura 1977). Modeling can occur via live demonstrations or through television, video tape, or film. As an activator, modeling involves presenting a specific behavioral message, sometimes with the announcement of a reinforcement contingency (i.e., the model receives a reward following a specific desirable response) or a punishment contingency (i.e., the model receives a penalty after displaying undesirable behavior). Environmental protection programs have essentially ignored modeling strategies, yet modeling (through television or videotape) has the potential of reaching and influencing millions of residents. Winett and his students (e.g., Winett et al. 1985) showed prominent increases in the conservation of electricity for home heating and cooling after residents viewed videotape or television presentations specifying the monetary benefits resulting from simple conservation behaviors by persons in situations similar to those of the viewers.

4. *Commitment and goal setting.* Commitment and goal-setting techniques request a verbal or written statement from individuals or groups, stipulating that they will emit a particular behavior (e.g., pick up litter or collect recyclables), stop emitting a certain behavior (e.g., littering), or reach a designated outcome as a result of one or more behaviors (e.g., use 25 percent less water, gas, or electricity). For example, "promise cards" could be available in a variety of settings which obligate the signers to engage in particular behaviors for a given period of time (cf. Geller and Lehman, 1991). Completed promise cards can become raffle tickets in a lottery, thus combining commitment and incentive approaches. Likewise, individuals or groups can set a particular environmental protection goal (e.g., in terms of a desired level of program participation, or savings from conservation efforts) and rewards can be offered for achieving the designated goals. Becker (1978) increased the effectiveness of using feedback to decrease home energy use by giving residents difficult but achievable group goals.

Some field researchers (e.g., Burn and Oskamp 1986; Pardini and Katzev 1984) found markedly increased participation in neighborhood recycling programs after residents signed cards pledging their participation; and the author and his students demonstrated substantial increases in vehicle safety-belt use after "make it click" promise cards were distributed and signed at industrial sites, a community hospital, and throughout a university campus (see review by Geller, Berry, et al. 1990).

5. *Engineering and design procedures.* Engineering and design activators for environmental protection involve the design or redesign of equipment, tools, or entire environmental settings to provide opportunities for environmental protective behaviors, or to facilitate (or encourage) the occurrence of such behaviors. For example, simple modifications in the design of an environmental setting or litter-collection device can increase the convenience of litter control or resource recovery (e.g., by increasing the availability or size of trash cans or by providing large, obtrusive, partitioned receptacles for depositing different types of recyclables); or design/engineering interventions can help to motivate trash-can disposals or litter pick-up (e.g., by beautifying trash receptacles or environmental settings). Some behavioral environmental psychologists have shown remarkable litter control effects of simple modifications in the appearance, positioning, and availability of trash receptacles, and others showed household recycling advantages of a "recycle-it" trash receptacle with separate compartments for paper, glass, and cans (see reviews by Geller 1986 and Geller et al. 1982). Also, Cope and Geller (1984) demonstrated litter-control benefits with a large "put-and-take litter bag receptacle" containing a large disposal chute for automobile litter bags and a litter bag dispenser that held 25,000 plastic litter bags. These investigators, however, found optimal benefits with their special trash receptacle when they combined this activator strategy with a consequence technique (i.e., soft drinks were given to fast food customers who used the litter bags dispensed by the special trash can).

Consequences for Environment Preservation

Behavior change interventions for preserving the environment have been more effective when rewards or penalties were consequences for the occurrence of a target behavior or for a particular outcome resulting from the occurrence of one or more target behaviors. Consequences have been distinct stimuli (e.g., a monetary rebate, a self-photograph, a speeding ticket, a verbal commendation or condemnation), or opportunities to engage in certain behaviors (e.g., the privilege to add one's name to an

"Energy Efficient" honor roll, use a preferred parking space, or attend a special litter-control workshop).

Federal, state, and local governments have traditionally used disincentives and penalties to protect the environment. These behavior modification attempts usually take the form of laws or ordinances (e.g., fines for littering, illegal dumping, excessive water use, or for polluting water, land, or air), and to be effective, these techniques usually require extensive enforcement and legal personnel. Applied behavior analysts have deemphasized the use of these approaches for large-scale behavior change, not only because enforcement is cumbersome and behavior change depends upon continual promotion of a disincentive (cf. Ross 1982), but also because negative attitudes often accompany attempts to mandate behavior change through disincentive/penalty tactics.

Although behavior analysts consider it is most cost effective to attack behaviors directly (rather than focusing on attitude change) when addressing environmental problems (as discussed at the start of this chapter), they are concerned with the attitude formation or change following behavior modification. Positive attitudes associated with one's change in behavior maximize the possibility for the desired behavior becoming a norm—the socially accepted rule of action. Positive attitudes are apt to follow incentive/reward strategies, since a positive reinforcement approach is generally perceived as "voluntary," and does not elicit perceived threats to individual freedom which can result from disincentive/penalty procedures (cf. Skinner 1971). A perception of threat to one's freedom can actually lead to overt noncompliance with a mandate, resulting in pleasant feelings of regained personal freedom or control (Brehm 1972). This phenomenon has been labeled "psychological reactance," and is illustrated in the scenario of the vehicle passenger throwing litter at the road sign announcing a $100 fine (i.e., a disincentive) for littering. Of course, drivers will only do this when it is unlikely the litter control ordinance can be enforced—that is, when a police officer is unavailable (which is necessarily most of the time).

Response-Contingent vs. Outcome-Contingent Consequences

The positive reinforcement consequences applied toward environmental protection have varied widely. Some rewards have been given following the performance of a particular desired behavior, whereas other reward contingencies did not specify a desired behavior but were contingent upon a given outcome (e.g., based on obtaining a certain level of energy conservation, water savings, or environmental cleanliness). As reviewed by Geller (1986, 1989) and Geller et al. (1982), the following *response-contingent* consequences increased significantly the frequency of the environment-protective behavior targeted: (1) raffle tickets per specified amounts of paper delivered to a recycling center; (2) $5 if a resident's room thermostat was set at 74°F or higher in the summer and all doors and windows were closed when the air conditioner was on; (3) a coupon redeemable for a soft drink following litter deposits in a particular trash receptacle; (4) a merchandise token (exchangeable for goods and services at local businesses) for riding a particular bus; (5) a posted self-photograph and $1 for collecting a specially marked item of litter; and (6) points redeemable for family outings and special favors following reduced use of home appliances.

Outcome-contingent consequences effective at increasing the frequency of behaviors beneficial to the environment have included (1) a tour of a mental health facility for reducing vehicular miles of travel 20 percent or more; (2) 10¢ for cleaning a littered yard to a specified criterion; (3) $5 for averaging a 10 percent reduction in miles of travel over twenty-eight days, and $2.50 for each additional 10 percent reduction, up to 30 percent; (4) $2 per week for a 5 to 10 percent reduction in home-heating energy, $3 for an 11 to 20 percent reduction, and $5 per week for reductions greater than 20 percent; and (5) a cash return to apartment residents of 75 percent of energy savings from expected heating costs for a master-metered apartment complex (see reviews by Geller 1986, 1989; Geller et al. 1982).

Feedback Interventions

A variety of energy conservation studies demonstrated beneficial effects of giving residents specific and regular feedback regarding their energy consumption (e.g., see reviews by Geller 1986, 1989; Geller et al. 1982). As an outcome consequence, feedback indicated amount of energy consumption in terms of kilowatt hours, cubic feet of gas, and/or monetary cost; and the clear display of energy use was rewarding (when the feedback reflected a savings in energy costs) or punishing (when the feedback implied an increase in consumption and costs).

Most of the feedback research by behavioral environmental psychologists targeted residential energy consumption, and for a majority of these field studies the feedback was given individually to particular residences. As reviewed by Geller (1986, 1989) and Geller et al. (1982), successful ways of delivering energy consumption feedback have included (1) a special feedback card delivered to the home daily, weekly, or monthly; (2) a mechanical apparatus illuminating a light whenever electricity use exceeded 90 percent of the household's peak level; (3) an electronic feedback meter with a digital display of electricity cost per hour; (4) the use of a hygrothermograph to give readings of room temperature and humidity; and (5) self-contained training programs for teaching and motivating residents to read their own electric meters regularly and graph their energy consumption.

Some feedback research studies addressed the conservation of transportation energy. One field study showed vehicular miles of travel (vmt) to decrease as a function of public display of vmt per individual; and other studies found vehicular miles per gallon (mpg) to increase with a fuel-flow meter indicating continuous mpg or gallons-per-hour consumption or with a public display of mpg for short-run and long-haul truck drivers (see reviews by Geller 1986 and Geller et al. 1982). One feedback intervention targeted litter control and showed a 35 percent average reduction in ground litter following daily displays of litter counts on the front page of a community newspaper (Schnelle, Gendrich, et al. 1980).

INCREASING THE IMPACT OF INTERVENTION PROGRAMS

My students and I have recently been researching and developing a system for evaluating the impact of behavior change techniques to protect the environment (Geller, Needleman, and Randall 1990) or improve driving behavior (Geller, Berry, et al. 1990). This has been a formidable task, especially considering the variety of environmental and individual factors that can moderate intervention effectiveness. Frankly, we have only cracked the surface at developing a practical intervention impact model to evaluate the cost-effectiveness of large-scale intervention programs and guide the development of more effective procedures to change behaviors for environmental protection. This process, including a comprehensive literature review, has led to the identification of five factors that determine the behavior change impact of an intervention program.

Specifically, we propose that the *immediate* impact of an intervention program is a direct function of (1) the transmission of specific *response information* (i.e., direction to emit a particular target behavior); (2) the amount of participant *involvement* promoted by the intervention; (3) the degree of *extrinsic control* defined by behavior modification procedures or response-consequence contingencies (i.e., incentive/reward or disincentive/penalty strategies); (4) the degree of participant *social support* encouraged by the intervention procedures; and (5) each individual participant's perception of *self-efficacy* (Bandura 1989), *intrinsic control* (Deci 1975), or *empowerment* (Byham and Cox 1988), all of which we presume to be essentially the same inferred construct and reflect the degree to which an intervention program allows the participants to feel a sense of personal freedom or autonomy.

To derive impact or effectiveness scores for various behavior change interventions, Geller, Berry, et al. (1990) defined each behavior change technique of an intervention program (a given program can apply several different behavior change techniques, as illustrated above), and then judged whether the procedures of each technique had the potential to include aspects of the five evaluation factors listed above, which are presumed to influence intervention impact. To do this, the following questions and issues per factor were addressed:

1. *Response information.* Does the behavior change procedure have the *potential* to offer new and specific information relevant to the target behavior(s)? Whereas all techniques have the potential of providing new response information, the response information of an intervention program depends upon the particular message used for the behavior change technique and each program recipient's prior knowledge of the target behavior. For example, written activators (e.g., signs or memos specifying desired behaviors) are often informative upon initial exposure to viewers; however, after individuals become aware of the appropriate behavior, the same activator essentially becomes a *reminder* (with less response information upon repeated presentations). Consequently, determining an information score for a particular behavior change technique in an intervention program requires an estimate of the participants' prior knowledge of the target behavior(s) and a consideration of all techniques used in a program.

2. *Involvement.* Does the behavior change technique promote overt participant action relevant to the target behavior? This factor can be

measured through direct observation of the amount of behavioral activity resulting from the intervention program, which is generally a direct function of the ratio between intervention agents and program participants (i.e., more intervention agents per participants usually promote greater program involvement).

3. *Extrinsic control.* Does the behavior change procedure manipulate a response consequence (i.e., a reward or penalty) in order to influence a target behavior? While disincentive/penalty contingencies are perceived as exerting more extrinsic control than incentive/reward programs (Skinner 1971), the amount of perceived enforcement of a disincentive/penalty program is also a powerful determinant of intervention impact (Ross 1982).

4. *Intrinsic control.* Does the technique offer an opportunity for personal choice or control? This factor is particularly important for estimating the long-term effects of an intervention program. That is, powerful extrinsic contingencies (e.g., large penalties and consistent enforcement) may motivate extensive behavior change while the program is in effect; but if the intervention program is withdrawn, the undesirable behaviors are likely to return, unless the participants gain an internal justification for performing the target behaviors. However, the degree of internal justification for a target behavior has been found to vary inversely with the amount of extrinsic control exerted in an intervention program (e.g., Lepper, Green, and Nisbett 1973).

5. *Social support.* Does the behavior change procedure include opportunities for continual program-relevant support from program participants or other individuals or groups (e.g., family, friends, or work groups)? For example, interventions that promote group or team interaction (e.g., consensus-building exercises or group goal setting) or promote group/team performance (e.g., group competition feedback or rewards) can influence social or peer support (or peer pressure) among the participants, thereby increasing individual motivation to emit the target behavior(s). Also, if the consequences of meeting the criteria of a reward contingency include prizes valued by several family members, it is likely that social or family support will be activated and add to the impact of the intervention program.

This has been only an introduction to the challenge of developing a reliable and valid system to guide the development of behavior change intervention programs for environmental protection. Although this research is still preliminary, the mission of this venture is actually critical for solving the human behavior aspects of each societal problem raised in this text. The enormity and urgency of changing human behavior to improve (or perhaps only to maintain) quality of life on Planet Earth require increasing resources and efforts to develop, evaluate, and implement intervention programs to change and maintain public behavior in desired directions. Thus, a reliable and valid taxonomy of behavior change techniques from which to choose particular intervention programs is urgently needed.

SUMMARY AND CONCLUDING COMMENTARY

Behavior change theory was first applied to environmental problems in the early 1970s, following the first Earth Day. During this period, numerous behavior change studies focused on the development and evaluation of interventions to reduce such environment-destructive behaviors as littering, lawn trampling, vehicle miles of travel, and the purchase of beverages in throwaway containers. Other behavioral studies showed how to increase such environment-preserving behaviors as picking up litter, collecting and delivering recyclables, composting, car pooling, and practicing a number of low-cost conservation techniques (e.g., installing insulation and shower-flow limiters, adjusting thermostat settings and wearing appropriate clothing, reducing the use of air conditioners, adjusting for peak-load demands, and increasing the use of mass transit). Several innovative behavior change techniques emerged from this research, many proving to be cost-effective for communitywide application. Although the results from this domain of behavior change research were encouraging, large-scale applications of the practical intervention programs were not to be. The textbooks (Cone and Hayes 1980; Geller et al. 1982) that reviewed this work were read by very few individuals besides students at the relatively few colleges or universities offering courses in environmental psychology. The failure to apply this knowledge is unfortunate, especially in light of the profound intensification of environmental destruction occurring since the first Earth Day.

There are many possible reasons for the lack of governmental, corporate, and societal interest in the behavioral environmental research of the 1970s, including ineffective dissemination of the practical research findings to agencies and audiences who were more intrigued with high technology and quick-fix approaches to solving environmental problems. Indeed, the theme of this behavior change research—conservation through low-technology community-based intervention—has been typically viewed as incompatible with big business and consumer convenience. This viewpoint was summarized succinctly by Clive Seligman, one of the behavior change researchers of the '70s: "Unless business can make money from environmental products or politicians can get elected on environmental issues, or individuals can get personal satisfaction from experiencing environmental concern, then individuals and organizations will simply do what ever competes with environmentalism if they see the payoff as greater" (C. Seligman, pers. comm., March 8, 1990, cited in Geller 1990).

National, state, and local governments have seemed content to pass environmental-control legislation and then penalize individual, group, or corporate infractions of such policy. This is partly because laws, policies, and ordinances are relatively quick and easy to implement and monitor; they represent the traditional governmental approach to behavior control, and the monetary fines from infractions provide funds for the mandating government, organization, or community (R. Foxx, pers. comm., March 22, 1990, cited in Geller 1990).

This paper has summarized a number of behavior change approaches to environmental protection that did not incorporate mandates, disincentives, or penalties—the techniques that should actually be used only as a last resort if public acceptance and positive attitude change are desired. Although this applied research focused on individuals in the residential/consumer sector, many of the lessons learned can be applied to the governmental/institutional and commercial/industrial sectors. Let us hope that Earth Day 1990 has begun an era of corporate and government concern and community empowerment for addressing environmental issues in sharp contrast to the corporate and individual greed of the 1980s, which occurred at the expense of community and environmental enhancement.

Unlike twenty years ago, it is now fashionable and profitable for companies to promote their products as being environmentally protective. Behavioral and social scientists can play an important role in increasing corporations' environmentally protective behavior by helping them develop more effective environmental programs with the low-technology behavior change interventions reviewed in this chapter. Along these same lines, the government should provide incentives and rewards (e.g., tax breaks) for companies demonstrating environment-preserving practices, and should establish funding for researchers interested in studying the human element of environmental issues. Such research support was essentially nonexistent for the behavioral environmental psychologists of the 1970s, and thus most of these researchers and teachers abandoned the field in the early 1980s (Geller 1990). There is cause for optimism, however, given the increased amount of media attention to environmental issues and the overwhelming expression of environmental concern by the public. These are promising signs that the culture is beginning to change toward a concern for environmental protection. Clearly, the Zeitgeist is ripe for governments, scientists, corporations, environmental groups, and citizens to work together to preserve the quality of environment we now enjoy. The future of our Planet Earth is indeed in our hands.

REFERENCES

Bandura, A. (1977). *Social learning theory*. Englewood Cliffs, N.J.: Prentice-Hall.

Bandura, A. (1989). Human agency in social cognitive theory. *American Psychologist, 44*, 1175–1184.

Becker, L. J. (1978). The joint effect of feedback and goal setting on performance: A field study of residential energy conservation. *Journal of Applied Psychology, 63*, 228–233.

Bell, P. A., Fisher, J., Baum, A., and Green, T. E. (1990). *Environmental psychology*. 3d ed. Chicago: Holt, Rinehart and Winston.

Brehm, J. W. (1972). *Responses to loss of freedom: A theory of psychological reactance*. New York: General Learning Press.

Burn, S. M., and Oskamp, S. (1986). Increasing community recycling with persuasive communication and public commitment. *Journal of Applied Social Psychology, 16*, 29–41.

Byham, W. C., and Cox, J. (1988). *Zapp: The lightning of empowerment*. West Caldwell, N.J.: William Morrow and Co.

Cone, J. D., and Hayes, S. C. (1980). *Environmental problems/Behavioral solutions*. Monterey, Calif.: Brooks/Cole Publishing Company.

Cope, J. A., and Geller, E. S. (1984). Community-based interventions to increase the use of automobile litter bags. *Journal of Resource Management and Technology, 13*, 127–132.

Deci, E. L. (1975). *Intrinsic motivation*. New York: Plenum.

Delprata, D. J. (1977). Prompting electrical energy conservation in commercial users. *Environment and Behavior, 9*, 433–440.

Dennis, M. L., Soderstrom, E. J., Koncinski, Jr., W. S., and Cavanaugh, B. (1990). Effective dissemination of energy-related information: Applying social psychology and evaluation research. *American Psychologist, 45*, 1109–1117.

Ehrlich, P. R., Ehrlich, A. H., and Holdren, J. P. (1977). *Ecoscience: Population, resources, environment.* San Francisco: Freeman.

Fishbein, M., and Ajzen, I. (1975). *Belief, attitude, intention and behavior: An introduction to theory and research.* Reading, Mass.: Addison-Wesley.

Geller, E. S. (1986). Prevention of environmental problems. In L. Michelson and B. Edelstein, eds., *Handbook of prevention*, 361–383. New York: Plenum.

Geller, E. S. (1989). Applied behavior analysis and social marketing: An integration to preserve the environment. *Journal of Social Issues, 45*, 17–36.

Geller, E. S. (1990). Behavior analysis and environmental protection: Where have all the flowers gone *Journal of Applied Behavior Analysis, 23*, 269–273.

Geller, E. S., and Lehman, G. R. (1991). The Buckle-Up Promise Card: A versatile intervention for large-scale behavior change. *Journal of Applied Behavior Analysis, 24*, 91–94.

Geller, E. S., Berry, T. D., Ludwig, T. D., Evans, R. E., Gilmore, M. R., and Clarke, S. W. (1990). A conceptual framework for developing and evaluating behavior change interventions for injury control. *Health Education Research: Theory and Practice, 5*, 125–137.

Geller, E. S., Lehman, G. R., and Kalsher, M. J. (1989). *Behavior analysis training for occupational safety.* Newport, Va.: Make-A-Difference, Inc.

Geller, E. S., Needleman, L. D., and Randall, K. (1990) "Developing a taxonomy of behavior change techniques for environmental protection." Paper presented at the First U.S. Conference on Municipal Solid Waste Management, Washington, D. C., June 1990.

Geller, E. S., Winett, R. A., and Everett, P. B. (1982). *Preserving the environment: New strategies for behavior change.* Elmsford, N.Y.: Pergamon Press.

Geller, E. S., Witmer, J. F., and Orebaugh, A. L. (1976). Instructions as a determinant of paper-disposal behaviors. *Environment and Behavior, 8*, 417–438.

Gifford, R. (1987). *Environmental psychology: Principles and practice.* Newton, Mass.: Allyn and Bacon.

Goleman, D. J. (1988). "The psychology of planetary concern: Self-deception and the world crisis." Keynote address at the meeting of the American Psychological Association, Boston, August 1988.

Ittelson, W. H., Proshansky, H. M., Rivlin, L. G., and Winkel, G. (1974). *An introduction to environmental psychology.* New York: Holt, Rinehart and Winston.

Kohlenberg, R. J., Phillips, T., and Proctor, W. (1976). A behavioral analysis of peaking in residential electricity energy consumption. *Journal of Applied Behavior Analysis, 9*, 13–18.

Lepper, M., Green, D., and Nisbett, R. (1973). Undermining children's intrinsic interest with extrinsic rewards: A test of the over-justification hypothesis. *Journal of Personality and Social Psychology, 28,* 129–137.

Lewin, K. (1958). Group decision and social change. In E. E. Maccoby, T. M. Newcomb, and E. L. Hartley, eds., *Readings in social psychology,* pp. 197–211. New York: Holt, Rinehart and Winston.

Pardini, A. U., and Katzev, R. A. (1984). The effect of strength of commitment on newspaper recycling. *Journal of Environmental Systems, 13,* 245–254.

Proshansky, H. M., Ittelson, W. H., and Rivlin, L. G., eds. (1976). *Environmental psychology: People and their physical settings.* 2d ed. New York: Holt, Rinehart and Winston.

Rifkin, J. (1980). *Entropy: A new world view.* New York: Viking Press.

Robertson, J. (1986). "Five views about the future." Keynote address at a special injury-control conference, "Social dynamics of change: Implications for traffic safety," Vancouver, B.C.

Ross, H. L. (1982). *Deterring the drinking driver.* Lexington, Mass.: Lexington Books.

Schnelle, J. G., Gendrich, J. G., Beegle, G. P., Thomas, M. M., and McNees, M. P. (1980). Mass media techniques for prompting behavior change in the community. *Environment and Behavior, 12,* 157–166.

Skinner, B. F. (1971). *Beyond freedom and dignity.* New York: Knopf.

Skinner, B. F. (1938). *The behavior of organisms.* New York: Appleton-Century-Crofts.

Skinner, B. F. (1987). *Upon further reflection.* Englewood Cliffs, N.J.: Prentice-Hall.

Stokols, D., and Altman, I., eds. (1987). *Handbook of environmental psychology.* 2 vols. New York: Wiley.

Winett, R. A. (1978). Prompting turning-out lights in unoccupied rooms. *Journal of Environmental Systems, 6,* 237–241.

Winett, R. A., and Neale, M. S. (1981). Results of experiments on flexitime and family life. *Monthly Labor Review,* November, 24–32.

Winett, R. A., Leckliter, I. N., Chinn, D. E., Stahl, B., and Love, S. Q. (1985). Effects of television modeling on residential energy conservation. *Journal of Applied Behavior Analysis, 18,* 33–44.

Zerega, A. M. (1981). Transportation energy conservation policy: Implications for social science research. *Journal of Social Issues, 37,* 31–50.

PART FIVE

EMPOWERMENT, ACTIVISM, AND COMMITMENT

Until one is committed there is hesitancy—the chance to draw back—always ineffectiveness. Concerning all acts of initiative and creation there is one elementary truth the ignorance of which kills countless ideas and splendid plans: that the moment one definitely commits oneself then Providence moves too. All sorts of things occur to help one that would never otherwise have occurred. A whole stream of events issues from the decision raising in one's favor all manner of unforeseen incidences and meetings and material assistance which no one could have dreamt would have come his way. Whatever you can do or dream you can— begin it. Boldness has genius, power, and magic in it. —*Goethe*

In our era of instantaneous global communication, new crises present themselves to us each day. We are challenged to respond, to take a stand, to demonstrate our concern, to use our skills and resources to make a difference. By what internal, psychological process do we either commit ourselves to involvement and action or choose not to respond?

In this part, this question is addressed from several different perspectives. Members of the Boston Women's Peace Research Group describe, in chapter 13, their personal struggles with integrating the "professional" and the "personal" in their peace activism and research, emphasizing the importance of connection, support, and validation in a group in their peace work. In chapter 14, Sally Mack describes her venture into the intense and empowering experience of participating with her family in nonviolent civil disobedience at the Nevada Nuclear Test Site, and the powerful effect of this experience on her relationships with family, friends, colleagues, and clients. In chapter 15, Susan Fiske examines the psychological survey data on people's beliefs and feelings about nuclear war, and reviews data on the possible psychological and social reasons for lack of involvement in antinuclear activities. She suggests strategies for psychologists who wish to increase activism. Finally, in chapter 16, Douglas McKenzie-Mohr identifies some of the psychological factors that either promote or inhibit activism on the issues of militarism and the environment, and proposes strategies for increasing activism in the general public.

13

Women and Peacemaking: The Importance of Relationships

The Boston Women's Peace Research Group (Susan M. Brooks, Sarah A. Conn, Priscilla Ellis, Sally A. Mack, Bianca Cody Murphy, and Janet Surrey)

Matters of social responsibility and peace have been central issues in the lives of women, manifesting themselves in such areas as family relationships, friendship groups, neighborhood and community projects, and governmental affairs. Along with the increasing awareness and development of feminist consciousness in the past thirty years, many more women have been taking initiative and assuming leadership in the struggle for social justice, environmental safety, peace, and nuclear disarmament. The Boston Women's Peace Research Group (BWPRG) consists of six women, all psychotherapists, who have been looking at different ways women are expressing themselves in peacemaking efforts and trying to learn what this expression reveals about women's psychological development and ways of functioning. Our experience has led us to believe that women become empowered to work for peace in the context of their relationships with others. In this paper we will introduce you to a theoretical framework that emphasizes the relational context of women's psychological development; to the views of research that frame our work; and to application of both in situations ranging from the college classroom to the Nevada Nuclear Test Site.

First let us introduce ourselves.

Susan ("Suz") Brooks is a clinical psychologist in private practice. She is a long-time social activist and has researched women's commitment to the antinuclear movement.

Sarah Conn is a clinical psychologist in private practice who teaches a course on global issues and psychotherapy. She is a parent of two teenage daughters.

Priscilla ("Prill") Ellis is a clinical psychologist in private practice, a co-director of the Atomic Veterans Family Project, and the mother of two young sons.

Sally Mack is a clinical social worker and an active member of Social Workers for Peace and Nuclear Disarmament. She promotes and studies the development of awareness and activism in social-political issues and has shared her struggles for peace and justice with her husband and three sons.

Bianca Cody Murphy is an assistant professor of psychology at Wheaton College who teaches a course on psychology in the nuclear age. She is a counseling psychologist, co-director of the Atomic Veterans Family Project, and an active member of Psychologists for Social Responsibility.

Janet Surrey is a clinical psychologist, teacher, and researcher in the area of women's psychological development. She conducts workshops on women's empowerment and peacemaking in this country and abroad. She is a board member of Women's Action for Nuclear Disarmament.

RELATIONSHIP AS A CONTEXT FOR SOCIAL CHANGE

The importance of relationship as a context for social change was demonstrated in the women's movement of the 1960s. Consciousness-raising groups seemed to develop spontaneously and ubiquitously, becoming a major force for personal and political change. They facilitated the development of connections among women, which led from movement out of silence, shame, and isolation into an increasing sense of empowerment through solidarity. The groups themselves, and the issues around which women mobilized, expressed the values women have traditionally "carried" for Western culture: the importance of relationships and a commitment to care, connection, and the preservation of life (Miller 1976). Long-term women activists in the peace movement emphasize the importance of relationships with others in both initiating and sustaining their activism (Brooks 1987). The affirmation and articulation of women's strengths and values through the women's movement have offered women new vehicles for personal and professional growth and new visions for social change.

When women are asked to describe their visions of peace, they do so differently than men. Surrey (1987) interviewed twenty men and women about experiences of peace in their daily lives. The women spoke about peace in terms of mutually empathic human relationships, and as a dynamic creative process. Men more frequently defined peace by what it is *not*—they saw peace as the absence of war. Women tended to experience peace in human relationships, whereas men tended to experience peace alone or with nature.

WOMEN'S DEVELOPMENT: EMPOWERMENT THROUGH CONNECTION

The women's movement has had a profound impact on theories about psychological development and human nature. In *Toward a New Psychology of Women* (1976), Jean Baker Miller presented a new analysis of the limits of our cultural vision of human nature. She suggested that women's experience is necessary and critical to an understanding of human experience:

> Humanity has been held to a limited and distorted view of itself, from its interpretation of the most intimate emotions to its grandest visions of human possibilities, by virtue of its subordination of women.
>
> Until recently, "mankind's" understandings have been the only understandings generally available to us. As other perceptions arise—precisely those perceptions that men, because of their dominant position, could not perceive—the total vision of human possibilities enlarges and is transformed. (Miller 1976, 1)

Miller (1976), Chodorow (1978), and Gilligan (1982) argue that new understandings of women's experience can lead to new paradigms of psychological health and development for both sexes and for the society as a whole. The Stone Center group (Miller, Jordan, Kaplan, Stiver, and Surrey)[1] has explored a model of "empowerment through connection" and is studying its implications for women, personally and politically. This model focuses on the centrality of relationships in fostering growth and empowerment for women. It focuses not on the self but on relationships as the context for psychological growth and movement.

In this paradigm, women's core sense of self is seen as rooted in relationships, and psychological growth depends on certain kinds of relational interactions. In this model, the motive to participate in a relationship is seen as fundamental and not reducible to other basic drives or needs. Individual authenticity and interpersonal connection develop together and enhance each other. The goal of development is seen as the capacity for engaging in relationships characterized by mutual empathy and mutual empowerment (Surrey 1985).

In a healthy, growth-promoting relational context, all participants are able to represent their feelings, thoughts, perceptions, and experiences. Personal authenticity and empowerment develop when each voice can be heard and responded to and becomes part of a shared vision and purpose. All growth and development in relationships must be mutual to be truly healthy. This dialogical creative process releases energy that is available to all participants as "power together" or "power through interaction" rather than "power over." Empowerment in the relationship and empowerment outside it are mutually nourishing. The whole of such a relationship is far greater than the sum of its parts.

BIRTH OF THE BOSTON WOMEN'S PEACE RESEARCH GROUP

Our experience in the Boston Women's Peace Research Group has from the beginning been a demonstration of the power of the relational context to stimulate the creativity and effectiveness of each individual participant while at the same time producing an effect as a whole through group action. Before we came together as a group, each of us had followed her own route into peace research or activism. Although a common element for each of us was the importance of relationships along the way, each of us came into the group with her own experiences and interests.

Our group of six began meeting in 1987 as the Boston Women's Peace Research Group (BWPRG) to explore our common interests in peace and social change, and particularly our shared search for factors that enhance or impede individuals' and groups' capacities for peacemaking. We each brought a history of social commitment, ebbing and flowing with the cycles of our lives; a curiosity about the sources of our own commitment and that of others; and a hunger for a creative process rooted in connections with like-minded women.

Our intention was for each woman to present her work to the group and receive feedback and support from the others. Every meeting began with a check-in during which each of us shared her personal struggles with the issues and with her work. Each person had had moments of feeling overwhelmed by the momentum of the arms race, and each person struggled continuously about ways to take effective action while holding on to some coherence in her life, relationships, and jobs. We found that time spent exploring these connections between "the personal and the political" had several benefits. It helped each of us to make better decisions and work more effectively as individuals. Our meetings went more smoothly after each woman had received some validation and support on the preoccupations she had brought with her. And the content of those meetings grew in richness and depth because they were grounded in our own experiences. Our meetings have often moved between tears and ideas, through empathic connection with the personal struggle of one of us to a theoretical exploration of the forces for and against peacemaking in the wider culture. For each of us, in different ways, the BWPRG has enhanced our involvement and commitment to peace work.

JAN: In 1978, I read Jean Baker Miller's book, *Toward A New Psychology of Women*. As I finished the book, I felt a sense that my perception of my life and the world would never be the same. Her analysis of women's development and reinterpretation of so-called weaknesses as potential strengths suddenly reframed my whole understanding of myself. This laid the foundation for my own empowerment as a woman, for reclaiming myself as strong—that is emotionally powerful, caring, and motivated to create and deepen connections. This convinced me that the study of women's experience could lead to a whole new psychology and language to describe our experience that could have enormous power in women's lives.

My theoretical study of women's psychological development has always been in the context of my commitment to the empowerment of women, personally and politically. It has been clear to me that learning to create and live in mutually empathic, mutually empowering relationships is necessary for peace and global survival. Thus it is necessary to study women's strengths and relational capacities for "peacemaking" and to bring these into the larger world. I began to study how men and women experienced peace in their daily lives and relationships and how they viewed themselves and other family members as "peacemakers." When I entered the group, it was an arena for presenting my fledgling work in "peace research." As a clinician, I saw research as the least developed aspect of my work, and the one in which I felt the most inadequate. The group has been extraordinarily important to me in supporting this research as well as my activism, but has also helped me to grow in ways I never would have foreseen. As the group has developed, I have begun to understand that my activities as a person, therapist, and activist were all part of doing "research," and were all part of my emerging identity as a peacemaker. I could see this in others before I truly accepted this about myself.

BIANCA: Jan and her colleagues at the Stone Center have described what they refer to as "growth-enhancing connections." It has been my relationship with *each* of the women in this group that has enabled me to think about peace and nuclear issues in my professional life—as a researcher, clinician, and teacher—and has led me to become an activist.

My first involvement was through research. Prill, one of my partners in group practice, told us about a presentation on atomic veterans—the 200,000 to 300,000 soldiers who were routinely exposed to radiation in above-ground atomic tests from 1945 to 1963. As family therapists we became interested in exploring the psychological impact of radiation exposure on both the men and their families. This led to the creation of the Atomic Veterans Family Project (Murphy, Ellis, and Greenberg 1990).

My interviews with the atomic veterans led to my becoming a peace activist. After hearing the stories of the vets and their families, I found I could not just "do research." I went to the Nevada Test Site, the place where many of the atomic veterans were exposed, to participate in nonviolent civil disobedience to protest the continued underground nuclear testing. Sally had been to the test site before and I was delighted to be able to go with her and join in her affinity group.

Peace issues permeated my clinical and teaching roles. With my cotherapist Jon Reusser, I wrote about how family therapists can address themselves to nuclear issues (Reusser and Murphy 1990; Murphy and Reusser, chapter 8, this volume).

My involvement with nuclear issues also led to my developing a course at Wheaton College entitled "Psychology in the Nuclear Age," which explores the contributions psychologists have made to the understanding of peace, war, and nuclear issues. Sarah was already teaching a similar course and it was important to have her collaboration and support.

In our group (BWPRG), Suz had shared her research on longtime women activists. I became interested in looking at the emergence of activism in college-age women and so I began to study how my students coped with the information they gained in my course on psychology and nuclear issues.

SALLY: In 1986, I had gone with my husband and our three grown sons to the Nevada Test Site to protest our country's continuing underground testing and development of nuclear weapons (see chapter 14). We had engaged in nonviolent civil disobedience as a family. That experience was deeply moving to me. I felt powerfully united with my family and the larger family of humanity as we trespassed across the line onto the test site. But only later did I fully realize what a significant breakthrough I had experienced.

I got in touch with my own terror and sadness at the nuclear threat, and a more personal pain from which I had been protecting myself from. Not only had I been holding off awareness of a potential nuclear holocaust, I also had been avoiding my memory—as a Jewish child of an immigrant father living in an anti-Semitic small town during World War II—of a secret and preoccupying terror that the fate of many European Jewish families might one day be our own.

It was fitting, then, that my husband and I chose to appeal our conviction for trespassing at the test site using the Nuremberg Defense, among other arguments. When our appeal was denied, I chose not to pay a fine, but to return to Nevada to serve a five-day sentence. My decision to do so was influenced by the discussions with our group (BWPRG), which encouraged me to describe and more fully appreciate the nature of our family action, its meaning for me, and its continuing and increasing significance in my personal development and ongoing political activities. At first I had felt defensive in this "women's group" because my recent personal and political growth and expression did not develop through my relationship with women, but rather through the love and meaningful experience with four men in my life (my husband and three sons). But the group affirmed my feelings about my family (including my valuing and caring about them as men) and helped me acknowledge that with each of them individually, as well as collectively, there had been through the years a mutual sharing of deeply felt personal, social, and political passions that informed the action we ultimately took together at the test site. We all seemed more fully to appreciate that the concept of "empowerment through connection" was not confined to women's relationships with each other, although perhaps a woman's greater readiness and ability to accept and react to being empowered helps her to influence others to respond similarly. I felt even further validated by the fact that Bianca had decided to join me at the next test site civil disobedience action.

My time in jail was itself an empowering experience, shared in true sisterhood with a close woman friend who had been the person who originally encouraged me to go to the test site.

PRILL: It was wrestling with the decision of whether to have a child that pushed the nuclear issue into the forefront of my awareness. How could I bring children into a world that was not only plagued with troubles, but possibly on the brink of extinction? If I were going to bring children into the world, then I would have to involve myself in the struggle to keep that world viable.

In her interviews with peace activists, Jan asks them to describe an image of peace from their own lives. My immediate image was of being in the hospital with my husband and newborn son in the hours after his birth: this was a moment of perfect peace and wholeness. In that image lies the paradox that shapes my life right now: children are the source of so much of my inspiration and commitment for this work, and also of the interruptions, postponements, and sense of fragmentation I struggle with.

The urgency and passion we feel in peace work are not unlike the passion we feel for our children and those we love. In daily life those passions can collide. (Even as I write this sentence, my six-year old is yelling "Mom!") How to manage those inevitable collisions I see as the challenge of the relational self. Jean Baker Miller (1976) speaks of the zest and vitality of the relational self; I often feel its exhaustion and fragmentation. Being connected means being pulled in many directions by sometimes warring and certainly competing commitments and relationships. At times I feel more like Dr. Doolittle's Pushme-Pullyu than an integrated human being.

The formation of BWPRG coincided with a demanding time in my own family life: the familiar struggle of the middle-aged woman with young children and ailing, elderly parents. My clinical and peace research work was already enormously enriched and supported by the "relational contexts" of my clinical group, Newton Psychotherapy Associates, and my research colleagues in the Atomic Veterans Family Project. So for me there were always the questions: "Why another group? Do I have the time and energy for this?" This has been my theme song in BWPRG.

Struggling with these competing demands and feeling overburdened at times, I have voiced in the group both my doubts about whether I should remain in it, and my view of "the other side" of the relational self: namely, the pushes and pulls that can make one feel fragmented, frustrated, and exhausted. Several times I came to a meeting intending to announce my withdrawal, and sometimes I even raised it hesitantly. Every time I was either met with a firm "you belong here," or I felt recharged and stimulated in hearing about other members' work and struggles. I think that this is what is meant by the mutual empowerment of the relational context.

Suz: In the late 1970s, I participated in the formation of a group called Interhelp, which was an organization of peace activists committed to integrating psychological and spiritual wisdom with peace efforts (Macy 1983). Being involved in the early formation of this organization helped me to focus on bringing together these disparate parts of myself. This progress toward integration added new zest to my commitment toward global responsibility. I came to graduate school with a long history of activism and I felt a tremendous conflict about channeling my energies away from direct peace work. I found myself incorporating issues related to peace or to the antinuclear movement in all my major papers. I chose a topic for my final project that allowed me to integrate peace activism and research. My project was looking at what factors went into mature women's commitment to the antinuclear movement.

Dissertation burnout and the topic of nucelar war meant I had to work for years with the angst that inevitably bubbles up during the act of creating, and the fears engendered from working with this topic. Often I found myself reading or writing and having to stop and just sob, particularly in reading about Hiroshima and Nagasaki. Other times, I found myself just wanting to make love for hours to affirm life. For me, the Boston Women's Peace Research Group was a continuing opportunity to attempt an integration of my activist beliefs, psychological theory, and my frustration with the traditional, and seemingly limited methods of Western scientific inquiry. My focus was then to allow these ideas and theories to meet in my spiritual practice, so that my head and heart were speaking from the same place. As a group we mirrored each other in the struggle for integration, each with her individual voice. I was with women who understood the power of angst and what was needed for creative movement. Bringing together unrelated aspects of ourselves was an exciting adventure stimulated by our sharing of both love and ideas.

Sarah: When my oldest child started elementary school and I went there to register her, I felt huge, much too big for the building. The last time I had been in such a building, I realized, I had been small enough to fit under a desk during air raid drills. As I sent my own child into the wider world in 1979, all my own fears from my childhood in the 1950s returned for me. With them came anxiety, anger, and isolation, feelings that propelled me in search of a larger community. I found that community among people in my city who were addressing the nuclear threat in grass-roots peace organizations.

For years, however, I kept my peace activism separate from my work as a psychologist and psychotherapist. I began to realize that I needed to heal that disconnection by bringing the two together. In 1985, I organized a conference for the Massachusetts Psychological Association (MPA) on the Psychology of Individual and Collective Survival, at which I presented the beginnings of my work on a model for the development of social responsibility. Through the organizational work for that conference, I met other psychologists who were engaged in teaching and research, connections that eventually led to my beginning to teach my own courses on nuclear and peace psychology. After presenting my work at that MPA conference, I began to meet other women who were activists, therapists, and researchers. Those connections eventually grew into the Boston Women's Peace Research Group. Hearing the experience of these women and sharing my own, as well as presenting my model to the group and working with others as each developed her work, has enhanced immeasurably my sense of integration and the creativity of my thinking.

A VISION OF RESEARCH

In those early days, we did not see ourselves primarily as researchers; at least we did not identify with conventional descriptions of what researchers did. Yet we were there to gather, record, synthesize, and interpret information. We began to realize what many feminist researchers (Cook and Fonow 1986, Harding and Hinitikka 1983; Mies 1983; Oakley 1981; Ribbens, 1989) had already discovered: that "research" is not only the objective Western scientific method. Research is a relational interactive process. We select material for study that matters to us deeply. When we conduct interviews, it is with a caring presence, not with illusions about depersonalized "objectivity." We frequently offer our observations back to our participants, both to validate our findings and in the hope that these insights might be useful. Each of us found opportunities for research in our peacemaking activities.

SALLY: I was in jail with six young women who had done a "back country action," walking for five days into the test site toward Ground Zero with fifty-pound survival packs on their backs and a vision of healing Mother Earth in their hearts.

When you're in jail, you have no way to distract yourself from your thoughts and feelings, so you face them. And when you're with other women, you share them. As I recognized that each of these women was telling me significant information and expressing deeply felt emotions (incidentally, I am approximately the ages of their mothers and they spanned the ages of my sons), I decided to ask them each over twenty questions that would form a set of data that might help explain what motivated and enabled them to take this action. This research initiative, which is not a customary approach for me, was my response to feeling glutted with powerful emotions and information that I both wanted to make sense of for myself and later be able to share (respecting confidentiality, of course) so that others could also look at what contributes to social-political activism. I asked them all I could about what had brought them there and where they got their strength. When I got out, I called each of their mothers and—after letting them know that their daughters were okay—had long conversations with them too about their daughters' backgrounds.

I saw that the commitment of these young women enabled them to struggle through their disagreements, jealousies, or competitiveness with one another. Potential and actual conflict had to be talked out, understood, and honored so that they could feel trusting and confident to do such an interdependent and potentially dangerous—and ultimately extremely powerful—action together.

The enthusiastic response of the peace research group to my interactions with the women in jail and the data I had collected spurred me on to renew contacts with them and to plan a follow-up study, which I hope to combine with the original data and publish in the near future.

SARAH: From observing my own development as a peace activist, I began to work on a model for the development of "global responsibility," the ability of individuals and groups to respond to global problems by changing their behavior. My emerging model is based primarily on observations of my own development, in part on the experiences of all of us in this group, and in part on the psychological literature on empathy, prosocial behavior, and family development. This model contains four equally important, interrelated components. The first, and most essential, is *awareness*, which refers both to the perception of global problems and the ability to "keep them in mind," to think about them, to take in information about them. A second aspect is *understanding*, the ability to integrate and analyze the information that comes into awareness. A third aspect is *direct experience*, which refers to the ability to feel and engage rather than becoming numb and dulled. A fourth aspect is *action*, the willingness to work actively for one's own and others' survival. These all emerge in a context of connection; they are ways of connecting the individual or group to the world around.

These aspects of global responsibility are interrelated and mutually reinforcing. When one aspect is emphasized, the others are affected. When one is ignored, the quality of the others suffers, as does the quality of the person's or group's overall effectiveness. With the support and encouragement of the BWPRG, I eventually published an article describing this model of the development of global responsibility (Conn 1990).

SUZ: For my doctoral dissertation, I interviewed eight long-time women antinuclear activists, intensively, twice each, to try to understand their subjective experience of commitment. The intensity of our topic created a very intimate and charged mood in many interviews; it engendered very deep feelings about the world and our part in its future.

I found that women experienced what I call a contextual understanding of their commitment. Contextuality is the organization of ideas and meanings around relationship(s), interconnections, and/or larger arenas. The contextual style of relating created a circular dynamic. A personal relationship of some kind engendered feelings of responsibility, care, and connection. Feelings of responsibility developed from the concern these women felt about the world and its interface with their personal relationships. Activism was the route through which these women's feelings of care and responsibility broadened into a larger context. In this way, global responsibility was born for the women in my study.

What was most wonderful for me was to see that the women all experienced their activism as a healthy, affirming commitment. It was not without pain and angst, but the actual commitment was something that helped them in their lives. And it was the women in my study who really empowered me to see this project through. The women in the BWPRG helped me to begin to heal from the experience of writing this final project. I felt beleaguered and unable to put voice to my ideas. The group offered a place to begin to do this in a nonthreatening way.

RATIONAL EMPOWERMENT IN ACTION

Our understanding of the importance for our empowerment of the relationships and connections in our lives grew as we focused on the content of our individual work, on our experience of doing it, and on our process as a group. Our excitement about our own process of mutual empowerment led us to make a presentation at a professional conference (Boston Women's Peace Research Group 1988a), where we not only described our individual work but illustrated our experience of relational empowerment. As each of us presented "her content" to the audience, two processes occurred that demonstrated the value of publicly acting together as a group. First, we listened with "new ears" in that setting. The expanded relational context, now including the audience, enabled us to appreciate even more fully each member's unique contribution. Second, a more powerful sense of "we" emerged through our relating as a group to others outside of it—so powerful that we were inspired to work toward a larger and longer gathering of women concerned with peacemaking later that year (Boston Women's Peace Research Group 1988b). Through this action, the group seemed to take a giant step toward a life of its own. The balance between the lively "I" and the larger "we" fueled our energy, empowering each of us as we took action in our lives.

BIANCA: The experience of my students at Wheaton College in a course, "Psychology in the Nuclear Age," demonstrates the importance of the relational context in the development of activism in young women. I ask the students to keep journals. I believe that it is important to understand what students themselves reported were the effects of the class on them.

When students first became aware of nuclear issues, they often reported feeling overwhelmed and scared. At the same time that the students were frightened by the information they were gaining, they also reported that their increased knowledge of nuclear issues made them feel better about themselves and enhanced their self-esteem. Their newly acquired knowledge and the feelings that went with it led to action—to their finding their own voice. And, their action often took place in the relational context. They began talking to their friends and roommates about nuclear concerns. Some of them went home and talked to their families. One woman interviewed three generations in her family; another spoke with her parents about her younger brother's knowledge of nuclear issues; a third talked to her siblings and then approached her parents with a plan for action.

Their actions went from smaller relational contexts of family and friends to the larger contexts of networking with other concerned students to affect the community at large. For example, one group of students contributed to a peace calendar being developed by Neil Wollman from Manchester College in Indiana.

The students themselves recognized the importance of the relational context in their actions. One group asked their fellow students whether they would ever take an activist position. One student said: "Only if I have others to march with. I need people to motivate me. I'm not sure why, maybe it's for support." Another said: "If I was encouraged or heard through others of ways of responding, I would want friends to join me and motivate me. I think it's related to psychic numbing as to why I alone wouldn't initiate it." And still another student said: "I realize that besides becoming more informed about nuclear disarmament issues, I need to do more psychological work building a sense that I can feel powerful in the face of this. It's [nuclear issues] something that hurts me inside and I need to feel safe and strong rather than helpless and hopeless. Please have small discussions to build a support group on campus. It is needed now."

Because of my interviews with atomic veteran families, I went to the Nevada Test Site and joined Sally Mack and others in one of the civil disobedience actions to protest the continued underground nuclear testing. The students knew about my planned trip because they had asked me how I coped with the stories that the atomic veterans had told me, and I mentioned that one of the ways I did this was by taking action. Some of the students said that they also wanted to go to Nevada to protest, but they could not afford to. Since many people around the country wanted to make their presence felt at the test site but were unable to go, the demonstration planners had suggested that we make handprints and put them around the test site. A student had all the handprints placed on one sheet of plastic, with the Wheaton emblem, drawn by her roommate, in the center. Faculty, students, and staff participated. I took it with me and hung it on the barbed wire surrounding the test site. It was a beautiful reminder for me of my connections with others as I crossed under the barbed wire where it hung.

This was a powerful example of the importance of the relational context in activism. One student commented: " A group activity signifies togetherness and community effort." Another said: "I wanted to trace my hand for Professor Murphy's journey because I felt that if I did that I would be doing something. I know it's not much but with the group also doing it, I felt united. By making this project a group activity, I feel like I'm not the only one concerned. Someone feels the same way I do." I think this so beautifully underlines the importance of mutual empathy and the relational empowerment for activism in these young women.

At the end of the course, students wrote in anonymous evaluations: "I feel educated about the issues. Now I feel that I can do something, I don't feel so helpless and I'm not as likely to ignore it." "I used to believe that nuclear war was inevitable, but now I see that action can be taken to prevent it."

At least for these women students, it was important that their actions were taken in a relational context. Is it because they are women that this relational context is so important? I can't really say. All I can do is share with you how these young women seemed to move from a sense of unawareness, denial, and despair to a place in which they were more aware and self-confident, feeling a sense of response-ability—the ability to respond. This took place within the context of a mutually empowering relationship with one another, their friends, their family, and, finally, the wider community.

PRILL: The project I am now working on, with Bianca and another colleague, Sarah Greenberg, evolved after the birth of my first child, when I was trying to find ways of integrating my personal, professional, and political interests. The Atomic Veterans Family Project is an attempt to understand how families respond to the reality of radiation exposure. Meeting and talking with the families of atomic veterans, many of whom are suffering from some kind of radiogenic illness, is a powerful emotional experience, a far cry from what many of us have been taught to believe constitutes research. We have also involved our "subjects" in the modification of the research "design"; the families, in other words, are co-participants and co-creators in the research process. My peace work, then, has been a form of "action research" as well as an attempt to bring together different parts of myself and my concerns.

I consider integrating the fragments and balancing the pushes and pulls to be among the biggest challenges that I face. To this end, I've come up with two things that have been helpful to me. One is maintaining a long-range perspective, recognizing that we are in this for the long haul, and that indeed there are going to be ebbs and flows in our energy and commitment. The second is taking a tolerant and forgiving attitude toward ourselves, recognizing that we can't do all that we want to do at every minute of the day or even every day. In the latter realization I have been greatly strengthened by the BWPRG.

Gradually, I took in the fact that the group was truly affirming the periodicity of my own life, validating the importance of the "personal" work I was doing in my family life. There was no sense that this work was inferior to my "public" work; indeed, such distinctions were not only arbitrary but were damaging to the visions we shared and the contributions we were trying to make toward a healthier, more peaceful world. Women, I think, can be especially sensitive to, and cognizant of, these interconnections among private and public spheres. If these interconnections are truly honored and valued, as they have been in BWPRG, there is a greater chance that we can carry these values into other contexts of our lives.

JAN: The group helped change my understanding of research, my personal identity, and the direction of my work. I have been involved in developing a theory of empowerment in relationships at the Stone Center at Wellesley College. I have used my theoretical work as the basis of empowerment workshops I conduct with Women's Action for Nuclear Disarmament. I have continued to do therapy, but have become more and more concerned with the global context of individuals' concerns. I began consciously to try to help my clients to see their lives and relationships as arenas for peacemaking, encouraging them to see themselves in more integrated and holistic ways.

This broader definition of my identity and work ultimately redirected me toward forming a new group to study and practice "global psychotherapy." This is a group of clinicians attempting to reframe the paradigms of psychological understanding to include the global context; redefine "mental health" to include awareness and empowerment on global issues; and to facilitate clients' sense of themselves as related to and capable of acting in the global arena.

How has this evolution come about? The group has been a precious source of energy, empowerment, understanding, and change. This has occurred through a process of relational empowerment, where each person can represent herself authentically, be responded to, and contribute to co-creating a new understanding. The dynamic of such a group is energy-releasing, forward-moving, and creativity-enhancing, because each person is an essential part of the new creation, and each person grows and develops herself through this process. I would certainly encourage the participation in such a group experience for all clinicians, teachers, activists, and researchers.

CONCLUSION

The Boston Women's Peace Research Group has embraced a vision that honors the values that women have traditionally carried in our culture: the centrality of relationships and the commitment to care, connection, and the preservation of life. The group has evolved in ways unanticipated by us when we came together. We have come to value the importance of sharing the concerns and details of our personal lives and relationships as well as taking action together as essential parts of the group process. As we presented our experiences and ideas to each other, the group process strengthened each of us individually. It has sustained our energy for peace research, deepened our passion for new "empowerment" models of participation in the world, and stimulated inquiry into the interconnection between our clinical work, our research, and our activism.

For each of us, the group has provided an arena of dialogue and action that has sharpened our understanding and vision of ourselves as "peacemakers" *and* "researchers," deepening our understanding of the relational and activist aspects of research. For each of us, the individual relationships with members of the group, as well as the group as a whole, have enhanced our development—personally, professionally, politically, and spiritually.

We have explored and affirmed that genuine mutuality in relationships promotes psychological growth and empowerment. We see such an empowering relational context as optimal for initiating, sustaining, and deepening peace activism in many arenas, from the kitchen to the classroom to the Congress.

NOTES

1. The Stone Center group has been meeting for ten years to explore women's psychological development. The group consists of Jean Baker Miller, Judith

Jordan, Alexandra Kaplan, Irene Stiver, and Janet Surrey. The group has published a series of Working Papers, available through the Stone Center, Wellesley College, Wellesley, MA 02181.

REFERENCES

Boston Women's Peace Research Group (1988a). Women and peacemaking: Work in progress. Panel presented at the Massachusetts Psychological Association Annual Meeting, May 6.

Boston Women's Peace Research Group (1988b). Women and peacemaking: Research and Action. A Conference at Wellesley College, October 29.

Brooks, S. (1987). Contextuality and commitment: A phenomenological study of eight women's experiences of their anti-nuclear activism. Ph.D. diss., Massachusetts School of Professional Psychology.

Chodorow, N. (1978). *The Reproduction of Mothering*. Berkeley: University of California Press.

Conn, S. A. (1990). Protest and thrive: The relationship between personal responsibility and global empowerment. *New England Journal of Public Policy* 6(1), Spring/Summer, 163–177. (Also available as a paper through the Center for Psychological Studies in the Nuclear Age, Harvard Medical School, 1493 Cambridge Street, Cambridge, MA 02138.)

Cook, J. A., and Fonow, M. M. (1986). Knowledge and women's interests: Issues of epistemology and methodology in feminist sociological research. *Sociological Inquiry*, 56(1), 2–29.

Gilligan, C. (1982). *In A Different Voice: Psychological Theory and Women's Development*. Cambridge, Mass.: Harvard University Press.

Harding, S., and Hinitikka, M. B., eds. (1983). *Discovering Reality: Feminist Perspectives on Epistemology, Metaphysics, Methodology, and Philosophy of Science*. Boston: D. Rieder.

Macy, J. R. (1983). *Despair and Personal Power in the Nuclear Age*. Philadelphia: New Society.

Mies, M. (1983). Towards a methodology for feminist research. In G. Bowles and R. Lein, eds., *Theories of Women's Studies*. Boston: Routledge and Kegan Paul.

Miller, J. B. (1976). *Toward a New Psychology of Women*. Boston: Beacon Press.

Murphy, B. C., Ellis, P., and Greenberg, S. (1990). Atomic veterans and their families: Responses to radiation exposure. *American Journal of Orthopsychiatry*, 60, 418–427.

Oakley, A. (1981). Interviewing women: A contradiction in terms. In H. Roberts, ed., *Doing Feminist Research*. London: Routledge and Kegan Paul.

Ribbens, J. (1989). Interviewing—An unnatural situation. *Women's Studies International Forum*, 12(6), 579–592.

Reusser, J. W., and Murphy, B. C. (1990). Family therapy in the nuclear age:

From clinical to global. In M. Mirkin, ed., *The Social and Political Contexts of Family Therapy*. Boston: Allyn and Bacon.

Surrey, J. (1985). The "self-in-relation": A theory of women's development. *Work in Progress #13*. Wellesley, Mass.: Stone Center Working Paper Series.

Surrey, J. (1987). The Psychology of Peace Making. Paper presented at the Stone Center, Wellesley College, Wellesley, Mass., June.

14

A Family Says No to Violence: Personal Empowerment through Nonviolent Civil Disobedience

Sally A. Mack

There comes a time when words are insufficient, pronouncements are vague, resolutions are inadequate, legislations are null and void, and such a time is right now. It is now time for action. —*The Reverend Tim McDonald, Southern Christian Leadership Conference, Nevada Test Site, June 2, 1986*

INTRODUCTION

On June 2, 1986, in Mercury, Nevada, my husband and I and our three sons participated in an act of nonviolent civil disobedience. We held hands and walked as a family across the boundary of the Nuclear Test Site, where our nation's nuclear weapons are tested in underground tunnels. We joined 144 other people trespassing on U.S. government property, all knowing we would be arrested for our action. Along with hundreds of other Americans who had come to the demonstration, we wished to protest our government's continuation of nuclear weapons testing in the face of the accidental nuclear explosion tragedy at Chernobyl and the Soviet moratorium on testing that had been going on for almost a year. Our ultimate goal was to prevent a nuclear war by helping to stop nuclear weapons development and encourage the adoption of a comprehensive test ban treaty.

One of the most dramatic, and perhaps instructive, forms of direct action to confront the social, political, and global issues of our times is that of nonviolent civil disobedience. NVCD, as we shall call it, is a physical action that calls attention to a problem and highlights its implications by confronting the physical embodiment of that problem. In our case the action was group trespassing, which led to automatic arrest at the Nuclear Test Site near Las Vegas, Nevada. An organization called American Peace Test has been organizing such actions periodically since 1986. These have been attended by crowds of participants ranging from hundreds to thousands, coming together from all over the U.S. and other parts of the world. Most of the group sets up camp in the desert, living and planning together for the "disobedient" act of stepping onto the test site and receiving the consequences of such action. These consequences usually include being arrested and handcuffed, held in a locked outdoor pen for several hours, transported to an arraignment, and given possible fines or a jail sentence. Prior to the action, leaders of APT have informed the local sheriff of their intended demonstration and reasons for it, and have indicated their respect for him and his men and their obligation to carry out their job.

MY EXPERIENCE AT THE TEST SITE

Prior to crossing onto the test site, my family and I had spent a day and a half becoming part of a spirited and close group: we attended a rally of speeches, entertainment, and group singing, standing outside in the 115° heat; we later learned about nonviolent civil disobedience, clarifying and agreeing *by consensus* how we would conduct ourselves, getting training on practical, safety, and legal matters. Divided into "affinity groups" of fifteen to twenty people to discuss our goals and how we wanted to carry them out, we had gotten in touch with what had moved us to come to this demonstration, sharing our anxiety about the potential hazards of the next day's action, and becoming a caring and determined working unit.

In the morning before our action, when we came together again as a total group, the spiritual and human motivation for our concerns became even clearer to me as I heard talks by a Franciscan priest, by Shoshone Indians living in their now-contaminated ancestral homes near the test site,[1] and by a Southern Christian Leadership Conference minister.

Together we all participated in a world prayer (we prayed for the people of all the countries on earth—all 163 of them) led by a young woman from Japan.

But despite my strong belief in our purpose, I began to experience a vague, but intense, anxiety and growing discomfort in my gut as we gathered to create the human line that would cross onto the test site. I felt detached from a deep dread that I couldn't identify. Gradually I realized that I had finally gotten in touch with my own terror and grief over the threat of nuclear war—that it had taken the actual physical experience of going to the test site and sharing the fear and love and conviction of hundreds of wonderful people, especially my own family, to enable me to do so.

It was not until I had left the test site and was on my way home that I recognized an unconscious memory that was background to my current terror.

In the past I had always stood at the edge of the nuclear terror, supporting others in my family who were more involved and active, but too busy with other very worthy causes to be active myself. What I really had been too busy to be was in touch with my emotions. It was liberating to experience them and then act on them and thus feel mastery over the emotions I had been avoiding. By the time I joined hands with my family to cross the boundary line, I felt tremendous strength and pride and belief that our action as a family could make a difference.

We were among three hundred people who formed a slow parade along the road to the boundary, holding hands and singing songs such as "America the Beautiful" and "We Shall Overcome." We were truly a cross-section of Americans: white-haired elderly, young mothers wearing placards with pictures of their children (one showed a delightful wind-blown toddler on a swing proclaiming "Let Meagan Live"), college students, disabled people walking with canes, secretaries, service workers, professors . . . a wave of beautiful, committed, hopeful humanity.

The sheriff stopped the five of us at the boundary line, as he did every group, and told us we would be arrested if we crossed. When my husband told him we were from Boston and had come as a whole family to do this, he looked at each of us and said: "You have fine-looking sons. You should be proud." I felt a strange, unexpected human bond with the sheriff and his men as I stepped across the line, let go of my sons' hands, and extended my arms.

We were handcuffed and led to buses waiting to take us to be arraigned. Most of the demonstrators were completely cooperative and were treated respectfully in turn. My husband and I had decided ahead of time, along with several others, to contest our arrest and have our case appealed through the Nevada court system, based on the Nuremberg Defense.[2] Therefore, we signed out on our own recognizance and were taken off the bus that would carry others to their arraignment. Although our sons jokingly mocked a tragic farewell to us, the good-byes struck a terrifying echo in me, and I felt my heart sink as their bus pulled away.

Only much later, in the plane on my way home to Boston, did I consciously realize that the separation reawakened an old fantasy of my childhood as a first-generation American Jew growing up during the Nazi holocaust: many times I had imagined how, if the German army overtook the United States, I would outsmart the guards if they tried to separate my parents and me for deportation to camps or gas chambers. Obviously, my deep dread before lining up for the march that morning was not only that of a possible nuclear terror which I had been trying to deny, but also the terror of a previous holocaust, which fear I had kept secret from my parents and rarely talked about or consciously remembered throughout my life.

Following the arraignment, about fifty people went to jail rather than pay a fine or agree to return for trial at a later date, my middle son among them. His personal conviction and courage were to have an ongoing influence on me.

Still very moving to me as I read them almost five years later are the words of inspiration and hope spoken to us just before our action by the Reverend Tim McDonald:

Today the Nevada Test Site will be transformed from a desert of death and destruction to an oasis of peace and goodwill. Today at the Nevada Test Site, we got to walk together, children don't you get weary. Talk together, children don't you get weary. Go to jail together, children don't you get weary. There's a great camp meeting at the Nevada Test Site. God bless you. We will change the course of this nation. —The Reverend Tim McDonald, Southern Christian Leadership Conference, Nevada Test Site, June 2, 1986

Does citizen action such as NVCD in fact help to change the course of a nation? My belief is that it does, and I will discuss the process and dynamics of change as they affect the individuals involved in the action, those they wish to influence directly, and the greater community—the nation and the world.

Let us begin with a look at the general principles of NVCD and some history of its use to create political change.

NONVIOLENT CIVIL DISOBEDIENCE

Nonviolence has been practiced throughout history. There have been numerous instances of people courageously and nonviolently refusing to cooperate with injustice. However, the fusion of mass struggle and non-violence is relatively new. It originated largely with Mohandas Gandhi (1869–1948) at the onset of the South African campaign for Indian rights in 1906.

Nonviolence was also used extensively during the civil rights movement, which began in the 1940s and reached a peak in the 1960s. During the Vietnam War, in the late 1960s and early '70s, and again in more recent years, nonviolent action has been employed in the struggles against nuclear technology, against U.S. policy in Central America and South Africa, and for the rights of farm workers, women, and people with AIDS, to name just a few.

Dr. Martin Luther King, Jr. (1929–1968), who provided such inspiring leadership during the civil rights movement of the '60s, wrote that the philosophy and practice of nonviolence has six basic elements: (1) non-violence is resistance to evil and oppression; it is a human way to fight; (2) it does not seek to defeat or humiliate the opponent, but to win his/her friendship and understanding; (3) the nonviolent method is an attack on the forces of evil and injustice, not an attack against the persons carrying out the evil and injustice; (4) it is the willingness to accept suffering without retaliation; (5) a nonviolent resister avoids both external physical and internal spiritual violence—not only refuses to shoot, but also to hate, an opponent; the ethic of genuine love is at the center of nonviolence; (6) the believer in nonviolence has a deep faith in the future; the forces in the universe are seen to be on the side of justice.

Gandhi's use of NVCD was built on the concept of *satyagraha*, which means "truth force." Through this concept, nonviolence is viewed as a creative, planned, positive, active force, which, because it does not use violence as a means of resolving conflict, is a truly revolutionary approach for those who seek social or political change. "Sat" implies openness, honesty and fairness, that is, truth. It is understood that each person's opinions and beliefs represent a part of the truth and that in order to see more of the truth we must share our truths cooperatively. Other concepts included *ahimsa,* which is an expression of concern that our own and others' humanity be manifested and respected; and *tapasya,* which says that one must always provide a face-saving "way out" for opponents. The goal is to discover a wider vista of truth and justice, not to achieve victory over the opponent.

In order to carry out NVCD effectively, the participants need to be prepared through group training. The purpose of training is for people to form a common understanding of the use of nonviolence. Training sessions provide a forum to share ideas about nonviolence, oppression, fears, and feelings. They allow people to meet, form "affinity groups," and get to know and trust each other. Participants plan and prepare for a particular action and its tone and learn about the legal ramifications. The training helps them decide whether, or in what capacity, they will participate in an action. Through role playing, people learn what to expect from police, officials, other people in the action, and themselves.

Nonviolence training can range from several hours to several months. Most typical in the United States are sessions that run up to eight hours and have ten to twenty-five people with two trainers leading the discussion and role-playing.

AMERICAN PEACE TEST

From the beginning, the APT used the principles of NVCD to create a systematic and sustained campaign as part of a comprehensive strategy to stop nuclear testing and achieve a Comprehensive Test Ban Treaty. The concept for this organization originated in 1985, when several members of the Nuclear Freeze Campaign's Direct Action Force participated in a four-day civil disobedience action at the Nevada Test Site. Inspired and empowered, they organized a month-long presence at the test site, urging the United States to join the unilateral Soviet testing moratorium, which began August 1, 1985.

In 1986 the APT published the following points of unity: We are united in

1. Our support for a Comprehensive Test Ban Treaty between the U.S. and the Soviet Union;
2. Our belief that a program of public education, legislation, and direct action, including civil disobedience, is essential to achieving our goals;
3. Our commitment to the practice of nonviolence; [and]
4. Our commitment to democratic, nonhierarchical decision making.

They developed guidelines for their organization, which stated that all activities must be strictly nonviolent in action and tone, and that the attitude conveyed through words, symbols, and action should be one of openness, love, and respect toward all people encountered. All participants must undergo nonviolence training; no property will be damaged; and all activities must be open and public, not secret. No participant will bring or use any drugs or alcohol. All participants must freely accept the legal consequences of their actions and must not seek to evade these consequences beyond legitimate legal recourse. All participants must agree to follow the directions of the decision-making body. In the event of a serious disagreement, participants agree to remove themselves from the action.

Furthermore, because the APT believes that a willingness to make personal sacrifice will serve as a catalyst to create a groundswell of resistance to nuclear testing, all those who commit civil disobedience are encouraged, if convicted, to serve at least two days in jail even if a fine is offered in lieu of jail time.

EFFECT OF ACTION ON MY FAMILY

Our family functioned as part of an affinity group of approximately fifteen people who came to the test site from the northeastern region of the United States. The geographical assignments were made so that we could meet or contact each other again for regional demonstrations—which in fact we did. One immediately apparent effect of our family participation was the opportunity to see and hear each other functioning as an affinity group member (and at times as a leader in the group) independent of the accustomed roles we have within our family. Our sons, Tony, Kenny, and Danny, were twenty-two, twenty-four, and twenty-six years old, respectively, at that time. Each was living away from home and pursuing his own academic or work interests. Our coming together at the test site was in the spirit of our commonly held values and a wish to support each other in the expression of those values.

We had come as equal participants as well as mutual supporters, and we worked together to set up tents, procure food, prevent sunburns, and retrieve forgotten and necessary items. A humorous, and actually poignant, moment for me was when Kenny, the most absentminded of my children when he was a youngster and the child whose jackets I always retrieved in the school's "Lost and Found" barrel, masterfully saved the day for me when he resourcefully found a car and raced back to our campsite to find my driver's license, which I would need to prove my identity after I got arrested.

Although we participated as a family unit, we also functioned as separate individuals, relating to a task that had major implications beyond the family and even the group. Our focus ultimately was the effectiveness and safety of the total community of demonstrators. I saw my husband and sons listening, attempting to persuade, calculating risks—and, most movingly, expressing their personal beliefs and aspirations for life in this world—with a group in which I was but one equally important member. In some way this identification with a group larger than our family—in fact, with all of humanity—made each of us, we all later agreed, more deeply appreciate the others' value and feel much closer as a family.

As individuals, each of us took from our NVCD experience a more focused consciousness and impetus to "make a difference" in the world. Soon after our action, Tony decided to leave college temporarily and to spend six months in Central America. He helped to build a soil-testing plant in Managua, Nicaragua, with a community of Americans and students from a local agricultural college, and he traveled to several other Latin American countries to learn about agricultural and political development in the region. After college he went to work for a foundation that sponsors grass-roots groups in Central and South America that are involved in self-help social and economic development programs. Kenny organized a major NVCD demonstration at the local (Boston) office of the Department of Energy[3] after he returned from the test site (and jail) and later wrote his thesis on the Nuclear Freeze Campaign. Eventually he went to law school with the intention of working in international relations.

The intensified, and ultimately continuing, power of his commitment to work for peace and justice was presaged in the statements Kenny made after he returned from jail and was on the way home from the airport, where my husband John had met him with a tape recorder in the car:

When Americans themselves are put in jail and have the experience of being in jail . . . the incredibly grounding, affirming experience of being in jail . . . when the people of the United States are actually serving time in jail, I just think the whole thing is going to turn around. . . . Martin Luther King said all direct action, nonviolent direct action, is not the end in itself. . . . Ultimately you're not going to shut down a test site by having these demonstrations physically shut it down. But one of the things he said was that a direct action complements legislation. You know that is the wonderful thing between the two, that it [direct action] forces legislation in a way that the Freeze [Nuclear Freeze Campaign] never could.

Danny returned to the test site the following year to help carry out a portion of the APT Mother's Day demonstration of 1987. He had initiated a plan for a "peace dance," a kind of empowerment ritual, in response to what he felt had been too much time and energy spent on decision making and a lack of wholeness and, especially, physical action in our preparation for the 1986 demonstration. Over the previous five years he had participated in many protest demonstrations and was also actively involved in dance, theater, and the creation of rituals that promoted spiritual consciousness. He was now especially interested in helping participants "stay in touch with the deeper meaning of their NVCD actions" and "to bring out the spiritual element, that is, to 'raise power,' . . . so that the group can focus on clearing themselves for the action." "We need to . . . find some way to remember our unity, remember our larger purpose." He explained that "the power of dancing, singing, and chanting, when it is done in a truly spirited way . . . is called 'raising power' and that is truly what it does. Martin Luther King spoke about this in reference to the freedom songs of the civil rights movement":

In a sense the freedom songs are the soul of the movement. . . . I have stood in a meeting with hundreds of youngsters and joined in while they sang "Ain't Gonna Let Nobody Turn Me 'Round." It is not just a song; it is a resolve. A few minutes later, I have seen those same youngsters refuse to turn around from the onrush of a police dog, refuse to turn around before a pugnacious police chief in command of men armed with power hoses. These songs bind us together, give us courage together, help us to march together (King 1964, p. 61).

More recently, Danny has focused his energy on the effort to better understand how immediate economic considerations affect human behavior and, while starting a business of his own, organized others in his community to work together to establish socially responsible business and economic practices.

When I asked Tony four and a half years later what the effect of our family NVCD action has had on him, his reply was:

The biggest thing is realizing what's possible. I never thought we'd do anything like that. But if we could do it, other families could do it. If you have individuals in a family who are activists, they could do it [act] together as a family and multiply the power of it. . . . But the idea does not occur to them that it can be a family occurrence. . . . People think of taking political action as an individual or with a political group. But a family group can be a political group. There have been plenty of family political groups . . . some of them have run our country. But acting with a sense of rebellion against authority—a family is not looked at in that light. It goes against [the idea of] what a family is. . . . There's a gap to be bridged.

Comparing the nature of families and political expression in the United States with Central America or other Third World countries, he pointed out that in our country we think of people being "enclosed within their home, [functioning on] a personal level, but not on a political level. That changes in Central America, where the family is the extended family and the extended family *is* the community."

John, who is a psychiatrist and medical school professor and had been active as a clinician and writer in the mental health field, began to take much more of a leadership role in examining and talking and writing about psycho-political aspects of peace and nuclear disarmament issues. A few months after our NVCD action, he addressed a group of Harvard undergraduates on the subject of "Action and Academia in the Nuclear Age," Mack, 1987. He explained that academics are in a position to analyze and critique current policy and to educate others and increase their awareness of basic principles and rights to object to dangerous government actions. He concluded his talk by saying:

The nuclear arms race threatens academic life and freedom and everything else we cherish. Some aspects of our education may enable us to see or understand the threat more clearly than others do. Surely we need to be better informed about the nuclear arms race so that we can efficiently challenge the basic tenets that have justified its perpetuation and escalation. But in addition to becoming better informed, we have the opportunity—the obligation—to do all we can to oppose this most terrible evil of our time. Each of us can do it in his or her own way. Nonviolent civil disobedience is traditionally American, but one must be prepared for the consequences. [Martin Luther] King said, "One who breaks an unjust law must do so openly, lovingly, and with a willingness to accept the penalty." For me, personally, there has been something liberating about this action. I recommend civil disobedience for your spiritual health.

In fact, he eventually became increasingly interested in spirituality and its role in his own life and in that of others, leading to what he experienced as a more profound ability as a psychiatrist to understand and help others deal with their suffering.

EFFECT OF ACTION ON MY PERSONAL DEVELOPMENT

In the four and a half years since our family action in Nevada, my newfound willingness to take risks have been repeated over and over again. I am more willing to "stand out," expressing myself in ways that might be rejected or ignored, but feeling in touch with my deeper self and my strongly held convictions. My self-confidence and resolve have continued to grow as I take on new challenges and initiatives in political activism, writing about my experiences and ideas, giving talks at political and professional meetings (and even at an elementary school), and starting a new group within our Social Workers for Peace organization called Families in Action in the Nuclear Age.

Because I had experienced a new kind of personal validation at the test site through sharing such intense emotions and meaningful actions with others, I felt identified with a community of people who were committed to working toward social and political change. This, in turn, has empowered me to assume leadership in helping to build an even larger community of people who share this awareness and dedication. I have encouraged others to join me in returning with APT to the Nevada test site and helped plan local vigils and demonstrations to raise public awareness of ongoing nuclear testing and development.

The experience of being more open and sensitive to issues of violence and injustice and disempowerment led me to develop a deeper awareness and commitment to other current social-political concerns, such as Central American problems. I began to appreciate how these issues had always been a basic component of my interests and efforts in social work, on both an individual and community level, and gradually I began to experience less of a split between my professional and social-political work—in fact, each informed and enhanced the other.

Although in the past I had never run for office in my professional organization, the National Association of Social Workers, I became a candidate and was elected to that body's 1990 Delegate Assembly. With like-minded colleagues I helped to persuade the assembly to vote for a peace and disarmament network as one of the program priorities for our 120,000 member organization. This committed NASW to provide resources that would enable our members to work for a shift in national expenditures from armaments to funding for human services and for promoting nonviolent resolution of national and international conflict.

In my social work practice, I find that I now have a greater awareness of social, political, and spiritual issues in the lives of people I work with —and more willingness to address them and help others do so. I am less afraid of helping others face feelings of rage and despair—not surprisingly, because I am now better able to face them in myself. As a therapist, I find that the people I counsel are now more willing to take responsibility and even risks to act on their own behalf and for their own beliefs. This may be a reflection of my own attitudes and approach, although some people I work with who know of my activism have acknowledged that they see my personal and political work as a model for themselves. I believe this kind of emotional and spiritual growth shows up in the work of others who participate in NVCD—not just mental health professionals, but teachers, doctors and nurses, lawyers, and businesspeople as well.

Perhaps the most striking example of my increased resolve and belief in myself is demonstrated by my response when I learned, a year and a half after our arrest, that our appeal was denied and we were expected to pay our $150 fine or go to jail. I still felt so strongly about the purpose and significance of our action (and I'm sure I was inspired by Kenny's courage and commitment and its effect on others) that I chose to return to Nevada and serve five days in the Tonopah jail. (See chapter 13 for a further description of this experience.)

Finally, and not surprisingly, there has been a change in my relationship with family members, as I am less the "you first" enabler of others and more the mutual partner in our interactions. In fact, I find a general change in my personal style: I view interpersonal frustrations and conflicts as a problem to address mutually, and because I have more belief that we can face them together, I am less likely either to give in or try to establish my separate power. What the experience of NVCD taught me in a dramatic way is that personal victory is not when you win power over others, but when you are faithful to yourself.

EFFECTS OF NVCD ON PARTICIPANTS AND THE COMMUNITY

I believe that the changes in attitudes and behavior that result from doing NVCD are not unique to me or the members of my family, but are seen in others who have participated in this type of social-political action.

The increased self-confidence and personal empowerment of NVCD participants appear to be, at least in part, a result of a holistic experience. Because they are involved on a physical, mental, and spiritual level, and especially on the powerful interpersonal, or sociopolitical, level, people have an integrating experience and resulting awareness that seems to strengthen their motivation and focus their behavior.

At the test site in the Nevada desert, there was also something else that occurred—an almost mystical connectedness with the Earth. Many people have described the serene natural beauty and stillness of the desert, and contrasted it with the technological violence that occurs at the test site. These NVCD participants felt a deep connection, belonging, and responsibility to the earth, to the desert that was being desecrated by the violent explosions and the cave-ins over the tunnels and by the toxic gases and radiation that resulted. Ultimately, we felt more deeply connected to the planet that would, if a nuclear war actually occurred, suffer the fate, many times over, of the test site lands and the surrounding communities with their highly increased incidence of plant, animal, and human diseases such as leukemia and birth defects.

We found that others in the community were particularly responsive to our having done NVCD as a family. Beginning with our fellow activists at the test site and continuing with family, friends, colleagues, and even strangers who merely read or heard about us, people reported feeling moved and inspired to further action as they got in touch with the connection between their attachment to their own families and the significance of the nuclear threat to their deepest concerns and primary motivations in life.

The resulting ability to break through and overcome denial and fear— the denial of the danger that threatens us and the fear of being ostracized or even physically harmed if we act—is contagious. Others see and hear about us and often identify with us: they begin to question their own complacency and avoidance. Some join us in direct action, others become more conscious of the issues and discuss them more openly. They may be more likely to write to their congresspeople or to their newspapers or even change their voting patterns. Elected officials are thus affected both directly and indirectly. Representative Pat Schroeder of Colorado has stated that she believed the passage of Congressional bill #HR3442, which mandated the cutting of funds for nuclear testing as long as the Russians were not testing, was influenced by the NVCD actions at the test site.

Judges have also been affected by the nuclear test site activists. During his arraignment in Beatty, Nevada, Ken told Judge William Sullivan that he thought that when whole families began to take action like this together, "that's when this thing's going to turn around." Judge Sullivan, obviously moved, stopped the proceedings and spoke to the packed courtroom. In an unusual expression of personal feeling, he told them cautiously, "I just want you all to know I think you are making progress through your efforts."

Along with testimony and arguments presented by NVCD demonstrators at their arraignments and during their appeals, former test site workers have also filed suits claiming that their higher incidence of cancer or other diseases were caused by nuclear weapons testing. The government claimed immunity from such lawsuits, but Federal Judge Roger Foley denied the government's appeal, stating, "At the highest level of government it was believed and decided that national security required for human safety to be subjugated to the greater national need of the nuclear weapons test." The government, he said, once felt it had the right to "sacrifice its citizens at the nuclear altar." But, "thank God, the government has found its conscience," he said, adding that evolving legal precedent and a heightened awareness among federal lawmakers had made such lawsuits "a whole new ball game" and that a trial should be held as soon as possible.[4]

Although nuclear weapons testing has continued to go on (in 1990, eight tests were carried out in the United States and one in the Soviet Union), public awareness of and protest against the severely debilitating effects of radiation and other types of nuclear accidents has finally found expression in the larger community, far beyond the originally small group of activists. Those issues that once seemed like exaggerated concerns of "fringe groups" about injustices imposed on citizens working in or living

near nuclear or other toxic facilities are now part of the everyday awareness of our ecologically minded society.

All social-political change begins with personal action—facing one's
fears and anxieties, taking risks to stand up to injustice and violence, and
learning to trust and work with others to build an effective community
movement. The result of such action is not only personal empowerment,
but also community empowerment.

Our psychologically minded society is finally aware that the expression
of much of the violence in the world—from the neighborhood to the
global arena—is based on violence learned at home. What better way to
counter such behaviors and attitudes than for *families* to confront violence and injustice through nonviolent actions.

NOTES

1. The Ruby Valley Treaty of 1863, an agreement ratified by the U.S. Senate
   and signed by President Ulysses S. Grant in 1869, stipulated that the federal
   government would compensate the Shoshone Nation for loss of the traditional use of their land. However, in the case of the Nuclear Test Site, the
   government neither negotiated permission for nuclear testing activities nor
   paid compensation to the Shoshones.
2. The Nuremberg Defense is a rule of international law established at the trial
   of Nazi war criminals after World War II. It states that one should be
   absolved from punishment for crimes that were committed to prevent even
   greater crimes against humanity.
3. The Department of Energy is the federal agency in charge of all nuclear
   weapons testing.
4. "Federal Judge Clears Way for Suit by Workers at Nuclear Test Site," *New
   York Times*, February 10, 1990, p. 10. Judge Foley apparently was referring
   not only to earlier decisions in the courts, which found the federal government negligent by failing to follow safety requirements during nuclear testing, but also to the Radiation Exposed Veterans Compensation Act (#HR
   1811) of 1988, which was the first federal legislation that awarded compensation to victims of radiation caused by nuclear testing.

REFERENCES

King, M. L. (1964). *Why We Can't Wait*. New York: New American Library.
Mack, J. E. "Action and Academia in the Nuclear Age." *Harvard Magazine*,
   Jan.–Feb., 1987, Vol. 89, No. 3, pp. 25–31.

15

People's Reactions to Nuclear War: Implications for Psychologists

Susan T. Fiske

My friend has cancer. She has reason to believe that she has a one-in-three chance of dying from it. Although she understands this diagnosis, her possible death remains somewhat hypothetical to her. She imagines her death mostly in the abstract, and she talks about missing the city and her occasional trips into the country. Strangely, she does not talk so much about missing the people in her life. She also believes she cannot do anything to change her odds. She does not worry about the cancer very often; it mostly is not salient to her. If asked about it, she reports fear and worry, and certainly she prefers effective treatment to nothing. But she does not change her life with regard to her cancer. She does not seek support. She does not join organizations. She does not discuss her situation publicly. She goes on about her normal life. Some people say she is marvelous, remarkable, life-affirming, brave, and adaptable. Other

This chapter is an updated, condensed version of an article that appeared in American Psychologist, *42, 207–217 (copyright 1987 by the American Psychological Association. Reprinted by permission). The updated material, indicated here by references to Schatz and Fiske (1991), resulted from a subsequent collaboration with Robert Schatz; a complete version of the new material, which also incorporates data from Europe, is contained in R. T. Schatz and S. T. Fiske, "World citizens' reactions to the threat of nuclear war: The rise and fall of concern in the eighties, available from the author. In the current chapter, some previously in-press and unpublished references have been updated from the original. The references that to my knowledge remain unpublished have been deleted in the current version.*

people say she is suppressing her fear, denying reality, and desensitized to her own death. Regardless of what people say, the experts say her reactions are fairly typical.

My friend is the average American citizen. Her cancer is the possibility of a nuclear war. This portrait of her reactions resembles the portrait I will draw of the ordinary person's reactions to the possibility of nuclear war. I have described it this way initially because it is difficult to have a fresh perspective on this issue, particularly for those likely to be reading this article—a point to which I will return in concluding. It may be useful to keep the analogy in mind while reading.

In this article I will first describe the average citizen's response to the possibility of nuclear war. Second, I will describe possible psychological and social sources of that response. And, third, I will contrast the average citizen with the antinulcear activist and the survivalist.

In describing adult responses to nuclear war, I will separately examine beliefs, feelings, and actions. This three-part distinction is standard in social psychology: Beliefs include conceptions of the likelihood of nuclear war, images of mushroom clouds and utter destruction, and expectations about one's own survival. People's feelings, for these purposes, consist of their reported emotional reactions and their nuclear-policy preferences. People's actions regarding the possibility of nuclear war include political activity and survival activity.

In the context of most political issues, people express beliefs and feelings, but they do not act. In the context of nuclear war, however, many observers cannot reconcile the major discrepancies between the ordinary person's beliefs about the horrific possibilities, on the one hand, and the ordinary person's relative lack of feelings and actions, on the other hand. Nuclear war seems like an issue to which people's response *should* be more active. Although this puzzle is not entirely new, there has been little effort to review the hard data concerning the modal person's beliefs, feelings, and actions and little effort to examine those data in light of people's standard responses to other political issues. The sources of data here include over 50 studies from social and behavioral science: mainly surveys of adults, with preference given to national findings, when available, over local findings; some questionnaire studies of college students; and a few experimental studies with college students. The data span the period from 1945 to the present, and they lend some new insights into the discrepancies among people's beliefs, feelings, and actions. Placing the data in the context of people's responses to other political issues demonstrates that their responses to nuclear war are not unusual, contrary to the perspective taken by some previous observers.

BELIEFS

For years, psychologists have documented people's beliefs about nuclear war, primarily using survey interviews and questionnaires. Psychologists have also drawn on the in-depth relationship of the clinical setting (for historical overviews, see Klineberg 1984; Morawski and Goldstein 1985; Wagner 1985). Immediately following Hiroshima-Nagasaki, the first surveys began to examine people's attitudes toward the bomb and its use. The use of attitude surveys ebbed and flowed over the next four decades, peaking after the Russians' first atomic test, after the creation of the hydrogen bomb, after the Bay of Pigs and the Cuban Missile Crisis, after the Nuclear Test Ban Treaty, after the Stratetic Arms Limitation Treaty (SALT) initiatives, and during the present unprecedented level of worldwide concern over nuclear weapons (Kramer, Kalick, and Milburn 1983). The use of surveys parallels variations in levels of public interest, according to indexed citation frequencies in the *Reader's Guide to Periodical Literature* (Polyson, Hillmar, and Kriek 1986). Complementing the survey efforts are observations by some clinical psychologists and psychiatrists on the intrusioin of concerns about nuclear war into ordinary people's preoccupations.

As I will show, surveys indicated that ordinary people's beliefs about nuclear war have remained remarkably stable over the four eventful decades since the bombing of Hiroshima and Nagasaki. Despite massive technological change in the power of the weapons and in their delivery time, despite their considerable proliferation, and despite dramatic fluctuations in the geopolitical situation, the adult American's response has endured with remarkable consistency. Moreover, people's responses differ surprisingly little across age, gender, race, education, income, and political ideology.

A primary component of people's beliefs is their view of the odds. People view nuclear war as not very probable, as a hypothetical event. The average person views nuclear war as "fairly unlikely" within the next 10 years. A local survey in Pittsburgh found that, on average, people estimated a one-in-three chance of a nuclear war within their lifetimes

(Fiske, Pratto, and Pavelchak 1983), and a local sample in Chicago put the estimate at 50/50 (Tyler and McGraw 1983).

National surveys indicate that expectations of war in general and nuclear war in particular peaked in the early eighties, with 50 percent of respondents believing it at least fairly likely within ten years; but these figures dropped off dramatically by the end of the eighties (Smith 1988; see Schatz and Fiske 1992 for a review).

Three decades ago, people were asked about the likelihood of another world war, which they overwhelming believed would be nuclear, they viewed such a war as somewhat more likely than people do now, but the average person still estimated the chances as 50/50 (Withey 1954). People are considerably more pessimistic about the possibility of nuclear war if a conventional war should erupt. Ever since 1946, the majority of Americans (between 63 percent and 79 percent) have believed that any subsequent major war would necessarily be nuclear (Kramer et al. 1983). But, on the whole, people apparently view nuclear war as unlikely.

Were the unlikely to occur, people think of it as horrific. As early as 1954 and as recently as 1982, survey respondents have described similar images of the event and its aftermath (Fiske et al. 1983; Withey 1954). Two features of these descriptions are notable. First, material destruction is described more than is human destruction, and second, abstract content outweighs concrete content. This primary emphasis on the material and abstract, rather than on concrete human devastation, is in marked contrast to the descriptions of Hiroshima survivors, who focus almost entirely on the human misery (e.g., Lifton 1968; Thurlow 1982; "What the Boy Saw" 1985).

The horrific hypothetical, for American citizens, involves images of material damage, mostly in the abstract—as complete ruin—or sometimes in the concrete—as a blinding light, buildings on fire, and subsequently dust, barren land, and no cities. References to death and injury also occur, mostly in the abstract but also sometimes as concrete references to the death of family and friends, to charred bodies, and to injuries such as mutilation, burns, bleeding, hair loss, sores, vomiting, and diarrhea. Three relatively abstract responses to one telephone survey (Fiske et al. 1983, 55) were

Nobody left. We'll just all be blown up. The loser will be gone completely.

It would destroy people. Everything in the world. All the beautiful things will be gone.

Death. Destruction. Chaos. Survival. Hiroshima.

Two relatively concrete ones were

I hope I die with everyone else. I can't see planning for it. Utter destruction, desolation, ruin.

Death. Buildings on fire. Screaming. Wondering what to do. Being scared. Take cover. Wondering what to do next.

In this survey setting, the typical images contained about twice as much abstract content as concrete content. People reported general impressions more than specific, sensory, proximate, personal impressions. And, as noted they focused more on material damage than on human damage. It seems quite possible that the abstractness and material focus of these reports are determined by the telephone survey context.

The highly personal, in-depth approach in a clinical setting provides another perspective on people's images. Some observers report that they and/or their patients have vivid images of nuclear holocaust (e.g., Nelson 1985). And Lifton (1983) described end-of-the-world imagery in literature and in some individuals. For example, a "vision of crashing skyscrapers under a flaming sky" (130) was reported by nuclear physicist and activist Eugene Rabinowitch, and "dreams of doom" (131) were reported by United Nations Secretary Dag Hammarskjold. Artists have depicted their visions of the Bomb and nuclear catastrophe (Boyer 1985; "What the People Saw" 1985). For example, James Agee created a fragment of a novel depicting official celebrations of the newly created bomb above ground, with twisted, menacing events below ground (as described in Boyer 1985).

Granted, these data provide an intimate view of a few people's concrete images. Nevertheless, it is not clear that these people are typical of the larger public, who are not artists, do not seek out a therapist known to be a peace activist, or are not themselves prominent peace activists. People with nuclear-war images oriented toward the concrete and the human may well be exceptional. Indeed, Lifton (1983) argued that vivid end-of-the-world imagery involves "an anticipatory imagination capable of sensitivity to a trend of events which other people have become numb to" (131). At the same time, most people do expect the total and complete annihilation of everything.

Included in the total annihilation of everything is annihilation of oneself. The ordinary person does not expect to survive a nuclear holocaust. Even the abstract references are clear in that respect ("utter destruction," "nobody left," "annihiliation"). Moreover, when specifically asked whether they personally would expect to survive, people on average rate their chances as poor (Gallup Poll 1983; cf. Kramer et al. 1983).

People's perception that they would not survive a nuclear war represents the only major change from their earlier beliefs. The number of people rating their chances of surviving as poor has steadily increased over the decades from about 40 percent in the 1950s to about 70 percent now (Gallup Poll 1983). In the early 1950s, survey respondents commented about the quality of life after an atomic attack, describing the possible psychological and economic aftermath (Withey 1954). They described the possibilities of panic, low or high morale, scarcity, production problems, and failed transportation systems. In describing these long-term effects of an atomic attack, the clear majority of people (68 percent) throught that the military would provide complete protection or at least prevent heavy damage. Today, people no longer believe that the United States military has the capacity to prevent heavy damage, probably because they believe that a nuclear war cannot be limited (Kramer et al. 1983; Yankelovich and Doble 1984). Thus, people used to comment about the quality of life in a post-nuclear-war world; now they do not expect to see it.

In sum, people think of nuclear war as somewhat unlikely, mainly imagining complete material destruction, in the abstract, and themselves as definitely not surviving.

FEELINGS

People commonly report quite bleak beliefs about a nuclear holocaust, which implies that they should also report some concomitant emotional reactions. When asked directly what emotions come to mind regarding a nuclear war, the typical person does report fear, terror, and worry (Fiske et al. 1983). On the whole, however, most people do not think about nuclear war very often (Fiske et al. 1983; Hamilton, Chavez, and Keilin

1986). The typical adult apparently worries seldom or relatively little about the possibility (Kramer et al. 1983). And such emotional responses do not vary dramatically as a function of social class or overall political ideology.

Some studies indicate that women report more anxiety than men do (e.g., Hamilton, Knox, Keilin, and Chavez 1987; Mayton 1986; M. D. Newcomb 1988). Note, however, that this may be due to reporting biases caused by gender-role differences in the perceived appropriateness of revealing one's feelings (e.g., Ruble and Ruble 1982). Many studies also report higher levels of concern among children (e.g., Chavez, Hamilton, and Keilin 1986; Escalona 1982; Goodman, Mack, Beardslee, and Snow 1983; Schwebel 1982; and see Beardslee 1986, for a review of representative sample surveys; Schatz and Fiske 1992, for a discussion of gender and age differences in worry.) Similarly, some college students report more distress then their parents do (Hamilton et al. 1986). Again, however, it is not clear how much this difference is due to reporting biases as opposed to actual levels of felt worry. Quite possibly, many of the same factors that determine one's willingness to report worry publicly also determine one's willingness to admit worry privately, but it would be difficult to evaluate this premise empirically. The available evidence indicates on the whole that the modal level of reported worry is not high.

Many observers have puzzled over the relatively low level of worry. Given people's consensual horrific images and their low estimates of personal survival, should they not be more worried? If one combines people's estimated probability of nuclear war and their estimated probability of dying if a nuclear war occurred, people are essentially saying that they have about one chance in three of dying from a nuclear attack. To return to the analogy used at the beginning of this article, if most people received a cancer diagnosis giving comparable odds, they would doubtless be considerably upset. One naturally wonders why people's understanding is so discrepant from their feelings.

People probably cope emotionally with the threat of nuclear war in different ways. Some preliminary survey evidence classifies people according to distinct cognitive/emotional stances that range from romanticist to hedonist to fatalist to deterrentist to disarmist; the data suggest that people's emotional reactions vary accordingly (Hamilton, Chavez, and Keilin 1986). For example, people are classified as romanticists if they report believing that fundamental human goodness will prevent nuclear war; these romanticists report little anxiety, worry, and thought about the issue. Hedonists believe that the prospect of nuclear war justifies immediate gratification, and they report a high degree of personal impact and a high probability of nuclear war but only moderate worry and moderate anxiety. Altruistic fatalists believe nuclear war is quite possible but not preventable so that they should work for the good of humanity meanwhile, and they report low levels of personal impact and anxiety. Deterrentists report some worry and anxiety, and they estimate a moderate probability of nuclear war. Disarmists report the highest levels of thought, worry, and anxiety.

Across the larger population, people's level of nuclear anxiety correlates with nonconforming attitudes, felt vulnerability, drug use, low self-esteem, and perceived lack of social support (M. D. Newcomb 1986). Similarly, nuclear anxiety is related to death anxiety (Hamilton, Keilin, and Knox 1987). Of course, the direction of causality is not clear. People who experience nuclear anxiety may therefore be more vulnerable socially and emotionally (e.g., Escalona 1982), but the reverse is equally possible: People who are vulnerable for other reasons may then focus disproportionately on nuclear threat. Perhaps the same people a century ago would have worried about catastrophes such as massive floods or fires.

Clinical interviews, which use less representative samples but have more depth, indicate that some individuals experience deep-seated worry, fear, and anxiety (Nelson 1985). These individuals are not typical of the larger population, however, so unfortunately we do not know whether the interviews uncovered something about those particular people or a deeper truth about all of us. The essential research requires both in-depth interviews *and* representative samples; it apparently remains to be done. Nevertheless, the best current evidence indicates that although people certainly report concern when asked, the issue simply is not emotionally central for most people most of the time.

However, people's policy preferences more dramatically reveal their feelings. The typical person clearly supports a mutual freeze on nuclear arms, although not a unilateral freeze (Gallup Poll 1983; Kramer et al., 1983). Support for a mutual freeze is remarkably consensual (77 percent agree); it is unusually broad-based, showing few differences across gender, age, income, and education (Milburn, Kramer, and Watanabe, 1984);

and it has held firm over the decades since 1945 (Ladd 1982). The typical person believes that the use of atomic weapons in Japan was necessary and proper but does not accept their use any longer (Kramer et al. 1983; Yankelovich and Doble 1984). Despite this widespread support for a bilateral nuclear freeze, the typical American feels that our level of defense spending is "about right" so it is not clear that most citizens are willing to give up nuclear weapons altogether (Schatz and Fiske 1992).

Men and older generations do, however, show more support for the use of nuclear force. For example, men and women have differed consistently, although not dramatically, in their acceptance of the use and risks of nuclear weapons ever since 1949, with women being less accepting. This fits with the 5 percent to 10 percent gender gap on other foreign policy issues related to force (e.g., "Women and Men" 1982). Political generations also differ in their approval of the use of force generally and in the nuclear case specifically (Jeffries 1974); there is a nuclear generation gap, with younger generations somewhat less accepting of using force. Income and education can influence attitudes toward nuclear force (Jeffries 1974), with increases in either leading to decreased support, although this is not found consistently (Milburn et al. 1984). Note that these gender, age, and class differences occur only in attitudes toward the use of nuclear force should the occasion arise, but not in basic support of a nuclear freeze (Milburn et al. 1984). In brief, then, people worry seldom, but they overwhelmingly favor a mutual nuclear freeze.

ACTIONS

Most people do nothing. They do not act in any way beyond, if asked, voicing support for the policy of a nuclear freeze (Fiske et al. 1983; Milburn et al. 1984; Tyler and McGraw 1983). Age, gender, and social class are not reliable predictors of activism, although political ideology may be. Most people simply do not write antinuclear letters to the editor or to their elected representatives, they do not join or financially support the relevant organizations, and they do not sign petitions.

From one perspective, given that people's beliefs about nuclear war include a low likelihood of personal survival and at least minimal worry, one might expect them to be more active. What is especially surprising, to some observers, is that people are inactive in a matter of such literally earth-shattering consequences. From another perspective, however, the inaction of ordinary citizens is not at all surprising, because most people most of the time pay scant attention to politics and almost never engage in political activity beyond voting, if that (Kinder and Sears 1985; Milbrath and Goel 1977; Nie and Verba 1975). Moreover, with regard to this particular issue, there is no evidence that people expect their actions to have consequences; that is, they have a low sense of political efficacy.

PSYCHOSOCIAL SOURCES OF PEOPLE'S REACTIONS

It seems evident, at first, that people's significant others would influence their responses to nuclear threat. Unfortunately, on this point the hard data are sparse. Moreover, they are limited to nuclear-policy attitudes, so the data do not describe the sources of people's more emotional responses, their beliefs, or their actions. As with most political attitudes, one might expect that the parents primarily socialize the child (Kinder and Sears 1985; Sears 1975), but the data on children's responses to nuclear war suggest that this may not be the case (Beardslee 1986). College students' stance toward nuclear war resembles the *perceived* but not the actual stance of their parents (Hamilton, Chavez, and Keilin 1986; Hamilton, Knox, and Keilin 1986). Thus, although they think they share their parents' perspective, they often do not. As noted earlier, young people are less accepting of the use of force, including nuclear force. This discrepancy is preserved by most families' reported failure to discuss nuclear issues (Hamilton, Knox, and Keilin 1986), a standard finding in all types of political socialization (Sears 1975).

Outside the family, people tend to have friends whose attitudes resemble their own, both because similarities attract and because friends influence each other; this point is well-documented (Berscheid 1985). Moreover, people perceive their friends to have similar attitudes to an even greater extent than they do (Levinger and Breedlove 1966; T. M. Newcomb 1961). Hence, it is likely that people perceive their attitudes toward nuclear war to be shared by their friends. Although the relevant evidence is slim, college students do perceive their friends to have similar attitudes (Hamilton, Chavez, and Keilin 1986)—whether they do or not is a separate question, as yet unanswered.

When directly asked the source of their responses to the possibility of nuclear war, people often cite media coverage (Fiske et al. 1983; Milburn et al. 1984). A recent media event allowed social researchers to investigate whether people's intuitions are right about this. Dozens of efforts examined the impact of the docudrama *The Day After*, which was televised in November 1983. The conclusions are intriguingly well substantiated by research a dozen years ago on the effects of the film *Hiroshima-Nagasaki: 1945* (Granberg and Faye 1972). Both films make the abstract concrete and bring the unthinkable into awareness. Both films demonstrate the specific ways the media can influence people: by making certain issues salient and by reinforcing people's prior reactions. *The Day After* had a remarkably clear impact on people's beliefs, emotions, and information seeking behavior, at least in the short term; it had remarkably little impact on their policy preferences and political behavior (cf. Oskamp 1986; Oskamp et al. 1985).

ANTINUCLEAR ACTIVISTS AND SURVIVALISTS

For most people, most of the time, nuclear war is not a salient concern. But for a tiny fraction of the population, it is. The tiny fraction for whom the issue is chronically salient is an important fraction: They tend to be active, and they create events that the media cover, so they potentially make the issue more salient for everyone (cf. Nie and Verba 1975). Salience exaggerates people's propensity to act in whatever direction they already would tend to act. Hence, two types of action can be spurred by salience, antinuclear action and prodefense action. In this section I will portray the typical antinuclear activist and the typical prodefense activist because they provide some clues to the discrepancy between people's bleak beliefs and their usual inaction.

As defined here, even the antinuclear activist's typical activities are few and modest: writing congressional representatives and donating money to an antinuclear group. Nevertheless, this is far more than the average person does and far more than people's usual levels of political activity. Even this humble degree of antinuclear protest is worth examining. Factors that motivate antinuclear protest most centrally include an extreme chronic salience of the issue and an unusual sense of political efficacy, as well as some attitudinal and demographic factors. Chronic personal salience of the nuclear issue clearly distinguishes the activist. Antinuclear activists report frequently thinking about the issue (Fiske et al. 1983; Hamilton, Chavez, and Keilin 1986), on the order of several minutes a day. Having the issue on their minds apparently creates detailed and concrete images of nuclear war (Fiske et al. 1983) like those mentioned earlier: images of dismembered bodies, people screaming, buildings on fire, miles of rubble, and barren landscapes. Presumably, their uniquely salient concrete images are motivating for antinuclear activists. Moreover, the combination of high perceived severity and high perceived likelihood of nuclear war is a good predictor of intent to become involved in antinuclear activity (Wolf, Gregory, and Stephan 1986).

A strong sense of political efficacy also distinguishes the activist (Hamilton et al. 1987; Milburn et al. 1984; Oskamp et al. 1985; Tyler and McGraw 1983); this is true of political activists in general (Nie and Verba 1975). The antinuclear activist believes that nuclear war is preventable, not inevitable, and that citizens working together can influence government action to decrease the chance of a nuclear war. The antinuclear activist is specifically motivated by a sense of personal political capability combined with a belief in the efficacy of political action (Wolf et al. 1986). The correlation between political efficacy and behavioral intent is substantial by social science standards (Schofield and Pavelchak 1985; Wolf et al. 1986). Moreover, although activists believe that governments create the risk of nuclear war, they also believe that citizens can and should be responsible for preventing it (Tyler and McGraw 1983). Not surprisingly, considering their strong sense of political efficacy, antinuclear activists tend to participate in other types of political activity as well (Fiske et al. 1983; Milburn et al. 1984; Oskamp et al. 1985). Thus, their antinuclear activity is not a special case.

Although activists believe nuclear war is preventable, they do not believe it is survivable (Tyler and McGraw 1983). Hence, their sense of efficacy is limited to political activity, not to their own ability to live through the holocaust should they fail.

People develop a strong sense of political efficacy through complex personal and social factors (Kinder and Sears 1985). The activists' sense of political efficacy is linked to a broad sense of personal, rather than external, control over life events in general (Tyler and McGraw 1983). Antinuclear activists, then, are people who think about nuclear war a great deal and think they can help prevent its occurrence, and they are fortified by a sense of personal control. Besides personal salience and efficacy, antinuclear activists are distinguished by some less clear-cut and less interesting predispositions. Activists, of course, have even stronger antinuclear attitudes than does the average citizens (Fiske et al. 1983). They sometimes report more worry, more anxiety, more anger, more outrage, and less hopelessness (Hamilton, Keilin, and Knox 1987; Hamilton, Knox, Keilin, and Chavez 1987; Milburn el al. 1984; Oskamp et al. 1985; Tyler and McGraw 1983). Antinuclear activists may be more likely to be liberals and Democrats (Oskamp et al. 1985; Tyler and McGraw 1983; Werner and Roy 1985), although this result does not always show up (Fiske et al. 1983). They may be more likely to be educated and well-off (Tyler and McGraw 1983), although again, not all researchers have found these results (Fiske et al. 1983; Milburn et al. 1984).

And finally, the jury is still out on activists' view of the likelihood of nuclear war. One might expect that frequently imagining the event would make it seem more likely (Carroll 1978). On the other hand, activity by oneself and others might be viewed as decreasing the odds of nuclear war, especially for people with a strong sense of efficacy. Some research indicates that antinuclear activists indeed do estimate a higher probability of nuclear war (Milburn et al. 1984; Tyler and McGraw 1983, but cf. Fiske et al. 1983). More data are clearly needed on all of these points.

Overall, antinuclear activists do not differ dramatically from the majority of Americans in their attitudes toward nuclear war; they express only somewhat more extreme attitudes and feelings than do ordinary Americans. Hence, it is mainly their activities, not their thoughts and feelings, that require explanation. Issue salience and political efficacy go some distance toward doing so in this as in other political arenas (Milbrath and Goel 1977; Nie and Verba 1975).

The prodefense activist is more of a mystery. In a sense, such people are doubly puzzling, for they are likely not only to oppose a nuclear freeze and favor a defense build-up, which puts them in a minority of Americans, but also to be active in the service of their attitudes, which also makes them unusual. One form of prodefense activism is survivalist activity that includes building a shelter, storing food and water, making family evacuation plans, and the like. Survivalists rate nuclear war as relatively probable (Tyler and McGraw 1983; but see Hamilton, Chavez, and Keilin 1986). Accordingly, nuclear war may well be a chronically salient issue for them, as it is for the antinuclear activist. In this case, however, salience catalyzes an entirely different sort of activity, in line with presumably different preexisting attitudes.

The efficacy of a survivalist also differs from that of ordinary people and antinuclear activists. Survivalists believe that nuclear war is not preventable but that it is survivable (Tyler and McGraw 1983). Hence, although survivalists believe nuclear war is likely, they do not report being worried about it (Hamilton, Chavez, and Keilin 1986; Tyler and McGraw 1983). Consistent with their belief that nuclear war is not preventable, survivalists are low on political efficacy. Surprisingly, they are also low on internal locus of control. Perhaps this is consistent with their belief that responsibility for nuclear war lies with historical forces, not with the ordinary citizen or the government (Tyler and McGraw 1983). More data are needed to describe not only the survivalist but also other types of more obviously prodefense activists.

IMPLICATIONS FOR PSYCHOLOGISTS

Psychologists have a long history of concern with nuclear war. Most members of the American Psychological Association (APA) report reading about the issue, discussing it informally, and signing petitions, according to a recent survey (McConnell et al. 1986). Most APA members agree with the 1982 APA Council of Representatives resolution to support a nuclear freeze (Polyson, Stein, and Sholley 1986). This concern, moreover, is not new. Psychologists decades ago anticipated people's fears about the bomb; they initially worked to assuage these fears, to prompt public trust in the atomic experts, and to examine civil defense from a psychological perspective (Morawaki and Goldstein 1985). But these efforts soon tapered off as it became clear that, surprisingly, the ordinary person was apparently less concerned than the researchers expected. Despite high levels of reported awareness about the issues, people report relatively little fear or worry, at least in survey interviews, and most people take no action to prevent nuclear war. Many observers in the psychological community have wondered publicly about the ordinary citizen's apparent indifference when confronted with the potential annihilation of humankind (e.g., Goldman and Greenberg 1982; Lifton 1982; Mack 1981, 1982). This contrast has prompted the enduring puzzle variously called "fear suppression," "psychic numbing," "denial," and "apathy," which has been attributed to people's feelings of impotence, helplessness, inefficacy, and the life. Moreover, direct empirical support for denial-like processes is mixed at best (Schatz and Fiske 1992).

The discrepancy between people's nuclear understanding and their elusive emotional and behavioral concern, however, is a puzzle only if the observer takes a prescriptive stance. Nuclear war *should* be one issue on which people act, because it involves the potential end of civilization and, more concretely, one's own death. Given the unbelievable magnitude of the potential event and the fact that most people understand this to a great extent, the discrepancy between their beliefs and their relatively unworried inaction seems intolerable. Some would call it irrational or even a major mental health issue (e.g., Goldman and Greenberg 1982).

This prescriptive stance, however, confuses the magnitude of the event with the realistic possibility of affecting its occurrence. One could argue, of course, that the unbelievably huge magnitude of the event requires action even given the smallest probability of affecting its occurrence. Nevertheless, no one really knows whether citizen action will help to prevent a nuclear war. It is not an empirical question. And informed opinions differ about the effectiveness of citizen action. Hence, the assumption that nuclear war is an issue on which people should be active is a prescriptive, moral statement, not a descriptive one. One danger of prescription is that it obscures accurate description.

Furthermore, our personal and professional involvement in this issue has a risk. It creates a danger of what social psychologists call a *false consensus bias* (Ross, Green, and House 1977). That is, it is all too easy to believe that the average citizen shares a sense of urgency, a sense that something must be done. Becoming aware of our false consensus bias means realizing that the issue is not all that salient for the average citizen. We must not overestimate the degree of disturbance in the average person. Although people are clearly aware and deeply concerned, nuclear war is mostly not on their minds. Readers who are worried cannot take it for granted that everyone shares their urgency but has somehow suppressed it. One sees this in some psychologists' claims that the average person is dramatically disturbed about the possibility of nuclear war. Unfortunately, clinicians and researchers may inadvertently overestimate the ordinary person's concerns because they themselves are professionally concerned with nuclear war (cf. Fischhoff, Pidgeon, and Fiske 1983; Flanagan and Sommers 1986; Hamilton, Chavez, and Keilin 1986).

The average person also has a low sense of political efficacy, probably in contrast to most readers of this article. Politically active readers cannot take it for granted that everyone shares their sense of efficacy but somehow avoids action. Most people believe, rightly or wrongly, that they can do nothing in regard to nuclear war. Of course, some people, although not many, do share active readers' sense of political efficacy. These are likely to be people who have been politically active before and can be mobilized to be active again. One role the active few serve is to keep the issue salient for everyone. But it is important to remember that most people's inaction is consistent with their understanding of political reality.

Remaining relatively unworried and inactive, despite the horrific possibility of nuclear war, is not irrational if people are correct in judging that their activism would have no consequences. The ordinary person does not possess the antinuclear activist's sense of political efficacy, that is, does not believe that nuclear war is preventable by citizen actions. And, by some lights, people are right about this: The activity of one ordinary person hardly makes a difference (cf. Converse 1975). And even collective public opinion rarely influences foreign policy; public opinion ranks far behind perceived geopolitical realities in influencing government leaders' decisions in this realm (Rosenau 1967). Some experts even argue that the public is not competent to judge in these matters anyway. If one accepts all these premises, then ordinary people's relative lack of worry and complete inaction, despite their horrific beliefs and clear expectation that they would die in a nuclear war, are not irrational. Viewed this way, one can come to the defense of the ordinary person, and there is no massive problem revealed by the nuclear discrepancy. Across most societies and most political issues, the average person is not politically active (Nie and Verba 1975; Milbrath and Goel 1977). Inactivity on nuclear issues is thus standard and to be expected.

For those inclined to be active in the service of their beliefs, there are apparently two key tasks that will encourage citizens to voice their perceptions of the horrific possibilities of a nuclear war. People do have feelings and beliefs about nuclear war, and these are not inappropriate, given what is known. Granted, the issue of nuclear war is not central for most people most of the time. When it is salient, however, people do respond to it. Because most of the country does report that nuclear war creates worry, fear, and sadness when they think about it and because most of the country supports a mutual freeze, it seems likely that the effects of continued activity on the part of some make the issue salient for the many. Keeping the issue salient is likely to accentuate people's existing worry and their preference for a mutual nuclear freeze.

This suggests some general strategies for psychologist activists. These come not only from the research reviewed here but also from the standard results of research on political participation. First, one must find a way to give people a sense of political efficacy or what I would call "hope through action." This is not easy. But one clear message from social psychology is that one must pair fear-arousing communications with possible action solutions for people (cf. Feshbach 1986; Wolf et al. 1986). The solutions must be perceived as politically effective and as something the ordinary person is capable of doing. Second, we must keep the issue salient by public events and by media converge of those events, which is, ironically, even more important. Keeping the issue alive may indeed help to keep us all alive.[1]

The current research also suggests an agenda for future researchers and for funders of such research:

1. We need to know more about people's reactions to nuclear war, in *broad context*. Many of the findings with regard to adult reactions to nuclear war are not surprising to political scientists; they should not be surprising to psychologists who trouble to examine the related literature. The issue should be studied not in isolation but rather along with people's beliefs, feelings, and actions regarding other serious political issues, other potential catastrophes, and other possibilities of their own deaths. Empirically comparing this issue to other issues is an antidote to viewing people's reactions to nuclear war as unprecedented when it is in fact the potential consequences that are unprecedented.

2. We need rigorous national surveys coupled with subsamples interviewed in depth. Too many of the surveys cited here suffer from convenience sampling, inexpert methodology, and ad hoc items that limit cross-study comparisons. It is a tribute to the researchers' perseverance that the surveys were conducted at all, because almost all were unfunded. And the existing data are certainly a start. But we have learned enough now that the survey data must be extended to a national scale and rigorous techniques used. Surveys alone will not suffice, moreover, for at least some people indicate different levels or worry in the privacy of clinical settings. The subjective nature of the in-depth clinical interview needs to be balanced against the impersonal nature of the more objective survey interview.

3. We need data on the sources of people's reactions. We have only the sparsest data on the influences of family and friends and on the impact of the media. Again, this research needs to be conducted with full knowledge of the standard findings on political socialization and media impact, to see how the nuclear issue compares.

4. We need more studies of activists, both antinuclear and prodefense. The primary motivation of many involved psychologists is the prevention of nuclear war. Studying the activists provides insights into how other citizens can make themselves heard.

5. Finally, we need funding. Countless studies contain apologies for shortcuts and limitations required by the investigator's out-of-pocket support. Many investigators have commented privately on their frustrated applications for support. It is not that excellent work cannot be done, for some already has been. One wonders whether psychological research on nuclear war seems too political for traditional funding agencies and too tame for peace-oriented funding agencies. It is a pity, for psychology has much to contribute, and much remains to be done before it is too late.

NOTES

Note: The literature review in this article was originally prepared for the Symposium on Medical Implications of Nuclear War, Institute of Medicine, National Academy of Sciences, Washington, D.C., September 1985.

The author would like to thank William Beardslee, Michael Milburn, Steven Neuberg, Mark Pavelchak, and Janet Schofield for their comments on an earlier draft of this article.

Correspondence concerning this article should be addressed to Susan T. Fiske, Department of Psychology, Tobin Hall, University of Massachusetts, Amherst, MA 01003.

1. Other relevant insights from psychology and related areas have been expertly collected by Ralph K. White (1986).

REFERENCES

Beardslee, W. R. (1986). Children's and adolescents' perceptions of the threat of nuclear war: Implications of recent studies. In F. Solomon and R. Q. Marston, eds., *The medical implications of nuclear war*, 413–434. Washington, D.C.: National Academy Press.

Berscheid, E. (1985). Interpersonal attraction. In G. Lindzey and E. Aronson, eds., *The handbook of social psychology*, 3d ed., 413–483. New York: Random House.

Boyer, P. (1985, August 12 & 19). How Americans imagined the bomb they dropped: The cloud over the culture. *The New Republic*, 26–31.

Carroll, J. S. (1978). The effect of imagining an event on expectations for the event: An interpretation in terms of the availability heuristic. *Journal of Experimental Social Psychology*, *14*, 88–96.

Chavez, E. L., Hamilton, S. B., and Keilin, W. G. (1986). "The Day After": A preliminary report on its effects on children [Comment]. *American Psychologist*, *41*, 722–723.

Converse, P. E. (1975). Public opinion and voting behavior. In F. I. Greenstein and N. W. Polsby, eds., *Handbook of political science*, vol. 4, 75–172. Reading, Mass.: Addison-Wesley.

Escalona, S. K. (1982). Growing up with the threat of nuclear war. Some indirect effects on personality development. *American Journal of Orthopsychiatry*, *52*, 600–607.

Feldman, S., and Sigelman, L. (1985). The political impact of prime-time television: "The Day After." *Journal of Politics*, *47*, 556–578.

Feshbach, S. (section ed.). (1986). Changing war-related attitudes. In R. K. White, ed., *Psychology and the prevention of nuclear war*, 511–523. New York: New York University Press.

Fischhoff, B., Pidgeon, N., and Fiske, S. T. (1983). Social science and the politics of the arms race. *Journal of Social Issues*, *39*, 161–180.

Fiske, S. T., Pratto, F., and Pavelchak, M. A. (1983). Citizens' images of nuclear war: Contents and consequences. *Journal of Social Issues*, *39*, 41–65.

Flanagan, R., and Sommers, J. (1986). Ethical considerations for the peace activist psychotherapist [Comment]. *American Psychologist*, *41*, 723–724.

Gallup Poll. (1983). *Public opinion 1983*. Wilmington, Del.: Scholarly Resources.

Goldman, D. S., and Greenberg, W. M. (1982). Preparing for nuclear war. The psychological effects. *American Journal of Orthopsychiatry*, *52*, 580–581.

Goodman, L. A., Mack, J. E., Beardslee, W. R., and Snow, R. M. (1983). The threat of nuclear war and the nuclear arms race: Adolescent experience and perceptions. *Political Psychology*, *4*, 501–530.

Granberg, D., & Faye, N. (1972). Sensitizing people by making the abstract concrete: Study of the effect of "Hiroshima-Nagasaki: 1945." *American Journal of Orthopsychiatry*, *42*, 811–815.

Hamilton, S. B., Chavez, E. L., and Keilin, W. G. (1986). Thoughts of Armageddon: The relationship between nuclear threat attitudes and cognitive/emotional responses. *International Journal of Mental Health*, *15*, 189–207.

Hamilton, S. B., Keilin, W. G., and Knox, T. A. (1987). Thinking about the unthinkable: The relationship between death anxiety and cognitive/emotional responses to the threat of nuclear war. *Omega: Journal of Death and Dying*, *18*, 53–61.

Hamilton, S. B., Knox, T. A., and Keilin, W. G. (1986). The nuclear family:

Correspondence in cognitive and affective reactions to the threat of nuclear war among older adolescents and their parents. *Journal of Youth and Adolescence, 15,* 133–145.

Hamilton, S. B., Knox, T. A., Keilin, W. G., and Chavez, E. L. (1987). In the eye of the beholder: Accounting for variability in cognitive/emotional responses to the threat of nuclear war. *Journal of Applied Social Psychology, 17,* 929–952.

Jeffries, V. (1974). Political generations and the acceptance or rejection of nuclear warfare. *Journal of Social Issues, 39,* 119–136.

Kinder, D. R., and Sears, D. O. (1985). Public opinion and political action. In G. Lindzey and E. Aronson, eds., *The handbook of social psychology,* 3d ed., pp. 659–741. New York: Random House.

Klineberg, O. (1984). Public opinion and nuclear war. *American Psychologist, 39,* 1245–1253.

Kramer, B. M., Kalick, S. M., and Milburn, M. A. (1983). Attitudes toward nuclear weapons and nuclear war: 1945–1982. *Journal of Social Issues, 39,* 7–24.

Ladd, E. (1982). The freeze framework. *Public Opinion, 5,* 20–41.

Levinger, G., and Breedlove, J. (1966). Interpersonal attraction and agreement: A study of marriage partners. *Journal of Personality and Social Psychology, 2,* 367–372.

Lifton, R. J. (1968). *Death in life: Survivors of Hiroshima.* New York: Random House.

Lifton, R. J. (1982). Beyond psychic numbing: A call to awareness. *American Journal of Orthopsychiatry, 52,* 619–629.

Lifton, R. J. (1983). *The life of the self: Toward a new psychology.* New York: Basic Books.

McConnell, S. C., Brown, S. D., Ruffing, J. N., Strupp, J. K., Duncan, B. L., and Kurdek, L. A. (1986). Psychologists' attitudes and activities regarding nuclear arms [Comment]. *American Psychologist, 41,* 725–727.

Mack, J. E. (1981). Psychosocial effects of the nuclear arms race. *Bulletin of the Atomic Scientist, 37,* 18–23.

Mack, J. E. (1982). The perception of U.S.–Soviet intentions and other psychological dimensions of the arms race. *American Journal of Orthopsychology, 52,* 590–599.

Mayton, D. M. (1986). Spontaneous concern about nuclear war by college students. *Basic and Applied Social Psychology, 7,* 185–193.

Milbrath, L. W., and Goel, M. L. (1977). *Political participation,* 2d ed. Chicago: Rand McNally.

Milburn, M. A., Kramer, B. M., and Watanabe, P. Y. (1984). The nature and sources of attitudes toward a nuclear freeze. *Political Psychology, 7,* 661–674.

Morawski, J. G., and Goldstein, S. E. (1985). Psychology and nuclear war: A chapter in our legacy of social responsibility. *American Psychologist, 40,* 276–284.

Nelson, A. (1985). Psychological equivalence: Awareness and response-ability in our nuclear age. *American Psychologist, 40,* 549–556.

Nelson, A. (1985). Psychological equivalence: Awareness and response-ability in our nuclear age. *American Psychologist, 40,* 549–556.

Newcomb, M. D. (1986). Nuclear anxiety and psychosocial functioning among young adults. *Basic and Applied Social Psychology, 9,* 107–134.

Newcomb, M. D. (1988). Nuclear attitudes and reactions: Associations with depression, drug use, and quality of life. *Journal of Personality and Social Psychology, 50,* 906–920.

Newcomb, T. M. (1961). *The acquaintance process.* New York: Holt, Rinehart and Winston.

Nie, N. H., and Verba, S. (1975). Political participation. In F. I. Greenstein and N. W. Polsby, eds., *Handbook of political science,* vol. 41–74). Reading, Mass.: Addison-Wesley.

Oskamp, S. (1986). Nuclear war on television: The impact of "The Day After." In G. Comstock, ed., *Public communication and behavior,* vol. 2. New York: Academic Press.

Oskamp, S., King, J. C., Burn, S. M., Konrad, A. M., Pollard, J. A., and White, M. A. (1985). The media and nuclear war. Fallout from TV's "The Day After." In S. Oskamp, ed., *Applied social psychology annual: Vol. 6. International conflict and national public policy issues.* Beverly Hills, Calif.: Sage.

Polyson, J., Hillmar, J., and Kriek, D. (1986). Levels of public interest in nuclear war: 1945–1985. *Journal of Social Behavior and Personality, 1,* 397–401.

Polyson, J., Stein, D., and Sholley, B. (1986). Psychologists and nuclear war: A survey. *American Psychologist, 41,* 724–725.

Rosenau, J. N. (1967). Introduction. In J. N. Rosenau, ed., *Domestic sources of foreign policy,* 1–10. New York: Free Press.

Ross, L., Greene, D., and House, P. (1977). The "false consensus effect": An egocentric bias in social perception and attribution processes. *Journal of Experimental Social Psychology, 13,* 279–301.

Ruble, D. N., and Ruble, T. L. (1982). Sex stereotypes. In A. G. Miller, ed., *In the eye of the beholder: Contemporary issues in stereotyping,* 188–252. New York: Praeger.

Schatz, R. T., and Fiske, S. T. (1992). International reactions to the threat of nuclear war: The rise and fall of concern in the eighties. *Political Psychology.*

Schofield, J., and Pavelchak, M. A. (1985). "The Day After": The impact of a media event. *American Psychologist, 40,* 542–548.

Schwebel, M. (1982). Effects of the nuclear war threat on children and teenagers: Implications for professionals. *American Journal of Orthopsychiatry, 52,* 608–618.

Sears, D. O. (1975). Political socialization. In F. I. Greenstein and N. W. Polsby, eds., *Handbook of political science,* vol. 4, 93–154. Reading, Mass.: Addison-Wesley.

Smith, T. W. (1988). The polls: A report: Nuclear anxiety. *Public Opinion Quarterly, 50,* 519–536.

Wagner, R. V. (1985). Psychology and the threat of nuclear war. *American Psychologist, 40,* 531–535.

Werner, P. D., and Roy, P. J. (1985). Measuring activism regarding the nuclear arms race. *Journal of Personality Assessment, 49,* 181–186.

What the boy saw: A fire in the sky. (1985, July 29). *Time,* 34-39.

What the people saw: A vision of ourselves. (1985, July 29). *time,* 54–57.

White, R. K., ed., (1986). *Psychology and the prevention of nuclear war.* New York: New York University Press.

Withey, S. B. (1954). *Survey of public knowledge and attitudes concerning civil defense.* Ann Arbor: Survey Research Center, Institute for Social Research, University of Michigan.

Wolf, S., Gregory, W. L., and Stephan, W. G. (1986). Protection motivation theory: Prediction of intentions to engage in anti-nuclear war behaviors. *Journal of Applied Social Psychology, 16,* 310–321.

Women and men: Is a realignment under way? (1982). *Public Opinion, 5*(2), 21–30.

Yankelovich, D., and Doble, J. (1984). The public mood: Nuclear weapons and the U.S.S.R. *Foreign Affairs, 63,* 33–46.

16

Understanding the Psychology of Global Activism

Douglas McKenzie-Mohr

Decades from now, if humanity survives, our children will look back upon the latter part of this century with contempt and horror. Future generations will wonder how it was possible that we knowingly allowed the atrocities that went on all around us to occur. They will wonder how we tolerated huge expenditures on the arms race while over one quarter of the world's population lived in absolute poverty. They will wonder how an intelligent species could be so utterly negligent of its environment that it would threaten the very existence of its children.

Theodore Roethke wrote in 1966 that "in a dark time the eye begins to see." If we are to alter the epitaph that our children will write for us, we must begin to see in this dark time. We must come to fully appreciate the gravity of our present state of militarization and environmental destruction. But just as importantly, we must come to understand the factors that affect individual actions as they relate to militarization and environmental destruction, and we must use this knowledge to enhance our survival.

THE PRESENT DANGER

It is estimated that a nuclear attack against the United States would result in tens of millions of deaths (Schell 1982), while in Canada between six to eight million individuals would be killed or seriously injured in the first few minutes of a nuclear holocaust.[1] Due to the lack of medical facilities, which would would have been destroyed in the initial explosions, those who were seriously injured would die in the next several days (Bates et al. 1983). In the months following a nuclear holocaust, initial survivors would be faced with an array of insurmountable problems. They would have to cope not only with the stress of having had tens of thousands of people around them die, but also with radiation fallout (see Lindop and Rotblat 1981), the spread of communicable diseases (see Abrams 1981), malnutrition, starvation, exposure, the absence of medical facilities, and the subsequent collapse of society (see Geiger 1981). Anyone who survived these hardships would still have to contend with the long-term effects of exposure to radiation (see Lindop and Rotblat 1981) and the ecological impact of nuclear winter brought on by thousands of nuclear detonations (see Sagan 1985).

Grim as this depiction might be, it is only half the picture. The ever increasing militarization of our planet not only threatens the future of humanity but also undermines the lives of millions without one missile or shot being fired. At present, world military expenditures exceed one trillion dollars a year (Sivard 1989). This is a difficult figure to grasp until the dollars are translated into the human suffering that could be alleviated by money now spent on militarization. For example, each and every day, forty thousand children die globally from preventable diseases. The World Health Organization has estimated that the amount of money required to save these children's lives is equal to that which is presently spent globally on the military every three weeks (Sivard 1989).

In addition to militarization, humanity is also threatened by a host of environmental problems. For example, we now have evidence that the ozone layer, which is located twenty to fifty kilometers above the earth's surface and is responsible for screening out hazardous ultraviolet radiation, is thinning as a result of humanity's use of chlorofluorocarbons (CFC's). As this shield thins, the amount of ultraviolet radiation that reaches the earth's surface increases. It has been estimated that a 1 percent reduction in ozone may lead to an additional fifteen thousand cases of skin cancer each year in the United States. Further, ozone depletion is linked to increases in the incidence of cataracts and damage to crops. Additional evidence of our destruction of the environment can be found in the Great Lakes. Over one thousand chemicals have been found in these waters which are utilized by over thirty-five million North Americans. In fact, contamination of Lake Ontario has reached such proportions that children and pregnant women are warned against eating its fish. These are but two of the ways that humanity is damaging its environment. Others include contamination of the air we breathe, global warming, toxic waste, and soil erosion, to name a just a few.

If we are to deal effectively with these issues, it is of paramount importance that we quickly come to understand how to mobilize the public to search out solutions to militarization and environmental destruction. In this chapter I intend to present some of the psychological factors that are related to activism on these two issues, and to suggest strategies for mobilizing the public.

PUBLIC RESPONSES TO THESE THREATS

Public concern with global militarization is reflected in the public's broad support for a number of arms control proposals (see Kramer, Kallick, and Milburn 1983). For example, a freeze of the arms race is supported by 77 percent of American adults (Gallup 1983; Kramer, Kallick, and Milburn 1983), while in Canada, public endorsement of a freeze reaches near unanimity at 86 percent (Gallup 1984). Not surprisingly, with such high levels of endorsement, support for a mutual freeze of the arms race is affected little by demographic variables such as gender, income, and education (Milburn, Kramer, and Watanabe 1984).

What is of concern, however, is that although the public overwhelmingly endorses such proposals, few work to promote their enactment (Milburn and Watanabe 1985; Mohr, McLoughlin, and Cohen 1987). Indeed, Susan Fiske (chapter 15 in this volume) reports that "most people do not write letters to the editor nor their elected representatives, they do not join or financially support the relevant organizations, and they do not sign petitions" (see also Mohr, McLoughlin, and Cohen 1987). Similarly, Locatelli and Holt (1987) conclude that the majority of the public respond as if there is no danger.

The discrepancy between individuals' attitudes toward militarization and their actual behavior has been commented on widely. Most writers have taken the prescriptive stance that this is the one issue on which people *should* be active (see chapter 15) Fiske, French, and Van Hoorn (1986), for example, have commented that the "most unhealthy psychological response" to the arms race may well be inattention. That the public is inattentive appears to be substantiated. A national survey of American adults found that only 3 percent of those surveyed chose the arms race as the news item to which they pay the most attention (*Los Angeles Times* Poll 1982).

As with militarization, the public reports high levels of concern with environmental destruction. For example, 94 percent of Canadian adults reported in recent Gallup polls that they were either somewhat or very concerned with the desecration of the environment (Gallup 1989a, 1989b). However, unlike public response to militarization, public concern with environmental destruction does not end here. As an illustration, 80 percent of municipal residences in the province of Ontario are participating in a recycling program that requires residents to leave recyclable materials at the curbside (*CTRC Bulletin* 1987). While the public does not always engage in actions congruent with their attitudes on environmental issues, such as driving less, attitudes and behavior have been shown to be consistent in several areas, such as the purchase of green consumer products and the joining of environmental protection groups.

Why is the public engaging in behavior consistent with its attitudes regarding the environment while failing to act accordingly regarding militarization? Ajzen and Fishbein (1977), in a review of the attitude-behavior literature, report that most research demonstrates a low or nonsignificant correlation between measures of attitudes and actual behavior. In response, recent theorists have argued that there is no necessary connection between attitudes and behavior (see Zanna, Higgins, and Herman 1982), and have turned to identifying the variables that moderate the attitude-behavior relationship (e.g., Fazio and Zanna 1981).

What variables might be leading individuals to engage in behavior congruent with their attitudes with respect to the environment but not with respect to the arms race? This is an important question since its answer will provide us with suggestions of how to more effectively mobilize the public on disarmament issues.

Lazarus's model of stress and coping is of particular interest in that it suggests factors that might influence peace and environmental activism (Lazarus and Folkman 1984).[2] Lazarus's model involves two steps. During the first step, primary appraisal, an individual asks the question, "What significance does militarization or environmental destruction have for me?" If either of these issues is perceived by the individual to be threatening, it is then necessary to evaluate coping strategies that may be employed to deal with the threat. In the second step, which Lazarus terms secondary appraisal, the individual asks, "What can be done?" According to Lazarus's model, when a person has appraised either of these issues as threatening, two options are available: problem-focused coping or emotion-focused coping. Problem-focused coping involves taking direct action in order to alleviate or alter the threat. With respect to militarization, joining a disarmament group, writing an elected representative, and participating in a rally are examples of problem-focused coping. With respect to environmental destruction, recycling, conserving energy, and re-using products would all be examples of problem-focused coping. On the other hand, emotion-focused coping refers to strategies employed by an individual to alleviate emotional distress. Denial, selective attention, and avoidance are examples of emotion-focused coping strategies with respect to both issues. If effective, these strategies can alter the subjective significance of the stressful event, and hence reduce distress. For example, an individual may deny the existence of the threat of nuclear holocaust or the severity of the environmental crisis, successfully altering the perceived threat so that it is no longer disturbing.

Lazarus's model is useful in illustrating why the public has responded so differently to these two issues. This model directs us initially to assess whether the public appraises both issues as threatening. Here the evidence is clear. As demonstrated by Fiske (chapter 15) in her review of research investigating public responses to the arms race, the vast majority of the public do not believe that nuclear war is probable. Further, the public worries about this issue infrequently. In contrast, if we look at public reactions to environmental destruction, a very different process occurs. For the most part, the general public believes that environmental destruction is a threat. Here, a wide segment of the population, as evidence by Gallup polls, believes that global warming, depletion of the ozone layer, and contamination of ground water, to name only a few issues, are serious threats. Indeed, in a study completed by Nemiroff and McKenzie-Mohr (1990), Canadian adults were found to worry five times more frequently about environmental destruction than the arms race. Therefore, in the first step of Lazarus's model, when an individual appraises the significance of both of these issues, the public has come up with two very different answers. For the most part, the public feels threatened by environmental destruction and is much less concerned about militarization.

Given the lack of perceived threat, for most individuals concern about militarization would go no further: having decided that the arms race was not a significant threat, there is no reason to consider what can be done about it. But what about the minority of the public who does feel threatened? How are these individuals likely to respond? Lazarus's model suggests that the level of empowerment an individual feels will largely determine whether an individual chooses to become active (a form of problem-focused coping) or deals with the threat by denying its existence or blocking out thoughts of it (forms of emotion-focused coping). The crucial question becomes then, How empowered does the public feel with respect to the arms race? The answer: not at all. In a study conducted by Mohr and Silver (1986), 82 percent of a random sample of Canadian adults reported feeling completely helpless to effect any type of change with regard to the arms race.

While many individuals feel threatened by environmental destruction, many also feel empowered to change these problems, as evidenced by the previously mentioned recycling program. Clearly, with respect to the environment, the majority of the public has concluded that they are threatened, but unlike the case of the arms race, has decided that they can have some control over the issue.

The differential public response to these two global issues suggests ways to mobilize the public more effectively. Specifically, I wish to provide several suggestions in this regard, and because mobilizing the public in the pursuit of an end to militarization is presently the more difficult and less successful of these two tasks, I will focus primarily on this issue.

REACHING THE PUBLIC

One of the primary concerns of those who are active in the peace and environmental movements is how to educate and mobilize the public most effectively. This is an acute concern in the peace movement, in which many activists lament that their attempts at education are reaching only the converted. Indeed, it was my own observation of the futility of most attempts to educate the public on peace issues that led me initially to research the determinants of peace activism. When I first became concerned with the arms race in the early 1980s, I attended a variety of public meetings sponsored by the peace movement. After attending these meetings, I began to realize that the same people were almost always in attendance. It did not appear to matter who sponsored the meeting; I saw the same people continually. Indeed, to call these events "public meetings" was misleading. In all truthfulness, they were events organized by peace activists and attended by peace activists. In short, peace activists were spending a great deal of time, money, and energy organizing public events, but only "the faithful" were showing up.

A decade of research on the determinants of peace activism is now beginning to answer the question of why primarily only the "converted" or presently active attend meetings sponsored by the peace movement. Lazarus's model suggests that only an individual who feels threatened by the arms race and at the same time empowered is likely to become active. As discussed previously, we now have a variety of studies that document that the majority of the public does not feel threatened by the arms race. Further, the vast majority of those who feel threatened feel helpless to effect any type of meaningful change. As a consequence, it should not surprise us that for the most part only the converted attend meetings sponsored by the peace movement. As McKenzie-Mohr and Dyal (1988) have demonstrated, those who are active in the peace movement feel significantly more powerful than those who share similar pro-disarmament attitudes but remain inactive.

How then might the peace movement more effectively reach the public? In answering this question, it is useful to reflect first upon how the public responds to the present educational efforts of the peace movement. While the majority of the public does not think that nuclear holocaust is likely to occur (Fiske, this volume, chapter 15), they nonetheless find thinking about the subject distressing (Mohr, McLoughlin, and Cohen 1987). In fact, when queried as to whether they believe they would survive a nuclear holocaust, most individuals correctly answer that their chances of survival would be slim. It shouldn't surprise us that the majority of the public avoids thinking about this issue, as demonstrated by the *Los Angeles Times* poll discussed earlier. If an individual feels both threatened by thoughts of nuclear holocaust and at the same time disempowered, she or he is likely to use emotion-focused coping as a strategy for dealing with thoughts of a nuclear holocaust. As a consequence, most of the public is likely to avoid any attempts to enhance their level of knowledge regarding global militarization. In short, any attempt to educate the public that involves the recipient actively choosing to expose himself or herself to information about militarization is unlikely to succeed. If the peace movement is to reach the public more effectively, it must bring its message directly to the public and the message must be empowering.

There are two primary ways in which the peace movement can attempt to reach out to the public more effectively. The first involves making direct contact with the public through paid advertisements. The second involves making direct contact with individuals in their place of work or residence. At least two studies show that directly contacting potential new members for the peace movement is an effective strategy. A study of British Columbia peace activists, carried out by the B.C. Chapter of Psychologists for Social Responsibility, revealed that almost half of the respondents were influenced to become involved as a result of knowing someone in the peace movement (Walkley, Erikson and Tilby, 1988). Further, this survey found that 53 percent of respondents made contact with a local peace group through a friend, acquaintance, or colleague. Frank and Nash (1965), in a study of peace activists, also found that the greatest influence in becoming involved came as a result of personal contacts. Hence, one way to circumvent the public's use of emotion-focused coping is to contact individuals personally. Such a strategy is, however, not without its shortcomings. The primary downfall of such an approach is the labor-intensive nature of essentially going door to door in pursuit of new members.

In approaching the public either directly or through the use of paid advertisements, what type of message is likely to be most effective? Lazarus's model suggests that the most effective messages will lead jointly to an appraisal of threat as well as one of efficacy. In research that I have conducted with Jim Dyal (McKenzie-Mohr and Dyal 1988), however, we have discovered just how difficult it is to alter individuals' appraisal of the likelihood of nuclear holocaust. Even after exposing individuals to new knowledge regarding the potential causes of nuclear holocaust, such as accidental breakdown of the computer systems that control nuclear weapons, short launch times, and launch on warning (see Barash 1987), individuals were very resistant to reappraising nuclear holocaust as being more likely. It may not be necessary, however, to increase public perceptions of the likelihood of nuclear attack in order for individuals to feel sufficiently threatened by militarization to consider becoming active. Simply pointing out to individuals the connections between militarization and the economy, and militarization and Third World development, may be enough to bring about an appraisal of threat.[3]

How should the peace movement go about empowering the public? Here is where the recent surge in activism on environmental issues can provide us with some clues. If you were to formulate a list of the activities that an individual could engage in with respect to the environment and militarization, you would quickly realize just how quantitatively and qualitatively different the lists are. A list of militarization activities might include such actions as writing letters to elected representatives, participating in rallies, joining or financially supporting peace groups, signing a petition, or voting for a political candidate who supports demilitarization. A list of environmental activities would include each of the activities just mentioned but in addition a whole host of other activities such as recycling, conserving energy, using recycled products, composting, driving less or carpooling, and buying environmentally friendly products. Indeed, there has been a recent proliferation of books that provide suggestions for actions to protect our environment. Clearly, quantitatively the environmental movement has articulated a much more comprehensive list of activities that each of us can engage in. But not only are there a greater variety of environmental activities, the majority of these activities are also qualitatively different. Most environmental activities can be conducted by an individual acting alone (such as recycling or driving less). Most environmental activities take little skill to perform and, perhaps most importantly, many are immediately reinforcing to the individual. Hence, if I wish to conserve energy I can turn down the thermostat and check that all nonessential lights are off. Further, these are relatively easy tasks to perform and my actions are immediately reinforced by the knowledge that I am producing less greenhouse gases and am also saving on my heating and electrical bills.

In short, the peace movement has failed to articulate for the general public activities that do not require a high skill level, can be performed individually, and are self-reinforcing. We have limited participation in the peace movement because we do not provide the public with such action strategies. Further, as we limit participation in the movement, we also serve to disempower the public. Empowerment regarding militarization issues rest upon a perception of collective control (McKenzie-Mohr and Dyal 1988): a belief that in working in consort with others, change is possible. By limiting the number of people who are active, we undermine perceptions of collective control.

If we are to enhance the number of people who are active on peace issues, we must begin to define "peace" more broadly and also clarify the connection between militarization and environmental issues. Unwittingly, peace activism has become synonymous with concern with nuclear holocaust. This is understandable to the extent that many of those who are presently involved became active as a result of the Reagan administration's rhetoric around winning a nuclear holocaust that was prevalent in the early 1980s. Nonetheless, this concentration on preventing nuclear holocaust marginalized many individuals by not recognizing within the scope of peace activism more accessible activities, such as raising children to favor nonviolent conflict resolution. Further, by not sufficiently linking peace issues with other global issues, the peace movement has again circumscribed the number of activities in which individuals can engage. For example, by drawing the connection between dependence on nonrenewable fossil fuels and international conflict (e.g., the crisis in the Persian Gulf), a whole range of behavior such as driving less and turning down the thermostat—activities that were previously seen as being only related to safeguarding the environment—suddenly become relevant to international conflict.

Further, by educating the public about the connections between peace and environmental issues, we ensure that the public will be more resilient to fluctuations in media attention. Three studies, with highly consensual results, have mapped attention to he nuclear arms race since 1940. Richard Paarlberg (1973), who used the number of magazine articles published yearly on the arms race as an indication of salience of the issue, found that the first three peaks in the number of articles correspond to the dropping of bombs on Hiroshima and Nagasaki (1945); the first Soviet atomic explosion (1949); and the acquisition of the hydrogen bomb by the Soviet Union (1953). Following the Bay of Pigs Invasion (1961) and the Cuban Missile Crisis (1962), there was a sharp decline in the number of relevant articles. This lull corresponds to the occurrence of a variety of diplomatic initiatives as well as various arms-limitations treaties. Similar results were obtained by Lowther (1973), who investigated the number of books dealing with the arms race that were published yearly.

It is important to note that from 1963 to 1971 the nuclear arms race nearly disappeared from the public's view. Paarlberg documents that the number of magazine articles on the arms race fell by a factor of eight. Similarly, Lowther found the number of new books on the arms race decreased by 50 percent after 1964. Indeed, Paarlberg notes the loss of attention was so severe that by 1970 the number of relevant magazine articles had fallen to a twenty-six-year low.

The results of these two studies, which demonstrate that in the forty years preceding 1982 there have been rapid increases and decreases in public attention to the arms race, are echoed in a more recent study. This latest study documents that once again public attention to the arms race is diminishing. Polyson, Hillmar, and Kriek (1986) have tracked the number of magazine articles on nuclear-related issues reported in the *Reader's Guide to Periodical Literature*. This guide covers a wide range of popular magazines (about 180 different periodicals). Their data document that the number of relevant articles has fallen from a high in 1982 of 595, to 284 articles in 1984, and 209 articles in 1985. Recently, I brought these figures up to date, and in 1987 the number of articles had dropped to 146, in 1988 to 100, and last year, the number of articles totaled just 95. In short, media attention, as measured by the number of magazine articles published yearly on the arms race, was six times as great in the early 1980s as it is presently.

Fiske (this volume, chapter 15), in a review of research on public responses to the threat of nuclear holocaust, argues that one of the primary impacts of high visibility of the arms race is to make the public more aware of their attitudes regarding nuclear weapons. When individuals are more aware of their attitudes regarding nuclear weapons, she asserts, they are more likely to engage in congruent behavior. Hence, those individuals who are supportive of nuclear disarmament will be more likely to engage in prodisarmament behavior when extensive media coverage of this issue keeps their pro disarmament attitudes salient. We can safeguard against those times in which media attention is less extensive by drawing connections between militarization and environmental issues and, in so doing, help the public to establish a global survival schema that contains information about each of these issues as well as the connections between them.[4] Hence, at a time in which the media is giving more attention to one issue, as it is presently doing with the environment, the attention given to the environment will prime the survival schema and help to keep both issues salient (see Taylor and Crocker 1981).

Finally, if the peace movement is to be more successful in mobilizing the public, it must deal with public concerns regarding national security. In addition to perceived threat and the availability of specific actions that are perceived as effective, it is also necessary that an individual perceive that one's specific actions would not significantly increase the likelihood of other negative events. For example, many disarmament initiatives of the peace movement are met with opposition because they are perceived as having a number of undesirable "side effects." These may include perceived outcomes as diverse as a decrease in national security, loss of jobs as a result of less military production, and economic retaliation from allied countries. To the extent that individuals view any of these consequences as likely, we expect that they will be less likely to engage in behavior that supports disarmament. Peace activists take competing threats very seriously. In fact, peace activists spend a large amount of time trying to dispel such claims. For example, arguments regarding a loss in national security as the result of disarmament have resulted in an avalanche of books by peace researchers dealing with alternative security (see for example, Galtung 1984; Sommer 1985).

The results of several studies indicate that a perceived decrease in national security as the result of nuclear disarmament is negatively related to support for such proposals. For example, White and Feshbach (1984) found that individuals who did not support a nuclear freeze were much more likely to fear and distrust the Soviet Union. Further, proposals to unilaterally freeze the arms race consistently receive minimal support (Feshbach and White 1986). In a review of public opinion data, Campbell (1986) found that Australians strongly support nuclear disarmament, but also fear the Soviet Union. In contrast, New Zealanders strongly favor nuclear disarmament, but see no threat posed by the Soviet Union. Campbell concludes that the lack of an external threat in New Zealand has permitted the public to carry out actions supporting the declaration of the country as a Nuclear Weapons Free Zone, while similar initiatives have met with strong opposition in Australia.

In conclusion, if the peace movement is to mobilize the public more effectively, it must alter perceptions of the threat posed by militarization and enhance the perceived efficacy of disarmament initiatives. Further, the peace movement must strive to show the connections between global issues. Effort to show the connections between global issues will be rewarded by a public that is more resilient to fluctuations in media attention to these issues. Finally, the peace movement must articulate a vision of the future in which grotesque militarization is a thing of the past. Such a vision must include a much stronger sense of common humanity, a strong resolve to settle international disputes through diplomacy and international law, and a new vision of security (see Dyal and McKenzie-Mohr, this volume chapter 18). Until the peace movement articulates this vision, the public will continue to lack the clarity of purpose that comes from being able to see in a dark time.

NOTES

1. Throughout this chapter the more conventional term "nuclear war" has been replaced with the more descriptive and accurate phase "nuclear holocaust." The word "war" engenders images of victory and defeat, which no longer apply since the advent of nuclear weapons. For a further discussion of the linguistics of the arms race, see Cohn 1987, Nelson 1985, Pentz 1986, and Weizenbaum 1987.

2. See Gilbert (1988) for an explanation of additional variables that are related to peace activism.

3. Military spending contributes to inflation by generating spendable income without increasing the availability of goods to the civilian sector, as well as by lessening the amount of capital available for civilian investment. These two factors combine to place a steady upward pressure on prices. Further, characteristics of military procurement, such as "cost-plus contracts" and rapid product change, have a direct inflationary impact.

   In addition to fueling inflation, military spending also increases unemployment. Military spending is frequently cited as a way of creating jobs. The question, however, is not whether military spending creates jobs—any form of spending creates jobs—but rather how many jobs does military spending produce relative to the same amount of money spent in the civilian sector? Military spending is highly capital-intensive and, as a result, produces relatively few jobs compared to the more labor-intensive civilian sector. How many more jobs would be created if the money were spent in the civilian sector? Mel Watkins, a renowned economist at the University of Toronto, has argued that spending an equivalent amount of money in the civilian sector would produce two to four times as many jobs, depending on where in the civilian sector the money was invested (Regher and Watkins 1983).

4. A schema is a cognitive structure that includes an individuals' knowledge,

beliefs and feelings around a specific issue such as the environment. At present, it is likely that most schemata for the environment do not include connections to militarization. Further, the reverse is also likely true; most schemata for militarization contain few, if any, connections to the environment.

REFERENCES

Abrams, H. (1981). Infection and communicable diseases. In R. Adams and S. Cullen, eds., *The final epidemic*, 192–218. Chicago: Educational Foundation for Nuclear Science.

Ajzen, I., and Fishbein, M. (1977). Attitude-behavior relations: A theoretical analysis and review of empirical research. *Psychological Bulletin, 84*, 888–918.

Barash, D. (1987). *The arms race and nuclear war*. Belmont, Calif.: Wadsworth.

Bates, D. G., Briskin, D. P., Cotton, L., McDonald, M., Panaro, L., and Polson, A. (1983). What would happen to Canada in a nuclear war? In E. Regher and S. Rosenblum, eds., *Canada and the nuclear arms race*, 171–190. Toronto: James Lorimer and Company.

Campbell, D. (1986). Public opinion and Australia's security challenges for the peace movement. *Peace Magazine Australia* (October–November), 37–41.

Cohn, C. (1987). Slick'ems, Glick'ems, Christmas Trees and Cookie Cutters: Nuclear language and how we learn to pat the bomb. *Bulletin of the Atomic Scientist, 43*, 17–24.

CTRC Bulletin (1987). *Canadian Tinplate Recycling Council*. Toronto, Ontario, October 1987.

Fazio, R. H., and Zanna, M. P. (1981). Direct experience and attitude-behavior consistency. In L. Berkowitz, ed., *Advances in experimental social psychology*, vol. 14. New York: Academic Press.

Feshbach, S., and White, M. J. (1986). Individual differences in attitude towards nuclear arms policies: Some psychological and social policy considerations. *Journal of Peace Research, 23*, 129–139.

Fox, D. L., and Schofield, J. W. (1989). Issue salience, perceived efficacy and perceived risk: A study of the origins of anti-nuclear war activity. *Journal of Applied Psychology, 19*(10), 805–827.

Frank, J., and Nash, E. (1965). Commitment to Peace Work: A preliminary study of determinants and sustainers of behavior change. *American Journal of Orthopsychiatry, 35*, 106–119.

French, P. L., and Van Hoorn, J. (1986). Half a nation saw nuclear war and nobody blinked? A reassessment of the impact of The Day After in terms of a theoretical chain of causality. *International Journal of Mental Health, 15*, 276–297.

Gallup (1983). *Public Opinion 1983*. Wilmington, Del.: Scholarly Resources.

Gallup (1984). *Public Opinion 1984*. Wilimington Del. Scholarly Resources.

Gallup (1989a). *Canadians increasingly concerned about the dangers of pollution*. Toronto, Ontario: Gallup Canada, Inc., June 19, 1989.

Gallup (1989b). *Environment and taxation most concern Canadian public*. Toronto, Ontario: Gallup Canada, Inc., July 31, 1989.

Galtung, J. (1984). *There are alternatives! Four roads to peace and security*. Nottingham: Russell.

Geiger, J. (1981). Illusion of survival. In R. Adams and S. Cullen, eds., *The final epidemic*, 173–181. Chicago: Educational Foundation for Nuclear Science.

Gilbert, R. K. (1988). The dynamics of inaction: Psychological factors inhibiting arms control activism. *American Psychologist, 43*, 755–764.

Kramer, B. M., Kalick, S. M., and Milburn, M. A. (1983). Attitudes towards nuclear weapons and nuclear war: 1945–1982. *Journal of Social Issues, 39*, 7–24.

Lazarus, R., and Folkman, S. (1984). *Stress, appraisal, and coping*, New York: Springer.

Lindop, P., and Rotblat, J. (1981). Consequences of radioactive fallout. In R. Adams and S. Cullen, eds., *The final epidemic*, 117–150. Chicago: Educational Foundation for Nuclear Science.

Locatelli, M. G., and Holt, R. R. (1987). Antinuclear activism, psychic numbing, and mental health. *International Journal of Mental Health, 15*, 143–161.

Los Angeles Times (1982). Nuclear Weapons (Study No. 51). *Los Angeles Times* Poll, March 14–17 Los Angeles: Los Angeles Times.

Lowther, M. P. (1973). The decline in public concern over the atom bomb. *Kansas Journal of Sociology, 9*, 77–88.

McKenzie-Mohr, D., and Dyal, J. A. (1988). Perceptions of threat, collective control, tactical efficacy and competing threats as determinants of pro-disarmament behavior. Paper presented at the 96th Annual Convention of the American Psychological Association, Atlanta, Georgia.

Milburn, M. A., and Watanabe, P. Y. (1985). Nuclear attitudes, images and behavior. Paper presented at the International Studies Association meeting, Washington, D.C.

Milburn, M. A., Kramer, B. M., and Watanabe, P. Y. (August, 1984). The nature and sources of attitudes toward the nuclear freeze. Paper presented at the 92nd annual meeting of the American Psychological Association, Toronto.

Mohr, D., and Silver, R. (1986). Coping with the threat of nuclear war. Paper presented at the Canadian Psychological Association meeting, Halifax, June 1985.

Mohr, D., McLoughlin, J., and Cohen, R. L. (1987). Threat and control as mediators of peace activism: A comparison of peace activists and community residents. Unpublished manuscript. University of Waterloo, Department of Psychology, Waterloo, Ontario, Canada, N2L 3G1.

Nelson, A. (1985). Psychological equivalence: Awareness and response-ability in our nuclear age. *American Psychologist, 40,* 549–556.

Nemiroff, L. S., and McKenzie-Mohr, D. (1990). Comparing environmental activism and peace activism. Paper presented at the 98th Annual Convention of the American Psychological Association, Boston.

Paarlberg, R. (1973). Forgetting about the unthinkable. *Foreign Policy, 10,* 132–140.

Pentz, M. (1986). To prevent nuclear war and promote nuclear disarmament: It's time for a new look. In T. L. Perry and J. G. Foulks, eds., *End the arms race: Fund the human needs,* 271–295. West Vancouver: Gordon Soules.

Polyson, J., Hillmar, J., and Kriek, D. (1986). Levels of public interest in nuclear war: 1945–1985. *Journal of Social Behavior and Personality, 1,* 397–401.

Regehr, E., and Watkins, M. (1983). The economics of the arms race. In E. Regehr and S. Rosenblum, eds., *Canada and the Nuclear Arms Race,* 63–84. Toronto: James Lorimer and Company.

Sagan, C. (1985) "Nuclear Winter: A report from the world scientific community." *Environment* (October), 12–15, 38–39.

Schell, J. (1982). *The fate of the Earth,* Avon: New York.

Sivard, R. L. (1989). *World Military and Social Expenditures 1989,* 13th ed. Washington, D.C.: World Priorities.

Sommer, M. (1985). *Beyond the bomb: Living without nuclear weapons.* New York: Expro Press.

Taylor, S.E., and Crocker, J. (1981). Schematic bases of social information processing. In E. T. Higgins, C. P. Herman, and M. P. Zanna, eds., *Social Cognition: The Ontario Symposium,* vol. 1. Hillsdale, N.J.: Erlbaum.

Walkley, A. M., Erikson, D. H., and Tilby, P. (1988). A profile of peace activists: demographics, attitudes, and opinions and motivational factors. Unpublished manuscript.

Weick, K. E. (1984). Small wins: Redefining the scale of social problems. *American Psychologist, 39,* 40–49.

Weizenbaum, J. (1987). Facing reality: Computer scientists and war efforts. *Technology Review* (January), 22–23.

White, M., and Feshbach, S. (1984). Nuclear disarmament in Middletown: Attitudinal, demographic and psychological variables. Paper presented at the 92d Annual Convention of the American Psychological Association, Toronto.

Zanna, M. P., Higgins, E. T., and Herman, P. C., eds. (1982). *Consistency in social behavior: The Ontario symposium,* vol. 2. Hillsdale, N.J.: Erlbaum.

PART SIX

PREPARING THE NEXT GENERATION

I know of no safe depository of the ultimate powers of society but the people themselves, and if we think them not enlightened enough, the remedy is not to take the power from them, but to inform them by education. —*Thomas Jefferson*

The psychological problem is how to make all people aware that whether they like it or not, the earth is becoming a single community. —*Jerome Frank*

How do we prepare youth for participation in the complex world that awaits them? How do we educate young people for effective engagement in the critical issues of our times? In chapter 17, Phyllis La Farge describes the newly developing field of "peace" or "nuclear age" education in our elementary and secondary schools. She defines its goals and the various types of content and process such education employs in its effort to create the "socially responsible" citizen. James Dyal and Douglas McKenzie-Mohr describe, in chapter 18, the role that education plays in shaping our worldviews and argue that we need to educate for new modes of thinking through "survival education," socially responsible educational efforts at the high school, college, and university levels. In chapter 19, Steven Zeitlin summarizes the psychological research on the effects of the nuclear age on young people and argues for the important benefits of communication within the family about feelings and attitudes related to the nuclear threat.

17

Teaching Social Responsibility in the Schools

Phyllis La Farge

Future generations may look back on the fifty years following Hiroshima as a period marking a watershed in consciousness. A growing awareness of the economic, environmental and political interdependence of the world has characterized this period along with an increased understanding that the destructive potentials of technology can no longer be contained by national boundaries, whether one thinks in terms of nuclear weapons, nuclear power accidents like Chernobyl, or the effect of chlorofluorocarbons on the ozone layer. Vital also to a new consciousness is the technology of television, which crosses boundaries in an unprecedented way—boundaries of time via instantaneous transmission, national boundaries, and the boundary between the family and the public realm.

It will take years, perhaps generations, before anyone will have the perspective to understand the full effect of the shift of consciousness that may be taking place—before anyone can try to answer the question, "Who have we become?"

Elementary and high school teachers, however, confronted as they are with young people every working day, do not have the luxury of pausing to ask, "Who are we becoming?"—let alone of trying to guess what the long-term answer may be. Nevertheless, a growing number of teachers, aware of a newly interdependent and risk-laden world, ask a more immediate and pragmatic question: "How can I help educate young people to be socially responsible citizens of a new world?" Depending on personal interests and professional expertise, individual teachers emphasize different answers; but if these were put together, they would begin to sketch a picture not of the new person we may be becoming (we don't know that for sure), but of the person many people of liberal persuasion believe we *should* become if we are to be equal to the challenges that face us. In their view, a number of qualities characterize this ideal citizen. He or she has

- the skill to work cooperatively
- the will and ability to work toward the nonviolent resolution of conflicts
- knowledge of other cultures, including those that exist within the boundaries of one's own society
- a capacity for empathy with individuals of other cultures (and by extension an appreciation of their rights)
- a sense of stewardship, particularly with respect to the environment and natural resources
- the ability to think critically about public issues and define one's position on an issue with respect to one's values
- the ability to translate knowledge and conviction into action as a citizen
- the ability to accept involvement in controversy about public issues, if possible without encouraging their polarization.

In a still not fully articulated way, educators have begun to see these qualities as aspects of a whole, and therefore to think of the educational expertise and techniques that attempt to foster them as interrelated and sharing a common goal, which with increasing frequency they call education for social responsibility.

THE RESPONSIBLE CITIZEN: NEW AND OLD CONCEPTS

Definitions of the socially responsible citizen are at least as old as Plato, but in recent years the phrase "social responsibility" has had special connotations. During the 1980s it was identified with the movement against nuclear weapons and the arms race in general, through its use in the names of certain organizations, such as Physicians for Social Responsibility and Psychologists for Social Responsibility. For educators, including those associated with the organization Educators for Social Responsibility, it has accumulated much wider connotations in the course of the last decade. A number of factors influenced this change: the difficulty of teaching about a subject as politically loaded as arms policy in public schools, a change in the prominence of the nuclear weapons issue in public consciousness over the course of the decade, and, perhaps most important, an increasingly sophisticated analysis of what is involved in promoting peace and decreasing danger in the world.

The qualities associated with the emerging definition of the socially responsible citizen are in some ways nearly identical with traditional conceptions of the good citizen, and in some ways novel. There is nothing new, for instance, about the notion of cooperative effort, but for generations there has been very little of it in American classrooms, where the emphasis has been on individual mastery. Nor is there anything new about an emphasis on thinking critically about public issues or about active, even controversial, engagement as qualities of responsible citizenship. However, until very recently it was only men and, in reality, only the white middle and upper middle-class men of our society who were encouraged to be active citizens and to think critically about public issues. Moreover, for the most part the civic mission of the schools has focused on the socialization of young people as loyal and patriotic citizens, rather than on their development as critical thinkers.

The notion of stewardship is not new, but the situation of the planet is new, requiring, as I will suggest below, a new definition of the good steward.

There are, however, two aspects of the evolving definition of the socially responsible citizen that are new and directly responsive to a sense of a changed world: (1) the emphasis on empathy for other cultures and knowledge about them, and (2) an emphasis on nonviolent resolution of conflict. These new characteristics of the citizen call for a profound psychological evolution as well as the modification of political attitudes. Traditionally, the good citizen was he (until recently always he) who could put aside whatever he might know or care (often very little) for someone whom he perceived as "other" enough to fight him if need be. In every era, and in the great majority of cultures, a process of socialization for patriotism—or, before the era of the nation-state, for loyalty to the tribe or local lord—helped assure that this would be so. Although the new ideal of the socially responsible citizen does not deny the importance of national loyalty or patriotism, it, in effect, puts the spotlight elsewhere. In this sense it differs from the traditional message of the public schools. In an interdependent world, the new ideal citizen is someone who understands that his or her own interests are not limited by national boundaries or a narrow sense of national purpose. Phrased more idealistically, the new citizen strives for empathy that crosses boundaries, once nearly absolute, of nationality, socioeconomic class, race, and gender.

Underlying the new definition of the socially responsible citizen is an ideal of democracy in which realpolitik would not play a part (or as small a part as possible), and one in which all members of society would have a political voice. This ideal is shaped by the concept of the universality of human rights and is informed by a long tradition of justice as equity. In its emphasis on empathy and stewardship, however, the new definition of the citizen adds—to speak in Carol Gilligan's terms—the concepts of care, caring, and carefulness, the pursuit of the greatest good for the greatest number (Gilligan 1982).

KEY AREAS OF LEARNING

How do teachers at the elementary and high school level go about encouraging a sense of social responsibility? How do they try to nurture the new ideal citizen? One way to answer this question is to note that much of their effort is concentrated in the following key areas:

- cooperative learning techniques
- the nonviolent management or resolution of conflict
- multicultural education
- environmental education
- global education
- the creation of a sense of community within a classroom or a school, or fostering stronger ties for the student with the community beyond the school.

Brief discussions of these specific fields follow below. Here I would like to point out that although these areas can be defined as separate entities for the purpose of discussion, in an actual classroom they often overlap. Moreover, three of the areas—cooperative learning, conflict resolution, and the creation of a sense of community—are concerned with how students engage in learning and how they live together, not with content in the same sense that math or geography is a traditional subject in a school curriculum. Several factors influence this emphasis on process over content (or, put another way, the treatment of process as content). Educators interested in fostering a socially responsible young person believe, first, that the structure of the classroom and school teaches lessons that are at least as powerful as those of the traditional curriculum, and they believe that the way in which most schools and classrooms are structured—favoring conformity, passivity, or from another point of view, tending to reward individual rather than cooperative effort—does not encourage the kind of empowered, responsible student they would like to see (Sarason 1971; Silberman 1970). Furthermore, they believe that attitudes and behavior that foster democracy and social change are not modified by information alone but by actual practice. The way in which their students learn and live in school is seen as practice and as a model in miniature for their future behavior as citizens.

COOPERATIVE LEARNING

Americans have always balanced uneasily between the ideal of the rugged individual and a stress on the efforts of a team: the lone farmer established his homestead on the frontier, but he needed his (distant) neighbors to raise the roof of his barn; the baseball pitcher is at the same time a star and a member of the team. In classrooms, however, the emphasis has been on individual effort and achievement rather than on cooperative effort. There is a strong movement among contemporary educators to change this. They realize that more rather than less work will be collaborative in an interdependent world, and that this is particularly true with respect to solving complex social and environmental problems.

Cooperative learning advocates aim to create what they refer to as "positive interdependence" in the classroom. (Graves and Graves 1985). By this they mean a situation where the success of one student is dependent on the success of another. They contrast this with a situation in which the success of one student is dependent on the relative failure of others, as occurs when students are graded on a curve. To achieve this goal they favor organizing students into small cooperative groups in which every member of the group contributes to achieving a common purpose. On a social studies project, for instance, the researchers might tell the writers what they have learned; the writers of the group would not be able to write until the researchers had done their work, and without the writers the work of the researchers would not result in a finished product. Finally, a reporter, dependent on the work of both writers and researchers, might describe to the whole class the group's work.

Considerable coaching may be necessary to make cooperative learning effective in a classroom. Communication skills must be developed—does the writer on a project know how to ask the researcher to clarify or expand on what he or she has said? A sense of individual accountability as well as accountability to the group is necessary, as is the ability to reflect on the way the group or team is functioning. It is not easy to initiate cooperative learning techniques, and it has been found that it is harder to do so with older students in whom "patterns of peer interaction have already been heavily engrained" (Pirtle 1990). Put-downs, complaints, and domination of a group by one member are some of the problems that occur. Specific coaching in interpersonal processes is helpful. Two experts on cooperative learning, Nancy and Ted Graves, have written: "When we are seeking to change an environment to make it more cooperative, and when we have limited time, these interpersonal processes need to be made explicit. . . . This can be done most effectively not by preaching, but by helping students to arrive at the insight for themselves" (Graves and Graves 1985).

Although instituting cooperative learning in the classroom adds to the teacher's burden, research on its results shows that it is valuable not only in promoting individual academic achievement but in building collaborative skills and more positive and heterogeneous relationships in the classroom. Individual teachers have commented that it is useful in helping students work with each other across racial lines (Slavin 1981; Pirtle 1990).

CONFLICT RESOLUTION

The high level of violence in American society, the media's reliance on violence as a staple of programming, and, more immediately, the deterioration of the social atmosphere in many schools have attracted many educators to an approach and a series of techniques useful in managing or resolving conflict without resort to violence (Johnson and Johnson 1987; Lewicki and Litterer 1985; Prutzman et al. 1988). These techniques were developed and refined in the worlds of business, law, and the human-potential movement. Underlying them is the view that conflict is a natural, inevitable aspect of life, that its outcome can be positive, and that such an outcome is more likely if one party to a conflict doesn't "lose" and the other "win." This perception has led to the notion of a "win-win" solution, that is, one which both parties perceive as meeting their needs. Theoretically at least, such a solution can be arrived at if both parties define the problem from their own point of view, truly take in the other's definition of the problem, generate a number of alternative solutions, and choose one that is not so much a compromise as satisfying essential issues for all concerned (Kriedler 1990).

Conflict resolution has entered the schools in three principal ways: (1) at all levels, through the infusion of its ideas into traditional subject matter of the curriculum; (2) through the way in which a classroom is managed; and (3) in the higher grades, through the training of student mediators for the resolution of conflicts, notably on the playground. In each of these approaches the student is encouraged to play an active role rather than be a passive consumer of information or discipline. Thus students would not simply learn what the textbook says about North-South tariff disagreements before the Civil War but brainstorm alternative solutions. Or they might be asked to draw up a set of rules for the efficient functioning of their classroom, and then asked to redraft them as need be. Or, on the playground, two student mediators might say, "Let's hear both sides of your story and then we'll help you resolve your conflict in a way that you can both live with."

An active role encourages a sense of empowerment, and it may be that this is at least as important an outcome for students as learning specific techniques for resolving conflicts.

"Teaching conflict resolution and intergroup understanding to young people is rewarding, but not easy," write Linda Lantieri and Tom Roderick, co-directors of the Resolving Conflict Creatively Program, one of the nation's most successful conflict resolution programs, which in the 1990–1991 school year was projected to involve one thousand teachers in New York City and thirty thousand students in seventy schools (Lantieri and Roderick 1990). One of the reasons for the program's success is its twenty-hour training program for teachers, followed by ten hours of visits by expert consultants. Lantieri and Roderick write:

From almost five years of work with RCCP, we've learned that it takes time for adults to integrate conflict resolution concepts into their own lives; it takes time for them to learn how to translate those concepts into the classroom; and it takes time for even the most effective classroom instruction to have an impact. Some of the most effective teachers in the RCCP have observed that it sometimes takes months for youngsters to begin integrating the concepts and skills in such a way that their behavior begins to change. (Lantieri and Roderick 1990)

Careful training and persistence can, however, yield results. An independent evaluation of the RCCP program found that 87 percent of participating teachers noted improvements in attitude or behavior in their students, less physical violence in their classroom, less verbal abuse, and an increase in leadership skills.

MULTICULTURAL EDUCATION

The roots of multicultural education, like many other aspects of teaching for social responsibility, lie in the 1960s. At that time concern with the effects of racism, sexism, and inequality of opportunity began to focus attention on the Euro- or even Anglo-centric nature of school curricula, particularly in social studies and literature. This curriculum, as it evolved since the nineteenth century, was based on the traditional premise that the maintenance of national identity required "melting" immigrants to the United States into the culture of the original, northern European, primarily English-stock settlers, whose descendants continued to play a politically dominant role until World War II. Activists of the sixties began to see in this "melting pot" approach a perpetuation of racial, ethnic, and gender prejudices with a concomitant undermining of self-esteem for those who were not of the old-stock European culture. They stressed that culture influences "life chances as well as life styles" (Lynch 1983, 12). This perception has led to the promotion of a new ideal of American national identity that is culturally pluralistic, rather than assimilationist, favoring equal respect and the preservation of cultural traditions. As American society becomes more diverse, this ideal takes on new importance, and, in fact, becomes a model for relations in the "global village" in which we are now all residents.

In recent years, teachers, sometimes under pressure from politically organized ethnic groups, have made the pluralistic ideal the inspiration for curriculum choices in literature and social studies and turned to it as a rationale for bilingual education. In doing so they aim to give students of minority backgrounds a voice and build their self-esteem (at the same time they wish to foster cross-ethnic understanding in students of the mainstream white, middle-class culture). Although their goal is unimpeachable, they have encountered criticism focused on the ways in which they have attempted to attain it.

This criticism is directed, first of all, to the problem of what should be included in a multicultural curriculum. Establishing criteria for choice is a "sensitive, controversial and difficult question" (Lynch 1983). The immediate dangers, Lynch noted, are a "soft, folksy tokenism," a poor use of educational resources, or a kind of relativism. (The latter is the allegation of conservative critics.) Thoughtful advocates of multicultural education stress that curriculum choices should be in line with universal values of the society: "I believe cultural pluralism must incorporate the universal values of equality, freedom, and democracy as well as the particularistic values associated with the maintenance of cultural diversity" (Lynch 1983). Far easier said than done, however.

Still other critics have pointed to potential shortcomings of multicultural education, arguing that for all its good intentions it can end up by shortchanging students, particularly when it takes the form of bilingual education (Bernstein 1990) or when it takes an extreme position, as with Afro-centric history. By depriving students of the knowledge they need to succeed in the society, it essentially defeats its own purposes. This criticism raises another issue: Have advocates of multicultural education chosen to stress one—undoubtedly important—ingredient of self-esteem at the expense of others? Isn't competence in the public culture as great a source of self-esteem as ethnic pride? The two need not be mutually exclusive, and it is possible to build ethnic pride and competence in the mainstream culture in classrooms serving minority students (Homan 1986), but to do so teachers must have high expectations for their students. It may be that neither advocates nor critics of multicultural education have paid sufficient attention to the way in which teacher expectations are the critical factor in building student self-esteem (Rosenthal and Jacobson 1968).

In a very interesting essay, Roger Homan reports on his study of a Seventh Day Adventist middle and secondary school in the London area. The school has a 98 percent black student population, and a very successful record in preparing students for higher education. In a key paragraph that speaks to the issue of teacher expectations and student success as well as combining "multicultural" with "mainstream" elements in the curriculum, he writes:

There are no concessions to relevance or immediacy of interest. History begins with the War of the Roses. There is no shunning of Shakespeare in English literature. Competence in standard English is expected and achieved. Black studies and its manifestations in various traditional school subjects supplement rather than replace these. The dialect poet is read and enjoyed. There is a whole term of Caribbean history at the end of the second year. And the next school play, currently being written by one of the teachers, documents the history of black people from slavery through colonialism to the present day. (Homan 1986)

In no area of teaching for social responsibility does the process of teaching matter more than it does in multicultural education. Suppose, for instance, that a teacher undertakes to teach standard English to a group of students speaking black English. She can point out each student's mistakes each time they occur and provide drill in correcting mistakes frequently made by the whole class. With this approach, students learns to code-switch. To the extent they do, their sense of competence, and therefore their self-esteem, will improve, but at the same time they will be internalizing images of themselves as deficient—images they very likely have internalized long since.

Following a quite different approach, the teacher can begin by asking the students to describe the audiences they might have occasion to address: a friend, a parent, a potential employer, the school principal. The teacher might then ask them to give examples of how they might address these different audiences, thus helping them to define and discover what they already know about code-switching. With this discussion as a basis, the teacher could then proceed to work with specific language.

In the first approach the teacher remains the authority, standard English is presented as having higher status than black English, and the students are defined as deficient. In the second approach the teacher plays a facilitating role when possible, hierarchy of language choice is played down in favor of appropriateness to specific context, and students are valued for what they can bring to the topic. Most important, they are urged to play an active role in their own learning (Grant and Sleeter 1989). Implicitly, the first approach takes the "melting pot" approach and favors the maintenance of the traditionally dominant culture. The second approach does not attempt to conceal the operation of power in the society or draw a veil over what is needed for success, but it does not ask minority students to reject their own culture.

ENVIRONMENTAL EDUCATION

Like multicultural education, environmental education has its roots in the 1960s, a decade when public awareness of humanity's dangerous impact on the planet became widespread. Its necessity has grown far more obvious, however, in the '80s in the wake of events like Chernobyl and Bhopal, the fear of global warming, the discovery of the destruction of the ozone layer, and increasing revelations about toxic wastes.

Whereas other aspects of teaching for social responsibility concern themselves with interhuman relationships, environmental education is concerned with our relationship to the natural world. It demands "that the boundaries of ethical and moral behavior must be extended from human relations to the relations between all living and inert things in their total natural context. This ethical challenge calls for a radical and fundamental revision of Judeo-Christian Western values and beliefs" (Gray 1985).

This "revision" entails a psychological and philosophical change from a relationship of dominion over nature to one of interconnectedness and interdependence. Traditionally, the good steward recognized that his well-being was linked to the well-being of his land and beasts, but his sense of himself as a steward was at the same time wedded—at least in Western culture—to a premise of dominion as ancient and deeply rooted as God's words in the book of Genesis: "Let us make man in our image, after our likeness; and let them have dominion over the fish of the sea, and over the birds of the air, and over the cattle, and over all the earth, and over every creeping thing that creeps upon the earth."

The intertwined influences of modern rationalism, the idea of progress and the triumphs of technology, have exacerbated this attitude of dominion with disastrous results—not only for our physical environment but, many would say, for our inner, individual sense of psychological and spiritual wholeness. The environmental crisis is forcing a reexamination of these attitudes and a new emphasis on the good steward's interdependent relationship with the land, the natural resources, and the creatures that support his life. (See John Mack, chapter 20 in this volume.)

Linked with the concepts of interconnectedness and interdependence, but not identical with them, is the idea of the importance of biodiversity —a diversity of seeds from which to develop future plants is only the most familiar form of that necessary for sustaining life on the planet, including human life. From the point of view of biodiversity, humans are central only to the Earth's destruction unless they change their ways very rapidly, including their patterns of reproduction and consumption.

Environmental education also calls for an understanding of "the law of limitation and irreversibility" (Hardin 1968) that is, understanding that resources are finite. This idea runs directly counter to the belief in progress that is basic to modern Western culture and, more narrowly, to the consumer culture.

To look at the challenge of environmental education from the more down-to-earth perspective of implementation in the elementary and secondary classroom, one of its difficulties is that it is of necessity cross-disciplinary. Suppose a class of elementary school students decides to study a hedge outside the school building that has recently been cut down by vandals; they will inevitably be looking at the human impact on the natural world (perhaps also discussing some reasons or motives for this impact, and what might have prevented it), the possible regrowth or replanting of the hedge, and the impact of its temporary destruction on insect and bird populations and on the human community as well (e.g., is the school yard a less pleasant place to play without it, a less safe or a safer place?) (Carson 1978). To handle a project of even this relative simplicity, the teacher is asked to lead students in the direction of information from several different areas of science, and from outside science as it has usually been thought of in the schools. Moreover, he or she needs to be confident and skilled enough to move outside the classroom, to help students survey a site and study it over time, or perhaps help them organize the replanting of the hedge. Curricular material and other information prepared by environmental activist organizations as well as by educators specializing in environmental studies will be of particular help in making the necessary connections. However, substantial forces are arrayed against the serious study of a multidisciplinary subject in the schools:

In a practical sense, the difficulty of dealing with science and society in a unified manner in school settings makes it pedagogically more appealing to avoid the issue than to confront it. . . . Schools are not organized to deal with multiple "subjects" (that is, with more than one of the traditional disciplines at the same time), regardless of the level of lip service that may be offered in terms of need importance, and so on. The flow of educational history is against it, as are teacher education patterns, procedures of curriculum design, and "academic rigor." (Disinger 1989)

Another difficulty environmental educators encounter is in the stark overtones of the issues they teach:

> By its nature, and certainly by its history, environmental education tends to take a negative perspective. It seeks to capture attention and is generally successful in doing so by focusing on what is wrong, not what is right, with science/technology/society/environment interactions as they exist, or are perceived to exist, in the real world. (Disinger 1989)

The starkness implicit in environmental education creates problems for the teacher that in some ways parallel those encountered early in the '80s by teachers who attempted to bring the issue of the arms race and nuclear weapons into the classroom. They found that some students were overwhelmed by the vision of massive destruction or extinction involved in learning about the potential threat of nuclear weapons, while many more guarded themselves against the full impact of this vision, keeping themselves "cool" but as a result unengaged with the issue (La Farge 1987). Learning about environmental degradation, about the rapid extinction of species and diminishing resources, does not have quite the same apocalyptic overtones that learning about nuclear weapons has, but it is a grim undertaking nevertheless. Students may react by "living at two levels"—at one level recognizing threats to the world and at another resisting awareness for fear that it will trigger depression or despair. This resistance (or a related desire to live as if there were no tomorrow out of a conviction that there will be no tomorrow worth living) poses difficulties for environmental educators, whose aim, after all, is to alter behavior as well as attitudes. Their task is further compounded by the complexity of making real progress on environmental issues:

> The complexity of the problems, a lack of society consensus as to what the proper, or even acceptable, solutions might be, and disagreement among "experts" as to appropriate methods of seeking solutions contribute to the difficulty facing the educational establishment in attempting to achieve closure on environmental education as a curricular entity. There is no panacea for these difficulties but they do point to the importance of developing critical thinking skills and to the necessity of including examples of successful ecological management when planning a curriculum for young people. (Vivian 1973)

GLOBAL EDUCATION

In the course of the '80s most states mandated the study of global issues in some form in the public schools, although the content of courses varies widely according to the teacher's background and abilities. A global studies course might look at a specific area of the world, and not differ very much from a traditional geography course. Those educators interested in fostering a sense of social responsibility use a more demanding approach and stress the interdependence of the world's peoples and their economic, political, and, to an increasing extent, cultural interconnections. They favor drawing parallels between issues on a world scale and in the student's own community or a nearby one. Thus, a unit on hunger in Africa might be accompanied by serving a meal or meals to the homeless in a nearby shelter (Bryan 1990). The participatory, community service element has the potential greatly to intensify learning.

They advocate teaching methods that involve the student as actively as possible in his or her own learning—once again the way something is taught as well as what is taught is important. An active or experiential approach increases the likelihood that the student will develop an understanding of issues that goes beyond a narrow grasp of information in the direction of developing empathy, or what has been called a "sympathetic imagination" for other peoples and the problems in which they are enmeshed—problems from which we can no longer consider ourselves separate (Bhiku 1981).

For instance, a unit on global cooperation for elementary students could be taught in a traditional manner: the teacher displays products that come from different parts of the world, shows on the map where these products come from, asks students to color maps and paste on pictures of products from the appropriate source country, and finally asks what would happen if we did not trade with those countries. In a paradigm that engages the student more experientially, however, the teacher divides the class into four "countries," each identified with a product. Each country team is supplied with cards for trade and must decide what trades to make. At a certain moment one country is decimated by bad weather or famine. The teams of the other countries must decide how to react. Finally, students are encouraged to reflect on how they felt as they solved the problem (Grant and Sleeter 1989).

Other examples, aimed at junior high and high school students, might involve them in simulations in which each student, after considerable background preparation, plays a role in a conflict situation involving a tropical rain forest, human-rights abuses, and a terrorist seizure of an embassy.[1]

For a small but increasing number of students, exchanges with foreign students, or encounters with young people such as those from war-torn countries participating in the Children of War Tour, bring global issues vividly alive.[2]

BUILDING COMMUNITY

The concept of community is key to understanding the thinking of educators who teach for social responsibility. Their preoccupation with community has several roots: a negatively critical attitude toward the self-absorption consecrated by the culture of the '70s and '80s; a somewhat wistful nostalgia for the small-scale neighborhoods, communities, and workplaces that have been lost or threatened by the large bureaucratic organizations and mass culture of our society, and the conviction that a sense of community is basic to the development of the qualities defining the good citizen in an interdependent world. For educators interested in fostering a sense of social responsibility, the latter point is salient. It informs their efforts in all the areas described in this chapter: cooperative learning, conflict resolution, and multicultural, environmental, and globally oriented educational initiatives.

The concept of community assumes a sense of shared purpose and therefore of a certain interconnectedness or interdependence. Teaching for social responsibility stresses that the problems faced by our particular society—and the world—can only be solved by joint efforts (in the case of the environment, immense efforts) around a sense of common purpose. Although they may not articulate it explicitly, teachers contrast this community-focused ideal with a narrowly defined and pursued ideal of self-realization.

From the practical point of view of effective pedagogy as well as from the viewpoint of guiding ideals, teachers interested in promoting social responsibility stress the importance of community. Many students are cynical about the possibility of social action and social change: they feel helpless or disempowered. Educators believe that one way to overcome these feelings is to give students an opportunity for service in the community, thus helping them to become more confident in believing they can make a difference. (See James Dyal and Douglas McKenzie-Mohr, chapter 18 of this volume.)

Another and more radical approach to empowering students calls for restructuring their relationship to the classroom, the teacher, and their own learning in the direction of playing a more active role. Entailed is the involvement of students in creating a "shared set of values or goals," participating in "decision-making about important issues that emerge," and learning to "pay attention to the group's process" (Berman 1990). As suggested earlier, the classroom is seen as a model or laboratory for democracy, a place that will not only provide the student with skills and practice essential to the actively engaged citizen but faith that such engagement is possible. To accomplish this, the teacher must to some degree modify his or her status, become more of a facilitator and less of an authority. In the classroom and in the wider school setting, students must be able to air their concerns and have a voice in finding solutions for problems. This need has led some teachers to experiment with "family meetings" or "community meetings" where issues can be aired and solutions can be brainstormed. However, if the teacher relinquishes some of his or her authority and students begin to share in decision-making, then the latter need to develop skills that will enable them to function responsibly and effectively in a more democratic environment. The skills they need have been defined in this way:

> There are four new skills young people need to learn. They need to learn ORGANIZING SKILLS so that they can work well in groups and in organizations to affect change. They need to learn CONSENSUS-BUILDING SKILLS so that they can transform oppositional debates into productive dialogues. They need to learn group PROBLEM-SOLVING SKILLS so that they can draw upon the diverse resources and talents in a group to come up with the constructive solutions to complex problems. And finally they need LONG-TERM THINKING SKILLS so that they can evaluate the impact that potential solutions may have upon future generations." (Berman 1990)

Communication and critical thinking skills undergird all these more specific skills. As in other areas of teaching for social responsibility, community-building in the classroom puts an emphasis on process as contrasted with the traditional content of instruction. No area is more demanding since it adds an extra dimension to what the teacher must accomplish; in no area is the support of the principal and good communication with parents more essential.

CONCLUSION

Recent years—1989 in particular—have seen far-flung triumphs for democracy, but this is no reason for a sense of assured victory, especially in a country—ours—where only 16.6 percent of eighteen to twenty-four-year-olds voted in the 1988 national election.[3] It seems probable that the reasons for this dismal statistic lie not only in complacency—the sense that basic rights are not threatened in the United States—but in a group of influences that contribute to making young people feel that "the odds of success seem overwhelming, the personal costs high, the disappointment inevitable" if they endeavor to play an active role as citizens (Berman 1990). Among these are the unedifying media spectacle of polarized interest group politics at the national level in which government leaders resist working toward a consensus, or even toward agreement on the common good; large-scale bureaucratic institutions in which change can be cripplingly difficult; a consumer culture in which the fulfilling action is defined as making purchases for private consumption; and a television culture rife with violence and perhaps even more insidious in the way it encourages the viewer to believe that seeing is an adequate substitute for doing. Moreover, the changes that education for social responsibility in all its forms calls for involves a modification of attitudes toward power, both national and personal. These are very basic attitudes, which change slowly if at all. These are the Goliaths against which, puny but valiant, teachers interested in developing a new kind of citizen for an interdependent world, are arrayed. The schools in which they work often do not help them in what they want to accomplish. Although some teachers have the backing of school principals, which is essential to innovation, many do not. Moreover, schools are notoriously resistant to change, usually incorporating only what has already been accepted by the mainstream of the culture, and then in a laggardly way. This is not to say that teachers seeking to foster the new citizen may not succeed in making a big contribution to his or her socialization—after all, David did get the best of Goliath.

NOTES

1. I am referring here to three simulations, "Hostage Crisis," "Death of a Dissident," and "Fire in the Forest," all created by The Moorhead Kennedy Institute of the American Forum for Global Education, 45 John Street, Suite 1200, New York, NY 10038

2. For information about this group, which brings young people from war-torn countries to tour American high schools, contact Children of War Tour, 85 South Oxford Street, Brooklyn, NY 11217.

3. Data is from the Committee for the Study of the American Electorate, 421 New Jersey Ave., S.E., Washington, D.C. 20003.

REFERENCES

Berman, Shelley (1990). The Real Ropes Course: The Development of Social Consciousness. Educators for Social Responsibility *Journal.*

Bernstein, Richard (1990). A War of Words. *The New York Times Magazine,* October 14, 1990, Section 6.

Bhiku, Parekh (1981). Sympathetic Imagination and the Multicultural Curriculum. In J. Twitchin and C. Demuth, eds., *Multicultural education: Views from the classroom,* 83–90. British Broadcasting Company.

Bryan, Dale A. (1990). Teaching for Global Responsibility through Student Participation in the Community. In S. Berman and P. La Farge, eds., *Promising Practices in Teaching Social Responsibility.* Albany: State University of New York Press. In press.

Carson, Sean McBride (1978). *Environmental education: Principles and practices.* London: Edward Arnold.

Disinger, J. (1989). Current trends in environmental education. *Journal of Environmental Education, 17* (2) 1–3.

Gilligan, Carol (1982). *In a different voice.* Cambridge, Mass: Harvard University Press.

Grant, Carl A., and Sleeter, Christine E. (1989). *Turning on learning: Five approaches for multicultural teaching plans for race, class, gender and disability.* Columbus, Ohio: Merrill Publishing Co. (This is an excellent, useful book, worth volumes of rhetoric.)

Graves, Nancy, and Graves, Theodore D. (1985). Creating a cooperative learning environment: An ecological approach. In *Learning to cooperate, cooperating to learn.* New York: Plenum Press.

Gray, David B., in collaboration with Richard J. Borden and Russell H. Weigel (1985). *Ecological beliefs and behaviors.* Westport, Conn.: Greenwood Press.

Hardin, G. (1968). *Exploring new ethics for survival.* New York: Viking Press.

Homan, Roger (1986). The all-black school: Development and implications. In

S. Modgil, G. Verma, K. Mallick, and C. Modgil, eds., *Multicultural education: The interminable debate.* London: The Falmer Press.

Johnson, D. W., and Johnson, R. T. (1987). *Creative conflict.* Edina, Minn.: Interaction Book Company.

Kriedler, William J. (1990). Conflict resolutionland: A round-trip tour. Educators for Social Responsibility *Journal.*

La Farge, Phyllis (1987). *The Strangelove legacy.* New York: Harper and Row.

Lantieri, Linda, and Roderick, Tom (1990). A new way of fighting. Educators for Social Responsibility *Journal.*

Lewicki, R. J., and Litterer, J. A. (1985). *Negotiation.* Homewood, Ill.: Richard D. Irwin.

Lynch, James (1983). *The multicultural curriculum.* London: Batsford Academic and Educational, Ltd.

Pirtle, Sarah (1990). Cooperative learning: Making the transition on many levels. In S. Berman and P. La Farge, eds., *Promising Practices in Teaching Social Responsibility.* Albany: State University of New York Press. In press.

Prutzman, P., Stern, L., Burger, M. L., and Bodenhamer, G. (1988). *The friendly classroom for a small planet: Children's creative response to conflict program.* Philadelphia: New Society Publishers.

Rosenthal, Robert, and Jacobson, Lenore (1968). *Pygmalion in the classroom: Teacher expectation and pupils' intellectual achievement.* New York: Holt, Rinehart and Winston.

Sarason, Seymour B. (1971). *The culture of the school and the problem of change.* Boston: Allyn and Bacon.

Silberman, Charles E. (1970). *Crisis in the classroom: The remaking of American education.* New York: Random House.

Slavin, Robert E. (1981). *Using student team learning: Sourcebook for environmental education.* New York: C. V. Mosby Co.

Vivian, Eugene V. (1973). *Sourcebook for Environmental Education.* New York: C. V. Mosby Co.

RESOURCES

Organizations offering specific materials and services to elementary and secondary educators:

Alliance for Environmental Education
2111 Wilson Boulevard, Suite 751, Arlington, VA, 22201

American Forum for Global Education
415 John Street, Suite 1200, New York, NY 10038

The Audubon Society
950 Third Avenue, New York, NY 10022
(Environmental education, chiefly at the elementary level)

Center for Teaching International Relations
University of Denver Denver, CO 80208
  (Teaching international relations at the elementary and secondary levels)

Committee for Children
172 20th Avenue, Seattle, WA 98122
  (Conflict resolution)

Community Board
149 9th Street, San Francisco, CA 94103
  (Conflict resolution, student mediation)

Educators for Social Responsibility
23 Garden Street, Cambridge, MA 02138
  (Conflict resolution, community building, international issues)

Educators for Social Responsibility—Metro
475 Riverside Drive, New York, NY 10027
  (Multicultural education)

Facing History and Ourselves
25 Kennedy Road, Brookline, Ma 02146
  (Holocaust studies, critical thinking)

International Association for the Study of Cooperation in Education (IASCE)
136 Liberty Street, Santa Cruz, CA 95090

The Moorhead Kennedy Institute of the American Forum for Global Education
45 John Street, Suite 1200, New York, NY 10038
  (Simulations for junior high and high school students on issues of dissidence,
  terrorism, human rights, the environment. Particular expertise on Middle
  Eastern issues)

National Association for Mediation in Education
425 Amity Street, Amherst, MA 01002
  (Conflict resolution, student mediation)

National Wildlife Federation
8925 Leesburg Pike, Vienna, VA 22184-0001
  (Environmental education, elementary and middle school level)

North American Association
P.O. Box 400, Troy, OH 45373
  (Environmental education)

Resolving Conflict Creatively Program
New York City Public Schools
Linda Lantieri, Coordinator
163 Third Avenue, Suite 239, New York, NY 10003
  (Conflict resolution, multicultural intergroup relations)

Selected organizations offering materials to a general audience:

American Friends Service Committee
1501 Cherry Street, Philadelphia, PA 19102

Center for Defense Information
600 Maryland Avenue, SW, Washington, D.C. 20024

Clergy and Laity Concerned
198 Broadway 10038, New York, NY 10038

Common Cause
2030 M Street, NW, Washington, D.C. 20036

Consortium on Peace Research, Education and Development
361 Lincoln Hall
University of Illinois at Champaign-Urbana
1702 Wright Street, Urbana, IL, 61801

Fellowship of Reconciliation
P.O. Box 271, Nyack, NY 10960

Friends of the Earth
1045 Sansome, San Francisco, CA 94111

Global Education Associates
552 Park East, Orange, NJ 07017

Institute for Peace and Justice
4144 Lindell Boulevard, Suite 400, St. Louis, MO 63108

Natural Resources Defense Council
1725 I Street, NW, Suite 600, Washington, D.C. 20006

World Hunger Education Service
13117 G Street, NW, Washington, D.C. 20005

18

Psychological Contributions to Education for Social Responsibility

James A. Dyal and Douglas McKenzie-Mohr

Human history becomes more and more a race between education and catastrophe. —*H. G. Wells*

Einstein observed at the beginning of the nuclear age that "the unleashed power of the atom has changed everything save our modes of thinking, and thus we drift towards unparalleled catastrophe" (quoted in Nathan and Norton 1968). He believed that if humanity was to survive, there would have to be a paradigm shift in our way of thinking. Clearly, we have yet to attain the new manner of thinking that Einstein believed was a requisite for survival. If we are to develop new "modes of thinking," education will play a crucial role in their attainment. Our purpose in this chapter is to introduce the role education plays in shaping the present worldviews of high school, college, and university students. Further, we will discuss the contributions that education can, and is, making in developing new worldviews with regard to the environment and militarization. Finally, we will discuss future directions in education for survival.

EDUCATION: SHAPING REALITY

The basic function of education within any society is to provide children, adolescents and young adults with a view of the world that is very similar to that of the preceding generation.[1] As such, education overlaps with and extends the socialization process that begins in the family. Educational methods can vary from the oral traditions of hunting and gathering societies to the pedagogical methods found in the university classroom. While the manner of education may differ dramatically, the basic purpose is the same: the creation of a societally approved version of reality.

While the primary purpose of education is to create a societally sanctioned view of reality, the paradox of education is that educational institutions are made up of the more cognitively oriented members of society. In short, they are the very people who are likely to question accepted worldviews and envision alternatives.

It is this dynamic tension between old and new ways of thinking within the educational process which permits the possibility of constructing new worldviews. Unfortunately, in this conflict between old and new ways of thinking, the societal forces are heavily arrayed on the side of convention. As a consequence, traditional worldviews are very resistant to challenge by alternative perspectives. Indeed, present worldviews function as cognitive lenses through which inconsistent information is filtered and frequently dismissed. Further, society is structured to punish deviant thinking and behavior. In fact, our beliefs often take on the quality of absolute truths that we defend unto death. This is especially true of cultural belief systems that are organized around questions of power, both religious and secular. As Roger Walsh (1984) has perceptively observed:

Faulty beliefs about beliefs can be downright dangerous. When people forget that their ideologies and political systems are beliefs and mistake them for "the truth," then they become willing to fight, kill, and die for them. This situation becomes even more dangerous when people forget that any belief is necessarily limited and only a partial statement of the truth. They then make claims that their beliefs are not only the truth, but the whole truth and the only truth. Inquisitions, executions, and wars get started, rationalized, and glorified in this way. (24)

One need think only of the resistance to change in South Africa, for example, to realize just how powerful these forces may be. Clearly, alternative perspectives will meet with strong opposition from those who are firmly entrenched in present worldviews. Nonetheless, the advancement of these "new modes of thinking" is critical for human survival. In the next two sections we will briefly introduce two alternative paradigms that are just beginning to challenge conventional thinking regarding the environment and militarization.

THE NEW ENVIRONMENTAL PARADIGM

Milbrath (1989) has written one of the most challenging presentations to our present worldview of our relationship with the environment. For example, Milbrath asserts, "Growth is not a value, it is destruction if pursued vigorously. Pursuit of many of the honorific words in modern society (productivity, progress, power, biggest, winning, superiority, and so on) actually turn out to be counter-productive for achieving our deepest values. We need to reexamine those values."

But even more importantly, he has suggested what we must learn in order to survive.[2] In the search for a value system that will support a sustainable, viable ecosystem, he argues that we "should assign top priority to preserving the viability of our ecosystem and second priority to nourishing the good functioning of our society. When those two systems are working well all creatures would have a decent opportunity to live a healthy and satisfying life" (68).

Milbrath (1984a, 1984b, 1989) contrasts the worldview that has dominated Western thought since the industrial revolution with the new way of thinking that he believes is required for human survival. Briefly, the dominant social paradigm values the human domination of nature and has compassion only for those who are near to us in social distance. Its proponents assert that environmental risk is acceptable in order to maximize wealth and that there are no limits to growth. Further, its proponents support the structure of present society, which emphasizes market values, hierarchy, efficiency, and competition in support of complex, fast life-styles whose ultimate values are materialistic (or, the whoever-dies-with-the-most-toys-wins mentality). Finally, supporters believe in the present political structures in which decision making is based on expert advice with emphasis on using the "normal" channels of influence such as political lobbyists.

In contrast, the new environmental paradigm values nature for its own sake, and environmental protection over economic growth. It values extending compassion toward people more socially distant as well as toward other species. It believes that science and technology are not guaranteed to provide a sustainable environment and that careful plans and actions supported by governmental regulation are necessary to reduce the risk of environmental deterioration. It emphasizes inherent limits to growth and values resource conservation. It asserts that we must quickly come to appreciate the impact that the dominant social paradigm is having upon nature and upon human well-being. Finally, it emphasizes cooperation, simpler life-styles, and a new politics founded on consultation, participation, foresight, and planning based on new environmental paradigm values.

THE NEW SECURITY PARADIGM

Just as the dominant social paradigm that shapes our view of our relationship with the environment is being challenged, so is the dominant paradigm that informs how nation-states should interact.

Proponents of the dominant paradigm assert that it is the prerogative of nations to use force to protect their interests when they conflict with those of another nation. This worldview is so thoroughly entrenched that the use of force by a nation is frequently supported by the majority of its public. To fully comprehend how antiquated and barbaric is the behavior of states in this regard, as well as the public's support for this behavior, attempt to imagine the majority of North Americans supporting the use of force, including murder, to resolve an interpersonal dispute. While it might be comforting to believe that nations are resorting to force less frequently, the opposite appears to be the case. Since the end of World War II, there have been 127 wars and 21,800,000 war-related deaths (Sivard 1989). The incalculable suffering caused by war and the tremendous resources squandered on militarization have led writers such as Deutsch (1983) to describe the behavior of states as a malignant social process. Central to this malignant social process are the states' use of enemy images and their perception of security. An enemy image is a perception of an adversary as thoroughly diabolical, aggressive, and untrustworthy (White 1984). Enemy images play a crucial role in war making in that they allow politicians and the public to see their adversary as subhuman and, therefore, violence toward the enemy as being justifiable. These images function as schemata, and as such lead individuals to selectively encode and recall negative actions of adversaries (Flamenbaum and Silverstein 1987; see also Silverstein, chapter 6 in this volume). Further, enemy images may lead political leaders to expect aggressive behavior from an adversary and, as a consequence, to act in a hostile manner solely on the basis of this expectation.

Enemy images combine with current views on security in an explosive mix. Since the dawn of the agricultural revolution and the rise of the state, military planners and politicians have evaluated the strength of their military relative to that of their adversary. National security has been equated with this evaluation, with the mistaken perception that a country is more secure if it is more powerful than its adversary. Since at present virtually all nations equate security in this way, not surprisingly nations are frequently competing with one another in a futile race to attain military advantage. For example, since the end of World War II the United States and the Soviet Union have competed with one another for military superiority. They are still in competition with one another. Although the recent thaw in the cold war has dampened the rhetoric, the annual cost to United States taxpayers still approaches 300 billion dollars (Sivard 1989). Regarding national security, Sommer (1985) writes that we must

> move to a naturally more inclusive concept that considers the fate of each party to the conflict and seeks to protect *all* from harm. We extend this concern for our adversaries not from sympathy but from self-interest. We know well enough that if we do not look to their safety, we will have none ourselves. We can no longer gain security at their expense. . . . Mutually protective strategies thus replace bids for unilateral advantage. The defense of one *includes* the defense of the other. What in the pre-nuclear age was a moral imperative has in the nuclear age become a practical necessity. (20)

In contrast to the conventional worldview, the new emerging paradigm, to which Sommer refers, is called "common security." Common security has as its major tenet that the security of a nation is closely tied to the security of its adversaries. Hence, any military endeavor needs to be evaluated simultaneously from the perspective of the nation engaging in the action (such as building a new missile system) as well as from the perspective of the adversaries of the nation. This dual focus increases the probability that a nation will engage in actions that simultaneously increase its security while at the same time increasing the security of its adversary. Such a change in focus reduces the tension that fuels enemy images and arms races. Further, common security suggests a new form of military strategy that is referred to as "nonprovocative defense." Under this new system of defense, a nation enhances its security by shifting its military strategy from offense to defense. Nonprovocative defense involves confining one's military abilities to the defense of one's own territory and eschewing the ability to successfully engage in war beyond one's borders.

This alternative military strategy has as a basic premise the rights of nations to self-determination free from military intervention by other states. As such, this offshoot of common security challenges the very nature of the present worldview.

While much has been written on this topic (see for example Hollins, Powers, and Sommer 1989) and many individuals embrace common security as our safest alternative to ever-increasing militarization, few nations have adopted the policy of common security. If alternative paradigms, such as the two just described, are to challenge and eventually supplant present worldviews, they must become an integral part of the education process. In the next section we will examine the foothold that alternative paradigms are establishing in education and what impact they are having upon students' attitudes and actions toward the environment and militarization.

EDUCATING FOR SOCIAL RESPONSIBILITY

Over the past two decades, an ever-increasing number of courses have been offered at the university and high school level that challenge the dominant environmental and security paradigms. Not surprisingly, these courses are often regarded with suspicion by those holding the traditional worldviews entrenched in the academic community as well as in society at large. As noted by Mack (1984),

Some nuclear educational programs have been opposed on the ground that they do not offer balanced treatment. . . . I believe that the deeper and truer reason for the avoidance of this topic in the school curriculum is fear of change and the challenge that education about nuclear issues is likely to pose to prevailing assumptions imbedded in the social system. . . . The most powerful resistance grows out of our identification with the prevailing purposes and ideology of the nation and its associated corporate and institutional structure, including the mass media, which tend to locate the problem elsewhere—in the past context in the Soviet Union. (266, 269)

It should be apparent that the question of "objectivity" versus "bias" depends heavily on the version of social reality that is being asserted. Given the social nature of reality construction, the question of bias is incapable of "objective" resolution. If humanity is to survive, however, we must begin to test our beliefs by the following criterion: "Is holding this particular belief functional for the long-term welfare and survival of humankind?" By this criterion, is it more functional to believe in "pacifism" or "militarism" as a basis for resolution of international conflict? Is it more functional to advocate "nuclear power" or "solar power" as a solution to the long-term energy crisis? While it is still possible to argue for either alternative, the application of the survival criterion changes the nature of the argument from short-term nationalistic considerations to long-term global considerations.

NUCLEAR EDUCATION IN THE UNIVERSITY

During the first term of the Reagan administration, the Soviet Union was branded as an "evil empire" and the tensions in the cold war increased. A substantial portion of the American people shared an apocalyptic worldview in which the Soviets were regarded as implacable enemies who were never to be trusted and with whom nuclear holocaust was inevitable. At the same time we feared and distrusted the Soviets, we also became increasingly aware of the consequences of nuclear war. By 1984 several national polls indicated that a vast majority of Americans held the view that there would be no winner in a nuclear war, that nuclear war would not remain limited, and that an all-out nuclear exchange could result in the elimination of all higher forms of life on earth. As noted by Oskamp (1985), a national poll by Yankelovich and Doble (1984) concludes that the normative American reality was characterized "by an impatient awareness that the old responses are not good enough, and a sense of urgency about finding new responses."

University professors responded to this challenge for a new awareness by implementing dozens of courses that examined the nuclear threat from a variety of perspectives (see Ehrlich 1987). Psychologists participated in interdisciplinary teaching as well as introducing courses into the psychology curriculum that specifically focused on the nuclear threat and psychosocial analyses of war, peace, and international relations (Nelson, Slem, and Perner 1986).

While such courses attracted enthusiastic students who were often deeply concerned, the enrollments were relatively small and thus did not provide a strong contribution to raising the general level of awareness among undergraduate students. In order to broaden the base of informed students, many professors chose to introduce peace issues into their regular psychology courses.[3]

What impact has the introduction of these courses into the psychology curriculum had upon the worldviews and behavior of students? Perhaps the most extensive efforts to evaluate the impact of this material has been made by Nelson and his colleagues (Nelson, Slem, and Perner 1986; Nelson 1988; Christie and Nelson 1988). Their research program has involved nuclear threat curriculum units delivered through lectures and relevant reading assignments. The length of the units has ranged from one-hour lectures in introductory psychology courses to full-length courses. Before and after these course units, Nelson measured student attitudes on a Nuclear War Policy Questionnaire (NWPQ). A rather consistent pattern emerged over the nineteen classes that he studied from 1984 to 1987. Nelson (1988) concludes that "these studies show that university teachers can be influential in shaping student's opinions about the Soviet Union and about nuclear weapons policies. Even brief exposure to information about Soviet behavior in the arms control arena influences students to believe more strongly that the Soviets desire arms control and generally comply with verifiable agreements."

We have repeated and extended Nelson's findings with university students in Canada (Dyal, Salvini, et al. 1990). We evaluated the impact of a five-hour unit of lectures and associated reading assignments. The unit focused on the reality of the nuclear threat, the relevance of action as a coping strategy, and the nature of beliefs and their relation to survival. We examined beliefs about the Soviets and nuclear war. We emphasized the self-fulfilling nature of beliefs and the consequent importance of believing that one's collective actions can indeed have an impact on policy decisions. Finally, we concluded with the film, *A Step Away From War*, in which Paul Newman argues persuasively for a Comprehensive Nuclear Test Ban.

Our measures included the NWPQ used by Nelson and our own nuclear threat questionnaire (Dyal, Morris, and McKenzie-Mohr 1990).

We compared responses obtained prior to the nuclear-threat instruction unit with those responses following the unit. There were significant shifts along most of the relevant dimensions. That is, following the nuclear threat unit, these students affirmed less need to maintain superiority over the Soviets, less support for "Peace through Strength," and less support for the necessity of balanced reductions in arms control negotiation. They showed significant increases in nuclear anxiety, in their support for disarmament through cooperation/negotiation, a stronger sense of citizen efficacy, and an increased belief that nuclear war was not survivable.

One year after completing the course, the students were sent a follow-up questionnaire. All of the attitudinal and affective changes that were present at the end of the course were either maintained, or increased, in the following year.

ENVIRONMENTAL EDUCATION

There is now a broad and deep layer of support for moving environmental issues into the top priority of our survival agenda. Although concern is growing, our level of knowledge is not commensurate with the seriousness of the problem. In an extensive survey of 3,207 high school students in New York, Milbrath, Hausbeck, and Enright (1990) found that while students were aware and concerned, they had "weak substantive knowledge about how the environment works, how societal and personal actions impact the environment or how environmental problems impact society" (25). It is clear that the combination of increased concern and limited knowledge constitutes a serious challenge to our educational efforts: "Present day environmental problems are so serious that they threaten the sustainability of our society and our civilization. There is even the possibility that our own species may become extinct. There is no more urgent a task facing our society and our schools than to promote swift and deep learning to help us confront this challenge" (28).

How are we to respond to this challenge? Hungerford and Volk (1990) argue that knowledge and issue awareness do not necessarily lead to environmentally relevant behavior and thus" instruction must go beyond an 'awareness' or 'knowledge' of the issues. Students must be given the opportunity to develop a sense of 'ownership' and 'empowerment' so that they are fully invested in an environmental sense and prompted to become responsible active citizens" (17).

In support of the assertions of Hungerford and Volk (1990), research on environmentally responsible behavior suggests that the most effective educational programs are those that include opportunities for discussion of real-world, problem-focused issues and that provide hands-on field experience that increases environmental sensitivity (Sivek and Hungerford 1990). This means that socially responsible education should go beyond mere informational knowledge to procedures for transforming that knowledge and concern into purposeful action. It implies that the traditional educational process in which students listen passively to teachers must be replaced by an active process of dialogue that focuses on concrete real-world problem solving. A similar argument has been made by Lyon and Russo (1990) regarding nuclear education.

While recognizing the importance of an interactive, problem-focused classroom, environmental education programs at the high school and college level have also emphasized the importance of critically examining education regarding belief systems and values (Caduto 1983; Iozzi 1989). Iozzi (1989) has reviewed the literature in this area and concludes that "environmental education is effective in teaching positive environmental attitudes and values when programs and methods designed specifically to accomplish these objectives are used" (5). It would appear that these changes are also rather persistent. For example, Edwards and Iozzi (1983) studied high school teachers who participated in a two-week workshop designed to make them more knowledgeable, more concerned, and more committed to action. They found strong increases along these dimensions. Further, follow-ups conducted one and two years later indicated that while there was a large decline in the amount of knowledge, the level of concern and commitment remained high.

FUTURE DIRECTIONS IN SURVIVAL EDUCATION

What can we conclude from the various evaluations that have been done of environmental and nuclear-education programs? First, we need to help our students learn how values and beliefs are acquired and function at the individual and societal levels. Further, we collectively must come to realize that while beliefs are useful guides to behavior, they are not chiseled in stone; they are not idols to be worshipped. Like scientific "truths," they should carry with them a rejoinder such as "valid until further notice," or perhaps they should be thought of as requiring a surgeon general's warning such as the following: "Unquestioning allegiance to any belief system can be harmful to your chance of survival."

A second implication is that a survival education should help individuals become aware of their personal values and beliefs. It is hard to question assumptions about the world that are primarily implicit. This means that value clarification techniques can be useful classroom devices for increasing personal awareness (Caduto 1983). As we become more aware of our beliefs, we will also recognize how strongly they have been affected by socializing agents (parents, teachers, political leaders, etc.). This recognition can potentially free us to revise our beliefs to better assure humanity's survival (Milbrath 1989). As Walsh (1984) has observed, "We are free to choose consciously what we want to believe. We do not have to be helpless victims of our beliefs, though the exquisite paradox is that we can choose to believe that we are. In choosing our beliefs we move from being their passive victims to being their active creators. This enables us to recognize and help change limiting and distorting beliefs, not only in our own lives but also in society and the world" (51).

A third implication is that survival education goes beyond changes in thinking and feeling to affect changes in behavior. Education for survival implies taking socially responsible actions. Environmental education has stressed responsible behavior as the major objective (see Geller, chapter 12 in this volume; Sivek and Hungerford 1990; Hungerford and Volk 1990). Similarly, A. Nelson (1985) has commented more generally that we need to achieve a state of "psychological equivalence," or a level of awareness and commitment to responsible action that is commensurate with the magnitude of the global survival problems we face.

A final implication is that socially responsible education for survival is not value neutral. As noted by Staub (1988), "Education inevitably affects children's values and social behaviors. Since the consequences are inevitable, the question is which values, characteristics and behaviors schools should promote? We must advocate the values of interconnectedness and cooperation" (90–91).

Why must we advocate values of interconnectedness and cooperation? First, because there is abundant psychological support for the belief that

cooperative behavior is more functional for long-term resolution of conflicts (especially in highly interconnected systems) than is competitive,
selfish behavior (e.g., Deutsch 1983). Second, all facets of our lives are
penetrated and impregnated by the globalization of our world. In particular, we are beginning to recognize that many of the threats to our
welfare and survival are global in nature. While awareness of interdependence is already influencing the thinking of many political and economic
leaders, the educational systems of the world are far behind in providing
a globally sensitive curriculum that understands and supports these developments. A socially responsible educational system cannot continue
to ignore the failures of our schools to keep up with global realities. As
noted by the Carnegie Report on Education:

A socially responsible educational system provides "global education" which
promotes greater understanding of the world as an interconnected aggregate of
human and natural systems. These systems operate within a single planetary life-
support system on which the destiny of human kind depends. The purpose of
global education is to promote long-term human survival by developing greater
respect for and cooperation with our fellow human beings and greater concerns
for the environment on which we depend. . . . If education cannot help students
go beyond themselves and better understand the interdependent nature of our
world each new generation will remain ignorant, and its capacity to live confi-
dently and responsibly will be dangerously diminished. (Grossman 1990)

In conclusion, we believe that it is clear that one effective way to meet
Einstein's challenge for a new way of thinking is through socially responsible educational efforts. We thus need to accept the challenge to introduce into our undergraduate psychology courses issues of global human
importance, as well as instruction in which the important role of belief
systems in organizing our worldview is recognized. An integral part of
such a unit should be the affirmation that it is important to believe in the
responsibility that each of us has to become mindful of our situation and
take skillful actions. We can in good conscience affirm the presence of
such a unit as an integral part of a mindful education. In the words of
Paulo Freire, such an education is a "process of becoming increasingly
aware of one's reality in a manner that leads to effective action upon it.
An educated [person] understands his world well enough to deal with it
effectively. Such [people] if they existed in sufficient numbers, would
not leave the absurdities of the present world unchanged" (quoted in
Dyal 1975).

NOTES

1. The derivation of the English word "educate" is from the Latin "e duce" which means lead.
2. The suggestions provided in this section are based on Milbrath's book, *Envisioning a sustainable society: Leading our way out.* We strongly encourage reading this book, which may be the most important continbution to your education for social responsibility.
3. Wagner, Bronzaft(1987) provided useful suggestions regarding the topics in social psychology and personality which seem particularly relevant to the analysis of war and peace, and other useful commentaries on integrating the nuclear issue into the psychological curriculum have been written by Nelson (1985), Sunday and Lewin (1987), and Markusen (1987).

REFERENCES

Caduto, M. (1983). A review of environmental values education. *Journal of Environmental Education, 14,* 13–21.

Christie, D. J. and Nelson, L. (1988). Student reaction to nuclear education. *Bulletin of the Atomic Scientists, 44 (6),* 22–23.

Deutsch, M. (1983). The prevention of World War III: A psychological perspective. *Political Psychology, 4,* 3–31.

Dyal, J. A. (1975). Educational issues for the seventies. In J. A. Dyal, W. C. Corning, and D. C. Willows, *Reading in Psychology: The Search for Alternatives.* 3d ed., New York: McGraw-Hill.

Dyal, J. A., Morris, P., and McKenzie-Mohr, D. (1990). Nuclear anxiety and issue-relevant behavior: Association with mental health. *Journal of Social Behavior and Personality, 5 (5),* 243–262.

Dyal, J. A., Salvini, P., Lewis, C., and McKenzie-Mohr, D. (1990). Meeting Einstein's Challenge: Let's try education. Paper presented at the meetings of the American Psychological Association, Boston.

Edwards, A., and Iozzi, L. (1983). A longitudinal study of the cognitive and affective impact on inservice teachers participation in an intensive environmental education. In A. Saks, L. Iozzi, and R. Wilke, eds., *Current Issues in Environmental Education and Environmental Studies.* Troy, Ohio: North American Association for Environmental Education.

Ehrlich, R. (ed.) (1987). *Perspectives on Nuclear War and Peace Education.* New York: Greenwood Press.

Flamenbaum, C., and Silverstein, B. (1987). *Exaggerated Enemy Images and the Selective Recall of the Actions of Nations.* Paper presented at the 95th annual meeting of the American Psychological Association, New York, August.

Grossman, D. L. (1990). Wanted: An education that keeps pace with global realities. *Centerviews, 8 (4)*, 1–6.

Hollins, H. B., Powers, A. L., and Sommer, M. (1989). *The Conquest of War*. Boulder, Colo.: Westview Press.

Hungerford, H. R., and Volk, T. L. (1990). Changing learner behavior through environmental education. *Journal of Environmental Education, 21 (3)*, 8–22.

Iozzi, L. A. (1989). What research says to an educator. Part one: Environmental education and the affective domain. *Journal of Environmental Education, 20 (3)*, 3–9.

Lyon, M. A., and Russo, T. J. (1990) Student concern and potential action regarding nuclear threat: A survey of junior high school and college students. Paper presented at the annual convention of the American Psychological Association, Boston, August.

Mack, J. E. (1984). Resistance to knowing in the nuclear age. *Harvard Educational Review, 54 (3)*, 260–270.

Markusen, E. (1987). Teaching about psychological and social dimensions of the nuclear threat. In R. Ehrlich, ed. *Perspective on Nuclear War and Peace Education*, 83–94. New York: Greenwood Press.

Milbrath, L. W. (1984a). *Environmentalists: Vanguard for a New Society*. Albany, N.Y.: SUNY Press.

Milbrath, L. W. (1984b). A proposed value structure for a sustainable society. *The Environmentalist, 4*, 113–124.

Milbrath, L. W. (1989). *Envisioning a sustainable society: Learning our way out*. Albany: SUNY Press.

Milbrath, L. W., Hausbeck, K. M., and Enright, S. M. (1990). An enquiry into environmental education: Levels of knowledge, awareness and concern among New York state high school students. Paper presented at the 13th annual scientific meeting of the International Society of Political Psychology, Washington, D.C., July.

Nathan, O., and Norton, H. (1968). *Einstein on Peace*. New York: Arnel.

Nelson, A. (1985). Psychological equivalence: Awareness and responsibility in our nuclear age. *American Psychologist, 40*, 549–556.

Nelson, L. (1985). Adding peace to the curriculum. In N. Wollman, ed., *Working for Peace*, 170–178. San Luis Obispo, Calif.: Impact Publishers.

Nelson, L. (1988). Influencing enemy perceptions and nuclear policy options with educational interventions. Presented at the annual convention of the American Psychological Association, Boston, August.

Nelson, L., Slem, C. M., and Perner, L. (1986). Effects of Classroom instruction about the nuclear arms race. Paper presented at the Ninth Annual Meeting of the International Society of Political Psychology, Amsterdam, July.

Oskamp, S., ed. (1985). International Conflict and National Public Policy Issues. *Applied Social Psychology Annual*, vol 6. Beverly Hills: Sage Publications.

Sivard, R. L. (1989). *World Military and Social Expenditures 1989*. 13th ed. Washington, D.C.: World Priorities.

Sivek, D. J., and Hungerford, H. (1990). Predictors of responsible behavior in members of the Wisconsin conservation organizations. *Journal of Environmental Education, 21 (2)*, 35–40.

Sommer, M. (1985). *Beyond the Bomb: Living without Nuclear Weapons.*, New York: Expro Press.

Staub, E. (1988). The evolution of caring and nonaggressive persons and societies. *Journal of Social Issues, 44 (2)*, 81–100.

Sunday, S. R., and Lewin, M. (1987). Integrating nuclear issues into the psychology curriculum. In R. Ehrlich, ed. *Perspectives on Nuclear War and Peace Education*, 97–100. New York: Greenwood Press.

Wagner, R. V., and Bronzaft, A. L. (1987). Sprinkling psychology courses with peace. *Teaching of Psychology, 14*, 75–81.

Walsh, R. (1984). *Staying Alive: The Psychology of Human Survival.* Boulder, Colo.: Shambala.

White, R. K. (1984). *Fearful Warriors: A Psychological Profile of U.S.-Soviet Relations.* New York: MacMillan.

Yankelovich, D., and Doble, J. (1984). The public mood: Nuclear weapons and the USSR. *Foreign Affairs, 63*, 33–46.

19

Intergenerational Dialogue about Global Concerns

Steven J. Zeitlin

In this chapter I will cover two areas: a summary of psychological thought and research on the ways in which living in the nuclear context affects young people, and a description of the main findings from my study of family communication presented in the book, *No Reason To Talk About It: Families Confront the Nuclear Taboo* (Greenwald and Zeitlin 1987). The data and observations from these sources strongly suggest that interaction between the generations is a crucial ingredient in cultivating qualities necessary to face the challenges of the next century.

INTRODUCTION

What do our children think about a world where leaders attempt to meet our basic need for security by preparing for global destruction? What do children think about a world where technological development threatens the air we breathe and the water we drink? For five years (1982–1987) my colleagues and I interviewed families about the threat of nuclear war. We found that children have much to say about this subject, if encouraged to talk, and that adults, despite not having "the answers," and despite their own feelings of helplessness, have much to offer.

I read a charming and unsettling cartoon during the 1988 presidential campaign which gives voice to what a nightmare it can be when political

381

leaders present only rhetorical responses to the profound problems we face. Ronald-Ann, the pigtailed teen-age philosopher from "Bloom County," has a dream. In each panel of the comic, Ronald-Ann surveys a more blighted and frightening landscape. She says, "They're cutting down the rain forests. There goes all our oxygen. They're dumping toxic and nuclear gross stuff in our ground and water." She looks perplexed, then continues, "Acid rain! Our lakes are going to croak! Ozone layer, greenhouse effect, air pollution, infected hypodermic needles on the beach." Then she appears in an oxygen mask. Through her mask she seems a possible savior, a presidential candidate. The candidate says to her, "I darned well pledge allegiance to the flag, for purple mountain's majesties, with liberty and justice for all." Another candidate-figure, looking like the first, appears and echoes, "Good jobs at good wages." Ronald-Ann, referring to the killer from the horror movie, *Nightmare on Elm Street,* says in conclusion, "Shoot, who needs Freddy Krueger?"

Ronald-Ann speaks an important truth. We are facing a menacing killer and no one in charge appears able or willing to do anything about it. In survey studies, the vast majority of adolescents report knowing about global threats and their consequences by age ten. As one ten-year-old in our study said when asked if he and his friends knew about the effects of nuclear war: "Yes, unless they don't have a TV or radio, don't get a newspaper or magazines, don't have a phone, or don't go to school." The media and popular culture are saturated with references to nuclear weapons and global threats.

Ronald-Ann's humor contains a valid and potent description of the experience of many of us. We know, intellectually and viscerally, that serious problems exist in our world. But we see our leaders—who might be in a position to address these challenges—responding with clearly inadequate formulas and blame rather than constructive proposals. These responses on the part of leaders induce those who are dependent on them to "tune out."

What we know is that most children report not talking with adults about these matters of grave concern. Most families do not discuss them. This silence is what fuels the nightmare. Psychological harm does not occur because of the existence of nuclear missiles or global pollution. Nor does it occur because of a lack of constructive political leadership. Psychological harm occurs when a central fact of life is avoided and children are alone with their thoughts and feelings, literally believing that adults are unconcerned about the issues. Children's capacity for trust is impaired.

Vulnerability evoked by global threats tends to draw out the most defensive kind of behavior. In our family interviews, when the first family member begins speaking candidly about thoughts and feelings about nuclear weapons, an almost reflexive sequence of blaming goes on. It may be directed by a teen-ager to parents or by adults at a spouse, the president, or a national adversary. Invariably, when sensitive emotions are unmasked, someone immediately responds with blame. However, it is my belief that facing such issues together as a family is an effective vehicle for surmounting blame. It can enhance trust between the generations, spark children's hopefulness about their own future, and increase their sense of responsibility toward making that future secure.

PSYCHOLOGICAL THOUGHT AND RESEARCH

As early as 1947, the sociologist Lewis Mumford addressed the psychological consequences of the nuclear age. He wrote:

The steady increase in atomic destructiveness reaches a point at which everyone realizes that enough potential energy has been stored to destroy all the living species of the planet. . . . These conditions must lead to grave psychological disruptions. We can posit the familiar forms of these regressive reactions: escape in fantasy would be one; purposeless sexual promiscuity would be another; quack religions and astrology, with pretensions to scientific certainty flourish, as do cults; belief in continuity, the sense of a future that holds promise, disappears; and the taking of drugs to produce either exhiliration or sleep becomes practically universal. (Mumford 1947)

The theorist who has done the most work on the psychological effects of the nuclear threat is psychiatrist Robert J. Lifton (1982, 1983). Ten years after the bombing of Hiroshima he moved his family to Japan and interviewed scores of survivors. In his book, *Death in Life*, Lifton developed the concept of psychic numbing, observing that the survivors walked around in a state of perpetual numbness, grossly impaired in their capacity to respond in a human, emotional way.

Lifton expanded the concept of psychic numbing to explain the current attitude of most people toward the bomb and its destructiveness. He argues that we are all psychically numb at times, resulting from the enormity of the painful, threatening emotions that are unleashed whenever we do get in touch with the reality of our predicament.

According to Lifton, psychic numbing not only blocks us from developing the concern, thought, and action required to find a solution to the threat, but once we numb ourselves regarding such an important aspect of our world, he believes we may be unable to experience our relationships as fully as we wish. For Lifton the connection between numbing and the increasing ennui and restlessness of the age is an important one.

Joel Kovel, a psychoanalyst, has critiqued Lifton's work in *Against the State of Nuclear Terror* (1983). Kovel shares Lifton's view that the nuclear threat has a major impact on our psyche, and even agrees that futurelessness and terror are primary reactions, but he sees them resulting less from the existence of the bomb itself than from the manipulation of the bomb and its control by politicians. He does not see the challenge as an intrapsychic process of connecting with our feelings, but rather one of breaking down the social isolation among people and developing the will for political action. He says: "There are many social sanctions against expressing the fears we experience inwardly concerning the nuclear-crisis. It is not considered 'manly' to do so, but 'womanish' . . . . This accounts for the sense of shame which many feel about their nuclear fears. To admit the helplessness we, in fact, feel is like confessing to castration." (See also Macy, chapter 2 in this volume.)

Amazingly, until the early '60s no research studies were conducted on how the nuclear threat might affect individual psychology. Granted, this is an enormously difficult subject to quantify. The variables are too great and uncontrollable. However, psychology is voracious in its appetite for studies, even on esoteric subjects. The fact that no attention was brought to bear upon this interesting and novel circumstance until Milton Schwebel (1965) asked a series of questions during the Berlin crisis of 1961 supports Lifton's notion that some level of numbing was operating that affected researchers as much as the general public.

Following the Cuban missile crisis and the comprehensive test ban treaty in 1963, researchers were silent on these matters for another fifteen years. When research began again in the late 1970s all that observers had to go on were the two earlier studies by Schwebel and one by Sibylle Escalona (1965).

Schwebel was wondering whether the nuclear threat could be contributing to such trends as the increase in family disruption, increasing drug abuse, heightened loneliness and alienation, and decline in scholastic performance among teens in the early '60s. During both the Berlin crisis of 1961 and the Cuban missile crisis of 1962 he gave three thousand questionnaires to junior and senior high school students in New York, New Jersey, and Pennsylvania. He asked them to respond in writing to the following questions: Do I think there is going to be a war? Do I care and why? What do I think about fallout shelters?

Schwebel delineated resentment, denial, and powerlessness as primary responses to his queries. These adolescents often felt they had the "most to lose." They felt "they would be denied a chance to live, to love, to work, to bear children, and raise a family." They did not wish to survive a nuclear war, largely because they envisioned their families gone. "If I allowed myself to think about it, I'd be miserable," remarks one teenager in Schwebel's sample. Another comments, "It's terrifying to think that the world may not be here in a half-hour, but I'm still going to live for now." Schwebel found that a significant number of respondents embraced what he termed "the illusion of power." For them it is unmanly to hold any but a superior position in any encounter. The result is an attitude that is trigger-happy, ready to shoot first.

In sum, Schwebel, who repeated his research in 1979 immediately after the Three Mile Island nuclear power plant accident, found consistently widespread awareness of the nuclear threat, with profound implications. He concludes a 1982 article, however, with a hopeful message: "If we survive, the nuclear threat that each generation inherits is going to be a factor in the forseeable future. Instead of its being a source of terror and trauma, it can, with adults' assistance and with adults as models, be transformed into social learning experiences that help rather than impede children's developing sense of identity, mastery, and strength" (Schwebel 1982).

Escalona (1965) also asked youngsters ages ten to seventeen an open-ended question. She was careful to avoid the topic of nuclear war in her queries so that she would not suggest the answers she wanted. Instead she asked her sample to "think about and describe the world as it may be ten years from now." She found that 70 percent mentioned the bomb or war spontaneously.

Escalona focused particularly on developmental influences of "growing up in a social environment that tolerates and ignores the risk of total destruction by means of voluntary human action . . . [This] tends to foster those patterns of personality functioning that can lead to a sense of powerlessness and cynical resignation" (Escalona 1965). Although she found that few children and adolescents lived in actual fear of the threat, except at moments of acute crisis, children are influenced to believe authority's assertions that the only way to survive and prosper is for this nation to have the most and biggest weapons. They hear that countries are set to attack us, but hear little about negotiations or respect for the wishes of other nations.

The results of these trends, Escalona argues, is to weaken readiness to invest energy and self-control in the attainment of distant goals. Living with the threat of imminent destruction interferes with the ability to view the self as a competent active agent which disrupts long-range planning as well as organized collective activity.

Taking the lead from these early pioneers, others have more recently attempted to study similar material. Probably the most widely known is one performed by child psychiatrists William Beardslee and John Mack (1982, 1983). Beginning in 1978, under the auspices of the American Psychiatric Association, they asked 1,151 high school students in Massachusetts, California, and Maryland the following questions: What does the word "nuclear" bring to mind? How old were you when you first became aware of nuclear advances? Have nuclear advances influenced your plans for marriage, having children, or other plans for the future? Have nuclear advances affected your way of thinking about the future, your view of the world, and time?

A majority of respondents showed a great deal of awareness and concern, while a significant minority indicated they were not worried. Beardslee and Mack concluded that "thoughts of nuclear annihilation had penetrated deeply into the consciousness of children and adolescents and that many expressed unease about the future" (1982).

About the time when the Beardslee and Mack study was reported in 1982, research in this area began to catch on all over the world. The development in the last eight years has been enormous. In 1982 only two articles were published in American psychology journals under the heading of peace. By 1990 there were so many psychologists involved in the psychological aspects of peace that a division of peace psychology had been formed by the American Psychological Association. Equivalent groups have been formed by other disciplines.

With the burgeoning of research, emphasis has been placed on increasing methodological rigor and statistical analysis. Early congressional testimony on these issues was criticized for using studies in which respondents knew the interests of the interviewers and for drawing conclusions about the impact on psychosocial development that could not be sufficiently supported by anecdotal data. Another source of criticism came from Robert Coles, a well-respected psychiatrist and author of books on children's struggles with poverty and discrimination, who suggested that nuclear anxiety was a phenomenon only among affluent youth (1984, 1985).

A study by Goldenring and Doctor (1985) addressed these criticisms and has served as the model for studies in other nations. From two California cities they recruited an ethnically and socioeconomically representative group. Respondents did not know about the researchers' interest in nuclear anxiety. It was concealed by presenting the study as an assessment both of students' views of and fears about the future. Students were asked, among other things, to list spontaneously their three greatest worries and to rank-order a list of twenty other worries, one of which was nuclear war. Goldenring and Doctor also collected measures of adjustment and self-esteem so that they could be correlated with measures of nuclear anxiety.

Findings from these methodologically controlled studies have been consistent and striking. Young people who think most often and are the most anxious about the nuclear threat and who communicate with adults and peers have better scores on various measures of adjustment and self-esteem, are more concrete and optimistic about individual life plans, and are more likely to believe that their efforts and the efforts of others will prevent nuclear war than the group that reports little thought, anxiety, and communication about the nuclear threat (Berger Gould, Moon, and Van Hoorn 1986; Dyal, Morris, and McKenzie-Mohr 1990; Goldberg et al. 1985; Goldenring and Doctor 1985; Solantaus et al. 1984; Van Hoorn 1986). This finding holds regardless of social class. The data suggest strongly that engaging the nuclear dilemma, psychically and interactively, has a positive developmental impact.

Studies since 1985 have attempted to tease out medating factors that might account for the high positive correlation between nuclear anxiety and self-esteem. Canadian (Goldberg et al. 1985), Swedish (Holmberg and Bergstrom 1985), and Finnish (Solantaus et al. 1984) studies have cited communication with peers and adults as a key ingredient in those with high nuclear anxiety and positive scores on measures of adjustment. Dyal, Morris, and Mohr (1990) found in an American college population that high nuclear anxiety alone did not correlate with high scores on a "ladder of life" measure of well-being. However, where high nuclear anxiety was associated with some kind of activity—whether it be conversations, reading, or political action—then well-being scores were significantly above average. Chivian et al. (1985), in a survey of Russian and American children, found both groups equally high on levels of nuclear anxiety, but Russian children expressed a significantly greater belief that their efforts and the efforts of others would prevent nuclear war. Chivian speculates that the extensive emphasis of the Russian government on peaceful rhetoric in the last decade may account for this difference. We know from yearly studies by Bachman (1983) that the overall level of nuclear anxiety rises in times of superpower tension and recedes in the absence of bellicose rhetoric.

Research confirms that intergenerational communications about these matters has a positive impact on development. What research also reveals, sadly, is that only a small minority of adolescents communicate with adults about their concerns. It was this discrepancy, the sense that the nuclear issue was still taboo, which motivated our work on family communication.

THE FAMILY COMMUNICATION STUDY

Between 1982 and 1985 thirty families were interviewed in our study, half by a team in Philadelphia led by David Greenwald and Wendy Forman, focusing on elementary school children, and half by a team in Boston led by me, focusing on families with adolescents. The sample was recruited by asking friends and colleagues to give us the names of ordinary families who were not political activists and who might be willing to talk with us together as a group about their thoughts about the nuclear threat. Once we were given the name of a family we telephoned one of the parents, explaining our interest in how families communicate about the world situation and the threat of nuclear war. In more than half the initial calls, parents told us that families had not discussed these matters (only two families reported discussing the subject more than superficially). People assumed that previous nondiscussion would disqualify them from our study. Although we did not use a hard-sell approach, we reassured families that few people spoke in any depth about these issues. We emphasized that we hoped by doing these interviews we might be helpful to other families and the public at large who are exposed to a steady stream of information about these issues and have to live with this situation for the foreseeable future. Two-thirds of the parents contacted in this manner were able to enlist the participation of the remainder of their household and agreed to be interviewed.

Our final sample was ethnically and racially representative of the two metropolitan areas from which they were drawn. However, the recruitment method, which involved using contacts in our own personal and professional networks, and the self-selection bias have prevented us from being able to generalize findings to Americans families as a whole or to a particular group of American families. It was our subjective impression that these families thought of themselves as better than average communicators; nonetheless the nuclear issue had been taboo.

The interview itself was conducted in the family's home. It lasted an average of ninety minutes and was filmed on videotape. We did six-month follow-up interviews with 25 percent of the families, which began with their seeing a brief segment of the first interview on videotape. Interviews began with specific questions to each family member about what thoughts and conversations relevant to these issues had occurred. Gradually, a more interactive conversation would arise, supported by occasional questions and comments from the interviewers. What is described below conveys our impressions of the impact of these family dialogues.

Toward the end of the Rogers family interview, we sought the children's reactions to their father's strong statements about his feeling of powerlessness.

INTERVIEWER: When your father says that he feels powerless to do anything, how do you feel about his saying that?

BETH (17): Yeah. It's kind of sad that he feels powerless. We shouldn't have to be in a position to feel, you know, that you're afraid of your future. Yet I can see where he feels that way, because what can you do?

KIM (15): Yeah, It's kind of scary though. If your parents feel that way too, you know.

MATT (11): Yeah, your leader, who you look up to. Your leader is powerless.

A few minutes after the vignette described above, Matt is asked by the interviewer how he feels about the conversation his family has been having. He responds enthusiastically, "I never knew what everybody felt about it before. Like I didn't think they really cared about it until tonight. And now I'm sure after this talk. . . . Now I know what everyone else thinks, so in a way it makes me feel good."

Following his reply, Matt's mother reminds him that he seemed troubled by his father's talk of powerlessness. His mother astutely inquires, "Does it make you feel more powerless yourself?" Matt answers emphatically, "No! Because now I know I have all the other family with me. Now that I know what their side is I know that I'm not alone."

The tremendous value of facing issues within one's family is that talking about powerlessness may make people *feel* more powerful. Matt's father had spoken in detail about feeling pained and apprehensive about the prospects of a nuclear holocaust and utterly "impotent" to do anything about it. However, Matt comes away from the discussion confident that other family members care about the issue, something he had not known before. He feels good about their caring and less alone.

In another interview Sarah, age eleven, hears an explanation of deterrence for the first time. When her father finishes explaining that a rough equality of nuclear forces is designed to help prevent war between the superpowers, Sarah responds, "It's such a relief to hear that. The whole thing has seemed completely crazy."

Sarah's experience of the world being out of control is typical for kids of her age. Johnny, age thirteen, is asked by his father why he has said nuclear war is more likely than not to occur in his lifetime. Johnny answers, after a thoughtful pause, "One little slip-up by one country. Maybe somebody will say they're going to bomb us and then we say we'll bomb them first. Or somebody just makes a mistake—if there are so many bombs, things like that could happen." At the end of the interview Johnny gets his father to agree to another long discussion of these matters as a way of addressing his anxiety.

Preadolescents and adolescents were extremely enthusiastic about these interviews. As the examples above suggest, they got relief from useful information, felt less isolated with their thoughts and feelings, and learned that other family members cared too about this potential menace to their future. About half the adolescents participating in the family study said that they thought little or not at all about the threat of nuclear war. However, a significant percentage of these still reported satisfaction with the family interview. One eighteen-year-old girl, who could not remember how she voted on a nuclear referendum in Massachusetts just three months before the interview in 1984, said that she was glad to hear her brother, the family "good time Charlie," sound so "intelligent" on these matters. Another fifteen-year-old girl, who inspired our book title, said that she and her friends never talked about nuclear war and that if the threat ever seemed imminent she would "just commit suicide and not worry about it." When asked about the interview, she said she was glad to get "things out on the table" and express her point of view. When the interviewer asked if she was just being polite, she said "definitely not, there's been nowhere to talk about this and no reason to talk about it."

While adolescent enthusiasm for these discussions was high, we noticed that discussions remained very difficult for the adults. Adults were unsettled because they did not have the answers to difficult questions; they did not, in fact, know much more than their teen-aged children, either in terms of facts about the arms race or of human wisdom about reversing it. Their ability to protect their children was challenged by this recognition.

In exploring the differences between adults' and adolescents' reactions, we were led back to Erik Erikson's work (1963) on the life cycle, and particularly to his notion of "generativity." Adults in the age group of most of the parents interviewed have a basic need to pass on something of value that can establish and guide the next generation. If that need is frustrated, they can feel stuck and stagnant. The nuclear threat is psychologically menacing to parents whose life is centered around the care and protection of children. It is this crack in the covenant among the generations that is so awful to confront and which may account for the nuclear taboo.

As the following examples illustrate, when an emotionally authentic concern about the nuclear threat surfaced in a family circle, there was often special reactivity on the part of the adults. These willing-to-communicate parents often resorted to blaming responses at these moments.

In the Gallo family, the fourteen-year-old daughter, Emilia, had been given an attitude survey on nuclear weapons at school. She had mentioned the experience at home, prior to the interview, but without detail or emotion. In the family interview she was asked for more information about the survey and her response to filling it out. Emilia mentioned the question, "Do you think there will be a nuclear war by the year 2000?" The interviewer pressed, "How did you answer that?" Emilia replied, "I thought there probably would be."

Both parents' reactions were immediate and emotional. The father, visibly upset, said, "That bothers me." The mother's reaction was, "People come around here with a lot of depressing news." To her husband, she added, "You get too worried." He countered that she did not take things seriously enough. In all this interplay, the adolescent's original statement was lost. For the next twenty minutes the girl had little to say. Our conclusion about such sequences, repeated in numerous families, is that when adults perceive a threat to their ability to protect their children they may naturally feel inadequate—like *bad parents*. They feel a finger of judgment pointed at them too sharply and painfully, and they reflexively try to free themselves from this sense of guilt or inadequacy by shifting the blame to someone else.

In another family, when a similar point was reached, triggered by a daughter's admission of increasing worry, her father immediately responded by disparaging his own father for protest actions that were too "idealistic." The grandfather had written letters to the president which were "pathetic," in the father's view, because the grandfather "wasn't a practical enough man." At this comment, a second daughter spoke up, "Why are you knocking grandpa? At least he doesn't just sit there."

A third example illustrates how family discussion surmounts these blaming sequences if allowed to run their course. In this family there was a twenty-one-year-old, Bill, who was not very well established in his life. Out of high school, he worked part-time and seemed to be floundering. This young man had never taken a stand on a public issue. For the first time, in the family interview, he revealed that he and some friends had thought of going to New York to take part in the massive 1982 rally for disarmament in Central Park. When he mentioned this, his father's initial response was disparagement disguised as humor: "You guys would have gone down there and gotten arrested and turned over cars."

At this point, Bill's mother entered the discussion and shifted the tone. She recalled the Cuban Missile Crisis, and shared the fact that this young man had been about three months old, sitting on her lap, when she listened to John F. Kennedy's speech, "We are in a grave situation. . . ." She said, "You know, I did—I thought—I wasn't sure the world would be there the next day." The revelation appeared to give tacit permission for the son to continue. He expressed more concerns about the arms race and his fears about having children in such a dangerous world. The father responded with reminders about how treacherous he considered the Soviets. The conversation continued in that fashion for several minutes, with Bill expressing his anxieties about the future and his father countering with anxieties about the Soviets.

What was remarkable, however, occurred at the end, when Bill's father was asked how he felt about the conversation. He replied, "This is fantastic . . . I like the idea that he [Bill] had, I mean, that he actually had thoughts. I remember the time they were talking about going to Canada, sneaking off, but I had forgotten it. . . . And then after that I never believed that you people had any conversation other than was the beer cold enough."

This vignette indicates that crucial connections may never be made if communication is absent. Parents and adolescents have highly stereotyped and inaccurate notions of each other's thoughts and feelings. Parents may think their children only care about frivolous pursuits like entertainment and popularity. Children may think their parents care only about work and material gains. The aspects of the self which are aware of and vulnerable to the social and political context are often closed off in the family situation, even if they are accessible to the individual. Discussion makes each family member's inner truth and experience more available. It is not safe to assume that one knows the viewpoint of another. At the close of the interview with Bill's family, his mother asks, "Didn't you know it would be okay for you to have these thoughts?" He answered, "Absolutely not. I thought you would think I was too radical."

CONCLUSION

These findings suggest that adults have a responsibility to create a context in which authentic discussion with their children is possible. Adults need to provide role models that help young people find positive avenues to express their caring for life on earth.

As a psychologist who works with families, I believe that we not only prevent harm to our children but also cultivate their best virtues by dealing with stressful issues as a family. I hope parents will feel encouraged by the data presented here to communicate with their children about global threats and concerns of all types. Parents need support and should ask for community programs, in schools and as part of religious education, to help them carry out this challenging task.

I want to close, however, in my capacity as a parent. I am doing this work because I am a parent; I doubt that I would ever have begun it if I were not. As a parent, I hope for a great deal more than I do as a professional. I hope that we can begin a process in which humanity will recognize that war has become obsolete as a means for settling political differences. It appears unlikely that my generation will live to see this task accomplished, but it is my belief that by asking our children to think about these questions we may give them the opportunity to develop new solutions to age-old problems.

REFERENCES

Bachman, J. G. (1983). American high school seniors view the military: 1976–1982. *Armed Forces and Society,* 10 (1), 86–104.

Beardslee, W. R., and Mack, J. E. (1982). The impact on children and adolescents of nuclear developments. In R. Rogers, ed., *Psychosocial Aspects of Nuclear Developments.* Task Force Report #20. Washington, D.C.: American Psychiatric Association.

Beardslee, W. R. and Mack, J. E. (1983). Adolescents and the threat of nuclear war: The evolution of a perspective. *Yale Journal of Biology and Medicine,* 79–91.

Berger Gould, B., Moon, S., and Van Hoorn, J., eds. (1986). *Growing Up Scared?* Berkeley, Calif.: Open Books.

Chivian, E., Mack, J. E., Waletsky, J., Lazaroff, C., Doctor, R., and Goldenring, J. (1985). Soviet children and the threat of nuclear war: A preliminary study. *American Journal of Orthopsychiatry,* 55, 484.

Coles, R. (1984). The doomsayers. Class politics and the nuclear freeze. *Boston Observer,* 3 (10), 1ff.

Coles, R. (1985). Children and the bomb. *The New York Times Magazine,* December 8, p. 44.

Dyal, J., Morris, P., and McKenzie-Mohr, D. (1990). Nuclear anxiety and issue-relevant behavior: Association with mental health. *Journal of Social Behavior and Personality,* 5(5), 243–262.

Erikson, E. H. (1963). Eight ages of man. In *Childhood and Society,* 247–274. New York: Norton.

Escalona, S. (1965). Growing up with the threat of nuclear war: Some indirect effects on personality development. *American Journal of Orthopsychiatry,* 52 (4), 600–607.

Goldberg, S., LaCombe, S., Levenson, D., Parker, K., Ross, C., and Sommers, F. (1985). Thinking about the threat of nuclear war: Relevance to mental health. *American Journal of Orthopsychiatry,* 55 (4), 503.

Goldenring, J., and Doctor, R. (1985). California adolescents' concerns about the threat of nuclear war. In T. Solantaus, E. Chivian, M. Vartanyan, and S. Chivian, eds., *The Impact of the Threat of Nuclear War on Children and Adolescents,* 112–133. Proceedings of an international research symposium. Boston: International Physicians for the Prevention of Nuclear War.

Greenwald, D., and Zeitlin, S. (1987). *No Reason to Talk about It: Families Confront the Nuclear Taboo.* New York: W. W. Norton.

Holmberg, P., and Bergstrom, A. (1985). How Swedish teenagers think and feel concerning the nuclear threat. In T. Solantaus, E. Chivian, M. Vartanyan, and S. Chivian, eds., *The Impact of the Threat of Nuclear War on Children and Adolescents.* Proceedings of an Informational Research Symposium. Boston: International Physicians for the Prevention of Nuclear War.

Kovel, J. (1983). *Against the State of Nuclear Terror.* Boston: South End Press.

Lifton, R. J. (1982). *Death in Life: Survivors of Hiroshima.* New York: Basic Books.

Lifton, R. J. (1983). *The Broken Connection: On Death and the Continuity of Life.* New York: Basic Books.

Mumford, L. (1947) Social Effects. *Air Affairs* (March), 370–382.

Schwebel, M. (1965). Nuclear cold war: Student opinion and professional responsibility. In M. Schwebel, ed., *Behavioral Science and Human Survival.* Palo Alto, Calif.: Behavioral Science Press.

Schwebel, M. (1982). Effects of the nuclear war threat on children and teenagers: Implications for professionals. *American Journal of Orthopsychiatry,* 52, 608–618.

Solantaus, T., Rimpela, M., and Taipele, V. (1984). The threat of war in the minds of 12–18 year-olds in Finland. *Lancet,* 1 (8380), 784.

Van Hoorn, J. (1986). Facing the nuclear threat: Comparisons of adolescents and adults. In B. Berger Gould, S. Moon, and J. Van Hoorn, eds., *Growing Up Scared?* Berkeley, Calif.: Open Books.

PART SEVEN

CONCLUSION

A human being is a part of the whole called by us "Universe," a part limited in time and space. He experiences himself, his thoughts and feelings as something separated from the rest, a kind of optical delusion of his consciousness. This delusion is a kind of prison for us, restricting us to our personal desires and to affection for a few persons nearest to us. Our task must be to free ourselves from this prison by widening our circle of compassion to embrace all living creatures and the whole of nature in its beauty. —*Albert Einstein*

In this concluding chapter, John Mack calls for a revitalization of the psychological professions. He calls for a profound self-examination by the psychological and mental health professions and challenges many of the basic assumptions and distinctions operating in these fields. He envisions a coming together again of the psychological and spiritual disciplines in ways that may contribute to the process of human transformation.

20

Toward a Psychology for Our Time

John E. Mack

INTRODUCTION: EVOLVING NOTIONS OF THE MIND

This book reflects, if not a revolution, certainly a dramatic evolution in the field of psychology itself. More than a century ago William James asserted that psychology is the science of "individual minds" (James 1890, 6). But if this is so, then the nature of psychology as a discipline must shift with our evolving notions of what an "individual," the "mind," or the "psyche" is. Knowledge from psychoanalysis, psychological research, psychedelics and other nonordinary states of consciousness, neuroscience, group and family psychology and psychotherapy, philosophy, theology, humanities and the social sciences, communication theory and computer science, and still other disciplines, together with the experience of living in the twentieth century, have refined and expanded our knowledge of the mind or psyche in many ways. Of particular concern to the authors of this volume is the increased awareness of how the social, political, economic, and technoscientific context affects the psychological problems we choose to address and the nature of the psyche itself. Although we understand it better now, this context-dependency of psychology was as true when Freud was developing the psychoanalytic method in response to the distresses presented by neurotic patients in the repressive culture of late Victorian Europe as when contemporary psychologists investigate gender differences of children in response to the Persian Gulf War of the 1990s. In each case knowledge is sought not purely for its own sake, but because questions have come into focus as the result of accumulated research and understanding and the impact of a particular contemporary sociopolitical or historical reality. Further, even the most "hard science" research, such as investigations of the functioning of the human brain, is motivated at some level by a concern for human well-being in addition to a purely intellectual curiosity. Whatever the complex combination of motives that propel psychological study, the likelihood that particular observations or insights will become part of our accepted professional or cultural understanding of the "mind," with its more objective and individual connotation, or "self," which has a more subjective and psychosocial implication, depends upon the contribution that this knowledge can potentially make to individual or social betterment.

CHANGING IDEAS OF THE SELF AND OF THE MENTAL HEALTH PROFESSIONAL'S TASK

The above assertions are basic starting points for what follows. The technological transformations of this century, particularly in the fields of communication, computer science, and globe-uniting weaponry of mass destruction, have created a multiplicity of challenges to psychology that derive from, or have as their common ground, a change in our idea of the self, especially the notion that "self" connotes a defined individual structure with clearly designated boundaries. Whether we consider the alter egos that our computers have become (Turkel 1984), the loss of privacy that has characterized this century, the invasion through television in our living rooms by war and terrorism, the interpenetration of the experience and artifacts of diverse cultures, the seepage of environmental devastation into our minds and bodies, or the heightening of human anguish through the increasing global awareness of economic inequality and injustice, the notion of the individual mind or self as a more or less discrete entity is being replaced by a view of the human psyche as a far-reaching field, interdependent, interconnected, and interpenetrated by other minds or psyches. Ironically, this shift in our notion of the psyche has brought the self of psychology closer to the idea of self or soul in religion and has connected (or reconnected) psychology and spirituality, from which it struggled so hard to separate itself under the leadership of John Watson, B. F. Skinner and other behaviorists in the 1920s and 1930s (Fuller 1986).

As other authors in this book have discussed, this means that mental health professionals, whether identifying themselves as psychologists, psychiatrists, or members of another discipline, are considering increasingly the social and political context in which their clients live, especially family and social disruption, material and relational privation, and political conflict, all of which are becoming the expectable environments of our time. The expanded self-awareness that is now demanded of the mental health professional or paraprofessional under such circumstances goes beyond the dynamic understanding that traditional psychotherapies have provided. It means a searching exploration of personal and political identity and values.

The work of Gill Straker, a white female psychologist providing mental health services to black youth in South Africa, illustrates this change clearly (Straker 1990). In order to build trust among these young people Straker had to "eschew temporarily my primary identity" and develop an expanded self as a mental health worker. She found that the disclosure of her value/ideological position was more important than her mental health orientation in building trust among her clients, challenging notions of therapeutic neutrality. Personally pacifistic in orientation, she had to reconsider the legitimacy of violence in the situation in which she and her clients found themselves. For the South African conflict was a youth rebellion, and armed struggle had been necessary for the survival of some of these young people. It had advanced the cause of their liberation from apartheid and may have expanded positively their sense of themselves. Straker was forced to wonder, for example, if she personally were to be attacked, as these youths had been, could she remain politically neutral or pacifistic? In this situation, "People who believe in pacifism have trouble not taking sides," she said, and "Sometimes reality overtook ethics and ideology." Straker listed several therapeutic aims for her work, which reflected her analysis of the complex challenges to the therapist's own self and the intermingling of inner and outer reality, of therapy and sociopolitical analysis, that the South African situation demanded:

1. Relate traumatic events to the interpersonal context and "break the silence."
2. Limit, if possible, the breakdown of psychological defenses.

3. Make sense of the total social and political situation.
4. Evaluate constantly one's own feelings and behavior.
5. Address the economic needs of the treatment population.
6. See if it is possible to increase the number of available options or choices of action of her clients.
7. Build on the "metaphor" of the freedom fighter to provide hope and affirmation.
8. Accept the reality of the war situation in which she was working and choose the least destructive alternative.

SPIRITUAL HUNGER, TRANSFORMATION, AND THE EMPTY SELF

We live in a time of profound spiritual hunger, a longing for connection with the sacred, and of social unrest. The idea of the "empty self" has become a kind of defining pathology of this contemporary state, much as was sexual conflict or neurosis toward the end of the nineteenth century (Cushman 1990). Addictions of various sorts are directly related to this condition. In a desperate effort to fill an inner void, people look to drugs and other addicting substances or stimulating behaviors, and to the accumulation of prestige, power, wealth, and material possessions as our desires are stirred and manipulated by the entertainment media and the advertising industry.

Lee Atwater, architect of George Bush's ruthlessly aggressive campaign for the presidency in 1988, captured eloquently this core affliction of our time in a dramatic recantation published in *Life* as he faced death from a brain tumor (Atwater and Brewster 1991). Here is some of what he said:

> My illness helped me to see that what was missing in society is what was missing in me: a little heart, a lot of brotherhood.
> The '80s were about acquiring—acquiring wealth, power, prestige. I know. I acquired more wealth, power and prestige than most. But you can acquire all you want and still feel empty. What power wouldn't I trade for a little more time with my family? What price wouldn't I pay for an evening with friends? It took a deadly illness to put me eye to eye with that truth, but it is a truth that the country, caught up in its ruthless ambitions and moral decay, can learn on my dime. I don't know who will lead us through the 1990s, but they must be made to speak to this spiritual vacuum at the heart of American society, this tumor of the soul.

I've come a long way since the day I told George Bush that his "kinder, gentler" theme was a nice thought, but it wouldn't win us any votes. I used to say that the President might be kinder and gentler, but I wasn't going to be. How wrong I was. There is nothing more important in life than human beings, nothing sweeter than the human touch.

It is all here, and more: the empty self; the spiritual hunger; the failed materialism, self-centeredness and competitiveness of the culture; the moral failings of our nation; the longing for relationship and intimacy; the connection of the inner self to the larger social and political context; the implication of the importance of social responsibility beyond one's own immediate needs and ambitions. But Lee Atwater's transformation occurred when he was suffering terribly and facing a death that was soon to befall him ("some nights I can't go to sleep, so fearful am I that I will never wake up again. . . . The terror of it all is blinding"), some time after he had conducted one of the most vicious political campaigns in American history, a campaign in which blatant racism was a central feature. It seems that we have to come to the point where our civilization is facing its own annihilation from instruments of mass killing or environmental destruction before we can embark upon the spiritual and social transformation that will be necessary to save us.

Social analysts have pointed to the various sociohistorical causes of breakdown in our culture. Behind all of these explanations, I believe, is the sense of separateness and fragmenting of relationship that is the natural consequence of the Newtonian/Cartesian materialist worldview that sharply divides self and other, subject and object. Spiritual hunger for connection beyond the individual self has been mistaken for the desire for some substance or thing. The repeated emphasis on the centrality of relationship in recent writings by feminist mental health professionals represents an important, and to my mind, healthy, effort to address and heal this fundamental disorder, as does the increasing involvement of mental health professionals in work with refugees and other victims of political violence.

SOCIAL RESPONSIBILITY AND THE TRANSFORMATION
OF PSYCHOLOGY

Social psychologist Brewster Smith has recently urged that psychologists become more socially conscious, provide pro bono human service, and do more to promote the public interest (Smith 1991). He writes: "I worry that insufficient scientific attention is being paid to the psychological aspects of the world-shaking issues of war and peace and environmental pollution and depletion, the essential life and death issues . . . and to the causes and consequences of poverty, which underlie so many human problems" (191). This is an important statement. But I would argue that the issue for psychology is still more fundamental. The global transformations documented in this book have resulted in such changes in the nature of the self or psyche that social responsibility is no longer simply an application of psychology to outside forces, a kind of add-on, to our regular professional lives. We are not giving pro bono for the benefit of others. As the boundaries of the self break down, or are penetrated by a flood of stimuli, threats, and information from the outside world, social awareness, connection, and responsibility have moved to the center of the psychological enterprise. Social responsibility is not simply about caring for the other outside of oneself; it means to be concerned for one's self in the other. Through the knowledge of the psyche that is our special journey, psychology and related disciplines can contribute uniquely to the life and planet-preserving activities that are now called for. Social responsibility is thus linked to our own survival and must soon become the core of our professional identity.

This process of transformation in the psychological disciplines is only at its beginning. Like all major societal change it is coming about gradually, and without universal acceptance. But unlike paradigm shifts of the past, which may have represented primarily changes in the scientific or world view, this one has a certain urgency relating to the imminence of the crises now confronting the planet. The change is thus "called for" in both an empirical and in a normative sense. Those of us who would speak for the importance of change need also to work to bring it about. Social transformation does not happen on its own.

Those of us who seek to transform the agendas of the psychological professions can best do so by challenging the restrictive assumptions and distinctions that now govern the practice of the disciplines themselves, even (perhaps particularly) when they have become time-honored and associated with institutional practices and rewards. Some of these distinctions still have limited utility. But they have lost much of their conceptual power or usefulness in relation to the compelling possibilities of the psyche or self and the demands that human beings now confront. Stated differently, old assumptions stand in the way of our ability to engage fully the challenges and threats, individually and collectively, with which humankind is now absorbed. They obstruct, for example, our ability to question conventional stereotypes, outmoded social hierarchies, or hurtful inequalities of power. They prevent us from seeing issues wholly or systemically.

The following are some of the assumptions and distinctions in psychology that need to be challenged wholly or in part:

1. *There is a clear distinction between inside and outside, or inner and outer reality.* We know from dreams, and from other experiences in nonordinary states of consciousness, that the distinction between the inner and outer worlds, or between material and psychic reality, though useful for navigatng in the everyday world, is fragile and can quickly give way to a compelling sense of our connection or oneness with others and with the earth itself. Our psyches merge with other minds; the self is coterminous with its environment.

2. *Conscious and unconscious experience are sharply differentiated.* This distinction, though compelling in Freud's time, has lost much of its power, as we have come to appreciate the complex, intricate levels of awareness of which human beings are capable. Further, we have yet to distinguish between the dynamic unconscious, the elements of mental life we keep out of awareness for personal defensive reasons, and what might be called the "contextual" unconscious, those forces and assumptions of which we remain unconscious because they are (like the items in this list or the prejudices of an ethnic group) the shared givens of a profession or culture.

3. *The distinction between the individual and the collective psyche.* The point here is not that there is no value in speaking of individuals, or of individual minds or psyches. But when we do so we put aside the powerful truth that our psyches are profoundly connected at all times with other minds to the extent that we may not know the source of our own views or initiatives, as when our minds are being manipulated by the mass media. One has only to observe the lock-step manner in which a nation of seemingly thinking beings can be led inexorably, as if mindlessly, to support its leadership in time of war. The poet Robert Bly observed that "the life of the nation can be imagined . . . not as some-

thing deep inside our psyche, but as a psyche larger than the psyche of anyone living, a larger sphere, floating above everyone" (Jones 1985, 133).

4. *The distinction between the psychological and the spiritual.* As it has participated in the prevailing materialist worldview of the twentieth century, the profession of psychology has striven to distance itself from spirituality or religion, especially by distinguishing its scientific or empirical methods from the subjective or contemplative epistemologies and ontologies of theology. But the relationship over the centuries of mind or psyche to spirit or soul has been, until the past century, much more intimate than it is now. Psyche has acquired the connotation of structure and boundary or separateness; spirit implies openness, boundarylessness, and merger. For when the self as observer or as an experiencing entity takes its own separateness as the object of awareness, or as a source of not knowing, the domain of experience can widen, boundaries dissolve, and we may enter the realm of deeper connection or love, and, ultimately, open ourselves to the numinous or sacred. When this happens, we enter a nonordinary state of consciousness; psyche, in effect, *becomes* spirit. Such experiences seem to have been much more of an everyday dimension of human life before our mechanistic or materialist worldview cut us off from the domain of the spirit.

5. *Objective versus subjective ways of knowing.* Philosopher Ken Wilber has set forth the epistemological category errors that derive from confusing the domains of reality to which sensory/empirical, conceptual/analytic, or intuitive/contemplative ways of knowing apply (Wilber 1982). There is an implicit hierarchical tradition in academic psychology that values empirical/sensory evidence or methods, thought to be more "objective," or lending themselves to proof, over more intuitive knowledge, considered to be "subjective" or vulnerable to distortion or error. The approaches to knowledge and understanding developed in this book might be thought of as holistic or integrative, encouraging us to explore the psychology of human beings, individually and collectively, through all of the ways of knowing of which we are capable.

A corollary to the apposition of objective and subjective knowing would be the distinction between empirical, experimental, or quantitative methods, also thought of hierarchically as being more scientific or objective, and narrative or case study methods, with their messy welter of data that reaches varying levels of consciousness, feeling, and reality.

6. *Cognitive versus affective domains.* Psychology has, historically, found the watershed dividing the cognitive and affective realms of mental activity especially compelling. Cognition, comprising more clearly identifiable mental functions, has traditionally attracted a great deal of graduate study and other research. The exploration of affect or feeling, more unruly and reaching into the deeper strata of being of student and study subject alike, has, until recently, been less studied. Affective and cognitive processes interrelate complexly. It would be difficult to understand our resistance to environmental responsibility or the passionate hold of nationalistic emotions upon our psyches unless the rich connection between ideas and feelings is appreciated. The term "hot cognition" has broken the confines of mind research, like lava bubbling through the frozen earth's crust.

7. *Action and Academia.* As long as academicians make it clear that their political activities are distinct from their academic identities or responsibilities—so goes the conventional professional cant—no one can *object* to their initiatives and actions on behalf of peace, environmental protection, or other issues. And it is true, of course, that actions like those Sally Mack writes of in this book are not, in themselves, part of the academic enterprise. But civil disobedience and other experiences related to social and political commitment put flesh on the bones of the scholarly life. They bring the experiencer into direct contact with social institutions, political issues, and collective forces. In some cases, as when anthropologists and psychologists have protested at nuclear weapons test sites, data gathering and social action may occur simultaneously or become a single enterprise.

When we take a stand on a social or political issue, we heighten and deepen our purpose and sense of responsibility. Direct involvement adds commitment and a greater awareness of what is at stake. Far from lying outside the academic enterprise, political action or participation may be the royal road to a fuller appreciation of sociopolitical injustice and institutional resistance, which are vast territories that we must enter and explore. For psychologists concerned with social responsibility, political action, such as protesting government actions perceived as dangerous to human health or well-being, is consistent with the practice of their professions.

BREAKING THE SILENCE

With what kind of psyche in what sort of world would we be left if these assumptions and distinctions could be effectively challenged? We would discover that the human psyche has thinner boundaries than we thought, and that our individual minds are interpenetrated by and connected with the minds of others. We would come closer to achieving that sense of global or species identity of which Lifton, Macy, and others in this book have written. Men might more readily acknowledge the feminine in themselves, enabling them to enter a variety of partnerships with women to confront more effectively social and political issues. The barriers to feeling would fall, especially for men. As we develop a deeper, fuller sense of ourselves, we—men and women together—would be able to take responsibility for the dark side of our natures, the pain and despair of which Macy writes, and the walled-off dimension of our collective psyches, all of which are lived out in social violence. We would not run from the "terrible knowledge" of the twentieth century of which Lifton and Lafarge write that has made us all, in effect, holocaust survivors. Through a deepening self-knowledge the psychological professions could help our fellow citizens question and resist the groupthink through which the dominant elite guides our minds and leads us to social consensus, especially in relation to matters of war or national security. Heightened social or political awareness, with all its anxieties, is a precondition of social or political responsibility. As Ervin Staub has shown, in one way or another we are all political actors, for whether we take active initiatives to produce change or remain passive bystanders, acquiescing in local and national policies with which we may disagree, our behavior will affect the outcome.

Nadia Mandelstam, widow of the Russian poet Osip Mandelstam who was murdered by Stalin in 1938, wrote that "silence is the worst crime" (Mandelstam 1970). Challenging basic assumptions can help us to break our silence and remove the taboos that surround sensitive political questions. We can learn to say no to all mass killing—not just with nuclear weapons—as a solution to political differences. We can learn to distinguish between an adversary that may be a real threat from enemies that national leaders using the mass media sometimes create by polarizing, manipulating our perceptions, and intensifying conflict (see chapter 6 by Silverstein). Education for a new kind of global citizenry needs to include a familiarization with our susceptibility to all the forms of polarized thinking, the readiness with which we can be mobilized to support aggression by fear, and the dehumanization of a designated other. The psychological and mental health professions can help educators become familiar with these forces and mechanisms. But we need to begin with the initial task of knowing our own blindness, including inner resistances we may have, as part of a professional elite, to taking stands that may make us conspicuous and therefore subject to criticism within our academic or other institutional structures.

WHERE DO WE GO FROM HERE?

What then are the implications of our confrontation with the terrible knowledge of this most murderous of all centuries? Stated differently, how do we translate our confrontation with global horror into self-knowledge that can transform our collective destiny? We can begin with the ownership, with the acceptance of responsibility for the central difference between this and other times, the fact that the disasters of recent decades—war and the threat of nuclear war, environmental devastation, even famine—are products of human invention, perpetration, and indifference. They are the result of appetites and neglect, organized and fulfilled through corporate, political, military, and other institutions, augmented by evolving technologies, through which we subdue the human and environmental obstacles to the realization of our desires. Furthermore, we need to appreciate that the arena in which much of our inner need finds its expression is increasingly global. Great powers in the military and economic sense will cross the globe to war against other countries that would monopolize oil or other vital resources. Corporate executives will command armies of laborers to destroy forests to supply wood to furnish homes on the opposite side of the earth. Through communication satellites we are entertained by singers and actors around the world and political leaders spread their messages to audiences thousands of miles away. If our psyches have not been "internationalized," we are surely affected on a day-to-day, if not moment-to-moment, basis by the decisions and actions of other human beings all over the earth.

This globalization of the human psyche compels us to redefine the scope and possibilities of a psychology of social responsibility. We begin with our basic human identity, which includes in the sense of self an ever widening and deepening of our awareness of connection and common purpose with diverse peoples. As psychologists we make explicit through analytical and experimental methods, beginning with ourselves, the structures of thought and feeling, resistances or obstacles, that restrict communication, empathy, and relationship. This applies not only to psychosocial research and education, but also means inclusion of a new sociopolitical awareness and responsibility in the tasks of therapy and healing. A sense of psychological wholeness or completeness has come now to include a commitment to future generations within a larger human community. Psychodynamic psychology has helped us become aware, especially, of resistances of a personal or individual nature. We are less familiar with what might be thought of as institutional resistances, the forces that limit our thinking and inhibit our initiatives or creativity, consciously and unconsciously, within our specialties and organizations, the fears and rewards that keep us swimming in the mainstream. Peace education and peace psychology, for example, may be resisted (whatever the reasons given) by psychology department faculties because its very nature will lead to the examination and questioning of established policies, values, and structures of power, dominance, and prestige within the society, including the university itself.

Indeed, our university departments and professional organizations may be especially resistant to the implications of this process of transformation. For they are among our strongest centers of power and tradition, and do not usually reward with promotion and funding intellectual endeavors that challenge the basic assumptions of their disciplines. Yet the pressures of the global crises, and their intrusion into each of our lives, may force even the most conservative academic institutions to reexamine their academic priorities and investigative methods. Researchers themselves are becoming increasingly engaged with their subjects. In the study of fundamental social issues like environmental destruction, homelessness, and the threat of nuclear war, the margin between advocacy and research is narrowing. Just as, for example, investigators of the psychology of the nuclear arms race have been among its most effective opponents, researchers of the human costs of homelessness have been particularly powerful advocates on behalf of homeless individuals and families. As Cartesian dualisms give way to more wholistic or systemic analyses, the high valuation of extreme distance and separateness of investigator and subject is giving way to a greater acceptance of their inevitable connection. Self-knowledge and awareness of bias or intense emotional involvement, and how these affect research findings, are replacing the pretenses of total objectivity or value-free social science.

THE STUDY OF POWER AND POWER RELATIONSHIPS

As crises on a global scale are invading our personal and collective lives and forcing the psychological disciplines to challenge their assumptions about the nature of the psyche and the boundaries of our professional endeavors, new fields of study are emerging. Some of these, like the psychology of human survival, of peacemaking and environmental destruction, and education for caring and global responsibility, are well represented in this book. Of central importance for most if not all of these new fields, as well as being a neglected topic in its own right, is the study of power and power relationships. Again, one reason the subject has been avoided is that it strikes so close to our professional "homes," the psychological, psychiatric, and related professions, which have themselves been sources or repositories of power and prestige for so many of us. Civil disobedience, as Sally Mack has written, can be an education in the several forms of power and a source of empowerment for its practitioners. All human beings seek power in some form. The need to feel that our lives have an impact, that in some way our existence makes a difference, is a basic dimension of human nature. Men's avenues to power have traditionally been through dominance and control, women's through relationship and connection. Knowledge of these differences does not mean that they will end. Men and women who are aware of the dangers of coercive forms of power, especially as these are augmented through life- and earth-destroying technologies, can work together to discover new forms of power in the service of social and political transformation. There are clear public policy implications contained in the ideas and observations presented in this book. As the definition of the appropriate domain of psychological, or psychospiritual, investigation and understanding extends further into the social and political arena, psychologists will be working increasingly with other social scientists and decision-makers in addressing public policy issues. The growing multidisciplinary field of political psychology is bringing clinical and analytic knowledge to social and political decision-making.

CONCLUSIONS

Intellectual historian Richard Tarnas has suggested that "a civilization cannot become conscious of itself, cannot recognize its own significance, until it is so mature that it is approaching its own death" (Tarnas 1991, 445). The revolution of awareness of which I am writing here may be in part the result for myself and others of our consciousness of the imminent death of our world. Yet we would prefer a kind of collective ego death— a confrontation with utter despair over the destruction of life and the vain hope that all-knowing leaders will rescue us from our plight—to the physical death of our planet. For out of this ego death, the shattering of our species arrogance, especially the destruction of the twin illusions that we are separate from one another and other peoples and that the earth belongs to the human race, we may find the courage and commitment to protect and preserve the life of future generations and the earth itself. The revitalization of the psychological professions, and the new priority they may give to social and political issues, may contribute usefully to this process. Human transformation grows fundamentally out of self-awareness, which has always been the first responsibility of the psychological and spiritual professions, which, understandably, are now growing closer. The emerging discipline of transpersonal psychology, developed by Abraham Maslow and Stanislav Grof, reflects the joining of psychology and spirituality. Christina and Stanislav Grof have written: "The modern term for the direct experience of spiritual realities is transpersonal, meaning transcending the usual way of perceiving and interpreting the world from the position of a separate individual or body-ego. There exists an entirely new discipline, transpersonal psychology, that specializes in experiences of this kind and their implications" (Grof and Grof 1990, 40).

The prescritions set forth here are not utopian or idealistic sentiments, but practical requirements. Our planet, and therefore the life that it supports, may now be entering a terminal phase of its existence as a living organism. But the fatal illnesses are man-made, and their treatment is in our hands. Perhaps if the emerging self-knowledge that this book reflects is urgently and fully applied, it may not yet be too late. The dark portent of these words might seem to destroy hope or discourage effective participation. Yet, paradoxically, our power and ability to act may emerge out of confronting the most painful feelings. I recently went through a terrible ordeal in preparing a talk for a conference on violence toward children and adolescents. Consciousness of the suffering of children in war zones around the world and in our cities seemed too much to bear. Yet when I presented the talk something else, more hopeful or empowering, must have come across. "How do you stay so optimistic?" someone asked in the discussion period. I, of course, shared the process that I had undergone, the feelings I had experienced, in preparing the talk. Perhaps when we are able to confront fully the despair that is the fitting response to the horrors of these times, we may move to a place of greater energy and power. And when we share truthfully the process we have undergone, we may enable others to take on the challenges before them and help build an authentic community that is committed to personal and global transformation.

REFERENCES

Atwater, L., and T. Brewster (1991). "Lee Atwater's Last Campaign." *Life* (February) 58–67.

Cushman, P. (1990). "Why the Self is Empty." *American Psychologist* 45: 590–611.

Fuller, C. (1986). *Americans and the Unconscious*. New York: Oxford.

Grof, C., and S. Grof. (1990). *The Stormy Search for the Self*. Los Angeles: Tarcher.

James, W. (1890). *The Works of William James: The Principles of Psychology*, vol. 1. Cambridge, Mass.: Harvard University Press, 1981.

Jones, R., ed. (1985). *Poetry and Politics: An Anthology of Essays*. New York: William Morrow.

Mandelstam, N. (1970). *Hope Against Hope: A Memoir*. New York: Atheneum.

Smith, B. (1991). "Psychology in the Public Interest." In M. B. Smith, *Values, Self and Society: Toward a Humanist Social Psychology*, New Brunswick: Transaction Publishers.

Straker, G. (1990). Panel "Reports from the Front." Children in War Conference, Hebrew University, Jerusalem, June 26.

Tarnas, R. (1991). *The Passion of the Western Mind*. New York: Harmony.

Turkel, S. (1984). *The Second Self: Computers and the Human Spirit*. New York: Simon and Schuster.

Wilber, K. (1982). *Eye to Eye: The Quest for the New Paradigm*. New York: Anchor.

Appendix A

Selected Resources

Never doubt that a small group of thoughtful committed citizens can change the world. Indeed it's the only thing that ever has. —*Margaret Mead*

The following is a brief list of organizations involved in issues of peace, social justice, and the environment, including those referred to by the authors represented in this volume.

PROFESSIONAL ORGANIZATIONS

Association of Humanistic Psychology (AHP)
325 Ninth St.
San Francisco, CA 94103
(AHP has a strong commitment to peace psychology issues)

American Ortho-Psychiatric Association (Ortho)
Nuclear Issues Studies Group
19 West 44th St., Suite 1616
New York, NY 10036

American Psychological Association (APA)
Division 48: Peace Psychology
1200 17th Ave. NW
Washington, DC 20036

Center for Psychological Studies in the Nuclear Age
1493 Cambridge St.
Cambridge, MA 02139

Educators for Social Responsibility (ESR)
23 Garden St.
Cambridge, MA 02138

International Physicians for Prevention of Nuclear War (IPPNW)
126 Rogers St.
Cambridge, MA 02142

Physicians for Social Responsibility (PSR)
1600 Connecticut Ave., Suite 800
Washington, DC 20009

Professionals Coalition for Nuclear Arms Control
1616 P St. NW, Suite 320
Washington, DC 20036

Psychologists for Social Responsibility (PsySR)
1841 Columbia Rd. NW, Suite 216
Washington, DC 20009

Social Workers for Peace and Nuclear Disarmament (SWPND)
National Association of Social Workers
14 Beacon St., #409
Boston, MA 02108

NATIONAL PEACE ORGANIZATIONS

American Friends Service Committee (AFSC)
1501 Cherry St.
Philadelphia, PA 19102

American Peace Test (APT)
309 K St. NE
Washington, DC 20002

Fellowship of Reconciliation
P.O. Box 271
Nyack, NY 10960

Interhelp/Despair and Empowerment Workshops
c/o Kevin McVeigh
54 Thayer Rd.
Greenfield, MA 01301

National Peace Institute Foundation
110 Maryland Ave. NE
Washington, DC 20002

Peace and World Security Studies
Hampshire College
Amherst, MA 01002
(Can provide listings of academic peace studies programs)

Sane/Freeze
1819 H St. NW
Washington, DC 20006

Women's Action for Nuclear Disarmament (WAND)
691 Massachusetts Ave.
Arlington, MA 02174

Women's International League for Peace and Freedom (WILPF)
1213 Race St.
Philadelphia, PA 19107

ECOLOGICAL ORGANIZATIONS

Earth First!
P.O. Box 5871
Tucson, AZ 85703

Environmental Defense Fund
257 Park Ave. South
New York, NY 10010

Friends of the Earth
218 D St. SE
Washington, DC 20003

Greenpeace
1436 U St. NW
Washington, DC 20009

Rocky Mountain Institute
1739 Snowmass Creek Rd.
Old Snowmass, CO 81654

Sierra Club
730 Polk St.
San Francisco, CA 94109

Worldwatch Institute
1776 Massachusetts Ave. NW
Washington, DC 20036

Appendix B

The Seville Statement on Violence

Introductory Remarks by David Adams

The Seville Statement on Violence is a scientific statement which says peace is possible, because war is not necessarily part of human nature. It was written by an international team of specialists in 1986 for the United Nations sponsored International Year of Peace. It has been adopted for dissemination by Unesco, the United Nations Educational, Scientific and Cultural Organization. It has been endorsed by scientific and professional organizations around the world, including the American Psychological Association and the American Anthropological Association.

The Seville Statement on Violence is important because young people who believe the myth that war is intrinsic to human nature are less likely to believe they can do anything for peace. They are also less likely to take part in action for peace. The myth is widespread. Studies in Finland and the United States in 1984 and 1986 found that 52 percent and 44 percent of students, respectively, believed that "war is intrinsic to human nature."[1] Similar results were obtained in 1969 when a major survey was conducted of 5,000 university students in 18 nations. In most of these nations between 40% and 60% of the students believed that "war is a result of the inherent nature of men."[2]

Believing that it is our responsibility to address from our particular disciplines the most dangerous and destructive activities of our species, violence and war; recognizing that science is a human cultural product which cannot be definitive or all-encompassing; and gratefully acknowledging the support of the authorities of Seville and representatives of Spanish UNESCO; we, the undersigned scholars from around the world and from relevant sciences, have met and arrived at the following State-

418

ment on Violence. In it, we challenge a number of alleged biological findings that have been used, even by some in our disciplines, to justify violence and war. Because the alleged findings have contributed to an atmosphere of pessimism in our time, we submit that the open, considered rejection of these misstatements can contribute significantly to the International Year of Peace.

Misuse of scientific theories and data to justify violence and war is not new but has been made since the advent of modern science. For example, the theory of evolution has been used to justify not only war, but also genocide, colonialism, and suppression of the weak.

We state our position in the form of five propositions. We are aware that there are many other issues about violence and war that could be fruitfully addressed from the standpoint of our disciplines, but we restrict ourselves here to what we consider a most important first step.

It is scientifically incorrect to say that we have inherited a tendency to make war from our animal ancestors. Although fighting occurs widely throughout animal species, only a few cases of destructive intra-species fighting between organized groups have ever been reported among naturally living species, and none of these involve the use of tools designed to be weapons. Normal predatory feeding upon other species cannot be equated with intraspecies violence. Warfare is a peculiarly human phenomenon and does not occur in other animals.

The fact that warfare has changed so radically over time indicates that it is a product of culture. Its biological connection is primarily through language which makes possible the coordination of groups, the transmission of technology, and the use of tools. War is biologically possible, but it is not inevitable, as evidenced by its variation in occurrence and nature over time and space. There are cultures which have not engaged in war for centuries, and there are cultures which have engaged in war frequently at some times and not at others.

It is scientifically incorrect to say that war or any other violent behavior is genetically programmed into our human nature. While genes are involved at all levels of nervous system function, they provide a developmental potential that can be actualized only in conjunction with the ecological and social environment. While individuals vary in their predispositions to be affected by their experience, it is the interaction between their genetic endowment and conditions of nurturance that determines their personalities. Except for rare pathologies, the genes do not produce individuals necessarily predisposed to violence. Neither do they determine the opposite. While genes are co-involved in establishing our behavioral capacities, they do not by themselves specify the outcome.

It is scientifically incorrect to say that in the course of human evolution there has been a selection for aggressive behavior more than for other kinds of behavior. In all well-studied species, status within the group is achieved by the ability to cooperate and to fulfill social functions relevant to the structure of that group. "Dominance" involves social bondings and affiliations; it is not simply a matter of the possession and use of superior physical power, although it does involve aggressive behaviors. Where genetic selection for aggressive behavior has been artificially instituted in animals, it has rapidly succeeded in producing hyper-aggressive individuals; this indicates that aggression was not maximally selected under natural conditions. When such experimentally-created hyper-aggressive animals are present in a social group, they either disrupt its social structure or are driven out. Violence is neither in our evolutionary legacy nor in our genes.

It is scientifically incorrect to say that humans have a "violent brain." While we do have the neural apparatus to act violently, it is not automatically activated by internal or external stimuli. Like higher primates and unlike other animals, our higher neural processes filter such stimuli before they can be acted upon. How we act is shaped by how we have been conditioned and socialized. There is nothing in our neurophysiology that compels us to react violently.

It is scientifically incorrect to say that war is caused by "instinct" or any single motivation. The emergence of modern warfare has been a journey from the primacy of emotional and motivational factors, sometimes called "instincts," to the primacy of cognitive factors. Modern war involves institutional use of personal characteristics such as obedience, suggestibility, and idealism; social skills such as language; and rational considerations such as cost-calculation, planning, and information processing. The technology of modern war has exaggerated traits associated with violence both in the training of actual combatants and in the preparation of support for war in the general population. As a result of this exaggeration, such traits are often mistaken to be the causes rather than the consequences of the process.

We conclude that biology does not condemn humanity to war, and that humanity can be freed from the bondage of biological pessimism and empowered with confidence to undertake the transformative tasks needed in this International Year of Peace and in the years to come. Although these tasks are mainly institutional and collective, they also rest upon the consciousness of individual participants for whom pessimism and optimism are crucial factors. Just as "wars begin in the minds of men," peace also begins in our minds. The same species who invented war is capable of inventing peace. The responsibility lies with each of us.

Seville, May 16, 1986

SIGNATORIES

David Adams, Psychology, Wesleyan University, Middletown, Connecticut, U.S.A.

S. A. Barnett, Ethology, The Australian National University, Canberra, Australia.

N. P. Bechtereva, Neurophysiology, Institute for Experimental Medicine of Academy of Medical Sciences of U.S.S.R., Leningrad, U.S.S.R.

Bonnie Frank Carter, Psychology, Albert Einstein Medical Center, Philadelphia, Pennsylvania, U.S.A.

José M. Rodríguez Delgado, Neurophysiology, Centro de Estudios Neurobiológicos, Madrid, Spain

José Luis Díaz, Ethology, Instituto Mexicano de Psiquiatría, Mexico D.F., Mexico

Andrzej Eliasz, Individual Differences Psychology, Polish Academy of Sciences, Warsaw, Poland

Santiago Genovés, Biological Anthropology, Instituto de Estudios Antropológicos, Mexico D.F., Mexico

Benson E. Ginsburg, Behavior Genetics, University of Connecticut, Storrs, Connecticut, U.S.A.

Jo Groebel, Social Psychology, Erziehungswissenschaftliche Hochschule, Landau, Federal Republic of Germany

Samir-Kumar Ghosh, Sociology, Indian Institute of Human Sciences, Calcutta, India

Robert Hinde, Animal Behavior, Cambridge University, United Kingdom

Richard E. Leakey, Physical Anthropology, National Museums of Kenya, Nairobi, Kenya

Taha M. Malasi, Psychiatry, Kuwait University, Kuwait

J. Martin Ramírez, Psychobiology, Universidad de Sevilla, Spain

Federico Mayor Zaragoza, Biochemistry, Universidad Autónoma, Madrid, Spain

Diana L. Mendoza, Ethology, Universidad de Sevilla, Spain

Ashis Nandy, Political Psychology, Center for the Study of Developing Societies, Delhi, India

John Paul Scott, Animal Behavior, Bowling Green State University, Bowling Green, Ohio, U.S.A.

Riitta Wahlström, Psychology, University of Jyväskylä, Finland

Correspondence concerning the Seville Statement on Violence or the UNESCO brochure should be addressed to David Adams, Psychology Department, Wesleyan University, Middletown, CT 06457.

NOTES TO INTRODUCTORY STATEMENT

1. Adams, D., and Bosch, S. The myth that war is intrinsic to human nature discourages action for peace by young people. In J. M. Ramirez, R. A. Hinde, and J. Groebel (Eds.), *Essays in Violence*. Seville, Spain: University of Seville, 1987.
2. Eckhardt, W. Crosscultural theories of war and aggression. *International Journal of Group Tensions*. 2, 36–51, 1972.

Name Index

Subject Index

Abuse, 109

Activism: effects of, within family, 296–300; among psychologists, 321–22, 407; psychology of, 11, 300–302; as response to nuclear threat, 296–300, 313–21; women and, 281–85. *See also* Global activism; Nonviolent civil disobedience (NVCD); Peace activism

Addiction, 68–69

Affinity groups, 291, 295, 296

AFTA. *See* American Family Therapy Association (AFTA)

Aggression, 89–102; in children, 106–13; genetic potential for, 92; instrumental, 95; motives for, 93–95; nongenetic bases of, 91–92; orientation toward, 98–99

Alienation, 42. *See also* Defense mechanisms

Altruism, 90, 92

American Family Therapy Association (AFTA), Nuclear Issues Task Force, 185

American Orthopsychiatric Association (ORTHO), Nuclear Issues Study Group, 185

American Peace Test (APT), 291, 295–96

American Psychological Association (APA), 5, 318; Division of Peace Psychology, 8–9, 138, 184

Anger, 94. *See also* Aggression

Antagonism, ideology of, 100–101

Anxiety. *See* Fear; Nuclear anxiety

APA. *See* American Psychological Association (APA)

Applied behavioral analysis, 249–51

APT. *See* American Peace Test (APT); Nonviolent civil disobedience (NVCD)

Arms buildup, 67, 77

Attachment, 108

Attention, and enemy images, 145–61

Attitude change, 250

Attribution, 130, 150–55; hostile motivations and, 154–55; situational pressures and, 151, 153. *See also* Enemy images

"Auschwitz self," 24–25

Authority, 98, 99, 110–11

Behavior change programs: activators for environmental preservation, 255–58; applied behavioral analysis and, 249–51; consequences for environment and, 258–61; environmental psychology and, 248–66; impact of, 261–66; target behaviors in, 252–55

Beliefs, 62–63, 71–74, 91, 307–10, 376

Boston Women's Peace Research Group, 274–80

Buddhism, 68

Bystanders, 101, 113, 169

Caring, 92

Center for Psychological Studies in the Nuclear Age, 193, 195

Change. *See* Behavior change programs; Social change

Chernobyl, 26